Of Population

Of Population

Of Population

AN
ENQUIRY
CONCERNING THE
POWER OF INCREASE
IN THE
NUMBERS OF MANKIND

*Being an Answer to Mr. Malthus's Essay
on That Subject*

By WILLIAM GODWIN

(1820)

REPRINTS OF ECONOMIC CLASSICS

Augustus M. Kelley, Bookseller
New York 1964

Library of Congress Catalogue Card Number
63-23523

Printed in the United States of America.

OF POPULATION.

AN

ENQUIRY

CONCERNING THE

POWER OF INCREASE

IN THE

NUMBERS OF MANKIND,

BEING AN ANSWER TO MR. MALTHUS'S ESSAY ON THAT SUBJECT.

By WILLIAM GODWIN.

Fond, impious man! thinkest thou yon sanguine cloud,
Raised by thy breath, has quenched the orb of day?
To-morrow he repairs the golden flood,
And warms the nations with redoubled ray.

LONDON:

PRINTED FOR LONGMAN, HURST, REES, ORME AND BROWN,
PATERNOSTER ROW.

1820.

PREFACE.

IT happens to men sometimes, where they had it in their thoughts to set forward and advance some mighty benefit to their fellow creatures, not merely to fail in giving substance and efficacy to the sentiment that animated them, but also to realise and bring on some injury to the party they purposed to serve. Such is my case, if the speculations that have now been current for nearly twenty years, and which had scarcely been heard of before, are to be henceforth admitted, as forming an essential branch of the science of politics.

When I wrote my Enquiry concerning Political Justice, I flattered myself that there was no mean probability that I should render an important service to mankind. I had warmed my mind with all that was great and illustrious in the republics of Greece and Rome, which had been favourite subjects of meditation with me,

almost from my infancy.   I became further
animated by the spectacle of the Revolutions of
America and France, the former of which commenced when I was just twenty years of age,
[though I never approved of the mode in which
the latter was effected, and the excesses which
to a certain degree marked its very beginning]
and by the speculations, which in England, and
other parts of Europe, among learned men and
philosophers, preceded, and contributed to, and
have in some measure attended upon, and accompanied, every step of these events.   I
thought it was possible to collect whatever existed that was best and most liberal in the science
of politics, to condense it, to arrange it more
into a system, and to carry it somewhat farther,
than had been done by any preceding writer.

The book I produced seemed for some time
fully to answer in its effects the most sanguine
expectations I had conceived from it.   I could
not complain that it "fell dead-born from the
press," or that it did not awaken a considerable
curiosity among my countrymen.   I was never
weak enough to suppose, that it would immediately sweep away all error before it, like a
mighty influx of the waves of the ocean.   I hailed
the opposition it encountered, direct and indirect, argumentative and scurrilous, as a symptom
(we will suppose, not altogether unequivocal) of

the result I so earnestly desired. Among other phenomena of the kind, I hailed the attack of Mr. Malthus. I believed, that the Essay on Population, like other erroneous and exaggerated representations of things, would soon find its own level.

In this I have been hitherto disappointed. It would be easy to assign the causes of my disappointment; the degree in which, by the necessity of the case, the theory of this writer flattered the vices and corruption of the rich and great, and the eager patronage it might very naturally be expected to obtain from them : but this makes no part of what it is my purpose to say. Finding therefore, that whatever arguments have been produced against it by others, it still holds on its prosperous career, and has not long since appeared in the impressive array of a Fifth Edition, I cannot be contented to go out of the world, without attempting to put into a permanent form what has occurred to me on the subject. I was sometimes idle enough to suppose, that I had done my part, in producing the book that had given occasion to Mr. Malthus's Essay [a], and that I might safely leave the comparatively easy task, as it seemed, of de-

---

[a] It is stated in the front of the Essay on Population, that it is to my writings that the work is indebted for its origin.

molishing the "Principle of Population," to
some one of the men who have risen to maturity
since I produced my most considerable performance. But I can refrain no longer. "I
will also answer my part; I likewise will shew
my opinion: for I am full of matter; and the
spirit within me constraineth me."

This is a task in which I am the more bound
to engage, because, as I have said, if the dogmas
which are now afloat on the subject of population are to become permanent, I have, instead
of contributing as I desired to the improvement
of society, become, very unintentionally, the occasion of placing a bar upon all improvements
to come, and bringing into discredit all improvements that are past. If Mr. Malthus's way of
reasoning only tended to the overthrow of what
many will call "the visionary speculations" of
the Enquiry concerning Political Justice, the
case would have been different. I might have
gone to my grave with the disgrace, to whatever
that might amount, of having erected castles in
the air, for the benefit, not of myself, but of my
species, and of then seeing them battered to
pieces before my face. But I cannot consent to
close my eyes for ever, with the judgment, as
the matter now seems to stand, recorded on my
tomb, that, in attempting one further advance
in the route of improvement, I should have

brought on the destruction of all that Solon, and Plato, and Montesquieu, and Sidney, in ancient times, and in a former age, had seemed to have effected for the redemption and the elevation of mankind.

It is not a little extraordinary, that Mr. Malthus's book should now have been twenty years before the public, without any one, so far as I know, having attempted a refutation of his main principle. It was easy for men of a generous temper to vent their horror at the revolting nature of the conclusions he drew from his principle; and this is nearly all that has been done. That principle is delivered by him in the most concise and summary manner. He says, that he " considered it as established in the first six pages. The American increase was related [in three lines]; and the geometrical ratio was proved [b]." Now, it stands out broadly to the common sense of mankind, that this was proving nothing. Population, and the descent, and increase or otherwise, of one generation of mankind after another, is not a subject of such wonderful simplicity, as to be thus established. It is in reality the complexity and thorniness of the question, that have had the effect of silencing Mr. Malthus's adversaries respecting it. They

---

[b] Essay on Population, Vol. III, p. 344, note.

seem with one consent to have shrunk from a topic, which required so much patient investigation. In the midst of this general desertion of the public interest, I have ventured to place myself in the breach. With what success it is for others to judge.

It may seem strange, that what was so summarily stated, and successfully asserted, by Mr. Malthus, should require so much research and labour to overthrow. The Essay on Population has set up a naked assertion; no more. I might have made a contradictory assertion; and, equitably speaking, the matter was balanced, and what Mr. Malthus had written ought to go for nothing. But this would not have been the case. "Possession," says the old proverb, "is nine points of the law;" and the Essay on Population had gotten possession of the public mind. This author entered on a desert land, and, like the first discoverers of countries, set up a symbol of occupation, and without further ceremony said, "It is mine." His task was easy: he gave the word; his vessel was launched, and his voyage completed. Like Cymochles in the Fairy Queen, he could say,

> My wandering ship I row,
> That knows her port, and thither sails by aim;
> Ne care, ne fear I, how the wind do blow;
> Both swift and slow alike do serve my turn.

But the task in which I have engaged has been of a different sort. It was necessary that my advances should be slow, and my forces firm. It was mine, not only to dislodge the usurper from his fastnesses and retreats; but further, by patient exertions, and employing the most solid materials, to build up a Pharos, that the sincere enquirer might no longer wander in the dark, and be liable to be guided by the first daring adventurer that would lead him into the paths of error and destruction.

I beg leave to repeat one passage here from the ensuing volume, [c] as containing a thought very proper to be presented to the reader in the outset of the enquiry. " If America had never been discovered, the geometrical ratio, as applied to the multiplication of mankind, would never have been known. If the British colonies had never been planted, Mr. Malthus would never have written. The human species might have perished of a long old age, a fate to which perhaps all sublunary things are subject at last, without one statesman or one legislator, through myriads of centuries, having suspected this dangerous tendency to increase, ' in comparison with which human institutions, however they

---

[c] P. 139, 140.

may appear to be causes of much mischief to society, are mere feathers [d].' "

In the following pages I confine myself strictly to Mr. Malthus's book, and the question which he has brought under consideration. My bitterest enemy will hardly be able to find in this volume the author of the Enquiry concerning Political Justice. I have scarcely allowed myself to recollect the beautiful visions (if they shall turn out to be visions), which enchanted my soul, and animated my pen, while writing that work. I conceived that any distinct reference to what is there treated of, would be foreign to the subject which is now before me. The investigation of the power of increase in the numbers of mankind, must be interesting to every one to whom the human species and human society appear to be matters of serious concern: and I should have thought that I was guilty of a sort of treason against that interest, if I had unnecessarily obtruded into the discussion any thing that could shock the prejudices, or insult the views, of those whose conceptions of political truth mighty be most different from my own.

I am certainly very sorry that I was not sooner in possession of Mr. Malthus's calculation for peopling the whole visible universe with human beings at the rate of four men to every

---

[d] Essay on Population, First Edition, p. 177 ; Fifth Edition, Vol. II, p. 246.

square yard, contained in his Principles of Political Economy [e]. A considerable portion of my work was printed, before the appearance of that volume. Several passages in these sheets will read comparatively flat and tame, for want of the assistance of this happy *reductio ad absurdum* from the pen of the author.

I cannot close these few pages of Preface, without testifying my obligations to one friend in particular, Mr. David Booth, formerly of Newburgh in the county of Fife, now of London. Without the encouragement and pressing instances of this gentleman my work would never have been begun; and the main argument of the Second Book is of his suggesting. But indeed the hints and materials for illustration I have derived from his conversation are innumerable; and his mathematical skill assisted my investigations, in points in which my habits for many years, were least favourable to my undertaking.—It is further necessary I should add, that Mr. Booth has scarcely in any instance inspected my sheets, and that therefore I only am responsible for any errors they may contain.

The reader will find, annexed to the end of the Second Book, a Dissertation on the Ratios

---

[e] See below, p. 135, *et seqq.*

of Increase in Population, and in the Means of Subsistence, which that gentleman had the goodness to supply to me.

This is all that is necessary for me to say in the way of Preface. Except that I feel prompted to make my apology in this place, if I shall appear any where to have been hurried into undue warmth. I know how easily this sin is accustomed to beset all controversial writers. I hold Mr. Malthus in all due respect, at the same time that I willingly plead guilty to the charge of regarding his doctrines with inexpressible abhorrence. I fully admit however the good intentions of the author of the Essay on Population, and cheerfully seize this occasion to testify my belief in his honourable character, and his unblemished manners.

LONDON,
October 21, 1820.

POSTSCRIPT

———

I think I should be guilty of a certain omission, with which, if my readers could detect it, they would have a right to reproach me, if I did not fairly state some of the discouragements under which my work was undertaken, and has been carried on to its completion. But this I cannot do without making free with the letters of my friends; and, as long as I carefully suppress their names, I hope they will pardon the liberty I take.

The following is an extract of a letter from one of the most intelligent and highly endowed merchants of the city of London.

"November 23, 1818.

"You guess rightly, in supposing that I should hear with pleasure of your intending to controvert Mr. Malthus's book on population, especially as I think his opinion both *true* and important. Your work will not fail to draw, not only mine, but the public attention, to the most interesting subject in the whole science of political economy. If you are victorious, you will deserve a civic crown."

A zealous friend from the North writes to me in these terms:

"February 24, 1819.

"I have now to report the opinion of a good friend of yours and of mankind, to whom I communicated the great object that at present employs your pen. 'Implore Mr. Godwin,' he exclaimed, 'not to be in a hurry in publishing, and not to dispute with Malthus the prolific principle of population in new countries. The great and conclusive argument against Malthus, is the increase of refinement, luxury, dissipation, debauchery, and great cities, in old countries.' [This appears to me to be Mr. Malthus's own statement, and not an argument against him.] I add further, several of your friends here are of the same opinion, and feel considerable solicitude about the view you seem to be taking of the question."

A gentleman of the most eminent literary attainments writes to me thus:

"September 9, 1819.

"Though I have a great esteem for Malthus, I shall certainly read your work with the most respectful attention, and I shall open it with the assurance that, if it does not *alter my opinion*, it will exercise and delight my mind."

I will add one more passage from an individual of the most earnest zeal for the welfare of his fellow creatures, and who was peculiarly shocked with the views exhibited in the Essay on Population.

" May 10, 1820.

" I wish your work on population success; the views of Mr. Malthus are very dreadful. He seems to have convinced almost all men of their absolute truth, and I am sorry to say that I do not perceive his statements to be false. I shall indeed rejoice, if they are shewn to be so."

To these private communications I will add a few lines from a speech of Mr. Brougham in the House of Commons, delivered December 16, 1819. *See the Morning Chronicle.*

" Mr. Brougham had no hesitation in stating that the excess of population was one of the great causes of the distress which at present afflicted the country. This proposition from the best consideration which he had been able to give to the subject, he was fully prepared to maintain. But it was among the most melancholy mal-practices of the low part of the press, to depreciate this which was the soundest principle of political economy. Nay,

a

the worst expedients were used to calumniate the writers by whom that principle was mainly supported [f], though among those writers were to be found men of the most exalted morals, of the purest views, of the soundest intellect, and even of the most humane feelings. Yet against the writers who sought to guard society against this great evil, the utmost obloquy was directed [g]. "

A decision so absolute, at the time that my book was already in the press, might well have startled me. It fell from the lips of one of the most enlightened speakers of the present day, standing in his place in parliament. I cheerfully subscribe to the high endowments and extensive information of Mr. Brougham : and, if I could have bowed to authority merely, on a subject which had for two years occupied my almost undivided attention, I should have suppressed my work.—There is certainly a wide difference between the being seduced (as so many men have been) by the specious simplicity of Mr. Malthus's system, and the case of him who is " fully prepared" to maintain its tenets.

---

[f] This seems to be an instance of the excessive multiplication in question. By what writer has the principle been " mainly supported," but Mr. Malthus ?

[g] See further to the same purpose, below, p. 517, 518, note.

CONTENTS.

BOOK I.

OF THE POPULATION OF EUROPE, ASIA, AFRICA. AND
SOUTH AMERICA IN ANCIENT AND MODERN TIMES.

BOOK II.

OF THE POWER OF INCREASE IN THE NUMBERS OF
MANKIND, AND THE LIMITATIONS OF THAT POWER.

BOOK III.

OF THE CAUSES BY WHICH THE AMOUNT OF THE NUMBERS OF MANKIND IS REDUCED OR RESTRAINED.

BOOK IV.

OF THE POPULATION OF THE UNITED STATES OF
NORTH AMERICA.

BOOK V.

OF THE MEANS WHICH THE EARTH AFFORDS FOR THE SUBSISTENCE OF MAN.

BOOK VI.

OF THE MORAL AND POLITICAL MAXIMS INCULCATED IN THE ESSAY ON POPULATION.

" Russia being mentioned as likely to become a great empire by the rapid increase of population :—JOHNSON. Why sir, I see no prospect of their propagating more. They can have no more children than they can get. I know of no way to make them breed more than they do. BOSWELL. But have not nations been more populous at one period than another? JOHNSON. Yes, sir; but that has been owing to the people being less thinned at one time than another, whether by emigrations, war, or pestilence, not to their being more or less prolific. Births at all times bear the same proportion to the same number of people."

BOSWELL, LIFE OF JOHNSON : anno 1769.

ENQUIRY

CONCERNING

POPULATION.

BOOK I.

OF THE POPULATION OF EUROPE, ASIA, AFRICA, AND SOUTH AMERICA, IN ANCIENT AND MODERN TIMES.

CHAPTER I.

INTRODUCTION.

MR. MALTHUS has published what he calls an Essay on the Principle of Population, by which he undertakes to annul every thing that had previously been received, respecting the views that it is incumbent upon those who preside over political society to cherish, and the measures that may conduce to the happiness of mankind. His theory is evidently founded upon nothing. He says, that " population, when unchecked, goes on doubling itself every twenty-five years, or increases in a geometrical ratio.[a] "

---

[a] Essay on Population, fifth edition, vol. I. p. 9.

B

If we ask why we are to believe this, he answers that, " in the northern states of America, the population has been found so to double itself for above a century and a half successively.[b] " All this he delivers in an oraculous manner. He neither proves nor attempts to prove what he asserts. If Mr. Malthus has taken a right view of the question, it is to be hoped that some author will hereafter arise, who will go into the subject and shew that it is so.

Mr. Malthus having laid down a theory in this dogmatical manner, a sort of proceeding wholly unworthy of a reflecting nation or an enlightened age, it is time in reality that some one should sweep away this house of cards, and endeavour to ascertain whether any thing is certainly known on the subject.

This is the design and the scheme of the present volume I shall make no dogmatical assertions ; or, at least I am sure I will make none respecting the proposition or propositions which form the basis of the subject. I shall call upon my reader for no implicit faith. I shall lay down no positions authoritatively, and leave him to seek for evidence, elsewhere, and as he can, by which they may be established. All that I deliver shall be accompanied by its proofs. My purpose is to engage in a train of patient investigation, and to lay before every one who

---

[b] Vol. I. p. 7.

will go along with me, the facts which satisfy my mind on the subject, and which I am desirous should convey similar satisfaction to the minds of others.

The consequence is, that I, the first, as far as I know, of any English writer in the present century, shall have really gone into the question of population. If what I shall deliver is correct, some foundation will be laid, and the principle will begin to be understood. If what I allege as fact shall be found to be otherwise, or the conclusions I draw from my facts do not truly follow from them, I shall have set before other enquirers evidence that they may scan, and arguments that they may refute. I simply undertake to open the door for the gratification of the curious, or, more properly speaking, of those who feel an interest in the honour and happiness of the human species, which hitherto in this respect has been shut. Conscious how little as yet is known on the subject, I attempt no more than to delineate Outlines of the Doctrine of Population.

The first point then that I have to examine, and which will form the subject of Three of the Six Books into which my treatise is divided, is respecting the Power of Increase in the Numbers of the Human Species, and the Limitations of that Power. This question, precisely speaking, is the topic of the Second Book only: though I have thought proper to prefix in a

First Book a view of the numbers of mankind
in Europe, Asia, Africa, and South America,
in ancient and modern times, where population
has generally been supposed not to increase;
and in another [the Fourth] to subjoin a view
of the United States of North America in this
particular, where from some cause or other the
population has multiplied exceedingly.

The result of our investigations into the subject of population, I believe, will afford some
presumption that there is in the constitution of
the human species a power, absolutely speaking,
of increasing its numbers. Mr. Malthus says;
that the power is equal to the multiplication of
mankind by a doubling every twenty-five years,
that is, to an increase for ever in a geometrical
series, of which the exponent is 2:—a multiplication, which it is difficult for human imagination, or (as I should have thought) for human
credulity to follow: and therefore his theory
must demand the most tremendous checks [their
names in the Essay on Population are vice and
misery] to keep the power in that state of neutrality, in which it is perhaps in almost all cases
to be found in Europe. I think I shall be able
to make out that the power of increase in the
numbers of the human species is extremely
small. But, be that as it may, it must be exceedingly interesting to assign the Causes by
which this Power is Restrained from producing
any absolute multiplication, from century to

century, in those many countries where population appears to be at a stand: and I have accordingly endeavoured to take the question out of the occult and mystical state in which Mr. Malthus has left it. This disquisition forms the subject of my Third Book; as it was necessary to give it precedence over 'the examination of the population of the United States, that we might_be the better enabled to see, how far the causes which keep down population are peculiar to us, and how far they extend their agency to North America.

Such is the outline of the most essential parts of the following work; and here I might perhaps without impropriety have put an end to my labours. But, as Mr. Malthus has taken occasion to deliver many positions respecting subsistence, and various other points of political economy, I have thought it might not be useless to follow him into these topics.

The question of subsistence indeed Mr. Malthus has made an essential member of his system, having stated the power of increase in the numbers of mankind as equal to a doubling every twenty-five years for ever in geometrical series, and the utmost power of increase in the means of subsistence as reaching only to a perpetual addition of its own quantity in similar periods, or a progression in arithmetical series. Thus,

Population 1 2 4 8 16 32 64 128 256
Subsistence 1 2 3 4 5 6 7   8   9

I have therefore devoted my Fifth Book to the consideration of the Means which the Earth Affords for the Subsistence of Man.

The topic I have reserved for my Sixth Book is, at least to my apprehension, in no way less interesting than the question of Subsistence. Dr. Franklin and other writers who have attributed to the human species a power of rapidly multiplying their numbers, have either foreseen no mischief to arise from this germ of multiplication, or none but what was exceedingly remote. It is otherwise with Mr. Malthus. The geometrical ratio is every where with him a practical principle, and entitled to the most vigilant and unremitted attention of mankind. He has deduced from this consideration several moral and political maxims, which he enjoins it upon the governors of the world to attend to. I am persuaded that the elements of our author's theory are unsound, and that therefore his conclusions must follow the fate of the principle on which they are founded. But I should have left my undertaking imperfect, if I did not proceed to expose these maxims; thus, in the first place, setting the system of the Essay on Population and its practical merits in the full light of day; and, in the second, holding up for the instruction of those who may come after, an example of the monstrous errors into which a writer may be expected to fall, who shall allow himself, upon a gratuitous and

wholly unproved assumption, to build a system
of legislation, and determine the destiny of all
his fellow-creatures.   An examination of the
Moral and Political Maxims Inculcated in the
Essay on Population therefore constitutes the
subject of my Sixth Book.

I might indeed have written a treatise in
which I should have endeavoured to trace the
outlines of the subject of population, without
adverting to Mr. Malthus.   But, in the first
place it was gratifying to me to name an author,
who, however false and groundless his theories
appear to me, has had the merit of successfully
drawing the attention of the public to the subject.   I think it but fair, so far as depends upon
me, that his name should be preserved, whatever
becomes of the volumes he has written.   If any
benefit shall arise from the discussion of the
Doctrine of Population, there is a propriety in
recollecting the person by whose writings the
question has been set afloat, though he has not
discussed.   And, in the second place, I know
that the attention of the majority of readers is
best secured by the appearance of a contention.
If I had delivered the speculations of the following pages in a form severely scientific, and still
more if I had written my book without Mr.
Malthus's going before me, I should have appeared to multitudes to be elaborately explain-
ing what was too clear for an argument, and

could not have expected to excite an interest, to which under the present circumstances, if I have done any thing effectually on the subject, I may be thought reasonably entitled.

CHAPTER II.

SURVEY OF THE CREATION FROM NATURAL HISTORY.

Ο δὶ Θεος και η φυσις ουδὶν ματην ποιουσιν.
Aristoteles, De Cœlo, Lib. I, *cap.* 4.

PREVIOUSLY to our entering directly on the subject before us, it will probably be found not wholly unworthy of attention to recollect, in how different a way the multiplication of the human species has ordinarily been regarded, by writers whose purpose it was to survey the various classes of existence that form the subject of natural history, and who were satisfied to discover " the wisdom of God in the works of creation," from the ideas expressed by Mr. Malthus. The following is the manner in which the subject is stated by Goldsmith, one of the latest of the number, in his History of the Earth and Animated Nature.

" We may observe, that. that generation is the most complete, in which the fewest animals are produced : Nature, by attending to the production of one at a time, seems to exert all her efforts in bringing it to perfection : but, where this attention is divided, the animals so produced come into the world with partial advantages. In this manner twins are never, at least while infants, so large or strong as those that come singly into the world; each having, in some measure, robbed the other of its right; as that support which Nature meant for one, has been prodigally divided.

"In this manner, as those animals are the best that are produced singly, so we find that the noblest animals are ever the least fruitful. These are seen usually to bring forth but one at a time, and to place all their attention upon that alone. On the other hand, all the oviparous kinds produce in amazing plenty; and even the lower tribes of the viviparous animals increase in a seeming proportion to their minuteness and imperfection. Nature seems lavish of life in the lower orders of creation; and, as if she meant them entirely for the use of the nobler races, she appears to have bestowed greater pains in multiplying the number, than in completing this kind. In this manner, while the elephant and the horse bring forth but one at a time, the spider and the beetle are seen to produce a thousand: and even among the smaller quadrupeds, all the inferior kinds are extremely fertile; any one of these being found, in a very few months, to become the parent of a numerous progeny.

"In this manner therefore the smallest animals multiply in the greatest proportion; and we have reason to thank Providence, that the most formidable animals are the least fruitful. Had

the lion and the tiger the same degree of fecundity with the rabbit or the rat, all the arts of
man would be unable to oppose these fierce invaders, and we should soon perceive them become the tyrants of those who claim the lordship
of the creation.   But Heaven, in this respect,
has wisely consulted the advantage of all.   It
has opposed to man only such enemies, as he
has art and strength to conquer ; and, as large
animals require proportional supplies, nature was
unwilling to give new life, where it in some measure denied the necessary means of subsistence.

" In consequence of this pre-established order,
the animals that are endowed with the most perfect methods of generation, and bring forth but
one at a time, seldom begin to procreate, till they
have almost acquired their full growth.   On the
other hand, those which bring forth many, engender before they have arrived at half their natural
size.   The horse and the bull come almost to
perfection before they begin to generate ; the hog
and the rabbit scarcely leave the teat before they
become parents themselves.   In whatever light
therefore we consider this subject, we shall find
that all creatures approach most to perfection,
whose generation most nearly resembles that of
man.   The reptile produced from cutting, is but
one degree above the vegetable.   The animal
produced from the egg, is a step higher in the
scale of existence : that class of animals which
are brought forth alive, are still more exalted.

Of these, such as bring forth one at a time are the most complete; and foremost of these stands man, *the great master of all*, who seems to have united the perfections of all the rest in his formation [a]."

---

[a] History of the Earth and Animated Nature, Part II. Chap. II.

CHAPTER III.

GENERAL VIEWS AS TO THE ALLEGED INCREASE OF MANKIND.

To take a just view of any subject, one rule that is extremely worthy of our attention is, that we should get to a proper distance from it. The stranger to whom we would convey an adequate image of the city of London, we immediately lead to the top of St. Paul's Church. And, if I may introduce an allusion to the records of the Christian religion, the devil took our Saviour " up into an exceeding high mountain," when he would " shew him all the kingdoms of the world, and the glory of them."

Mr. Malthus has taken his stand upon the reports of Dr. Franklin, and Dr. Ezra Styles. He repairs with them to the northern parts of the United States of America, and there he sees, or thinks he sees, " the population doubling itself, for above a century and a half successively, in less than twenty-five years," and that " from procreation only [a]." He does not discover an ample population even in this, his favourite country. Far from it. The reason why the population goes on so rapidly in North America is, accord-

---

[a] Essay on Population, vol. I. p. 9.

ing to him, because there is " ample room and
verge enough" for almost all the population that
can be poured into it. He sees, in his prophetic
conception, that country, some centuries hence,
full of human inhabitants, even to overflowing,
and groaning under the multitude of the tribes
shall dwell in it.

Would it not have been fairer to have taken
before him the globe of earth at one view, and
from thence to have deduced the true " Principle
of Population," and the policy that ought to direct the measures of those who govern the world ?

How long the race of man has subsisted, unless we derive our opinions on the subject from
the light of revelation, no man knows. The
Chinese, and the people of Indostan, carry back
their chronology through millions of years.
Even if we refer to the Bible, the Hebrew text,
and the Samaritan which is perhaps of equal authority, differ most considerably and fundamentally from each other. But Mr. Malthus is of
opinion, that, in reasoning on subjects of political economy, we are bound to regulate our ideas
by statistical reports, and tables that have been
scientifically formed by proficients in that study,
and has accordingly confined himself to these.

But, though we know not how long the human race has existed, nor how extensive a period
it has had to multiply itself in, we are able to
form some rude notions respecting its present
state. It has by some persons been made an

objection to the Christian religion, that it has not become universal. It would perhaps be fairer, to make it an objection to the " Principle of Population," as laid down by Mr. Malthus, that the earth is not peopled.

If I were to say that the globe would maintain twenty times its present inhabitants, or, in other words, that for every human creature now called into existence, twenty might exist in a state of greater plenty and happiness than with our small number we do at present, I should find no one timid and saturnine enough to contradict me. In fact, he must be a literal and most uninventive speculator, who would attempt to set bounds to the physical powers of the earth to supply the means of human subsistence.

The first thing therefore that would occur to him who should survey " all the kingdoms of the earth," and the state of their population, would be the thinness of their numbers, and the multitude and extent of their waste and desolate places. If his heart abounded with " the milk of human kindness," he would not fail to contrast the present state of the globe with its possible state; he would see his species as a little remnant widely scattered over a fruitful and prolific surface, and would weep to think that the kindly and gracious qualities of our mother earth were turned to so little account. If he were more of a sober and reasoning, than of a tender and passionate temper, perhaps he would not weep, but I should think he would set himself seriously to enquire, how the populousness of nations might be increased, and the different regions of the globe replenished with a numerous and happy race.

Dr. Paley's observations on this head are peculiarly to the purpose. " The quantity of happiness," he says, " in any given district, although it is possible it may be increased, the number of inhabitants remaining the same, is chiefly and most naturally affected by alteration of the numbers : consequently, *the decay of population is the greatest evil that a state can suffer ;* and the improvement of it is the object, which ought in all countries to be aimed at, in preference to every other political purpose whatsoever [b]."

Such has been the doctrine, I believe, of every enlightened politician and legislator since the world began. But Mr. Malthus has placed this subject in a new light. He thinks that there is a possibility that the globe of earth may at some time or other contain more human inhabitants than it can subsist; and he has therefore written a book, the direct tendency of which is to keep down the numbers of mankind. He has no consideration for the millions and millions of men, who might be conceived as called into existence, and made joint partakers with us in such happiness as a sublunary existence, with li-

---

[b] Moral and Political Philosophy, Book VI. Chap. xi.

berty and improvement, might impart; but, for the sake of a future possibility, would shut against them once for all the door of existence.

He says indeed, " The difficulty, so far from being remote, is imminent and immediate. At every period during the progress of cultivation, from the present moment to the time when the whole earth was become like a garden, the distress for want of food would be constantly pressing on all mankind [c]." He adds it is true in this place, " if they were equal." But these words are plainly unnecessary, since it is almost the sole purpose of his book to shew, that, in all old established countries, " the population is always pressing hard against the means of subsistence."

This however—I mean the distress that must always accompany us in every step of our progress—is so palpably untrue, that I am astonished that any man should have been induced by the love of paradox, and the desire to divulge something new, to make the assertion. There is no principle respecting man and society more certain, than that every man in a civilized state is endowed with the physical power of producing more than shall suffice for his own subsistence. This principle lies at the foundation of all the history of all mankind. If it were otherwise, we should be all cultivators of the earth. We should none of us ever know the sweets of leisure; and all

---

[c] Vol. II. p. 220.

human science would be contained in the knowledge of seed-time and harvest. But no sooner
have men associated in tribes and nations, than
this great truth comes to be perceived, that comparatively a very small portion of labour on the
part of the community, will subsist the whole.
Hence it happens that even the farmer and the
husbandman have leisure for their religion, their
social pleasures, and their sports ; and hence it
happens, which is of infinitely more importance
in the history of the human mind, that, while
a minority of the community are employed in
the labours indispensibly conducive to the mere
subsistence of the whole, the rest can devote
themselves to art, to science, to literature, to
contemplation, and even to all the wanton refinements of sensuality, luxury, and ostentation.

What is it then, we are naturally led to ask,
that causes any man to starve, or prevents him
from cultivating the earth, and subsisting upon
its fruits, so long as there is a portion of soil in
the country in which he dwells, that has not
been applied to the producing as much of the
means of human subsistence, as it is capable of
producing ? Mr. Malthus says, it is " *the Law of
Nature.*" " After the public notice which I
have proposed, if any man chose to marry,
without a prospect of being able to support a family, he should have the most perfect liberty to
do so.   Though to marry, in this case, is in my
opinion clearly an immoral act, yet it is not one

which society can justly take upon itself to prevent or punish.   To the *punishment of Nature*
therefore he should be left d."   And elsewhere,
" A man who is born into a world already possessed, if he cannot get subsistence from his parents, and if the society do not want his labour,
has no claim of right to the smallest portion of
food, and in fact has no business to be where he
is.   At *Nature's mighty feast* there is no vacant
cover for him.   *She* tells him to be gone, and
will quickly execute *her own* orders e."

Never surely was there so flagrant an abuse of
terms, as in this instance.   Mr. Malthus is speaking of England, where there are many thousands
of acres wholly uncultivated, and perhaps as
many more scarcely employed in any effectual
manner to increase the means of human subsistence; for these passages occur in chapters of
his Essay where he is treating of our Poor-laws,
and the remedies that might be applied to the

---

d Vol. III. p. 180.

e This passage, which occurs in the Second Edition in quarto, p.
531, is not to be found in the Fifth Edition of the Essay.   But I beg
leave once for all to observe, that those sentences of our author, the
sense of which he has never shewn the slightest inclination to retract,
and the spirit of which on the contrary is of the essence of his
system, I do not hold myself bound to pass over unnoticed, merely
because he has afterwards expunged them, that he might not " inflict an unnecessary violence on the feelings of his readers [Quar-
terly Review for July 1817.]," or that he might " soften some of the
harshest conclusions of the first Essay [Malthus, Preface to the
Second Edition.]."

defects he imputes to them. I grant him then, that it is *Law* which condemns the persons he speaks of to starve. So far we are agreed. This Law Mr. Malthus may affirm to be just, to be wise, to be necessary to the state of things as we find them. All this would be open to fair enquiry. Great and cogent no doubt are the reasons that have given so extensive a reign to this extreme inequality. But it is not *the Law of Nature*. It is *the Law of very artificial life*. It is the Law which " heaps upon some few with vast excess" the means of every wanton expence and every luxury, while others, some of them not less worthy, are condemned to pine in want.

Compare this then with Mr. Malthus's favourite position, in opposition to what he calls " the great error under which Mr. Godwin labours," that " political regulations and the established administration of property are in reality light and superficial causes of mischief to society, in comparison with those which result from the *Laws of Nature* ꜰ."

But to return, and resume the point with which this chapter commenced. If Mr. Malthus's doctrine is true, why is the globe not peopled? If the human species has so strong a tendency to increase, that, unless the tendency were violently and calamitously counteracted, they would every where " double their num-

---

ꜰ Vol. II. p. 245.

bers in less than twenty-five years," and that for ever, how comes it that the world is a wilderness, a wide and desolate place, where men crawl about in little herds, comfortless, unable from the dangers of free-booters, and the dangers of wild beasts to wander from climate to climate, and without that mutual support and cheerfulness which a populous earth would most naturally afford?   The man on the top of St Paul's would indeed form a conception of innumerable multitudes : but he who should survey " all the kingdoms of the world," would receive a very different impression.   On which side then lies the evidence? Do the numbers of mankind actually and in fact increase or decrease?   If mankind has so powerfⁱl and alarming a tendency to increase, how is 't that this tendency no where shews itself in general history? Mr. Malthus and his followers are reduced to confess the broad and glaring fact that mankind do not increase, but he has found out a calculation, a geometrical ratio, to shew that they ought to do so, and then sits down to write three volumes, assigning certain obscure, vague, and undefinable causes, why his theory and the stream of ancient and modern history are completely at variance with each other.

CHAPTER IV.

GENERAL VIEW OF THE ARGUMENTS AGAINST
THE INCREASE OF MANKIND.

MR Malthus's theory is certainly of a peculiar
structure, and it is somewhat difficult to account
for the success it has met with.

The subject is population.

It has been agreed among the best philosophers in Europe, especially from the time of
Lord Bacon to the present day, that the proper
basis of all our knowledge respecting man and
nature, respecting what has been in times that
are past, and what may be expected in time to
come, is experiment. This standard is peculiarly applicable to the subject of population.

Mr. Malthus seems in one respect fully to con-
cur in this way of viewing the subject. There
are two methods of approaching the question,
the first, by deriving our ideas respecting it from
the volumes of sacred writ, and the second, by
having recourse to such enumerations, statistical
tables, and calculations, as the industry of mere
uninspired men has collected; and Mr. Malthus
has made his election for the latter. Dr. Robert Wallace, an able writer on these subjects,
whose works have lately engaged in a considerable degree the attention of curious enquirers,

has taken the opposite road. He begins his
Dissertation on the Numbers of Mankind in Ancient and Modern Times, printed in 1753, with
the position that the whole human race is descended " from a single pair," and, taking that
for the basis of his theory, proceeds to calculate
the periods of the multiplication of mankind.

Mr. Malthus, on the contrary reposes throughout his Essay on the pure basis of human experience and unenlightened human reason ; and I
have undertaken to write a refutation of his
theories.   He has chosen his ground ; and I follow him to the contest.   He had made no allusion to Adam and Eve, and has written just as
any speculator in political economy might have
done, to whom the records of the Bible were unknown.   If there is any thing irreverend in this,
to Mr. Malthus, and not to me, the blame is to
be imputed.   He has constructed his arguments
upon certain *data*, and I have attempted nothing
more than the demolishing of those arguments.
If any one shall be of opinion that the whole
question is in the jurisdiction of another court,
the Treatise I am writing has nothing to do
with this.   I design nothing more than an investigation of mere human authorities, and an
examination of the theories of the Essay on Population ; and I leave the question in all other
respects as I found it [a].   To return.

---

[a] See further on this subject, Book II. Chapter II. note a.

It will appear, I think, in the course of our discussion, that population is a subject with which mankind as yet are very little acquainted. But let us first recollect what it is that we are supposed to know. And I will first state those things which are admitted by Mr. Malthus, and which appear to make very little for the support of his system.

The globe we inhabit may be divided into the Old World and the New. Our knowledge of the history of Europe and Asia extends backward some thousand years. We know a little of the history of Africa. America was discovered about three hundred years ago, but has not in many of its parts been by any means so long a place of reception for European colonies. Mr. Malthus does not venture to carry his appeal on the subject of population there, farther back than one hundred and fifty years [b].

Well then, how stands the question of population in the Old World? Mr. Malthus freely and without hesitation admits, that on this side of the globe population is, and has long been, at a stand; he might safely have added that it has not increased as far back as any authentic records of profane history will carry us. He brings forward some memorable examples of a striking depopulation [c]: he might have added many more: he would certainly have found it difficult

---

[b] Vol. I. p. 7.   [c] Vol. I. p. 255. et seqq.

to produce an example equally unequivocal, of an increase of population, in any quarter of the Old World.

As to South America, and the indigenous inhabitants of North America, it is hardly to be disputed, and Mr. Malthus is very ready to admit, that they have sustained a melancholy diminution since the voyage of Columbus [d].

Such then is, so far, the foundation of our knowledge, as afforded us by experience, on the subject of population.   Mr. Malthus has brought forward an exception to all this, which I shall hereafter take occasion fully to examine, in a certain tract of the globe, now known by the name of the United States of America, and he affirms this exception to spread itself over a period of one hundred and fifty years.   The entire foundation of his work lies in one simple sentence : " In the Northern States of America, the population has been found to double itself for above a century and a half successively, in less than twenty-five years. [e] "

The pith of Mr. Malthus's book therefore, and a bolder design has seldom entered into the mind of man, is to turn the exception into the rule, and the whole stream of examples in every other case, into exceptions, that are to be accounted for without detracting from the authority of the rule.

---

d Vol. II. p. 289.   e Vol. I. p. 7.

The Essay on Population is the most oddly constructed, of any book, pretending to the character of science, that was perhaps ever given to the world.

It consists, in the copy now lying before me, of three volumes.

The first chapter, containing sixteen pages, comprises the whole doctrine upon which the work is founded. He that should read the first chapter, and no more, would be in possession of every thing in the book, that is solid and compressed, and bears so much as the air of science.

The next 698 pages,[f] the most considerable portion of the work, are wholly employed in assigning causes why every region of the globe, in every period of its history, part of the United States of America for the last one hundred and fifty years excepted, appears to contradict the positions of Mr. Malthus's theory. This is done by exhibiting certain checks on population, the whole of which, as will more fully appear hereafter, falls under the two heads of vice and misery. The remainder of the work treats of the different systems or expedients which have been proposed or have prevailed, as they affect the evils which arise out of the author's principle of population[g], and of our future prospects respecting the removal or mitigation of these evils[h].

Now upon this shewing, I affirm that Mr.

---

[f] Book I. and II.   [g] Book III.   [h] Book IV.

Malthus is the most fortunate man that ever lived, Sterne's king of Bohemia himself not being excepted[i]. Notwithstanding this glaring rottenness and fallacy in the first concoction of his work, the author has carried the whole world before him; no other system of thinking on the subject is admitted into the company of the great; hundreds of men who were heretofore earnest champions of the happiness of mankind have become his converts; and though, I believe, from thirty to forty answers have been written to the Essay on Population, not one of them, so far as I know, has undertaken to controvert the main principle and corner-stone of his system.

The strength of Mr. Malthus's writing wholly depends upon his intrenching himself in general statements. If we hope for any victory over him, it must be by drawing him out of his strong hold, and meeting him upon the fair ground of realities.

The hypothesis of the Essay on Population is this. The human species doubles itself in the United States of America every twenty-five years : therefore it must have an inherent tendency so to double itself : therefore it would so double itself in the Old World, were not the

---

[i] " The corporal forthwith began to run back in his mind, the principal events in the king of Bohemia's story, from every one of which it appeared that he was the most fortunate man that ever existed in the world." *Tristram Shandy*, vol. VI.

increase intercepted by causes which have not yet sufficiently engaged the attention of political enquirers.

To clear up this point let us consider how many children may be allowed to a marriage, upon the supposition that the object is barely to keep the numbers of the human species up to their present standard. In the first place it is clear, that every married pair may be allowed two upon an average, without any increase to the population, nay, with the certainty of diminution if they fall short of this. In the next place it is unquestionable, that every child that is born, does not live to years of maturity, so as to be able to propagate the kind ; for this condition is necessary, the children who die in their nonage plainly contributing nothing to the keeping up the numbers of our species. I should have thought therefore, that we might safely allow of three children to every marriage, without danger of overstocking the community. It will hereafter appear that all political economists allow four, it being the result of various censuses and tables of population, that one-half of the born die under years of maturity [k]. To this number of children to be allowed to every marriage upon an average, the purpose being barely to keep up the numbers of our species to the present standard, something must be added,

---

[k] Franklin, Works, 1806, vol. II. p. 385.

in consideration of the known fact, that every man and woman do not marry, and thus put themselves in the road for continuing their species.

When Mr. Malthus therefore requires us to believe in the geometrical ratio, or that the human species has a natural tendency to double itself every twenty-five years, he does nothing less in other words, than require us to believe that every marriage among human creatures produces upon an average, including the prolific marriages, those in which the husband or wife die in the vigour of their age or in the early years of their union, those in which the prolific power seems particularly limited, and the marriages that are totally barren, eight children [1].

All this Mr. Malthus requires us to believe, because he wills it. Let it never again be made one of the reproaches of the present day, that we are fallen upon an age of incredulity. I am sure no false prophet, in the darkest ages of ignorance, could ever boast of a greater number of hoodwinked and implicit disciples, than Mr. Malthus in this enlightened period.

How comes it, that neither this author, nor any one for him, has looked into this view of the question? There are such things as registers of marriages and births. To these it was natural

---

[1] " If in Europe they have but four births to a marriage, we in America must reckon eight."—Franklin, *ubi supra.*

for Mr. Malthus to have recourse for a correlative argument to support his hypothesis. The writer of the Essay on Population has resorted to certain statements of the population of the United States, and from them has inferred that the number of its citizens have doubled every twenty-five years, and as he adds, " by procreation only :" that is, in other words, as we have shown, that every marriage in America, and by parity of reasoning, in all other parts of the world, produces upon an average eight children. For the difference between the United States and the Old World does not, I presume, lie in the superior fecundity of their women, but that a greater number of children are cut off in the Old World in years of nonage, by vice and misery. We double very successfully (if they double) in the first period ; but we do not, like them, rear our children, to double over again in the second. Naturally therefore he would have produced a strong confirmation of his hypothesis, by shewing from the registers of different parts of the world, or of different countries of Europe, that every marriage does upon an average produce eight children : and if he had done this, I think he would have saved me the trouble of writing this volume. Something however has been done in the way of collating the registers of marriages and births ; and of this I shall make full use in my Second Book.

It may however be objected, that there are

two ways in which an increase of population may be intercepted; either by the number of children who shall perish in their nonage, through the powerful agency, as Mr. Malthus informs us, of vice and misery; or by certain circumstances which shall cause a smaller number to be born: it may not therefore be merely by the ravages of an extensive mortality, that population in the Old World is kept down to its level.

Mr. Malthus himself has furnished me with a complete answer to this objection.   In the first edition of his book [m] he sets out with what he called " fairly making two *postulata*: first, that food is necessary to the existence of man: secondly, that the passion between the sexes is necessary, and will always remain nearly in its present state."

This indeed is one of the " passages, which the author has expunged in the later editions of his book, that he might not inflict an unnecessary violence upon the feelings of his readers [n]." or, as he himself expresses it, is one of the places, in which he " has endeavoured to soften some of the harshest conclusions of his first Essay—in doing which he hopes he has not violated the principles of just reasoning [o]."   But, as Mr. Malthus has retained to the last all the conclu-

---

[m] P. 11.   [n] Quarterly Review, No. XXXIV, p. 374.

[o] Preface, Second Edition, p. vii; Fifth Edition, p. ix.

sions drawn from these *postulata*, and as his argument respecting the impracticability of a permanent state of equality among human beings, founded upon the parity of these two propositions, stands in the Fifth Edition *verbatim* as it stood in the first P, I cannot myself consent to his withdrawing his premises, at the same time that he retains the inferences built upon them.

Again: in compliance with " the feelings of certain readers," Mr. Malthus has added in his subsequent editions, to the two checks upon population, *viz.* vice and misery, as they stood in the first, a third which he calls moral restraint. But then he expressly qualifies this by saying, " the principle of moral restraint has undoubtedly in past ages operated with very inconsiderable force q;" subjoining at the same time his protest against " any opinion respecting the probable improvement of society, in which we are not borne out by the experience of the past r."

It is clearly therefore Mr. Malthus's doctrine, that population is kept down in the Old World, not by a smaller number of children being born among us, but by the excessive number of children that perish in their non-

---

p First Edition, p. 184 to 209 ; Fifth Edition, vol. II. p. 251 to 270.

q Second Edition, p. 384. See this question more fully discussed in Book VI. of the present work.

r Preface, p. ix.

age through the instrumentality of vice and misery.

Let us then proceed to illustrate this proposition, in its application to our own beloved country of England. We will take its present population at ten millions. Of this population we will suppose five millions to be adults. There must then, according to the statement of Dr. Franklin and other calculators, be ten millions of children, born and to be born from these five millions of adults, to give us a chance of keeping up the race of Englishmen. Of these ten millions five millions must be expected to die in their nonage, according to the constitution and course of nature. Surely this, together with the incessant uninterrupted mortality of the middle-aged, and of the more ancient members of society, may be regarded as sufficiently rendering the globe we inhabit " a universe of death."

But Mr. Malthus demands from us, by virtue of his geometrical ratio, ten millions of children more than our unsuspecting ancestors ever dreamed of, that is, eight children for every pair of adults. I say eight, because, if in countries where they have room and every facility for rearing their children, two perish in their nonage out of the first four, there can be no reason that I can apprehend, why as many should not perish out of the second four. Thus it appears that, for every five millions that grow up to the estate

D

of man and woman, twenty millions of children
are born, of which fifteen millions, every where
in the Old World, perish in their infancy.   The
first five millions of those who die in this manner, constitute a mortality that we must be contented to witness, since such, it seems, is the condition of our existence.   But the next ten millions I should call a sort of superfetation of al-
ternate births and deaths, purely for the benefit
of the geometrical ratio.

But where is the record of all this ?   In most
civilized countries some sort of register is kept
of births, marriages, and deaths.   I believe no
trace of these additional births which Mr. Malthus has introduced to our acquaintance, is any
where to be found.   Were all these children sent
out of the world, without so much as the ceremonies of baptism ?   Were they exposed among
the wilds of Mount Taygetus, or cast into the
Barathrum, or hurled from the Tarpeian rock, or
carelessly thrown forth, as Mr. Malthus says
the Chinese infants are in the streets of Pekin ?
For my own part, I am disposed to require some
further evidence on the subject, than merely to
be told they must have been born and have died,
in defiance of all received evidence on the subject, because such is the inference that follows
from the principles of the Essay on Population.

In reality, if I had not taken up the pen with
the express purpose of confuting all the errors of
Mr. Malthus's book, and of endeavouring to in-

troduce other principles, more cheering, more
favourable to the best interests of mankind, and
better prepared to resist the inroads of vice and
misery, I might close my argument here, and
lay down the pen with this brief remark, that,
when this author shall have produced from any
country, the United States of North America
not excepted, a register of marriages and births,
from which it shall appear that there are on an
average eight births to a marriage, then, and not
till then, can I have any just reason to admit his
doctrine of the geometrical ratio.

CHAPTER V.

NUMBERS OF MANKIND IN ANCIENT AND
MODERN TIMES.

Les hommes ne multiplient pas aussi aisément qu'on le pense.
VOLTAIRE, *Histoire Générale*, CHAP. I.

IT is not a little singular, and is proper to be
commemorated here, that a controversy existed
in the early part of the last century, as to the
comparative populousness of ancient nations, or
the contrary. One of the leaders in this debate
was the celebrated Montesquieu; and what he
says on the subject is so much to the purpose,
that I shall translate the passage.

" To amuse in some part," says one of the cor-
respondents in the Persian Letters to another,
" the time of my visit to Europe, I devote myself to the perusal of the historians, ancient and
modern; I compare the different ages of the
world; I am pleased to make them pass, so to
speak, in review before me; and I fix my attention particularly upon those great changes, which
have rendered some ages so different from others,
and the world so unlike to itself.

" You perhaps have not turned your thoughts,

upon a thing that to me is altogether surprising. How happens it that the world is so thinly peopled in comparison with what it was formerly? How is it that nature has wholly lost that prodigious fecundity which she boasted in earlier times? Is it that she is in her decrepitude, and is hastening to her final extinction?

" I have resided more than a year in Italy, and I have seen there only the ruins of that Italy which was anciently so famous. Though its present population is confined to the towns, they are themselves mere vacancy and a desart: it seems as if they subsisted for no other purpose, than to mark the spot where those magnificent cities formerly stood, with whose policy and whose wars history is filled.

" There are persons who pretend that Rome alone formerly contained a greater population than any one of the most powerful kingdoms of Europe does at present. There were single Roman citizens, who possessed ten, and even twenty thousand slaves, without including those they used for rustic employments: and as the numbers of the citizens alone amounted to 4 or 500,000, we cannot calculate the entire population of this great city, without reaching to a number at which the imagination revolts.

" Sicily, in times of old, contained within its shores flourishing states and powerful kingdoms, which have entirely disappeared: it is now considerable only for its volcanoes.

" Greece is so wholly deserted, as not to contain the hundredth part of the number of its former inhabitants.

" Spain, formerly so abundant in men, exhibits nothing at the present day but a variety of provinces, almost without inhabitants; and France is an unpeopled region, compared with that ancient Gaul which Cæsar describes to us.

" The north of Europe is in a manner stripped of its people. The times are no more, when she was obliged to separate her population into portions, and to send forth, as in swarms, colonies and whole nations, to seek some new spot where they might dwell at large.

" Poland and Turkey in Europe are almost without inhabitants.

" In America we do not find more than the two-hundredth part of the men who formerly composed its mighty empires.

" Asia is not in a much better condition. That Asia Minor, which boasted so many powerful monarchies, and so prodigious a number of great cities, has now but two or three cities within her limits. As to the Greater Asia, that part which is subject to the Turk is in no better condition, and for the part over which our monarch reigns [Persia], if we compare it with its former flourishing condition, we shall see that it contains but a very small residue of the population which anciently furnished the innumerable hosts of Xerxes and Darius.

" As to the smaller states, which are placed in the vicinity of these great empires, they are literally unpeopled; such for example are Imiretta, Circassia and Guriel. All these princes, with the extent of country over which they preside, have scarcely in their subjection so many as fifty thousand human beings.

" Egypt has not suffered less than the countries I have mentioned.

" In a word I review the different nations of the earth; and I find nothing but destruction. I seem to see a race of beings, just escaped from the ravages of an universal plague, or an universal famine.

" Africa has always been so unpenetrated, that we cannot speak of it with the same precision as of other parts of the globe; but, if we turn our attention only to the coasts of the Mediterranean, the portion of it which is known, we see at once how wretchedly it has sunk, since the period in which it formed a Roman province of the first order. Its princes are now so feeble, that they are strictly the smallest powers in existence.

" Upon a calculation, the most exact that matters of this sort will admit, I am led to think that the earth does not contain now fully the fiftieth part of the human beings, that inhabited it in the time of Cæsar. What is most astonishing is, that its population every day grows thinner; and if it goes on at the same rate, in one thousand years more, the race of man will be extinct.

" Here then, my dear friend, we are presented with the most fearful catastrophe that imagination can form.   Yet it is hardly attended to, because it proceeds by insensible degrees, and spreads itself over such a series of ages. But that very thing proves incontestibly, that there is an innate vice, a concealed and inaccessible poison, a wasting disease, which clings to our nature, and cannot be removed [a]."

It is surprising, if the Persian Letters ever fell in the way of Mr. Malthus's juvenile reading, that this impressive representation should not a little have startled him, amidst his anxieties and alarms for the excessive and ruinous multiplication of mankind. It would seem to require considerable strength of nerve, in the face of such a picture, to preach his *doctrine of depopulation;* for such in the sequel it will be discovered to be.

I know that this representation of Montesquieu has been controverted, and that among others it has fallen under the acute examination of Hume. But the most I think that Hume has effected, is to throw some portion of uncertainty on the subject.

---

[a] *Lettres Persanes, Lettre* CVIII. The ideas delivered here are resumed, and made the subject of further discussion in *L'Esprit des Loix, Livre* XXIII. *chap.* xix. *et seqq.*

It may be worth while to remark how gross and obvious are the mistakes into which a careless observer inevitably falls upon this question of population.

He goes into a village or a little town, and he is struck with the number of children he sees, playing, skipping, laughing, crying, paddling in the dirt, and almost running under his horse's feet, as he passes along. From this phenomenon he sagaciously concludes, " There is no fear for the future population of this village."

If he made an enumeration of the inhabitants of the village, would he find that the number of children taken together exceeded the number of inhabitants arrived at years of maturity? The result of the American census, as we shall presently see, is that half the inhabitants are under, and half above sixteen years of age. But, it has appeared from all the Tables, that if the present race of grown men and women did not produce children to the amount of double their own number, the race of mankind could not be kept up, consequently, if at any given period, as in America, the children only equal the adults in number, we must depend upon the recruits to be added every year, for the preservation of our species. If those that have already become mothers universally ceased to become mothers in future, and devolved the task wholly upon their offspring, and this were repeated from period to period, it would be a matter of no difficult cal culation to determine the precise era at which the human race would be extinct.

And what is the ground of this general mistake? Simply that we see those who are born, but do not see those who die. They are consigned to the silent grave, and we soon learn almost to forget that they ever existed. Hence Mr. Malthus and others would terrify us with the spectre of an imaginary overpopulation. Xerxes, I suspect, understood this matter much better, when he wept to think that, of the millions of men that passed in review before him in his march into Greece, not one would be alive at the end of one hundred years. Every old man is accustomed to the remark, that he sees all his contemporaries dying from around him, and that he is left in a manner alone in a new world. We depend entirely and exclusively upon the rising generation for the future population of the earth. In a few years I and my present readers of the year 1820 will have all left the stage, and the children that live under our roofs, or that we see in the streets, will be the only men and women, to conduct the affairs, and continue the race, of human kind. Mr Malthus, and men like Mr. Malthus, who have been accustomed to look with a jealous eye, and with certain feelings of terror and alarm, upon the number of little children they meet with, would, if they maturely considered this, contemplate the spectacle with a very different sentiment.

CHAPTER VI.

ILLUSTRATIONS FROM THE HISTORY OF CHINA.

NOTHING can be more ludicrous than that part of Mr. Malthus's book, in which, for 698 successive pages, he professes to treat of the checks by which population has actually been kept down to the level of the means of subsistence, whether in ancient or modern times. He acknowledges that in most countries population is at a stand. He takes little notice of the many instances, both in ancient and modern times, in which it has glaringly decreased. And he affirms, upon what evidence it is one of the special objects of this book to examine, that population, if unchecked, would go on, doubling itself every twenty-five years, or in a much shorter period, for ever.

Now, if Mr. Malthus had intended a fair and full examination of this question, he should have set down, in the first place, in each country how many children, in the natural order of things, would be born, and then have proceeded, in the second place, to show how they were cut off. This would have been to have reasoned like a mathematician, like a genuine political economist, and like a philosopher. But the first of these points Mr. Malthus has uniformly omitted. He has therefore appeared to walk over the course at an easy pace, somewhat like Bobadil in the play, calling for "twenty more, kill them too," simply by directing the keeper of the lists on no account to give entrance to a real combatant.

Since the author of the Essay on Population has omitted this essential part of the consideration, I will endeavour to supply the defect.

The fairest instance on many accounts to begin with, is that of China. In Mr. Malthus's book there is a chapter, entitled, " Of the Checks to Population in China and Japan [a]:" and the author, having spent a number of smooth sentences on the subject, to the amount of thirty-four pages, seems well satisfied that he has shewn that the actual state and history of China and Japan serve fully to confirm his opinion, that the population of the world would go on, unchecked, at the rate of doubling itself every twenty-five years or sooner.

China is a country that is supposed to be more fully peopled than any other country in the world. According to Mr. Malthus the population of that empire has been wholly at a stand for the last hundred years: for he quotes Du Halde in the beginning of the last century, to confirm the enumeration of Sir George Staunton at the end of it, and concludes that these two

---

[a] Book I. Chapter xii.

authorities substantially agree with each other [b]. Now China is a country of so uniform a tenour, its manners, its customs, its laws, its division of property, and its policy continuing substantially the same, that, if the population has been at a stand during the last century, there is every reason to suppose it has been at a stand, perhaps for ten centuries. China therefore is the most desirable instance that can be taken, of any old country, upon which to try the doctrine of the geometrical ratio.

China has other advantages of no mean importance to the application of our argument. First, that in this empire " extraordinary encouragements have always been given to marriage [c]." Hume states, that every man in China is married before he is twenty [d]. Mr. Barrow, a recent traveller, who accompanied Lord Macartney in his embassy in 1793, says, " Public opinion considers celibacy as disgraceful, and a sort of infamy is attached to a man who continues unmarried beyond a certain time of life. As an encouragement to marriage, every male child may be provided for, and receive a stipend from the moment of his birth, by his name being enrolled on the military list." He adds, " In China there are few of those manufacturing cities, which among us produce so

[b] Vol. I. p. 292, 3.   [c] P. 300.
[d] Essay on the Populousness of Ancient Nations.

great a waste of human life. No great capitals are here employed in any one branch of the arts. In general each labours for himself in his own profession. The still and inanimate kind of life which is led by the women, at the same tim : that it is supposed to render them more prolific, preserves them from accidents that might occasion untimely births ᵉ." So that here full scope is afforded to the principle of population.

It is somewhat remarkable that in this country, where the principle of population might reasonably be expected to have been first understood, if not in the exact period of its duplication, at least in its tremendous tendency to excess, no remedies should ever have been thought of by the governors of the country. China is something like the republic of Venice, as it stood for a period of a thousand years, famous for the profoundness of its policy, and the rigidness of its regulations. The great length of time during which its political economy has remained unchanged, implies this. All human things are subject to decay. The law of mutability is so powerful within us, that scarcely any thing is of force enough to control it. But there is somewhat of so vivifying nature in the constitution of China, as to bid defiance to corruption.

Mr. Malthus every where, up and down in

ᵉ Barrow, Chap. IX.

the Essay on Population, preaches against the
extensive use that we make of the institution of
marriage, and seems to think that the great remedy we have for the miseries of mankind as
arising from the principle of population, is to be
found in discountenancing marriage among the
poor.   How shallow then are the politicians of
this ancient empire, who have uniformly afforded the most " extraordinary encouragements to
marriage !"

Another circumstance is scarcely less miraculous.   The exposing of children is a very common practice in China.   So far, so good; this is
an obvious way of keeping down population ;
though Mr. Malthus seems in some places to
doubt its efficacy.   But the shallow politicians
of China again set themselves against this; and
edict after edict has been published to put an
end to it [f].

The statesmen of China have confessedly had
the knowledge and experience of several thousand years : but experience is thrown away upon
some people.   The government is celebrated for
the paternal spirit displayed by the head of it
towards his subjects : but some fathers, though
with no want of love, become the authors of
misery to their children by their injudicious conduct.

I proceed however to supply that which, as

---

[f] P. 314, 15.

before stated, Mr. Malthus has omitted, *viz.* an account how many children, upon the hypothesis of the Essay on Population, would be born, that we may afterwards proceed, with the more perfect preparation, to consider how they are cut off.

Mr. Malthus takes the population of China at 333,000,000 ᵍ. For the sake of a more convenient and compendious arithmetic I will put it down at three hundred millions. Now the doctrine of the Essay on Population is, that " population, when unchecked, goes on doubling itself every twenty-five years." Therefore in China, after every proper deduction has been made for balancing the number of deaths by an adequate number of births, that so the population may not decrease, there must be an additional number of births, or a sort of superfetation, to the amount of three hundred millions

---

g P. 293. This amount was regularly delivered in to Lord Macartney, in the form of an abstract of a census, taken in the preceding year, and digested under seventeen heads, for the different provinces of China within the Great Wall. " We had always,' says Mr. Barrow, " found the officer who delivered it, a plain, unaffected, and honest man, who had on no occasion attempted to deceive or impose on us ; and we could not consistently consider it in any other light than as a document drawn up from authentic materials."

It is necessary however to be observed in this place, that my argument does not in any degree depend on the question, whether this is the true rate of the population of China. If the real number of the inhabitants is one-third or one-half less than is here put down, we have only to reduce the following numbers accordingly ; the proportions, every moral consideration, and every consideration drawn from credibility, will remain the same.

every twenty-five years, to provide for the
doubling required by the Essay on Population.

In other countries, we will suppose, population
is more or less kept down by the various discouragements to marriage held forth in those countries, and, according to Mr. Malthus, by the late
period of life at which marriage frequently takes
place.   But in China extraordinary encouragements are given to marriage, and every man is
married before he is twenty.   We may be secure therefore that in that country the full number of children is born, whatever may become of
them afterwards.

Hereafter, perhaps before the close of the present century, we shall know something of the
population of the United States of America.
But, in the mean time, and while, in the sense
of genuine statesmen and legislators, we know
nothing, Mr. Malthus informs us, and lays it
down as the corner-stone of his portentous and
calamitous system, that " the population there
has been found to double itself, for above a century and a half successively, in less than twenty-
five years," and that this " has been repeatedly
ascertained to be from procreation only."   How
many children on an average to a marriage are
produced in the United States?   No one has
pretended authentically to inform us.   Are they
more than in the old countries of Europe? Probably not.   What number of those that are

E

born, die before ten or sixteen years of age? Of all this we are ignorant.

But whatever be the number of the children born in the United States of America, that die before they arrive at maturity, we know that in China three hundred millions of children more in proportion than in America, die every twenty-five years. This is as certain, as the doctrine of the Essay on Population is true.

The human mind is but ill adapted to grapple with very high numbers; and I am persuaded that important errors have been committed by theoretical writers in consequence of this infirmity. I will therefore endeavour to conform myself to the limited nature of human faculties, by reducing these numbers. It has already appeared, that three hundred millions of *extra*-infants must perish in China every twenty-five years, beyond the proportion of the number of infants that would perish in the United States. Now, if we divide this number by twenty-five, we shall find that twelve millions of *extra*-infants must perish annually in China, to support the doctrine of the Essay on Population.

This surely is a portentous sort of proposition to be built upon a theory, without a single foundation in the records of the country to support it. Mr. Malthus indeed says, that the exposing of children is a very common practice in China, and that about two thousand are annually exposed in the city of Pekin[h]. Alas, what is this to the twelve millions of *extra*-infants that it is absolutely necessary should perish annually in that country ? What a scene of devastation does Mr. Malthus's doctrine lead us to see in China! They must lie on heaps, like what we read of human bodies in the plague of Marseilles. As fast as a certain number of these infants waste away in the streets, an equal number supplies their place, so that the scene of putrescence and the noisomeness of the stench are made perpetual. Does any traveller relate that he has witnessed this ?—And all this time the legislators of the country know nothing of the matter, and go on from century to century, giving extraordinary encouragements to marriage, and prohibiting the exposing of children.

But all this has no existence but in Mr. Malthus's book. It must be true, because in the United States of America " the population has been found to double itself, for above a century and a half successively, in less than twenty-five

---

[h] P. 316. It is not unworthy of notice that Mr. Ellis, the last traveller in China, who accompanied Lord Amherst in 1816, says, " Of that degree of distress which might drive parents to infanticide there was no appearance, nor did any fact of the description come to my knowledge." He adds in a note, " It is by no means my intention to deny the existence of the practice, but to express some doubt of the asserted frequency." Ellis, Chap. VII. The modesty of the note, in all reason, inforces the statement in the text. It shews that Mr. Ellis is not a man who has devoted himself to the support of a theory.

years, and that from procreation only." I shall
hereafter proceed to consider the population of
America. I have no doubt that one of these
propositions is as true as the other.

I am well aware that we know nothing of the
population of China, and almost as little of that
of the United States. I have therefore taken
these statements almost entirely from Mr. Malthus himself. It is for him and his disciples to
explain and to reconcile them.

From all that has been said however it is perfectly clear, that the statesmen and legislators of
China, who have proceeded with a steady, and
perhaps I may add an enlightened, attention to
the subject for centuries, not only have no suspicion of the main principles taught in the Essay on Population, but are deeply impressed
with the persuasion that, without encouragement
and care to prevent it, the numbers of the human
species have a perpetual tendency to decline.

Upon the whole therefore it is as certain as
any thing can be, from the shewing of Mr. Malthus himself, that the empire of China has never
been subject to the operation of the geometrical
ratio.

CHAPTER VII.

INDIA.

The history of India bears a striking resemblance to that of China; and therefore it seems necessary to say something on that subject. The learning of the Bramins is not less ancient; and the history of their improvements and their sciences is lost in the abyss of antiquity. The natives of Indostan strongly resemble the Chinese in the unchangeableness of their institutions; what is to-day, equally existed yesterday, and has remained without alteration, as far back as their annals, their laws and their literature can carry us. The Chinese were conquered by the Tartars; but their records present to us the singular spectacle of the conquerors adopting the manners, the customs, and the institutions of the people they conquered. India has been less fortunate. Their Mahometan invaders fixed an empire among them, claiming a superiority over the nations they found there, rejecting their systems of policy and religion, and looking down with ignorant disdain upon their science and literature. But the Hindoo institutions have survived amidst these disadvantages.

The population of India does not seem to be less considerable than that of China. I have

conversed with a few persons, the best informed,
and the most learned as to every thing that relates to India, that are to be found in Great Britain, and they are decisively of that opinion [a].
There are forests that exist in China, and there
are large tracts of waste land in India; but the
districts favourable to population are not less
thickly inhabited in the latter than in the former. This statement I find strongly corroborated
in a paper in the Asiatic Researches [b], entitled,
A Statistical View of the Population of Burdwan, and Some Neighbouring Districts of the
Government of Bengal, by W. B. Bayley, late
Judge and Chief Magistrate of Burdwan. His
statement is, that " the district of Burdwan contains 262,634 dwelling-houses, of which 218,853
are occupied by Hindoos, and 43,781 by Maho-
metans: allowing therefore $5\frac{1}{2}$ inhabitants to each
dwelling, the total population of Burdwan will
amount to 1,444,487 souls. The area of the
district of Burdwan, as its boundaries are
at present arranged, comprises about 2400 English square miles. On an average therefore
each square mile contains a population of more
than 600 persons." He adds, " The total population of England gives an average of near two
hundred inhabitants to each square mile; but,

---

[a] Among others, I would beg leave to name Mr. H. T. Colebroke,
President of the Asiatic Society in London.

[b] Asiatic Researches, vol. XII. No. xiii.

if some particular counties are selected, the proportion will be found to approximate much more nearly to that of Burdwan. The county of Lancaster, for instance, furnishes, according to the last population reports of 1811, an average of 476 inhabitants to a square mile."

The situation of India then, as far as the subject I am here examining is concerned, is precisely the same as that of China. The great men who founded her institutions had no apprehensions of the evils of over-population. These institutions are grey with the hoar of many thousand years; and yet in all that time no one of her politicians and statesmen has ever suspected the tremendous mischief Mr. Malthus has brought to light. The Ordinances of Menu, as translated by Sir William Jones, treat marriage as one of the first duties of a citizen, and the begetting a son as a debt which every man owes to his country. And yet, if population is at a stand in India, and if marriage, and " early marriage [c]," as Mr. Malthus states it, is almost universal, then, upon the hypothesis of the geometrical ratio, it is indispensible that six children out of every eight, and fifteen millions out of twenty that are born, must perish in years of nonage. God knows how much vice and misery may be necessary to effect this purpose, which however, upon Mr. Malthus's principles,

---

[c] Vol. I. p. 277.

always is effected. But every sober and reflecting man must infallibly conclude that this is not so. And every rational man must stand astonished, when he enquires by what evidence the author of the Essay on Population endeavours to make out this the most revolting and incredible of all propositions. Mr. Malthus observes that India " has in all ages been subject to the most dreadful famines d." But what is this to the purpose? If all marry, and if, wherever marriage is " very greatly encouraged e," a sufficient number of children are born to support a doubling of population every twenty-five years, then, wherever that population is at a stand, fifteen out of twenty millions of children that are born, must perish in years of nonage. Does Mr. Malthus think, that the famines, here and there, or if he will frequently, scattered through the history of India, are sufficient to account for this? We have nothing to do, in the case of so monstrous an hypothesis as that of the Essay on Population, but to keep the object of our contemplation fixed, and to look into it intently, and it will speedily vanish from our sight, and sink into nothing.

---

d P. 278.   e P. 269.

CHAPTER VIII.

SOUTH AMERICA.

OF what I may denominate the ancient history of America, we know infinitely less, than of the history of China and of India. These latter countries still exist in a state very similar to their ancient state, and have been made the subject of investigation, the former to a succession of travellers, and the latter to a number of gentlemen for the last thirty or forty years, who have studied its ancient and esoteric language, and have devoted a considerable part of their lives to the investigation of the Hindoo policy and literature. But the Spaniards in their invasion of America, were, I suppose, the most merciless destroyers any where to be found in the annals of mankind: all knowledge, all history, all antiquities sunk before their savage barbarities. Yet there is something so much to the purpose of our present enquiry, in the histories of Mexico and Peru in particular, that I cannot persuade myself to pass them over in silence.

Nothing is more slow than the progress of nations. The beginnings of things are involved in impenetrable darkness; and exclusively of the light of revelation, we can annex no very dis-

tinct idea to the word, beginning. But, on this
subject of population, I shall follow the example
of Mr. Malthus, and reason only upon the facts
of political economy, and such philosophical
principles as we are able to found on these.
What we seem to know best on this subject, is
that, the further we go back, the more numerous
was the population of the globe.

The population of the New World, when it
first became known to Europeans, is put down
by Montesquieu and Montaigne at four hundred
millions at the lowest [a]. The original discoverers
are at a loss for expressions to do justice to what
they saw. They tell us, that the continent of
South America swarmed with human beings as
an ant-hill does with ants [b], and that the population reached to the utmost extent of possible
numbers. The island of Hispaniola, when first
discovered by Columbus in 1492, contained three
millions of people [c], though at the period when

---

[a] *Lettres Persannes, Lettre* 108 : Montaigne, *Liv. III. Chap. vi.*
It will of course be understood that I place no reliance on these numbers. It is contrary to every idea I entertain on the subject, to suppose that any thing can be precisely known respecting it, unless
after a long and patient investigation, checking every preceding report by the reports which follow, and the deductions which such collation shall afford. I therefore merely take the figures above put
down, as the representative of some very high, but uncertain number, and as standing for the testimony of all those who first visited
America, of whatever class or denomination, however barbarous, or
however humane, as to the extraordinary populousness of the countries they saw.

[b] Las Casas, *Destruycion de las Indias.*

[c] *Ibid.* Voltaire, *Histoire Générale, Chap.* 122.

its history was sketched by the virtuous and illustrious Las Casas in 1542, the number of its
natives did not exceed two hundred persons.

The Mexican empire, we are told, had been
founded only about one hundred and thirty
years before the invasion of Cortez in 1521; and
Montezuma was the ninth monarch in the order of succession who had swayed its scep-
tre d. But for this we need far other evidence,
than that of the soldiers by whom this people
was exterminated, and the priests, the object of
whose fanatical zeal was to establish what they
called the Christian religion, upon the ruin of
all monuments and all antiquity that were to be
found in the country. The Mexicans, it appears,
did not possess the art of writing, though in
many other arts they had reached to a pitch of
improvement altogether surprising. It would
have needed therefore the observation of travellers, imbued with the very soul of philosophy,
and who should have spent their lives in the
search, to have handed down to us the true records and history of this wonderful people. If
the Portuguese had been enabled to burn, massacre and exterminate the Chinese nation, in the
manner in which they and the Spaniards treated
the inhabitants of South America, what should
we have known of the curious institutions, the

---

d Robertson, History of America, Book VII.

great discoveries, and the endless annals and history of that illustrious monarchy [e]?

The South Americans were not willing to "sing the Lord's song" in the ear of their cruel invaders.   They were never questioned with kindness, nor by gentle degrees encouraged to call forth a frank and communicative spirit. All that we know of their history, was extorted under the influence of terror, and listened to with the supercilious scorn which the brutal consciousness of superior strength, and the sanguinary spirit of bigotry and persecution are so well qualified to inspire.   In no long time, so completely were these poor people subdued by the hardhearted avarice of their masters, that they felt no pleasure in recollecting what Mexico had been, and the tales perhaps of revolving ages of glory that their infancy had heard.   From an industrious and ingenious people, among whom astronomy had deposited her secrets, and the profoundest mysteries of policy and government were familiar, they sunk into a state of imbecility and helpless despondence, upon which the wild and active savage in the woods might look down with a well founded sense of superiority.

Here then, as well as every where else, we are struck with the profound ignorance which has existed on the subject of population.   The historians of South America, to a man, have found

---

* Raynal, *Liv. VI.*

no difficulty in believing that an empire, which boasted that it could lead three millions of warriors into the field [f], was sprung from some petty wandering tribe, that three hundred years before had come down " from some unknown regions towards the north and north-west[g]," and settled themselves in this delicious climate.

From Mexico let us pass to Peru. Nothing can be more extraordinary than the institutions of that empire. They had no such thing as individual property. They had the institutions of the rigid Spartans, combined with a mildness of character hardly to be paralleled in any other age or country. The surface of the territory they inhabited was divided into three equal portions, one devoted to the service of religion, another to the maintenance of the government, and the third to the subsistence of the nation. The fertility of the soil, and the favourableness of the climate rendered the labours of the Peruvians light. They repaired to their occupation with the sound of musical instruments and with songs. Every thing among them was cheerful and serene. The monarch always considered himself as the father of his people, and was regarded accordingly. The whole nation was divided into decurias and centuries ; and a perpetual vigilance and admonition were exercised by those in authority through the whole empire.

---

[f] De Solis, Book III, Chap. xvi.   [g] Robertson, *ubi supra.*

It is well observed by abbé Raynal, that nothing can be more unreasonable than to question
the truth of this story. Who among the destroyers of this empire was sufficiently enlightened, to frame a fictitious system of policy, so well
combined, and so consistent? Where could he
have borrowed the idea of many institutions in
legislation and police, to which at that time there
was nothing parallel in any other part of the
world? By what motive could he have been
induced to pen so bitter a satire upon his own
exploits, and to draw down upon himself and his
companions the execration of all enlightened posterity? Would not his story have been contra-
dicted by a multitude of contemporary witnesses,
instead of which we find among them the most
marvelous consistency and consent [h]?

Robertson very properly remarks that among
the Peruvians famine was unknown. The whole
wealth of the nation consisted in the produce of
the earth. As this was divided into three equal
parts, one for religion, one for the incas, and one
for the people, there was always a sufficient quantity in reserve, which the government might
distribute as they saw necessary. The quantity of soil under cultivation was not left to the
discretion of individuals, but was regulated by
public authority with provident attention to the
demands of the state [i].

---

[h] Raynal, Liv. VII.   [i] Robertson, *ubi supra*.

We know nothing of their institutions respecting marriage. But the negative evidence
on this head is abundantly sufficient. No reasonable man will believe that their laws on this
subject were substantially different from those
of China and Indostan. We have no account of
abortions, or the exposing of infants. We know
that at no time was there any deficiency of provisions. The Peruvian government was distinguished from all others, by its paternal care and
tenderness towards the people. And, as the
whole wealth of the state consisted in the fruits
of the earth, it follows that every additional labourer given to the community, was so much
added to the general stock.

Such was the population of the New World,
at the disastrous moment when a native of
Europe first set his foot on her shores. The depopulation was so rapid, that human imagination finds itself incapable of keeping pace with
it. According to Las Casas [k], who relates only
what he had every day an opportunity to see,
nothing can exceed the wanton folly and bru-
tality with which the Spaniards at first destroyed her inhabitants merely for their sport. If it
be true, as he has asserted, that in fifty years
three millions of the inhabitants of Hispaniola
were reduced to two hundred (and no other authority dissents from his, at least as to the final

---

[k] *Destruycion de las Indias.*

term of the progression), it is such a waste of human life, as perhaps no other period of history can produce [1].

The original population however of Mexico and Peru has not been absolutely exterminated, as was the case with the inhabitants found by the Spaniards in the Greater Antilles. Robertson estimates the number of Indians, according to the latest accounts, in Mexico at 2,000,000, and in Peru at 2,500,000 [m].

" In proportion," according to this author,

---

[1] Pinkerton, in his Geography, proceeding upon the authority of Estalla, the writer of a book of fictitious travels, would have us believe that, " deficient as the native population of Peru is at present, it was still more thin before the Spanish conquest." Modern Geography, third edition, Vol. II. p. 564.

Having referred to this geographer, I cannot dismiss the mention of him, without a passing observation upon the spirit in which his account of South America is written. He says [p. 304], " Certainly the Spaniards never sacrificed more victims than the Mexicans devoted to their Gods; and the clamours of pretended philosophy will often be found in opposition to the real cause of humanity which it aspires to defend. The cruelties of the Spaniards must by candour be partly imputed to the profusion of torture and human blood which every where met their eyes in this unhappy country; as such scenes change the very nature of man, and inflame him like the carnage of a field of battle." To say nothing of the gross misrepresentation contained in these lines, will Mr. Pinkerton assert that " the cruelties of the Spaniards" were greater in Mexico, than among the innocent Peruvians, and the harmless Indians of Hispaniola?

A few pages after that in which he thus extenuates " the Spanish cruelties," Mr. Pinkerton exclaims [p. 320] against the *infamous* practice of smoking:" affording us between the two an admirable example of his notions respecting the moral sense.

[m] Book VIII.

" as the Spanish court discovered the importance of its American possessions, the necessity of new modelling their whole administration became obvious.   There was otherwise reason to apprehend that, instead of possessing countries peopled to such a degree as to be susceptible of progressive improvement, Spain would soon remain proprietor only of a vast uninhabited desert [n]."   " The court of Madrid," he adds, " began at this time to display a humane solicitude and tender concern for the good treatment of the natives [o]."   " In no code of laws," he asserts, " is a greater attention manifested, or precautions multiplied with more prudent concern, for the preservation, the security, and the happiness of the subject, than we discover in the collection of the Spanish laws for the Indies [o]."   Among the instances of this, he specifies the " hospitals which have been erected in Lima, in Cusco, and in Mexico, where the Indians are treated with tenderness and humanity [o]."   To this I may add from Montesquieu, that " the Spanish administrators will not suffer any native above fifteen years of age to live unmarried ; nay, that the set time of wedlock appointed for them is, at fourteen years for the male, and thirteen for the female [q]."

In this brief review of the history of South America there are many things worthy of our observation.

---

[n] Book VI.   [o] Book VIII.
[q] *Esprit des Loix, Liv. XXIII. Chap. vii.*

F

In the first place, we are struck with the consideration, how little the inhabitants of the New World, as well as of all other parts of the globe, were aware of the mischiefs of overpopulation. South America, says Las Casas, " was found by us, swarming with human beings, as an anthill swarms with ants." To be sure we are told that the South Americans were a very unrefining and unreflecting people ; but yet one would have thought that so broad and glaring an evil could not have been overlooked by them. The moment a small number of voracious Europeans came among them, they felt the seriousness of the grievance. But, till then, they appear to have done extremely well. They did not tear each other to pieces, to see who should obtain possession of the means of subsistence. They were not aware of the tremendous consequences of having a family. The inhabitants of the Greater Antilles appear to have been the mildest and most inoffensive people any where to be read of. The innocence of the Peruvians has grown into a proverb. All was right and serene and prosperous among them, even by the confession of those very marauders by whom this fair scene of things was for ever subverted. It is sufficiently memorable, that in all the most populous parts of the globe, the policy of discountenancing marriage was never once thought of, but the contrary. This expedient for increasing the happiness of the human race, is a conception, the originality of which is fairly ascribable to Mr. Malthus.

It is proper however that in this place we should once again apply the calculation, which I regard as one main criterion of the truth or falshood of the principle of the Essay on Population. Hispaniola contained three millions of inhabitants. Consequently, to each generation of these inhabitants must be born six millions of children; and of these children, supposing the population to be at a stand, four millions and a half must perish under the age of puberty. Is it possible to imagine any thing, that requires a greater degree of implicit faith to receive? The Hispaniolans were in a state of the utmost simplicity. Their fine climate and their fertile soil had the effect of freeing them from almost all care for to-morrow. Where were they to find the vice and misery that might opportunely deliver them from the burden of a superabundant offspring? They went on carelessly, unapprehensive that they stood in need of such a remedy: but God, we must suppose, came in the night, and took away their children, even as in the history of the Jews he smote the first-born of Egypt. And, be it observed, that the greatness of the numbers of the people of Hispaniola has nothing to do with the question. If we reject the three millions asserted by the Spanish historians, and, with Robertson q, reduce them

q Book III.

to one million, we have then only to make a correspondent alteration in the figures above stated,
the effect will remain the same.

Another observation that ought not to be
passed over in silence, is the facility with which
this population was reduced.   In 1492 Hispaniola contained three millions of Indians. These
are gradually traced by Robertson as decreasing
to 60,000, to 14,000, and in no long time as being
wholly " extirpated" and " extinguished [r]."
Such depopulation would make every impartial
friend to the human race think seriously whether there might not be some danger on that side
of the question.

The next thing that strikes us in this survey
of the South American history is the results attending upon the permanent administration of
the Spanish vice-royalties of Mexico and Peru,
when the first violence of conquest and cruelty
had passed away.   The attention of the government has now been directed for more than two
hundred and fifty years, to the keeping up or increasing by every means they can devise the
numbers of the native race.   But, notwithstanding all the " humane solicitude and tender concern" that have been lavished for this purpose,
notwithstanding the excellence of their code of
laws, and the exemplary conduct of their hospitals, to which we must add the provisions by

---

r *Ibid.*

which early marriage is universally inforced, it will, I suppose, be admitted, that the native race has not been at best any wise increased during these two hundred and fifty years.

The same observation may be applied on the subject of negro slavery, as it exists in America and the West Indies. A multitude of precautions have been employed, particularly in South America, where the Spanish policy rates the negroes as a superior class of men to the descendants of the ancient holders of the empires of Mexico and Peru [a], to multiply the race, but always with inadequate success. A constant succession of new importations from Africa has been judged to be indispensible.

Lastly, it is but just that some notice should be taken of the effects produced upon the mother-country, by the tide of emigration to Spanish America that then prevailed. This is an experiment that is past and over; and it is reasonable that we should endeavour to derive from it such instruction as may be applicable to the similar tide of emigration that has now been flowing for at least fifty years to the English settlements in North America.

One of the most notorious facts of modern history is the tremendous state of weakness and depopulation that has characterised the Spanish nation for the last two hundred years. Voltaire

---

[a] Robertson, Book VIII.

says, " If the discovery of America was a source
of present advantage to Spain, it also inflicted on
her great calamities. One of these was the depopulation of the parent-state by the number of
emigrants necessary to give stability to her colonies [t]."   The following is the view Robertson
exhibits of this change[x]. " The Spaniards, in-
toxicated with the wealth which flowed in annually upon them, deserted the paths of industry to which they had been accustomed, and repaired with eagerness to the regions from which
this opulence issued. By this rage of emigration the strength of the colonies was augmented,
by exhausting that of the mother-country."
And again [x], " The inconsiderate bigotry of Phi-
lip III. expelled at once near a million of his
most industrious subjects [the Moors], at the
very time when the exhausted state of the kingdom required some extraordinary exertion of
political wisdom, to augment its numbers, and
to revive its strength."

---

[t] *Histoire Générale, Chap.* 122.   [x] Book VIII.

CHAPTER IX.

PARAGUAY.

To the examples which have now been detailed I cannot resist the inclination of adding the case of Paraguay, one of the most memorable establishments in the history of the world. The institutions of this portion of the New World emanated from a cultivated and learned fraternity, and whatever relates to them admits of an evidence the most complete and irresistible. The author of the Essay on Population passes over the affair of Paraguay in a smooth and quiet manner, with an incidental mention of half a page; a proceeding, I own, that appears to me a little suspicious, when I consider that the example of Paraguay would to many persons be alone sufficient to decide the question of Mr. Malthus's theory.

Paraguay was a settlement formed by the Jesuits in the interior of South America on the banks of the Rio de la Plata. They were shocked, as it was natural that religious men, and men separated from the contagion of the world, should be, at the atrocities acted by the Spaniards in this part of the world; and they formed a strenuous resolution to endeavour, by an experiment

of the utmost gentleness and humanity, to atone
to the unhappy natives, for the cruelties acted
upon their countrymen in other parts of the continent. They took for their model the history
and the happy constitution of Peru under the
rule of her incas, and the whole of the transac-
tion will redound to their immortal honour.
Their establishment began about the year 1610,
and the Jesuits were finally expelled from it by
authority of the king of Spain in 1767.

What abbé Raynal says on the subject is so
much to my purpose, that I shall do little more
than transcribe it.

" It might be expected, that mankind would
have most extraordinarily multiplied themselves,
under a government where no individual was
idle, and none were destroyed by excessive labour ; where the nourishment was wholesome,
abundant, and equally distributed to all; where
all were fully supplied with necessary clothing ;
where old men, widows, orphans, and the sick,
were tended with a care unknown to the rest of
the world ; where every one married of choice, and
without motives of interest ; where a numerous
family of children was a consolation, without the
possibility of being a burthen ; where a debauchery, inseparable from idleness, and which
assails equally the rich and the poor, never hast-
ened the approach of infirmities or old age ;
where nothing occurred to excite the artificial
passions, or to oppose those which are conform-

able to nature and reason ; where the advantages
of commerce were reaped, without bringing in
their train the vices of luxury ; where abundant
magazines, and succours mutually communicated
from tribe to tribe, insured them against famine
and the inconstancy of the seasons ; where the
administrators of justice between man and man
were never reduced to the sad necessity of con-
demning one individual to death, to disgrace, or
to any punishment but what was momentary;
where taxes and law-suits, two of the great
sources of affliction to the human race, were utterly unknown : such a country, I say, might
have been expected to prove the most populous
on the face of the earth.   It was not so.

" It was for a long time suspected, that the
Jesuits understated the number of their subjects
on account of the tribute at so much *per* head
which the court of Spain imposed on them ; and
the council at Madrid manifested some uneasi-
ness on this point.   The most exact researches
dissipated a suspicion not less injurious than
groundless.

" Those who gave the society no credit for the
integrity of their motives, spread a report that
the Indians did not multiply, because they were
consigned to the destructive labour of the mines.
This accusation was more or less urged, for more
than one hundred years.   But the further the
Spanish administration sought into the mat-

ter, the more they were convinced that there
was no such thing.

" The oppressiveness of a government administered by monks, was sufficient, according to
others, to arrest the multiplication of the Indians.
This is surely abundantly incompatible with the
charge which was also made against the missionaries, that they inspired the Indians with too
blind a confidence in, and too excessive an attachment for their instructors. In the history of
Paraguay it is found that numerous tribes repeatedly came with an importunate request that
they might be admitted into this happy association, while no one of their districts ever shewed
the smallest inclination to throw off the yoke.
It would be too much to suppose that fifty Jesuits could hold two hundred thousand Indians
in a forced submission, when they had it in their
power at any time to massacre their pastors, or
to fly into the woods.

" There are persons who have suspected that
the Jesuits spread among their Indian subjects
the doctrine of celibacy, which was so much ve-
nerated in the dark ages, and which has not yet
entirely lost its reputation in the world. On the
contrary, the missionaries never attempted to
give their novices the idea of this mode of acquir-
ing a place in heaven, against which the climate
opposed insurmountable obstacles, and which
would alone have sufficed to involve their best
institutions in abhorrence.

" In fine, certain politicians have alleged, that the want of the institution of private property is alone sufficient to account for the smallness of the population of Paraguay. But this institution will always be found to detract from, as much as it forwards the cause of population ; while the Indians of Paraguay, having always an assured subsistence, enjoyed the benefits of such an establishment, without its evils ᵃ."

Having, one by one, refuted these different solutions for the difficulty, abbé Raynal, who nevertheless adheres to the received and orthodox opinion, that if a race of men have every advantage and every blessing afforded them for that purpose, they will not fail greatly to increase in numbers, though he did not dream of their increasing in a geometrical ratio, is reduced to strain his invention to account for so unexpected a phenomenon. The cause that he seems principally to rely on as having kept down their numbers, is the small-pox.

Mr. Malthus faintly hints, that such a thing had been heard of in Paraguay as scarcity, and adds, " On these occasions some of the missions [that is the Indian tribes] *would have perished from famine, but for the assistance of their neighbours* [b]." Though how this could have happened in a country, where, as in Peru, the crops were divided into three equal portions, one for the purposes of religion, one for the expences of the government, and one for the subsistence of the people, it is not easy to divine.

ᵃ *Histoire des Deux Indes, Liv. VIII.*   [b] Vol. I, p. 87

CHAPTER X.

SPARTA.

AN accurate and instructive experiment on the subject of population appears to be afforded us by the institutions of Sparta. There is nothing more memorable in the history of mankind, than the code of laws digested by Lycurgus for that people; and this code seems to have operated in full vigour for five hundred years. Lycurgus, we are told, divided the entire lands of the republic into 39,000 equal portions; of which thirty thousand were distributed to the rural citizens of the state, and nine thousand to the inhabitants of the capital [a]. One of the leading principles of his code was to regard marriage as a duty, and the having a family of children as honourable. The age of marriage was fixed; and is conjectured by Barthelemi [b] to have been thirty for the males, and twenty for the female citizens.

" Those which would not marrie," says Plutarch [c], " Lycurgus made infamous by law. For it was not lawfull for such to be present, where

---

[a] Plutarch, *in Vita Lycurgi.*   [b] *Voyage d'Anacharsis.*
[c] Life of Lycurgus : North's Translation.

those open games and pastimes were shewed naked. Furthermore the officers of the citie compelled such as would not marry, euen in the hardest time of the winter, to enuiron the place of these sportes, and to go vp and downe starke naked, and to sing a certaine song made for the purpose against them, which was : that justly were they punished, because that law they disobeyed. Moreouer, when such were old, they had not the honour and reuerence done them, which old married men vsually receiued. Therefore there was no man that misliked, or reproued that, which was spoken to Dercillidas : albeit otherwise he was a noble captaine. For, coming into a presence, there was a young man which would not vouchsafe to rise and do him reuerence, nor to giue him place for to sit downe : And worthily, quoth he, because thou hast not gotten a son, who may do so much for me in time to come."

Here then, if any where, we may expect to find a nation, the population of which should increase at an extraordinary rate. There were no poor under the institutions of Lycurgus. All were fed at a common table ; all slept in public dormitories. The citizens received every encouragement, nay, as it appears, were absolutely enjoined, to marry ; and they certainly felt no anxiety about the subsistence of their future offspring.

All this must be exceedingly puzzling to the

followers of Mr. Malthus; were it not that they
are relieved from the consequences of the institutions of Lycurgus generally considered, by the
recollection of one of these institutions, which
they may regard as of sufficient force to check
the evils of an overgrowing population. This
was a law which prescribed the exposing of infants. We have already seen to what an extent
this exposing must have been carried, if there is
any truth in Mr. Malthus's hypothesis. Half
the born at least must have constantly been destroyed by the operation of a positive statute.
It is truly extraordinary, that Lycurgus should
have overlooked so enormous an evil, and should
have ordained that such multitudes of infants
should be continually born into the world, for
the mere purpose of being murdered. It is still
more extraordinary that no one should have
existed for five hundred years, with humanity
enough to remedy so atrocious a mischief.

But let us consider for a moment this law concerning the exposing of infants, as it was practised in the republic of Sparta. We have been
told by some travellers from China, that the private individuals of that country are in the habit
of having recourse to this expedient, to get rid
of the trouble of maintaining their offspring, and
that they continue to do this, notwithstanding all
the precautions used by the government to prevent it. No practice resembling this ever took
place among the Spartans. It is sufficiently evi

dent, that Lycurgus entertained no apprehension of being overstocked with citizens, and that his law had no such object in view. " After the birth of euery boy, the father was no more maister of him ; but he himselfe carried him to a certaine place called Lesche, where the eldest men of his kindred being set, did view the child : and if they found him faire, and well proportioned of all his limmes, and strong, they gaue order he should be brought vp. Contrariwise, if they found him deformed, misshapen, or leane, or pale, they sent him to be throwne in a deepe pit of water, which they commonly called Apothetes : holding opinion it was neither good for the child, nor yet for the commonweale, that it should liue, considering from his birth he was not wel made, nor giuen to be strong, healthfull, nor lustie of body all his life long. For this cause therefore the nurse, after their birth, did not wash them with water simply (as they do every where at that time), but with water mingled with wine : and thereby did they proue, whether the complexion or temperature of their bodies were good or ill. For they suppose that children, which are giuen to haue the falling sicknesse, or otherwise to be full of rewmes and sicknesse, cannot abide washing with wine, but rather dry and pine away : as contrarily the other which are healthfull, become thereby the stronger and the lustier d."

---

d Plutarch, *ubi supra.*

Two inferences clearly follow from this statement: first, that the laws of Lycurgus had in
their view no purpose to keep down the numbers of mankind: secondly, that a proceeding of
this sort, though it might diminish, and that probably in an inconsiderable degree, the number of
citizens in a given generation, was very indifferently adapted to reduce the number of births by
which the next generation was to be supplied.
In the same spirit Plutarch further relates:
"First of all, Lycurgus willed that the maidens
should harden their bodies with exercise of running, wrestling, throwing the lance, and casting
the dart, to the end that the fruite wherewith
they might be afterwards conceiued, taking nourishment of a strong and lusty body, should
shoot out and spreade the better; and that they
by gathering strength thus by exercises, should
more easily away with the paines of child-bearing [e]."

It is surely therefore of great importance to
any theory on the subject of population, to watch
the effects of the institutions of Sparta. And
here fortunately we possess information from the
highest authorities among the ancients, no less
than those of Thucydides and Aristotle.

It appears plainly from the history of Thucydides, that the republic of Sparta was in the
practice of increasing the number of her citizens

by foreign accessions; and we may distinguish two modes in which this recruiting was effected. First, by admitting certain of the Helots, or slaves, to the rights of citizenship; and secondly, by enrolling among her denizens individuals selected for this purpose from among the allies of Sparta. These latter were designed by the appellation of Neodamodes [men added to the ranks of the state]. In his history of the eleventh year of the Peloponnesian war, Thucydides expressly distinguishes these two species of recruits from each other[f] : and the Neodamodes are again mentioned by him in his account of the nineteenth year of the war[g]."

Aristotle is still more explicit. In the chapter of his Politics in which the republic of Lacedæmon is examined[h], he states that, " Though the territory of the Lacedæmonians was sufficient for the maintenance of one thousand five hundred horse, and thirty thousand foot [and in this estimate we may be sure he does not include the Helots, or slaves, by whom all the mechanical labour of the community was performed], yet the actual number of the citizens of the capital had fallen to one thousand. Thus," continues he, " the republic of Sparta fell, not by any single and particular calamity, but perished through the diminution of its numbers. In the earlier period of its history it is understood that they

---

[f] *Lib V, cap.* 34.   [g] *Lib. VII, cap.* 58.   [h] *Lib. II, cap.* 7.

G

gave the rights of citizenship to the natives of other Grecian states, that by reason of their long wars their numbers might not be too much reduced; and I have heard that the people of the capital only, at one time amounted to ten thousand."

Aristotle indeed imputes the reduced numbers of the citizens of Sparta to a defect in the institutions of Lycurgus, who, he says, forbade that any citizen of Sparta should sell his own property, or buy that of another, but allowed them to give or bequeath it to any one they would: in consequence of which in process of time the lands of the republic fell into the hands of a few.   But in this representation he stands alone. Plutarch, to whom posterity is principally indebted for the details of the subject, expressly states: " Lycurgus was not deceiued of his hope; for his city was the chiefest of the world in glory and honour of gouernement, by the space of fiue hundred yeares.   For so long his citie kept his lawes without any change or alteration untill king Agis, the son of Archidamus, began to reigne.   Now in the reigne of king Agis, gold and siluer beganne first to creepe in againe to the citie of Sparta, by meanes of Lysander i," in the close of the Peloponnesian war.

And again, in the Life of Agis, the son of Eudamidas, one hundred and fifty years later:

---

i Life of Lycurgus.

" Then began the state of Lacedæmon first to
be corrupted, and to leaue her ancient discipline,
when the Lacedæmonians, hauing subdued the
empire of the Athenians [that is, under Lysan-
der], stored themselves and countrey both, with
plenty of gold and siluer. But yet reseruing
still the lands left vnto them by succession from
their fathers, according vnto Lycurgus first ordinance and institution for diuision of lands
amongst them : which ordinance and equalitie
being inuiolably kept amongst them, did yet pre-
serue the common wealth from defamation of
diuerse other notorious crimes. Vntill the time
of the authoritie of Epitadeus, one of the Ephores,
a seditious man, and of proud conditions, who
bitterly falling out with his owne sonne, preferred a law, that euery man might lawfully giue
his lands and goods whilest he liued, or after his
death by testament vnto any man whom he
liked or thought well of. Thus this man made
a law to satisfie his anger, and others also did
confirme it for covetousnesse sake, and so overthrew a noble ordinance."

Plutarch himself speaks, in the time of the
latter Agis, of the citizens of Sparta as amounting only to seven hundred persons.

We have here therefore an evidence, such as
must be of great weight with every reasonable
man, respecting the population, or number of citizens of Sparta, during the successive periods of
the history of that republic. It is certain that

Lycurgus employed every means he could devise, to insure a numerous and healthy population. He encouraged marriage; he fixed a stigma on celibacy; and he provided for the support and education of the children that should be born, from the funds of the public. His institutions continued unimpaired for the space of five hundred years. Yet it is apparent that "the state perished through the diminution of its numbers." During the interval in which Sparta makes the most splendid figure in the page of history, it was reduced to employ various expedients for the purpose of increasing the amount of its citizens by extrinsic accessions. In the period of which Aristotle treats the free inhabitants of the capital were reduced from ten thousand to one thousand men; and in the reign of the latter Agis, about one hundred years later than Aristotle, they counted no more than seven hundred citizens. These are phenomena which I conceive to be utterly incompatible with any hypothesis that affirms the rapid multiplication of the human species.

CHAPTER XI.

ROME.

FROM Sparta let us pass to the republic of ancient Rome. In this state the subject of population seems to have been more studied and sys-
tematically attended to, than in any other upon
record. The institution of the Census of which
we have lately heard so much, as if it were a
thing altogether new, together with the name,
took its rise in this city. The original regulation was, that the citizens capable of bearing
arms, or in other words, all the males of a certain
age, and entitled to the privileges of a Roman
citizen, should be numbered every five years;
and, though this ceremony was often interrupted through the occurrence of extraordinary affairs, yet its seventy-second repetition took place
in the year of Rome 707, two years after the
battle of Pharsalia.

As this is a species of document to which hitherto there exists no parallel, I have thought it
worth while to insert here the sums of as many
of the enumerations as are to be found in Livy,
adding to them such as occur in the epitomes
which remain of the lost books of Livy. I am
not sure that the common construction, which I

have adopted, is the true one, that these numbers represent the citizens capable of bearing
arms; since to the enumeration for the year of
Rome 288 it is added, that this was the true
number, exclusive of male and female orphans [a],
and to Metellus's enumeration for 622, that this
was the true number, exclusive of minors and
widows [b]. But, whatever the numbers did or
did not represent, and whatever uncertainty may
exist on that head, they are plainly useful inasmuch as they enable us to compare one period
with another. I will still less undertake, as Mr.
Malthus does respecting the population of North
America, that these increasing numbers, where
they increase, are procured " from procreation
only." It is not my intention to treat here of
the various methods upon record, employed by
the Roman government to recruit the number
of her citizens. But we at least owe so much to
the illustrious and singular example of the Roman republic, as not to forget her enumerations,
whenever we desire to speculate fairly on the
subject of population.

The first Census, or Lustration of the people
of Rome, was made by Servius Tullius, the sixth
king, who is said to have reigned from the year
of Rome 174 to 219. The sum of his enumeration was 80,000 citizens. The rest are as follow :

---

[a] Livius, *Lib. III, cap.* 3.   [b] *Epitome LIX.*

Lustrum.	Year of Rome.	Numbers.
9	288	124,215
10	294	132,409
30	459	262,322
31	464	273,000
32	473	278,222
33	478	271,224
37	501	297,797
38	506	251,221
43	533	270,213
44	544	137,107
45	549	214,000
47	559	143,074
48	564	258,308
51	579	269,015
52	584	327,022
55	599	324,000
57	611	328,342
58	617	323,000
59	622	313,823
60	628	390,736
62	638	394,336
68	683	450,000
72	707	150,000

It is a subject therefore of some interest to enquire what were the laws of this celebrated republic upon the subject of population, to which
their attention was so perpetually recalled. The
old law, according to Dionysius of Halicarnassus,
which he says was in full force in the year of
Rome 277, required every citizen to marry, and
to rear all his children[c]. The laws further attached certain privileges to the state of a married

---

[c] Dionysius, *Antiquitates*, *Lib. IX, sub anno.*

man, others to him who had offspring, and others
still more extensive to him who had three
children. The citizen who had the greatest
number of children, had on all occasions the preference, whether in suing for office, or in the
exercise of office when obtained [d]. The consul
who had the most numerous offspring, had the
priority in the magistracy, and took first his
choice of the provinces, when his year was ex-
pired; the senator who had the largest family,
was named first in the catalogue of senators, and
was first called upon to give his opinion on the
subject in debate. In the year of Rome 622,
fifteen years after the destruction of Carthage,
the censors Metellus and Quintus Pompeius,
finding the number of citizens reduced between
this and the last enumeration, from 323,000 to
313, 823, took occasion to inforce the old law,
and decreed, that " all should be obliged to marry, for the sake of procreating children [e]." Julius Cæsar, during his first consulship, and afterwards, adopted measures of a similar tendency.
In a division he made of lands he reserved twenty thousand shares for such citizens as should
have three or more children [f]; and forbade the
ladies, who were unmarried, or childless, to wear
jewels : an excellent plan, says Montesquieu, for

---

d Tacitus *Annales, Lib. II, cap.* 51 ; *Lib. XV, cap,* 19. See further Lipsius, *Excursus ad Taciti Annales, Lib. III, cap.* 25.

e Livius, *Epitome LIX.* f Suetonius, Julius Cæsar, *cap.* 20.

pressing the vanity of the fair into the service of the state g.   Augustus went still farther. He imposed new penalties on the unmarried, and increased the rewards of those who had children. He caused the speech of Metellus the Censor in the year 622 to be recited in the senate h, the tenor of which was, " If the human race could be perpetuated without women, we should be delivered from a great evil : but, as the law of nature has decreed that we can neither live happily with them, nor subsist as a species without them, it is the duty of all to sacrifice their immediate repose to the good of the state i."   To which Augustus subjoined : " The city of Rome, of which we are so justly proud, does not consist of its houses, its porticoes, and public buildings ; it is the men of Rome that constitute the city. We must not expect to see, what we read of in old fables, human beings spring forth out of the earth to undertake the business of the state. The object of my care is to perpetuate the commonwealth ; and in this I call upon each member of the community to contribute his part k."

It was in the same spirit, that the civic crown, given to him who should save the life of a citizen, was considered as the most glorious of all rewards among the Romans.   Nor am I sure,

---

g *Esprit des Loix, Liv. XXIII, Chap. xxi.*

h Suetonius, Augustus, *Cap.* 89.   i Aulus Gellius, *Lib. I. Cap.* 6.

k Dion Cassius, *Lib. LVI.*

that the Porcian law, passed in the year of Rome 453, which forbade the infliction of stripes or death on a Roman citizen, did not owe its existence, at least in part, to this principle.

There has indeed often been quoted on the other side, the practice of which we read in the Roman history, of the exposing of infants. But this was subjected to regulations of the same nature in Rome, as in Sparta, from whence, according to Dionysius, the Romans are to be considered as deriving their origin [l]. If a child was born monstrous or deformed, it was permitted to the father to expose it; but he was previously required to shew the child to five of his nearest neighbours, and obtain their sanction [m].

To sum up the whole of what relates to this subject in the republic of Rome. I see no cause why we should not reason as confidently upon the records of the Census in the Roman history, as upon the Census of the United States of North America, or the enumerations of the island of Great Britain. The latter are affairs of yesterday. The American Census has been taken three times in a period of thirty years; the Enumeration of Great Britain twice. The United State of America have afforded a scene of continuous emigration, unparalleled in the

---

[l] *Vide apud* Montesquieu, *ubi supra.*   [m] Dionysius, *Lib. II.*

history of the world. The difference of the two Enumerations in Great Britain is not more than may fairly be accounted for from the novelty of the experiment. The numbering of the citizens of Rome took place seventy-two times in a period of five hundred years.

In Rome every encouragement was given to marriage. The magistrates were perpetually anxious for the multiplication of her citizens. The number of her denizens was frequently augmented by enrolling fresh recruits from among her allies. Yet we see to what perpetual fluctuations it was exposed.

A single city affords certainly a very imperfect criterion respecting the multiplication of mankind. Many will be continually retiring from the town into the country. Many more will flow from all parts of the country to people the metropolis. The stock of her population will be in a state of continual change. I do not think that the Roman Census supplies a demonstrative argument against the increase of mankind. But I think it is beyond comparison the most ample document from ancient history to prove, that if they increase at all, that increase must be effected by degrees very slow, if not almost insensible.

CHAPTER XII

MISCELLANEOUS OBSERVATIONS.

SUCH was the policy, and such the experience of the most celebrated nations of antiquity on the subject of population. But Mr. Malthus has brought forward certain maxims of a very different tenor from Plato and Aristotle, writing of an imaginary republic: and upon them he remarks, " From these passages it is evident that Plato fully saw the tendency of population to increase beyond the means of subsistence [a].' And, again, " If he could propose to destroy certain children, and to regulate the number of marriages, his experience and his reasonings must have strongly pointed out to him the great power of the principle of increase, and the necessity of checking it [b]." To which he adds, " Aristotle appears to have seen this necessity still more clearly."

Now, all this is surely sufficiently memorable. We have Lycurgus, and Romulus, and Metellus, and Julius Cæsar, and Augustus, and all the practical politicians of antiquity, marshalled on one side ; and Plato and Aristotle, who

---

[a] Vol. I. p. 333.   [b] P. 334.

amused themselves with framing imaginary re
publics, on the other : and Mr. Malthus chooses
to adhere to the Utopian notions, or, as he
phrases it, the " experience and reasonings" of
the latter.

He calls Plato and Aristotle wise, because he
thinks they fell into the same blunder as he has
done. Would not any reasonable man wonder
how the " experience of Plato" came to be so
much greater than that of the immortal legislators of the republics of Sparta and of Rome, and
of those who administered those republics for
several hundred years after the frail bodies of
their institutors had crumbled into dust ?

But the fact is, that Plato and Aristotle never
thought about the matter. They dreamed neither of a geometrical series, nor of any other
series. They were guilty of no refinement in
all this. They fixed the number of citizens in
their imaginary republic ; and all they meant in
the passages the sagacity of which Mr. Malthus
applauds, was, that if you are determined to
have no more than five thousand citizens, you
must take care not to have six.

Thus far I have been enquiring merely into
the human population of the world, or, more
accurately speaking, of those parts of the world
known by the names of Europe, Asia, Africa,
and South America ; and certainly in these we
have found no reasons to persuade us to believe
in Mr. Malthus's doctrine of the stupendous and

alarming multiplication of mankind. Let us now take the question upon a somewhat larger scale. Let us look abroad, and see what happens among inferior animals.

In the first edition of the Essay on Population Mr. Malthus found no powers to check the calamitous multiplication of mankind, but vice and misery; to which he has since added moral restraint. No one of these three applies to the lower orders of animals. They are incapable of vice: I think Mr. Malthus will not say, that they refrain from procreation from a principle of prudence: and they are seldom found starved to death. Mr. Malthus has ventured to intrude himself into the mysteries of the administration of the universe, under the sole guidance of his geometrical and arithmetical ratios; and I shall not hazard much in asserting that this is a science of another order.

If there was no principle at work in the world but Mr. Malthus's " Principle of Population," I should expect to find things much otherwise than they are. I know not that we have the smallest reason to suppose the animal world more numerous than it was three thousand, or (putting revelation out of the question, and supposing the earth to have subsisted so long) thirty thousand years ago. Every blade of grass, it may be, is peopled; but we may wander for days together in some parts of the world, without seeing an animal so big as a ferret or a hare. Why is this? Why is not nature

——strangled with her waste fertility,
The earth cumbered, and the winged air darked with plumes?

The spawn of fishes is most copious, but we know not how much of this is ripened into perfect animals. All we seem to know is, that the eaters are not more numerous than they have been from the earliest records of time, and that the small animals which serve for food to the large ones, are not produced in so much greater plenty than formerly, as to occasion any disturbance to the goodly order of the universe. We know that several species of animals have totally perished. We read of the unicorn, the leviathan, the behemoth, the mammuth, and many others, and of some of them the skeletons, in whole or in part, subsist to this day. What animal was to prey on the mammuth, or to keep down the enormous multiplication of his species, by making use of him for food? If Mr. Malthus's system were true, the earth long ere this, ought to have been a habitation for mammuths only; or rather this enormous animal, after having devoured every other species, ought himself to have perished, and the globe to have become one vast solitude.

It is not my intention to pursue this speculation respecting the animal tribes. It is enough for me to have started the hint for the use of future enquirers. I return therefore to the topic of human population.

There is something much more mysterious in the principle by which the race of mankind is perpetuated, than any man has yet distinctly remarked: and he that shall sufficiently attend to it, instead of wondering that the globe has not long ago been overstocked with inhabitants, and seeking for vague and indefinite causes to account for the thinness of its population, will be apt rather to wonder why the human race has not by this time become extinct.

What are the lessons that experience teaches us on this subject? Of the families that I knew in the earliest stage of my recollection, the majority have perished. The persons to whom I refer were men in the middle station of life, and who lived at their ease. Why has their race become extinct? How few can trace their descent in the direct male line through many generations? The persons of the name of Smith, or White, or Brown, are indeed numerous; for these are not one family, but the name of old was given at random to many. But take any name that is singular, Shakespear, or Malthus, or Gildon, how many of that name will you find in the muster-roll? Upon the principle of the Essay on Population, the inhabitants of this country ought long ago to have been a people of nobles: the nobility with us, like the mammuth in the brute creation, ought to have eaten up the rest; for they had ample encouragement to multiply, which the peasant and the mechanic could scarcely in the smallest degree partake. Yet our nobility are in a striking degree new families, scarce any of them taking precedence of the bastards of Charles the Second. Such is the order of the universe. " One generation," as Solomon says, one family, and one race of men, " passeth away, and another cometh;" but the human race survives these vicissitudes. In Scotland, titles are old, because they descend to heirs-general, and surnames are widely diffused, because it was the custom of the head of a clan to give his own name to all his followers.

A passage extremely to this purpose, on the subject of the town of Berne, occurs in Mr. Malthus's Essay, who has indeed always appeared to me a man of a candid mind; so much so, that in my opinion it would not have been difficult for any one of sufficient leisure and perspicacity, to construct an answer to the Essay on Population from the Essay itself. The passage purports to be an extract from the *Statistique de la Suisse*, in four volumes, octavo, published at Lausanne, in 1766. " In the town of Berne, from the year 1583 to 1654, the sovereign council had admitted into the *Bourgeoisie* 487 families, of which 379 became extinct in the space of two centuries, and in 1783 only

108 of them remained. During the hundred years from 1684 to 1784, 207 Bernese families became extinct. From 1624 to 1712, the *Bourgeoisie* was given to 80 families. In 1623 the sovereign council united the members of 112 different families, of which 58 only remain [c]."

It has sometimes occurred to me whether Mr. Malthus did not catch the first hint of his geometrical ratio from a curious passage of Judge Blackstone, on consanguinity, which is as follows:

" The doctrine of lineal consanguinity is sufficiently plain and obvious; but it is at the first view astonishing to consider the number of lineal ancestors which every man has within no very great number of degrees : and so many different bloods is a man said to contain in his veins, as he hath lineal ancestors. Of these he hath two in the first ascending degree, his own parents ; he hath four in the second, the parents of his father and the parents of his mother; he hath eight in the third, the parents of his two grandfathers and two grandmothers ; and by the same rule of progression, he hath an hundred and

---

[c] Vol. I. p. 484. There is an observation in Fuller, the celebrated historian of the Worthies of England, under the article, Huntingdonshire, much to the same purpose.

" I meet with this uncomfortable passage in Mr. Speed's description of this shire : *Thus, as this city, so the old families here have been with time outworne, few only, of the many formerly, now remaining, whose sirnames before the reign of the last Henry were in this shire of any eminency.*",

twenty-eight in the seventh; a thousand and twenty-four in the tenth; and at the twentieth degree, or the distance of twenty generations, every man hath above a million of ancestors, as common arithmetic will demonstrate.

" This will seem surprising to those who are unacquainted with the increasing power of progressive numbers; but is palpably evident from the following table of a geometrical progression, in which the first term is 2, and the denominator also 2; or, to speak more intelligibly, it is evident, for that each of us has two ancestors in the first degree; the number of which is doubled at every remove, because each of our ancestors had also two immediate ancestors of his own.

Lineal Degrees.	Number of Ancestors.
1	2
2	4
3	8
4	16
5	32
6	64
7	128
8	256
9	512
10	1024
11	2048
12	4096
13	8192
14	16384
15	32768.
16	65536
17	131072
18	262144

$$
\begin{array}{ll}
19 & 524288 \\
20 & 1048576 \,^{d} .\text{''}
\end{array}
$$

This argument however from Judge Blackstone of a geometrical progression would much more naturally apply to Montesquieu's hypothesis of the depopulation of the world, and prove that the human species is hastening fast to extinction, than to the purpose for which Mr. Malthus has employed it. An ingenious sophism might be raised upon it, to shew that the race of mankind will ultimately terminate in unity. Mr. Malthus indeed should have reflected, that it is much more certain that every man has had ancestors, than that he will have posterity, and that it is still more doubtful, whether he will have posterity to twenty, or to an indefinite number of generations.

Another remark also it is proper to make on this extract. Judge Blackstone does indeed shew, that the population of the world is, in one sense, the proper subject of a geometrical ratio. But his ratio is essentially different from that of Mr. Malthus. The Commentator on the Laws of England does not pretend to assign any period of time, any precise numbers of years, to his doubling; whereas the Essay on Population not only affirms a doubling by direct generation, which is not true; but it is also of the es-

---

d Commentaries on the Law of England, Book II. Chap. 14.

sence of the doctrine there delivered, that this doubling shall take within a limited and assignable portion of time.

In treating on this subject of population, and considering whether the small number of the present inhabitants of the earth is altogether to be ascribed to the inroads of vice and misery, it is certainly not wholly unworthy of our attention to observe, that some of those countries from which we have drawn our examples of the scarcity of men, were among the countries in which liberty and equality most abounded, and where distress was the least known. The two most flourishing states of ancient Greece, were Sparta and Athens; and in both the laborious occupations were assigned to slaves, while the free citizens lived in comparative idleness. In Sparta there was little motive to industry, as all property was in common : a citizen was there thought to be disgraced, if he practised any of the arts. In Athens Solon made an exception in favour of statuary and painting, which were therefore termed liberal arts [e]. Some of the citizens of Athens were enterprising, and sought to accumulate wealth; but the greater part were contented with the condition in which they were born. In the Symposium of Xenophon, a curious representation of the state of the Athenians in this respect is put into the mouth of

---

[e] Hill, Essays on Ancient Greece, Essay XIII.

one Charmides. " When I was wealthy," says
he, " I was exposed to perpetual demands for
the support of government, or for the expences
of the theatre. I could not go beyond the confines of Attica, without incurring the suspicion
of the magistrates, and was obliged to court the
favour of the vilest informers. Now, on the
contrary, that I have become poor, I go where
I chuse; I am treated with respect and deference by the rich, who regard me with the same
terror I once felt for others; and, when in want,
I can require of the state to support me." These
were the countries in which to have tried the
geometrical ratio; and it was tried. The constitution of Sparta endured five hundred years;
with what effect we have seen. The government of Rome was perhaps the happiest for its
citizens, and certainly produced, while in its
vigour, the greatest quantity of true energy and
heroic virtue, of any government that ever existed. Nor will the government of the canton
of Berne be cited among those that have most
oppressed their citizens.

In the Grecian republics the increase of mankind could not have been kept down in their citizens by want, for every citizen had a right to
call on the state to support him. And in Sparta
when the citizens had all been fed, there was a
numerous train of Helots, by whom the mechanical labour of the community was performed,
and who we may be sure would not all be

starved. The citizens therefore, the decrease of whom I have exemplified in striking instances, were, it is certain, always plentifully fed, and in that, and every other way that might seem to have the greatest promise of success, encouraged to multiply their species.

Of Hispaniola and Peru, such as they were when first visited by their European invaders, our accounts are not perhaps perfectly satisfactory and accurate: but I think we know enough to enable us to pronounce that, if vice and misery were all they had to depend upon for the stability of their condition, and the well being of the whole, they were very slenderly provided in these respects. The case is different with respect to the missions of Paraguay. These fall properly and fully within the province of history. We labour under no want of records respecting them. And I should therefore apprehend that, as far as the evidence of general history is to be admitted for proof, the doctrine of the geometrical ratio was fully tried in that celebrated establishment.

It should seem then that vice and misery are not altogether such powerful agents, and have by no means done so much for the well being of society as Mr. Malthus imagines. All the political establishments which have just been enumerated, contrived to do with a very small portion of them; and we have no reason to believe respecting any one of them, that they were overwhelmed with the multitude of their citizens. Indeed it is a strange hypothesis, so violent that one wonders that it could for a moment have imposed on human credulity, so shocking that it might drive all reasonable beings to despair, to suppose the agency of vice and misery to be so active and gigantic, that by those alone or, as Mr. Malthus expressively terms it, by " every cause which in any degree contributes to shorten the natural duration of human life [f]," three times as many children die in years of nonage in the Old World as in the United States of America, and that thus and thus only our population is kept down to a level, while, if we were as virtuous and happy as the citizens of that republic, it would not fail to double itself in less than twenty-five years. Every reader, I apprehend, who has gone thus far along with me, will feel satisfied, that there is some gross mistake in Mr. Malthus's statement respecting the population of North America: and it will be the business of the Fourth Book of the present work to endeavour to lay open the sources of that mistake.

---

[f] Vol. I, p. 21.

CHAPTER XIII.

VIEWS OF MAN AND SOCIETY WHICH RESULT FROM THE PRECEDING FACTS.

I TURN now from the dreary speculations of Mr. Malthus, to the venerable recollection of what has been the creed of all ages and nations upon this interesting subject.

Mr. Malthus's doctrine is directly calculated to bring our human nature into " hatred and contempt;" a crime I should think somewhat greater than that which Mr. Pitt made a law to counteract, " the bringing hatred and contempt upon the government of the united kingdom." One of his distinguishing positions is the neces- sity of warning men of the evil of marrying, ex- cept the few who, in the vicissitude of sublunary things, shall conceive they have a fair " prospect of being able to support a family :" and he re- commends that those who slight this warning, shall, with the innocent offspring they bring in- to the world, be " left to the punishment of Nature, the punishment of want." Almighty author of us all ! what a thing is man that thou hast made, the existence of which, in great num- bers, and without strict limitations, is to be counteracted by such sharp menaces, menaces that it is recommended should by no means be left as a dead letter [a] !

What is the idea we were taught of old to conceive of this creature, man ?

" Thou hast made him a little lower than the angels, and hast crowned him with glory and honour. Thou madest him to have dominion over the works of thy hands ; thou hast put all things under his feet ; all sheep and oxen, yea, and the beasts of the field, the fowl of the air, and the fish of the sea [b]."

" I am fearfully and wonderfully made : marvellous are thy works ; and that my soul knoweth right well. Thine eyes did see my substance, yet being imperfect ; and in thy book all my members were written, which in continuance were fashioned, when as yet there were none of them [c]."

I know not whether I shall be excused in putting the modern language of an uninspired writer, by the side of these venerable authorities.

Shakespear says : " What a piece of work is man ! How noble in reason ; how infinite in faculties ; in form and moving how express and admirable ; in action how like an angel ; in apprehension how like a God ; the beauty of the world ; the paragon of animals !"

---

[a] Essay on Population, Vol. III, p. 175, *et seqq.*
[b] Psalm VIII.   [c] Psalm CXXXIX.

An author of infinitely inferior talents has delivered a similar idea with exquisite beauty.

> I like thy frame : the fingers of the Gods
> I see have left their mastery upon thee ;
> They have been tapering up thy human form ;
> And the majestic prints at large appear d.

It has accordingly been held in all ages, that it was one of the first duties of a citizen, to give birth to his like, and bring offspring to the state. It is the voice of nature, and the law of nature, that every man should rejoice in posterity ; however perverted institutions may have often turned this blessing, as it stands in the law of human feelings and human understanding, into a calamity.

As such it is perpetually spoken of in the records of the Christian religion.

" As arrows in the hand of a giant," says David (and be it remembered that he was a statesman, a legislator, and a king)," even so are little children. Happy is the man that hath his quiver full of them : he shall not be ashamed, but he shall speak with the enemies in the gate e."

Again : " Blessed is he that feareth the Lord : his wife shall be as a fruitful vine in the sides of his house ; his children shall be like olive plants round about his table f."

Solomon, the son and successor of David, was plainly of the same opinion. He says, " Children's

---

d Lee, Junius Brutus. e Psalm CXXVII. f Psalm CXXVIII.

children are the crown of old men; and they are the glory of their father ᵍ."

The historian of the Judges of the Jewish nation has recorded his opinion on this subject, by his manner of narrating a fact. Of Abdon, one of the Judges, he has handed down the memory merely in one brief patriarchal painting. " He had forty sons, and thirty grandsons, which rode on threescore and ten asses' colts ʰ."

It has already appeared that all the great legislators and enlightened statesmen that ever existed, have seen the subject of population in the light in which it is here exhibited. It is only a few speculators in their closets, a Plato, an Aristotle, and a Malthus, that have regarded it in different points of view.

The language of Augustus is that of all practical politicians. " The city of Rome does not consist of its houses, its porticoes, and its public buildings; it is the men of Rome that constitute the city. The object of my care is to perpetuate the commonwealth; and in this I call upon each member of the community to contribute his part."

The amiable and enlightened author of Telemachus expresses himself thus. [The admonition is addressed by Mentor, to a king who had been spoiled by false ideas of greatness and renown.] " Know that you are a king, only just

---

ᵍ Proverbs, Chap. XVII.   ʰ Judges, Chap. XII.

so far as you have men over whom you reign.
It is not extent of territory that makes the monarch, but the number of human beings by whom
that territory is peopled. Let the country in
which you rule be moderate in extent; cover it
with innumerable inhabitants; let those inhabitants be sober, industrious and active; and your
power, your prosperity, and your glory will be
greater, than those of all the conquerors that ever
existed [i]."

Sir Richard Steele, in the Spectator [k], has
treated the same subject, in that fine vein of deep
feeling and pure *bonhommie* in which he so mar-
vellously excelled. " There is," says he, speaking in the person of an imaginary correspondent,
" another accidental advantage in marriage which
has fallen to my share; I mean the having a
multitude of children. These I cannot but regard as very great blessings. When I see my
little troop before me, I rejoice in the additions I
have made to my species, to my country, and to
my religion, in having produced such a number
of reasonable creatures, citizens, and Christians.
I am pleased to see myself thus perpetuated;
and as there is no production comparable to that
of a human creature, I am more proud of having
been the occasion of ten such glorious productions, than if I had built a pyramid at my own

[i] *Télémaque, Liv. XII.*   [k] No. 500.

expence, or published as many volumes of the finest wit and learning."

How refreshing is this! It is a return to nature and human feelings. It is in the nature of a letter of licence, permitting man to be man, allowing him to enlarge himself, and to spread into all the ramifications of social existence. Let not the system of the universe be calumniated! There is a sublime harmony between man as an individual, and man collectively considered. Private and public feelings, our love of ourselves and of all that is nearest to us, and our love of our country and our species, all operate to the same end. The interests of the one and of the other, through the whole extent of their great outline, coincide.

For twenty years the heart of man in this island has been hardening through the theories of Mr. Malthus. What permanent effect this may have upon the English character I know not: but I am sure it was high time that it should be stopped. We were learning, at least as many of us as studied the questions of political economy, and these are by no means the most despicable part of the community, to look askance and with a suspicious eye upon a human being, particularly on a little child. A woman walking the streets in a state of pregnancy, was an unavoidable subject of alarm. A man, who was the father of a numerous family, if in the lower orders of society, was the object of our anger.

We could not look at a human being with the eye of a painter, as a delicious subject of contemplation, with the eye of a moral philosopher, as a machine capable of adorning the earth with magnificence and beauty, or with the eye of a divine, as a creature with a soul to be saved, and destined to the happiness of an immortal existence. Our first question, and that regarded as a most difficult one, was, how he was to be maintained? It was not enough that he was born with the implements and the limbs, by which exuberant subsistence is to be produced. It was not enough that there was room for many millions of human beings more than now exist on the face of the earth. We were reduced (oh, miserable slavery!) to enquire, whether he was born among the easier orders of society, whether he was the son of a father, who had a fair " prospect of being able to support a family." We were learning fast to calumniate the system of the universe, and to believe that the first duty it required of us was to prevent too many human beings (that last work of God, that sole ornament and true consummation of the orb we dwell in) from being born into the world.

The great tendency and effect of Mr. Malthus's book were to warn us against making mankind happy. Such an event must necessarily lead, according to him, to the most pernicious consequences. A due portion of vice and misery was held out to us as the indispensible preservative of society, at the same time that the author himself did not venture to tell us how much of these murderous ingredients was necessary. His doctrine immediately led to the reversing all that had hitherto been held to be genuine politics, or sound moral philosophy. The theories of Mr. Malthus then being destroyed, the science of politics returns to its just and legitimate purpose, the enquiring how mankind in society, by every means that can be devised, may be made happy. Let us dismiss, now and for ever, the heart of flint that has disgraced the beginning of the nineteenth century, and take to ourselves hearts of flesh, and pulses that shall beat responsive to all that can interest or agitate any one of our fellow-creatures.

The law against murder has two sources. First, as all law is, or is intended to be, expressive of the will of the community, murder is forbidden, because the safety of each is the interest of all; that which is perpetrated on one, may next be the lot of him, or me, or any. So far it is a question of selfish calculation, on the narrowest seale. But the law is also founded upon a deep feeling of the worth and estimation of man in the abstract; a feeling confirmed by reason, and recognised, as has already been said, by all enlightened legislators. " Who kills a man, kills a reasonable creature, God's image."

If I quench thee, thou flaming minister,
I can again thy former light restore,

Should I repent. But once put out thy light,
Thou cunningest pattern of excelling nature,
I know not where is that Promethean heat,
That can thy light relume.

The sentiment that teaches us to hold the life of man at a cheap rate, has been the source of all the crimes of statesmen and warriors. We have been told of monopolists, who have bought up all the corn of a country in a period of famine, and seen with indifference thousands perishing around them, while they accumulated an immense fortune. Bonaparte in the year 1812 marched with an army of nearly four hundred thousand men into Russia, and, after a campaign of four months, escaped alone with difficulty back to Paris, while scarcely a remnant of his army survived the disasters into which he had led them : his pursuit was glory. But that of the disciples of Mr. Malthus is almost without a motive : they proceed with all the coldness of calculation, and expect neither wealth nor fame as the reward of their achievement. The check which the Author of the Essay on Population requires to keep down the numbers of mankind, is summed up by him in this expressive phrase [1]; "Every cause, which in any degree contributes to shorten the natural duration of human life :" in other words, whatever thing, that by sickness, by pain, by hunger, by hard-

---

[1] Vol. I, p. 21.

I

ship and calamity, wastes away, and slowly, with
agony and throes, extinguishes the. taper of existence.

Fortunately however the system of the universe is guiltless of these calculations.   An in-
experienced philanthropist might have wished
for the human species an easy mode of multiplication.   Looking upon the vast tracts of the
earth that have been naked and abandoned for
ages, and considering that, at the lowest computation, the globe of earth would subsist twenty
human beings for one of that handful that is at
present scattered on its surface, he might have
wished for a rapid mode of filling its desolate
places.   Of the hundreds of speculative men
who have ascribed to our nature the power of
such multiplication, scarcely one, till within
these twenty years, has prognosticated any evil
to result from it.   But that power from which
the human species derived its existence, has
disposed of the matter otherwise.   There are two
considerations by which any commodity may be
rendered precious.   One is its intrinsic beauty
and excellence; and the other the difficulty with
which it is to be procured.   In both ways the
price of our human nature seems to be enhanced.
We are not only " fearfully and wonderfully
made," the adapted dwelling of exquisite beauty
and indescribable grace, if only the external form
of man is considered, and by our mind capable
of all excellent and astonishing things : but, be-

CHAP. XIII.   VIEWS OF MAN AND SOCIETY.   115

side this, it to this day remains a problem, whether the numbers of our species can be increased. We are warned therefore to make much of this precious creature, man, to nourish it in want, to support it in distress, to relieve it by every attention and every liberality, on no account to waste a treasure so inexpressibly more estimable than the mines of Peru ; and, which is most of all, to raise this only inventive creature on the face of the earth, this creature susceptible of unlimited improvement, to all the perfection, whether of wisdom or happiness, whether in his individual or social capacity, that all our vigils and all our meditations can suggest to our performance.

ENQUIRY

CONCERNING

POPULATION.

BOOK II.

OF THE POWER OF INCREASE IN THE NUMBERS OF
THE HUMAN SPECIES, AND THE LIMITATIONS OF
THAT POWER.

CHAPTER I.

PROOFS AND AUTHORITIES FOR THE DOCTRINE
OF THE ESSAY OF POPULATION.

THE object I proposed to myself in the preceding Book was to bring together such views
on the subject of population, as might be inferred from the actual numbers of mankind in
Europe, Asia, Africa, and South America, either
in ancient or modern times, as far as any clear
notions might be obtained on that subject; and
hence to conclude what was the amount of pro-

bability, as arising from those facts, for or against Mr. Malthus's theory.   And I am willing to believe, that every reader who has thus far gone along with me, is satisfied, that, as far as probability goes, nothing can be more improbable, or do greater violence to all the facts handed down to us in history, than the principles of the Essay on Population.

I shall now attempt to go more deeply and scientifically into the question, and endeavour to ascertain what is the law of our nature respecting the increase of our species or otherwise, so far as that law can be inferred from the different documents and statistical tables, which the curiosity of governments, or the industry of men writing on the subjects of political economy, have accumulated and given to the world.

The whole system and doctrine of Mr. Malthus's Essay proceeds upon a very simple position; the tendency of human beings to multiply beyond the means of subsistence : and he plainly thinks that he grants to his opposers more than in argument they are entitled to claim, when he states that " population, where it is unchecked, goes on doubling itself every twenty-five years, or increases in a geometrical ratio [a] ;" while " the means of subsistence, under circumstances the most favourable to human industry, could not possibly be made to increase faster than in an

---

[a] Vol. I, p. 9.

arithmetical ratio b," that is, to " be increased every twenty-five years by a quantity equal to what it at present produces c."

To make this idea more intelligible to every reader, Mr. Malthus proceeds to state the effect of his two ratios in figures, and observes, " If we take the whole earth as the subject of our calculation, emigration will of course be excluded. Let us suppose the present population of the earth equal to a thousand millions; the human species, if the principle of population remained unchecked, would increase every twenty-five years, as the numbers 1, 2, 4, 8, 16, 32, 64, 128, 256, and the subsistence as 1, 2, 3, 4, 5, 6, 7, 8, 9. In two centuries the population would be to the means of subsistence as to 256 to 9; in three centuries as 4096 to 13; and in two thousand years the difference would be almost incalculable d."

As Mr. Malthus's position is simple, his proof is not less distinguished for brevity e. It is, I think, all summed up in the following sentence: " In the Northern States of America [meaning I believe, the northern parts of the republic, known under the name of The United States of North America], the population has been found to double itself, for above a century and a

---

b P. 14.   c P. 13.   d P. 15.

* In the Introduction to Book I, I have said, " He neither proves, nor attempts to prove what he asserts." And this is the accurate state of the case.

half successively, in less than twenty-five years [f]." To which he adds presently after : " This is a rate of increase in which all concurring testimonies agree, and has repeatedly been ascertained to be from procreation only [g]."

This, and this only, is the entire basis upon which Mr. Malthus's doctrine relies for its stability. He has added however certain authorities, upon which he founds his expectation of inducing the public to acquiesce in his statement. They are these :

1. Dr. Franklin. The statement of this author as quoted by Mr. Malthus [h], is, " There is no bound to the prolific nature of plants or animals, but what is made by their crowding and interfering with each other's means of subsistence. Were the face of the earth vacant of other plants, it might be gradually sowed and overspread with one kind only, as for instance with fennel : and were it empty of other inhabitants, it might in a few ages be replenished from one nation only, as for instance with Englishmen."

The Essay from which this extract is taken, is entitled, " Observations concerning the Increase of Mankind, Peopling of Countries, &c." It occupies nine pages in the late edition of Franklin's Works, 1806 [i], and was written in 1731, when the author was twenty-five years of age.

2. Dr. Ezra Styles. This gentleman publish-

---

[f] P. 7.   [g] P. 9.   [h] P. 3.   [i] Vol. II, p. 383.

ed in Boston, New England, in 1761, a Sermon on Christian Union, " some extracts from which Mr. Malthus has had an opportunity to see [k]." Dr. Styles, it seems, " speaking of Rhode Island, says, that though the period of doubling for the whole colony is twenty-five years, yet that it is different in different parts, and within land is twenty and fifteen years [k]."

3. Dr. Price [l]. This however seems not to be an authority distinct from the preceding. Dr. Price, in a letter to Dr. Franklin, which was read to the Royal Society, April 27, 1769, and published in the Philosophical Transactions, Vol. LIX, and again republished by the author in his Observations on Reversionary Payments [m], ...ays to his correspondent, " A doubling of population in eighty-four years is, as you, sir, well know [probably referring to Dr. Franklin's Observations concerning the Increase of Mankind above-quoted], a very slow increase, compared with that which takes place among our colonies in America [n]." At the bottom of the page Dr. Price refers us for further information to Dr. Styles's Sermon.

4. Euler. Who, in a Table inserted in Sussmilch's *Gottliche Ordnung*, " calculates, on a mortality of one in thirty-six, that if the births

---

k Essay on Population, Vol. II, p. 194.
l Vol. I, p. 7; Vol. II, p. 194.   m Vol. II, p. 3. seventh edition.
n Price's Observations, Vol. II, p. 49.

be to the deaths in the proportion of three to one, the period of doubling will be only twelve years and four-fifths o."

5. Sir William Petty. Who " supposes a doubling possible in so short a time as ten years p."

Being dissatisfied with Mr. Malthus's authorities, and finding some of his references inaccurate, I addressed that gentleman in the following letter :

SIR,   *October* 24, 1818.

I am at this moment engaged in a careful examination of your Essay on Population, and may probably commit something to the press on the subject.   I therefore take the liberty to request your answer to the following question.

In page 7 of the fifth edition, Vol. I, you say, " In the northern states of America, ——— the population has been found to double itself, for above a century and a half successively, in less than twenty-five years." Will you have the goodness to state to me by letter your authority for this assertion ?

I am, Sir, very respectfully,

your most obedient servant.

---

o Essay on Population, Vol. I, p. 8.

p *Ibid.* Mr. Malthus refers us for this statement to Sir W. Petty's Political Arithmetic, where it is not to be found. It occurs in his Essay concerning the Growth of the City of London.

To this letter Mr Malthus returned me an immediate answer.

East India College, Hertford,
Dear Sir,   *Oct.* 25, 1818.

Upon referring to the passage you mention in your letter, I find that the authorities on which I principally rest, are the details mentioned by Dr. Price in his Observations on Reversionary Payments, pp. 282, &c. P, and the pamphlet of Dr. Styles to which he particularly refers I afterwards saw some statements and calculations, which make the period of doubling only twenty years from the first settlement of America to the year 1800. But in the fifth edition, I find that the reference is made wrong, and that it should have been, Book ii. Ch. 13, instead of 11.

To this note, which occurs Vol. II, p. 194, of the fifth edition, I would refer you for my principal authorities at the time I published the quarto edition ; but since that, the late Statistical View of America, by T. Pitkin, in which are contained the three regular Census's of 1790, 1800, and 1810, together with an estimation in 1749, more than confirms what was there stated. Comparing the two Census's of 1790 and 1810 together, it appears that the population during

---

q I believe, Vol. II, p. 3, &c. of the Seventh Edition.

that period doubled itself in about twenty-three years; and from the estimate in 1749, in about the same time or less. This would admit of ample allowance for foreign immigration.

Truly yours.

CHAPTER II.

ANIMADVERSIONS ON MR. MALTHUS'S AUTHORITIES.

HAVING thus therefore got together all the authorities that Mr. Malthus has produced, or is able to produce, in support of his fundamental positions, let us proceed to examine into their validity and amount.

The first is Dr. Franklin. What he says on the subject of fennel, is of a very vague nature I do not imagine that any one will ascribe to this bare assertion the force of demonstration If I had heard it for the first time in conversation, and without having previously reflected on the subject, I should have answered, " Very likely." No more. The proposition is specious enough : but appearances are sometimes deceitful. Probability is not always on the side of truth. We are not sufficiently acquainted with the natural history of fennel, and of fennel-seed, to entitle us to pronounce positively. He that should undertake to " overspread the whole earth" with fennel, and that felt quite confident of the success of his experiment, I should have been apt to pronounce a very bold man.

But, when Dr. Franklin proceeds from this

hazarded assertion about fennel, to say, " Were the earth empty of other inhabitants, it might in a few ages be replenished from one nation only, as for instance with Englishmen," he makes a very wide step indeed.   There is a great difference between the sowing of seed, and the multiplication of men.   I have myself counted eighty grains of corn, growing on one stalk, from a single seed, in the course of a season. The sowing of vegetables is a very simple thing ; and we are apt to think that we can calculate with some certainty on the result.   And yet, I own I cannot feel an undoubting confidence in Dr. Franklin's crop of millions of acres of fennel.

The multiplication of mankind however is an affair of another sort, and governed by different laws.   It has by many persons been believed that we do multiply ; but what was the rate of increase, no one, till the year 1731, had ventured to pronounce.   It may be that I want the robust nerves of Dr. Franklin and Mr. Malthus ; but I own, if the human species were by some tremendous casualty swept from every other part of the globe, except this island, I should not like to witness the experiment, whether or no its present population could be replenished with Englishmen only.

I do not know how the world was peopled at first.   We are told, that we are all descended from a single pair : but we are not entitled to reason from this memorable history, to the every-day occurrences of life. The creation of the world, and the peopling of the earth, are all a miracle. The settling of countries and the dispersion of mankind were conducted by the immediate hand of the creator. Besides, human life, it is written, was originally of the duration of nearly a thousand years; and this may be supposed to have made a wide difference in the rate of multiplication.

But Dr. Franklin and Mr. Malthus are both of them calculators and philosophers. They do not pretend to appeal to miracles for the truth of their theories. Mr. Malthus in particular deals largely in statistical tables, and collections of the registers of births, marriages and deaths, in these latter ages of the world; and to these I shall presently take leave to accompany him.

Dr. Franklin I own has obtained a great name. But, when he launches into assertions so visionary as those here recited, and above all, when I recollect what tremendous and heart-sickening consequences Mr. Malthus has deduced from these assertions, I must say that a great name goes with me for nothing, and I must subject his positions to a strict examination.

Dr. Franklin is in this case particularly the object of our attention, because he was the first man that started the idea of the people of America being multiplied by procreation, so as to "double their numbers every twenty years." Dr. Franklin, born at Boston, was eminently an American patriot; and the paper from which these extracts are taken, was expressly written to exalt the importance and glory of his country.

The following is the way in which he supports his hypothesis respecting the population of America. "If it is reckoned in Europe that there is but one marriage *per annum* among one hundred persons, perhaps we may here reckon on two; and if in Europe they have but four births to a marriage [a], we may here reckon eight." It were to be wished, that Dr. Franklin had given his reasons for this amazing superiority in the fruitfulness of the marriage-bed on the other side the Atlantic. Is it any thing in the climate? Dr. Franklin says something respecting the late marriages of Europe; and this we shall shortly have occasion to examine. But he could hardly have thought that all European brides were so old, as from that circumstance

---

[a] The knowledge of this fact of the average of four children to a marriage, seems to be one of the oldest positions in political economy. Derham, in his Physico-Theology, Book IV, Chap. X, fifth edition, has constructed a Table for different parts of Europe, founded, as he tells us, on Major Graunt's Observations on the Bills of Motality, and Mr. King's Remarks on the First of Dr. Davenant's Essays, from which he draws the same conclusion: and on this he builds an inference, that the numbers of the human species have been for the most part at a stand, ever since that miraculous longevity of man ceased, which, he says, "was of absolute necessity for the more speedy peopling of the new world."

alone to account for their having no more than half the offspring of the brides of America. If this paper were without a date, I should have thought it had been written long before twenty-five years of age.

It is not a little curious, that the next authority upon which we are called upon to believe in Mr. Malthus's fundamental positions, is a Sermon delivered sixty years ago, by a puritanical preacher in Connecticut, which Sermon Mr. Malthus never saw.

To make a just estimate of the authority of Sir William Petty, it is necessary to quote his words. " Suppose there be 600 people; in natural possibility this number may yield near 75 births annually. For by some late observations the teeming females between 15 and 44 years of age, are about 180 of the said 600, and the males of between 18 and 59, are about 180 also, and every teeming woman can bear a child once in two years; from all which it is plain, that the births may be 90 per annum, and (abating 15 for sickness, young abortions, and natural barrenness) there may remain 75 births, which is an eighth of the people; which births by some observations we have found to be actually but a two-and-thirtieth part, or but a quarter of what is thus shewn to be naturally possible. Now, according to this reckoning, if the births may be 75 of 600 annually, and the burials but 15, then the annual increase of the people will be

60; and so the said 600 people may double in 10 years."

Now in this passage three things are assumed : first, the amount of teeming women in any given number of people; secondly, the amount of deaths annually ; and thirdly, the amount of births annually, that are, according to Sir William, " in natural possibility." Without going into the accuracy of the amounts in the two former instances, the first thing worthy of notice is that these two amounts are given as founded upon actual observations, while for the third the author confessedly has resort to the regions of possibility.   But in this there is no parity.

And what does Sir William Petty mean by " natural possibility ?"   How can we know any thing of possibilities, as to the natural history of man, but from actual observation? Sir William Petty assumes that every female between 15 and 44 years of age is what he calls a teeming female, or in other words capable of bearing a child once in two years, and that 15 out of 90 is an ample allowance for natural barrenness, for abortions, and for such indisposition, of whatever sort, on the part of the female, as should produce a temporary incapacity for child-bearing.   He further supposes that each female shall be the mother of fourteen children, or, more accurately speaking of fourteen children and a half; for, if the teeming women are constantly in the proportion of 180, and the number of children born annually stands as Sir William Petty has set it down,

K

then it is obvious that every teeming woman,
in other words, every woman between 15 and
44 years of age, must bear a child every second
year. Now where does Sir William find this?
And, if I were to say, that it is a " natural impossibility," that every woman between these
ages should do thus, should I not have as much,
or rather a great deal more, reason on my side?

So much for Sir William Petty's " possible
doubling of mankind in so short a time as ten
years."

I next proceed to consider the authority of
Euler, who, according to Mr. Malthus, " calculates, on a mortality of 1 in 36, that if the
births be to the deaths in the proportion of 3 to
1, the period of doubling will be only 12 years
and 4-5ths."

The name of Euler is truly imposing. He is
one of the most eminent mathematicians of modern times, and is worthy to be ranked with
the greatest geniuses in that science in ages
past. But it is truly to very little purpose that
the name of Euler is introduced into this question. And I am persuaded, if he could have
been aware of the use that would be made of
his authority, he would have taken effectual
care that it should not be employed for the purpose of imposing unfounded theories on the
world.

Euler never wrote a book on the population
of the earth, and the multiplication of the hu-

man species. If he had, I cannot but believe that he would have looked with a penetrating eye and a persevering temper into the subject. He would not have been discouraged by its intricacies ; but would have spent years of patient labour in collecting all the documents and tables that could be found, and by careful comparison have endeavoured to deduce from them such results as might be worthy of the confidence of future generations. He has done no such thing.

How comes his name then to be mixed up with the subject of which Mr. Malthus treats ?

A writer, to whose pages we are considerably indebted, and who appears to have been extremely assiduous in the execution of his task, John Peter Sussmilch, member of the Royal Academy of Sciences at Berlin, undertook a work, entitled, *Die Gottliche Ordnung, &c.* ; or, The Order of Divine Providence, as Displayed in the Births, Deaths, and Increase of the Human Race, which was first published in 1765 in two volumes octavo, and has since been enlarged into three. This work is replete with statistical tables ; and the author was at indefatigable pains in collecting all the documents that could throw light on his subject. His volumes are therefore of great value as a book of reference. The professed object of Sussmilch was, first to demonstrate the possibility of an increase in the population of the earth, and then to recommend the adoption of such means as he was able to suggest for realising that increase.

The great merit of this writer is patience and perseverance; and he appears to have been laudably diffident of his own abilities in matters of mathematical calculation. He therefore applied to Euler. Euler was a man of the highest reputation in the exact sciences, and had been employed by Frederic the Second, in the beginning of his reign, to assist in remodelling and giving new life and vigour to his Academy. Euler, with that liberality which ought always to be the characteristic of a man of genius, lent himself to the request of his brother-academician. For this purpose it was no wise necessary that he should study the subject of population; nor did he attempt to do so. He was responsible only for the fidelity of his calculations. Sussmilch gave him certain questions, gratuitous and arbitrary suppositions as to an imaginary multiplication of mankind; and Euler worked the sums. Every one therefore may easily judge, with what propriety Euler is brought forward as an authority on the occasion. As well might Bonnycastle in his Introduction to Algebra be cited to prove that a gentleman gave four millions five hundred thousand pounds for a horse, because he has shewn that, upon a certain computation, if adopted, that would actually have been the price ot the horse.

The computation of Euler to which Mr.

Malthus refers, stands thus. " If in any country there are 100,000 persons living, and the annual mortality is one in thirty-six, then, supposing the annual proportion of deaths to births to be variously, as 10 to 11, 10 to 12, and so on, up to as 10 to 30, what will be the numbers of persons who will yearly be added to the society, and what will be the number of years required for the original 100,000 persons to become 200,000 ?" Euler's answer is that " the period of doubling on the first supposition would be 250 years, and—on the last would be twelve years and four-fifths [b]." This question certainly did not require the extraordinary abilities of Euler to solve. If the sum were worked upon the Rule of Compound Interest, to be found in any of the common books of arithmetic, the answer would be exactly the same as it is in Euler's Table.

Surely the reading part of the public have seldom been so egregiously trifled with, as when Mr. Malthus gravely placed this calculation of Euler among his authorities for the rapid multiplication of mankind.

The question which the real politician is called upon to examine, is not what would be the result upon certain arbitrary suppositions, but what does actually happen in the community of mankind.

---

[b] This Table is printed in the Essay on Population, Vol. II, p. 167.

Mr. Malthus indeed adds, " This proportion [*viz.* the proportion on which Euler calculates a doubling in twelve years and four-fifths] has actually occurred for short periods in more countries than one [c]."

This the Essay on Population asserts in its usual Laconic style.

Surely it is not thus, that the gravest question (if at all grave) which was ever presented to the consideration of mankind, ought to be treated. Let it be remembered, that the corollary from this and the like propositions, is that vice and misery, and nothing but vice and misery, are the indispensible guarantees for the existence of our race.

I cannot for myself consent to admit such a proposition with such a corollary, without the minutest and the strictest examination. One line, or even six pages [d], will never satisfy me in a question of this sort. If Mr. Malthus had named his countries and his periods, it would then have been open for me to ascertain what peculiar circumstances might have occasioned this doubling for the confessedly " short periods" our author speaks of.

But what have we to do with " short periods ?" The speculations of the Essay on Population, with which the world has been made drunk for twenty years, treat of nothing less than in-

---

[c] Vol. I, p. 8.   [d] Vol. III, p. 344, note.

finity. The main proposition of the author is that "population, if unchecked, will go on doubling itself every twenty-five years, or increase in a geometrical ratio :" that is, will go on for ever: when it has once begun, nothing can stop it totally but the consummation of all things, or partially but some of those checks which fall under the heads either of vice or misery. Indeed Mr. Malthus has recently told us, that, " if any person will take the trouble to make the calculation," he may easily ascertain how long a time, upon his principles, will be necessary, to people the whole visible universe with human beings at the rate of four men to every square yard e. What have " short periods" of increase to do with this ?

It will more fully appear as we proceed that short periods of increase afford no foundation whatever upon which to found our conclusion as to any ratio of increase in perpetual series f.

But it is worth while to dwell a little upon this doubling in infinite series, which is the corner-stone of Mr. Malthus's system. The rules for calculating such a series are to be found in every common book of arithmetic : but hitherto it has been regarded by almost all sober men, as

---

e Principles of Political Economy, p. 227. See below, p. 484.

f See Mr. Booth's Dissertation on the Ratios of Increase, inserted p. 243.

an exercise in calculation, a mathematical recreation, and nothing more.

Mr. Bonnycastle, as above quoted, has ascertained the price of a horse, if he were purchased by the rule of a geometrical progression, of which the exponent is 2, and if the progression, beginning at a farthing, were carried on through thirty-two steps. Dr. Price has calculated the produce of one penny put out at our Saviour's birth to five *per cent.* compound interest, and finds that in the year 1791 it would have increased to a greater sum than would be contained in three hundred millions of earths, all solid gold[g]. But did any one ever think of applying this to the affairs of real existence? Has any one ever given four millions sterling for a horse? Did any one ever, by dint of compound interest, for himself and his successors, turn a penny into three hundred millions of earths, all solid gold? Is it worth our while, except as a puzzle to sharpen the wits of school-boys, to talk either of the one or the other? As little, be sure, are Mr. Malthus's ratios worthy to be thought of by statesmen, or acted upon even by the overseers of parish-workhouses, to which, according to our author, they eminently belong[h].

There is such a thing, well known among lo-

---

[g] Observations on Reversionary Payments, Vol. I, p. 314.

[h] See below, Book VI. Chapter III, *et seqq.*

gicians, as an argument, that proves too much, and by so doing is universally set down as proving nothing. If ever there was such an argument, such is Mr. Malthus's argument from " the American increase ;" or, in other words, such is " the American increase" as expounded by Mr. Malthus. A sound and well regulated mind, that is engaged in other matters than mathematical puzzles and wonders, soon comes to a stand amidst the luxuriances of an infinite series.

In this respect we may perhaps consider ourselves as substantially indebted to Mr. Malthus for the illustration, introduced into ·his last work, of peopling the whole visible universe at the rate of four men to every square yard. There is no bubble so brilliant, that, if you attempt to blow it up to too vast a size, will not presently burst, and shew to every bystander that it was but a bubble all the while.

There is, says Mr. Malthus, a tendency in the human species, susceptible of the effect of in no long time peopling all the stars. And yet, according to his own shewing, this tendency has never displayed itself, but in one insignificant period of one hundred and fifty years, in one remote corner of the world, and with what circumstances of evidence we shall presently have occasion to enquire. *Credat Judæus Apella.*

If the principle of population had gone on

unchecked for eighteen hundred years, it would have produced men enough to fill the whole visible universe with human creatures as thick as they could stand : this is in so many words the doctrine of our author. The earth is at this moment computed to contain 600,000,000 of human beings. I wish Mr. Malthus has put down his numbers, that, by subtracting the one from the other, we might see by a glance of the eye, how many had been crushed in the egg, or destroyed in infancy. But I have shewn in the proper place, that, upon the reasonings of the Essay on Population, they were not crushed in the egg, but were actually born, and actually died in childhood [i].

Let us however treat the doctrine of our author fairly. God forbid that we should crush the " principle of population" under the weight of numbers that do not belong to it! It is true that, upon our author's principles, all in every generation are born that can be born. But, for as many as die in their infancy, we cannot count upon their progeny. This progeny is only crushed in the egg. Granted : yet I must be allowed to set on the other side the age of the world. It would need only eighteen hundred years to people the whole visible universe at the rate of four men to every square yard : but the world has lasted according to the most moderate

---

See above, pages 30, 31, 32.

statements six thousand years; according to the Indians and Chinese many hundred times as long. Oh, for a sober philosopher to count up the innumerable infinities (how shall I express the idea!) of children that have died for the benefit of the geometrical ratio—beside all that mortality, which the records of countries or the sad ruminations of the moralist, had recognised, and thought they had completed the tale, little suspecting the discovery which has since been made of Mr. Malthus's ratios! Millions become as insignificant as units, when applied to this consideration. Dr. Price's three hundred millions of earths all solid gold, are nothing. Three hundred millions of earths all solid men, would not constitute the millionth part of that company which is set before us, when Mr. Malthus draws up the curtain, and shews us the geometrical ratio.—I must again repeat, How do we know this? Upon what evidence is it to be received? Upon one solitary experiment (and I must be allowed to add, a most equivocal one) of one bare hundred and fifty years, in one infant colony, as I may call it, in an obscure nook of the New World; and this replied to and refuted, with one voice, and with an evidence the most consenting and astounding, by all ages and countries, by all sects of religion and forms of government, that were ever heard of or devised.

If America had never been discovered, the

geometrical ratio, as applied to the multiplication of mankind, would never have been known. If the British colonies had never been planted, Mr. Malthus would never have written. The human species might have perished of a long old age, a fate to which perhaps all sublunary things are subject at last, without one statesman, or one legislator through myriads of centuries, having suspected this dangerous tendency to increase, " in comparison with which human institutions, however they may appear to be causes of much mischief to society, are mere feathers." There have been new lights in religion ; and there are new lights in politics : a spark struck out fortuitously, but carefully, gathered up and preserved by men anxiously solicitous for the public weal. " The light shineth in darkness."

But it may be said, though Mr. Malthus should be wrong in his calculations, and the power of increase in the numbers of the human species should not be altogether so prodigious as is above stated, it may nevertheless be sufficiently great to authorise all the practical inferences and precautions insisted on in the Essay on Population.

When once I have brought the reader to this point, I consider myself as having gained my cause.

The law of arithmetical and geometrical progression is one of the clearest things in the whole compass of human knowledge. It is altogether as certain, considered as matter of abstract science, as it is absurd and inapplicable, when we attempt to connect it with real life and the ebbs and flows of sublunary things. It admits no half-measures. It is like the *vis inertiæ*, which sir Isaac Newton has set down as a principal law of the *phenomena* of matter. Once set in motion, it moves for ever, and for ever with the same force.

Mr. Malthus's discovery is built on " the American increase." He " considers it as proved, as soon as related [k]." " The population has been found to double itself, for above a century and a half successively, in twenty-five years, and that by procreation only." " The American increase" proves the geometrical ratio of increase, or it proves nothing. The whole fabric of Mr. Malthus's theory rests upon this simple proposition; and it is the exceeding simplicity, and apparent cogency of its principle, to which it has been mainly indebted for its universal reception. If the numbers of mankind have not been found so to double in periods short, defined, and equal in duration, and to go on doubling, the Essay on Population is turned into waste paper.

This idle and extravagant hypothesis therefore being removed, the whole science stands just as it did before Mr. Malthus wrote; and we are brought precisely to the position most fa-

---

[k] Vol. III, p. 344, note.

vourable to the speculations of the following pages. The Essay on Population has done nothing, and worse than nothing. The geometrical ratio, as applied to any known state of mankind is a dream. "The American increase," as explained by our author is a blunder. Let us then proceed to scrutinize the subject of population, as a theory in which no advances have been made for a century past, and endeavour to draw sound inferences concerning it from authentic and incontrovertible documents.

Such then is the system that has gained a success in the world wholly unprecedented. A superstitious man might think it was prophesied of in the following passage of the Revelation of St. John. "And I stood upon the sands of the sea; and I saw a beast rise up out of the sea, having seven heads and ten horns. [Were there not seventeen states in the confederacy from which Mr. Malthus draws his example?] And they worshipped the beast, saying, Who is like unto the beast? who is able to make war with him? And there was given unto him a mouth, speaking great things and blasphemies: and power was given unto him, to continue forty and two months. And all the world wondered after the beast." And again: "In the latter times some shall depart from the faith, giving ear to seducing spirits, forbidding to marry."

The additional authority in behalf of the geometrical ratio, which has occurred to Mr. Malthus "since publishing his quarto edition," *viz.* "the three regular censuses, printed in Pitkin's Statistical View," will be fully considered by me in the Fourth Book.

CHAPTER III.

PRINCIPLES RESPECTING THE INCREASE OR
DECREASE OF THE NUMBERS OF MANKIND.

HAVING thus entered into an impartial review of Mr. Malthus's theory and the authorities upon which it is founded, I proceed to that
which is most properly the object of my volume. The Essay on Population has left for me
a clear stage in this respect : it has touched upon
none of those topics from which a real knowledge of the subject is to be acquired. Its author from a very slight and unsatisfactory evidence has drawn the most absurd and extravagant consequences ; and, having done this, he
closes the account, fully convinced that he has
shewn in " the laws of nature and the passions
of mankind ª " an evil, for which all remedies are
feeble, and before which all courage must sink
into despair.

My business is therefore with those topics
which Mr. Malthus has named, and only named :
" the laws of nature, and the passions of mankind." I will beg leave to consider something

---

ª Vol. II, p, 246.

of these, and particularly of the former, before I proceed to the millions to be found in a table of censorate; and, when I come to those tables, I will not look at them solely *en masse*, but will endeavour to analyse their contents.

The inquisitive and scientifical part of the human species are not wholly ignorant of the natural history of man. We know, in the first place, from experience, how long this fabric of the human frame is in the majority of cases capable to endure. " The days of our years are three-score years and ten." We know, in the next place, from the same source of experience, how many years in ordinary cases precede the period of our maturity, for how long a time we retain our full vigour and manhood, and how many years belong to the period of decrepitude and decline.

There is another particular relative to our species, which does not deserve the name of science, but which is of the most vital importance to the subject under consideration; and that is, the distinction of mankind into two sexes, male and female.

In the disquisition in which we are engaged, relative to the procreation and multiplication of our species, it is essential that we should recollect, that the female only is concerned in the business of bringing children into the world. This is the law of our nature; the germ of the human species can be matured by the female, and by her only. Women, if I may be allowed so to illustrate my principle, are the soil from which human creatures are produced. The rest of the society, men, young and old, and children of the male sex, [exclusive of such a number of males, as might be found necessary to give activity to the prolific power in the females] are absolutely of no account in relation to the point we are here considering.

Another distinction it is also incumbent upon us to recollect. We just now divided the life of man into three periods, immaturity, perfect manhood, and decline. This distinction is still more conspicuously applicable to the female sex. The line which divides the three periods in the life of the male, so far as the propagation of the species is concerned, is very uncertain. Not so in the female. It is, I conceive, well settled as a general rule, that the age of child-bearing is over, by the time the female has completed the forty-fifth year of her age. A line is also capable of being ascertained, if not for all females universally, at least variously for the different climates and races of mankind, fixing the age at which the power of child-bearing is found to commence. I believe I may add, that the distance between these two periods may be ascertained to be nearly the same in all cases, the female who in certain climates arrives at an earlier maturity, being seen to grow old, and to cease from the power of child-bearing, sooner than in the milder and more temperate climates which we inhabit.

It happens in many subjects, the understanding of which is of the greatest importance to the welfare of mankind, that the elements of our knowledge respecting them are so simple, as to be overlooked by the thoughtless, and contemned by the superficial. Just so it is in the question we are here considering.

The principle which has now been delivered will probably be found to be of the highest importance in leading us safely through the mazes of the question of population. If, in the enquiry respecting the increase of the numbers of mankind from one generation to another, the females of an age capable of child-bearing are alone to be considered, it follows, that a census or enumeration of human beings in any given country, or over the whole globe, can never constitute any term in the progression. Such an enumeration will consist of men, women and children, of every different age, from the infant in the cradle, to the male or female who from old age is tottering on the brink of the grave, and therefore can afford no solid ground from which to conclude as to the number of human beings that shall be found in.that country, or on this globe, after the lapse of twenty-five, fifty, or one hundred years. At all events it must be a very long series of observations, and these of a sort in which the difference of numbers can be in no wise imputed to the inaccuracy of early enumerations, and the superior exactness of those which follow, that can supply materials for any safe inference in this way. They must also relate to a country, not distinguished at least for any remarkable influx of emigrants from other parts of the world.

The males in the community we are considering (with the single limitation which has been above named), the old women, and the female children who are doomed never to arrive at the age of maturity, are the mere drones of the hive, so far as the enquiry respecting the progressive increase of the numbers of mankind is concerned. They may be useful; they may be ornamental; they may be entitled to all our respect and all our tenderness; they may be the boast of the whole earth for intellect or for virtue. But, for just so long a time as we would reason upon the abstract power and possibility of population, we must, though under a very different impression, and for the purpose of arriving at a very different conclusion, be as rigorous in excluding from our thoughts all that is most lovely and most honourable in human nature, as Mr. Malthus is when he supposes, that men in a perfectly virtuous and happy state of society, would ruin that state in the shortest practicable period, by an unreflecting conformity to the impulses of a brutal appetite.

The principle which is here laid down will be made in some respects more intelligible, if we illustrate it by a supposition, which has the further advantage of being peculiarly applicable to

Mr. Malthus's conception as to the United States of America.

Let us suppose a colony of one thousand persons to be transported into a country hitherto void of inhabitants.   Let us suppose this colony to consist of five hundred men and five hundred women, and that further every one of them shall be between the ages of twenty-five and thirty years. Here we get rid at once of all those useless or doubtful members of the community, so far as procreation is concerned, that fill up the extreme ranks of society in all settled countries, the ranks of childhood and of advanced life. Here are five hundred females, who, except so far as an allowance is to be made for cases of barrenness, are all of them qualified to add to the numbers of the next generation.

Let us now take the period assigned by Sir William Petty, who states that " it is possible to double the number of the members of a community in the short period of ten years."   In the colony I have described I can easily suppose this, and will even grant him, if required, a still larger amount. Well then : here will we fix our foot, and take this as the basis of a geometrical ratio.   In ten years this colony, which at first consisted of one thousand souls, has become two thousand. Therefore upon the principle here assigned, in twenty years it will become four thousand.

But what is the actual state of the case? The colony at first consisted of one thousand persons :

it now amounts to two thousand. But every individual of the last thousand, and much more (for many more than a thousand children must have been born, and have lived to a certain age, to compensate for the inevitable mortality of the seniors), is under ten years of age. The number of persons capable of bringing children into the world, has not experienced the smallest increase. Perhaps none of the original stock, from which an increase of the numbers of the community was to be expected, have yet arrived at that stage, when the spring of the constitution is so far exhausted, that they can no longer be relied on, as belonging to the class of those who shall give children to the colony. If however we had taken the period a little longer, such would infallibly have been the case. And at all events we may be perfectly sure, that the number of persons capable of becoming mothers, must in the course of ten years have been greatly diminished by death.

I will not at present pursue this illustration further: we shall have abundant occasion to resume the subject as we proceed. Enough has here been alleged, to afford a strong confirmation of the maxim of Voltaire, which I took as the motto of an early Chapter: *" Les hommes ne multiplient pas aussi aisément qu'on le pense* b." " The multiplication of the numbers of mankind is not quite so easy an affair as some have imagined."

CHAPTER IV.

ACCOUNTS WHICH ARE GIVEN OF THE POPULATION OF SWEDEN.

HAVING thus delivered what may perhaps be found to be the fundamental principle of our subject, we may profitably proceed to the examination of such documents, as the assiduity of political governors, or the industry of authors who have for whatever reason concerned themselves with the numbers of mankind, has collected on the subject of the populousness of nations.

It will be clear from what has been said, that tables of population for any very limited period, which do not distinguish the sexes and the different ages of the inhabitants of a country, are absolutely of no use in determining the question of the power, generally, or in any particular case, of progressive increase in the numbers of mankind. The two enumerations therefore, which were made of the people of Great Britain in 1801 and 1811, are merely so much labour thrown away.

Having taken some pains to look through all that is known of the population of countries, I can find nothing that affords a chance of reasonable satisfaction, except the accounts which have been published of the population of Sweden. To them therefore for the present I shall particularly direct my attention.

Sweden is a *regio pene toto divisa orbe.* It receives few emigrants, and sends forth few colonies. In the period to which the accounts relate that I am about to produce, this kingdom has enjoyed a great portion of internal tranquillity; and, as will more fully appear in the sequel, has possessed almost every imaginable advantage for the increase of its inhabitants by direct procreation.

Of the people of Sweden I find an account to have been taken, from three years to three years, in the enlightened manner above suggested, that is, under separate heads as to sex and age, from the year 1751, to, I believe, the year 1775. From that period it has been continued to the present time, with an interval of five years between each enumeration.

The collectors of the Swedish enumerations have further presented us with Tables of the annual births, marriages and deaths; and have even, in two instances, proceeded to compare the population as it is, with the population as it ought to be: thus,

For the year 1780.

Ought to be - - - - - 2,780,334

Is - - - - - - - - - - 2,782,168

And again for 1795.

Ought to be - - - - - 3,078,308

Is - - - - - - - - - - 3,043,731 [a].

Now the upper line in each of these examples, I conceive, can mean nothing else, than that, if we add the report of the intermediate births to the preceding enumeration, and subtract the intermediate deaths, the result ought to be as here stated. If this be the case, it is certainly worthy of remark, how near the computatory and the actual enumerations come to each other, and consequently how high a degree of credit is due to the Swedish Tables.

A judicious abstract of the information then existing on the subject, was published in the Swedish language, in the Memoirs of the Royal Academy of Sciences at Stockholm for the Year 1766, by Mr. Peter Wargentin, secretary to that institution. A continuation of Mr. Wargentin's paper has appeared, but somewhat irregularly, in the subsequent volumes of the same collection. I will set out with exhibiting an ample specimen of these Tables of population [b].

[a] Memoirs of the Royal Academy of Stockholm, for the Year 1799.
[b] Of the Tables I have here inserted, the first four are to be found in the volume of the Swedish Memoirs for 1766, the fifth in the volume for 1809, and the 6th in the volume for 1776. The seventh is a Table of my own construction, founded generally on the enumerations I met with dispersed in different volumes of this work.

TABLE I.

Containing an Abstract of the Bills of Mortality for the Years 1755, 1756, and 1757, and a Summary of the Enumeration for 1757.

Annual Deaths, being an Average of Deaths during the Years 1755, 1756, 1757.	Males.	Fem.	Number of the Living in 1757.	Males.	Females.
Still-born	1301	950	Born	44795	42999
Died under 1 year	10542	9348	Under 1 year	33731	33459
Between 1 and 3	3884	4027	Between 1 and 3	63954	64883
3 — 5	1922	1800	3 — 5	64380	65045
5 — 10	1639	1566	5 — 10	123984	125175
10 — 15	739	716	10 — 15	114605	114203
15 — 20	635	607	15 — 20	95254	100087
20 — 25	826	716	20 — 25	91460	104873
25 — 30	845	836	25 — 30	86947	99781
30 — 35	909	1014	30 — 35	82716	90880
35 — 40	819	757	35 — 40	68516	75563
40 — 45	1012	967	40 — 45	58990	65443
45 — 50	899	774	45 — 50	50658	58162
50 — 55	1090	941	50 — 55	43500	51973
55 — 60	1102	1100	55 — 60	39091	48599
60 — 65	1214	1481	60 — 65	29557	39580
65 — 70	1222	1693	65 — 70	22293	33559
70 — 75	1390	2009	70 — 75	16390	24913
75 — 80	1056	1593	75 — 80	9236	14679
80 — 85	733	1244	80 — 85	4060	6786
85 — 90	412	673	85 — 90	1690	2932
Upwards of 90	240	407	Upwards of 90	583	1026
	33130	34269	Males	1101595	1221600
			Females 1221600		
			Total 2323195		

TABLE II.

Average Deaths during the Years 1758, 1759, 1760.			Number of the Living in 1760.		
	Males.	Fem.		Males.	Females.
Still-born	1183	869	Born	44174	42331
Died under 1 year	9239	7789	Under 1 year	37323	37272
Between 1 and 3	3020	2861	Between 1 and 3	66034	66860
3 — 5	1549	1482	3 — 5	65828	66923
5 — 10	1605	1435	5 — 10	128627	129332
10 — 15	756	691	10 — 15	121525	119514
15 — 20	673	639	15 — 20	97621	101683
20 — 25	862	772	20 — 25	88752	103613
25 — 30	932	957	25 — 30	85001	100614
30 — 35	1020	1151	30 — 35	81433	92154
35 — 40	957	918	35 — 40	70773	79066
40 — 45	1150	1184	40 — 45	61158	68645
45 — 50	1160	990	45 — 50	51407	59339
50 — 55	1251	1167	50 — 55	43897	51872
55 — 60	1378	1307	55 — 60	37224	46402
60 — 65	1401	1749	60 — 65	32329	42647
65 — 70	1306	760	65 — 70	21438	30169
70 — 75	1432	2275	70 — 75	15102	25299
75 — 80	1187	1825	75 — 80	9096	14265
80 — 85	846	1341	80 — 85	4418	7387
85 — 90	410	669	85 — 90	1513	2571
Upwards of 90	223	392	Upwards of 90	555	1019
	32357	33354	Males	1121053	1246545
			Females	1246545	
			Total	2367598	

TABLE III.

Average Deaths during the Years 1761, 1762, 1763.			Number of the Living in 1763.		
	Males.	Fem.		Males.	Fem.
Still-born	1324	988	Born	45892	43904
Died under 1 year	11172	9850	Under 1 year	36094	35453
Between 1 and 3	4393	4336	Between 1 and 3	66059	67234
3 — 5	2206	2249	3 — 5	66454	67711
5 — 10	2151	2057	5 — 10	130019	130758
10 — 15	933	834	10 — 15	126696	128021
15 — 20	711	658	15 — 20	108312	109985
20 — 25	834	756	20 — 25	92299	105115
25 — 30	883	863	25 — 30	88056	101003
30 — 35	1020	1146	30 — 35	85936	95811
35 — 40	955	923	35 — 40	74826	81453
40 — 45	1180	1170	40 — 45	67448	74854
45 — 50	1099	938	45 — 50	52398	59551
50 — 55	1280	1113	50 — 55	47298	56646
55 — 60	1177	1097	55 — 60	37086	45537
60 — 65	1586	1721	60 — 65	34892	44925
65 — 70	1237	1566	65 — 70	20649	28964
70 — 75	1322	2041	70 — 75	15454	23159
75 — 80	1092	1695	75 — 80	8858	13556
80 — 85	917	1446	80 — 85	4620	7487
85 — 90	414	650	85 — 90	1508	2694
Upwards of 90	215	379	Upwards of 90	527	988
	36777	37488	Males	1165489	1280905
			Females	1280905	
			Total	2446394	

TABLE IV.

Account of the Births, Marriages, and Deaths in the Kingdom of Sweden for Fifteen Years.

Years.	Births.	Marriages.	Deaths.
1749	76766	19045	61483
1750	82360	20927	58939
1751	89341	21335	57663
1752	84110	20922	60456
1753	84406	20089	54977
1754	90021	21994	64715
1755	91767	21472	64982
1756	89739	20007	69161
1757	81878	18799	68054
1758	83299	19484	74370
1759	85579	23210	62662
1760	90635	23383	60083
1761	90075	22421	63183
1762	89162	21467	74520
1763	90152	20927	85093

TABLE V.

Enumerations of the People of Sweden for 1800 and 1805.

	1800.		1805.	
	Males.	Fem.	Males.	Fem.
Under 1 Year	41,515	40,424	47,688	47,413
Between 1 & 3	83,903	84,253	87,374	88,982
3 - 5	86,536	87,352	83,387	84,672
5 - 10	167,795	168,316	174,332	174,736
10 - 15	154,455	153,392	169,054	168,529
15 - 20	137,972	142,292	143,232	147,582
20 - 25	130,552	141,914	134,518	144,432
25 - 30	113,470	125,059	127,503	135,583
30 - 35	109,649	120,134	108,152	118,076
35 - 40	100,052	110,302	100,714	112,212
40 - 45	93,442	101,597	95,743	106,057
45 - 50	81,703	91,244	82,968	92,779
50 - 55	68,856	77,980	75,046	84,680
55 - 60	52,221	61,066	56,953	67,302
60 - 65	41,881	51,480	43,888	52,499
65 - 70	31,961	41,125	29,965	39,785
70 - 75	20,768	27,787	21,167	29,494
75 - 80	10,667	15,009	11,372	16,345
80 - 85	4,087	6,249	4,827	7,396
85 - 90	1,151	1,884	1,280	2,095
to 95			273	437
100			45	66
101, 2, 3	213	424	5	6
104			—	2
106			1	1
08			—	1
	1,532,849	1,649,283	1,599,487	1,721,160
	3,182,132		3,320,647	

TABLE VI.

Population of the Diocese of Upsal.

Years	Number of the Living			Subsisting Marriages	Widowers	Widows	Unmarried above 15		Under 15		Households.
	Males.	Fem.	Total.				Males.	Fem.	Males.	Fem.	
1749	90503	105926	196429	36279	2083	11846	21059	25818	31650	31412	29494
1752	93441	108752	202193	37474	1750	11774	21381	27432	32564	32544	28014
1755	97355	110949	208304	38872	2055	11537	22282	27209	33652	33874	29007
1760	95966	113384	209350	38851	2148	12621	21726	27325	33629	34199	29262
1763	99933	114112	214045	40492	2223	11874	21825	26921	35063	35154	30568
1766	102949	117057	220006	41273	2328	12267	23438	27827	35962	35638	33417
1769	104824	118671	223495	42055	2158	12202	24564	28139	36079	36242	33688
1772	105564	119081	224645	41652	2671	12381	25455	28989	35792	36053	33580
1773	103989	116725	220714	40682	3151	12033	25826	29330	34357	34654	32944

TABLE VII.

A General View of the Increase of the Population of Sweden.

Years.	Population	Interval.	Increase.	Proportion.
1751	2,229,611			
1757	2,323,195	6 years	93,534	$\frac{1}{24}$
1760	2,367,598	3 years	44,403	$\frac{1}{53}$
1763	2,446,394	3 years	78,796	$\frac{1}{30}$
1775	2,630,992	12 years	184,598	$\frac{1}{13}$
1780	2,782,168	5 years	151,176	$\frac{1}{10}$
1795	3,043,731	15 years	261,563	$\frac{1}{10}$
1800	3,182,132	5 years	138,401	$\frac{1}{22}$
1805	3,320,647	5 years	138,515	$\frac{1}{23}$
or without Finland				
1805	2,424,874			
1810	2,377,851	5 years	Diminution	
1815	2,465,066	5 years	87,215	$\frac{1}{27}$

Total Increase in 54 years, from 1751 to 1805,
1,091,016, or $\frac{1}{2}$ nearly.

THE first remark that suggests itself on these tables is, that they constitute the only documents which prove from actual observation, and in the compass of ordinary history, that there is a power of numerical increase in the human species. Exclusively of this evidence, all is conjecture merely; and one man has as much right to believe, with Montesquieu, that the race of mankind is by a fatal necessity rapidly verging towards extinction, as another to embrace the wild and chimerical opinions of Mr. Malthus, and the far-famed doctrine of the geometrical ratio.

In Sweden there has been for a certain period a progressive increase of population; and we have great reason to believe that this increase is chiefly or solely the effect of the principle of procreation. To judge from what has appeared in fifty-four years, from 1751 to 1805, we should say that the human species, in some situations, and under some circumstances, might double itself in somewhat more than one hundred years.

This is all that is known on the subject, which is in the smallest degree calculated to afford a foundation for Mr. Malthus's theories. For it will fully appear, when we come to treat of the United States of North America, that they do not yield him the slightest support.

This is all that is known in any degree favourable to Mr. Malthus's theories. What then is there that is known on the other side?

Every thing which has been brought together in the former book. We have not the smallest reason to believe, that the population of the earth has increased, or that the human race is in any way more numerous now, than it was three thousand years ago. This is a fact worthy of the most serious consideration:

Mr. Malthus dismisses this question in the slightest manner, and in his usual summary and dictatorial way pronounces that it is vice and misery that keep down the numbers of mankind. As his theory is delivered in three lines, " Population, when unchecked, goes on doubling itself every twenty-five years, or increases in a geometrical ratio:" so his answer to every objection lies also in three lines, " The positive checks to

M

population are various, and include every cause
whether arising from vice or misery, which in
any degree contributes to shorten the natural
duration of human life[e]."

It is not thus that the subject will be treated
in after-ages, and when philosophy shall have
extended its empire over this topic as over others.
Mr. Malthus has taken his contemporaries by
surprise, and, partly by the dazzling simplicity
of his hypothesis, and partly by its tendency,
supporting as it does, and furnishing the apology
of, almost all human vices, and particularly those
of the rich and great, has gained a countless number of adherents.

But what he has here delivered has not even
the semblance of science.   And patient men, I
will venture to predict, will hereafter arise, who
will look narrowly into the subject, and will endeavour from clear and intelligible principles,
not by one sweeping and unlimited clause, to
account for the facts brought together in my
first book.

The question then will be, to consider, What
is the reason that the multiplication of mankind,
such as we find it for fifty-four years in Sweden,
has never prevailed for any very extensive period of time, in any country of the world[d]. This

---

e Essay on Population, Vol. I. p. 21.
   d It may be worth while to illustrate this proposition in figures,
thus:

question necessarily involves with it another, and infinitely important question, Whether it is in any way the duty of political governments, or of those who possess power over their fellow-men, to meditate or provide any purposed or intentional checks against the increase of the human race?

My concern in the present Book is with the question, after what rate it is possible, judging from facts and actual experience, for the race of mankind, under the most favourable circumstances, to increase. It will be the object of the Third Book, to put together such hints as I have been able to collect, and such reflections as

The population of Sweden in 1805, as appears from the actual enumeration, amounted to   3,320,647

Now let us take half this number
as the population of 1705   1,660,323

By the same rule the population
will be

	in 1605	830,162
	in 1505	415,081
	in 1405	207,540
	in 1305	103,770
	in 1205	51,885
	in 1105	25,942
	in 1005	12,971
	in 905	6,485
	in 805	3,242
	in 705	1,621
	in 605	810
	in 505	405

So that by this way of calculation Sweden contained, at the time of the destruction of the Western Empire in 476, little more than three hundred souls, and when this part of the globe began to send forth its hordes, which destroyed the power of the Romans, and changed the face of the world, it could scarcely boast a human inhabitant.

have occurred to me, that may be calculated to afford a methodical and satisfactory solution of the fact generally as to the non-increase of the human race. At least I shall hope, as I said in a former instance [e], that "some foundation will be laid by me, and the principle will begin to be understood." I am anxious to " set before other enquirers evidence that they may scan, and arguments which, if convincing, they may expand, and if otherwise, which they may refute." I am anxious to furnish the materials of a solution, if not a solution in all its forms, of the phenomenon of the non-increase of the human race so far as the records of authentic profane history extend.

CHAPTER V.

INFERENCES SUGGESTD BY THE ACCOUNTS OF
SWEDEN.

THE labours however of the Swedish administrators on the subject of population, do not stop
at the barely acquainting us with the possible
progress of increase in the human species. By
their elaborateness and their apparent accuracy
they enable us to arrive at some fundamental
ideas on the subject. To understand this let us
here resume and apply the maxims delivered in
the Third Chapter.

The principle there laid down, and which is
the pole-star that must guide us in every sound
disquisition on the real or possible increase of
mankind, is that the multiplication of our species
can only be carried on by women, already arrived
at, and not having yet gone beyond, the age at
which they are capable of child-bearing. These
are the soil or *nidus*, in which the successive generations of mankind are reared ; and we cannot be wrong in expressly directing our attention to this quarter.

To apply this principle to the subject in hand,
no proceeding can be more obvious, than to have
recourse to such Tables of Population, as profess
to specify the sex, and most especially the ages,
of the persons numbered, and from thence to en-

deavour to ascertain the proportion borne by the number of females capable of child-bearing in successive periods to each other. This number, to whatever it may amount, must be doubled, before we shall have reached the first step in Mr. Malthus's geometrical ratio for the increase of mankind by procreation only.

In adjusting the amount of women capable of child-bearing in any community, we must determine a certain limit in the flow of human life, before the beginning and after the close of which a woman is not entitled to be placed in the class under consideration. I will take this interval as beginning at twenty, and ending at forty-five years of age. I am sure that, in assuming a period of twenty-five years I am making a very ample allowance. I might indeed have commenced my date earlier. But premature marriages are not found favourable to the producing a numerous offspring. And the falling off of women from child-bearing before they reach forty-five years of age, is at least as frequent, as the examples of females who have become mothers before they had completed their twentieth year. This is most especially the case in countries where the season I have assigned for marriage is greatly anticipated. Thus in Persia, where a woman frequently marries at twelve, she is often found to be old and past child-bearing at thirty.

That we may treat of man as he is, and human societies as they are to be found, we must take some certain period of time and tract of country, with indifferent and impartial selection, and not some imaginary state of society which has perhaps never been found to exist. I will hereafter offer a few observations on such a society [b]. But our present business is with the number of child-bearing females, that are actually found, or may be supposed to be found, in any established and settled community. They will be of all ages, from twenty to forty-five years. This will naturally and reasonably form the first term in our progression for the increase of mankind; and, as has just been said, this number must be doubled, in the tract of country we have chosen for our point of observation, before any substantial and permanent population in that country, built upon procreation only, can be doubled.

In Sweden, according to Mr. Wargentin's Tables, the number of women capable of child-bearing was as follows.

In 1757.

Between the ages of 20 and 25	104,873
25 and 30	99,781
30 and 35	90,880
35 and 40	75,565
40 and 45	65,443
Total	436,542

In 1760.

Between the ages of 20 and 25	103,613
25 and 30	100,614

[b] See below, Mr. Booth's Dissertation.

30 and 35	92,154
35 and 40	79,066
40 and 45	68,645
Total	444,092

In 1763.

Between the ages of 20 and 25	105,115
25 and 30	101,003
30 and 35	95,811
35 and 40	81,453
40 and 45	74,854
Total	458,236

One observation which suggests itself on the inspection of these Tables is, that the number of women proper for child-bearing, in each of Mr. Wargentin's enumerations, is to the numbers of the whole community in a proportion under one fifth, or, more accurately speaking, is as one to five and one-third nearly. This remark indeed is not decisive of the subject. The proportion will of course be varied, as the climate or season shall on the one hand be inauspicious for the rearing the born, or on the other be favourable to the increase of human longevity. It belongs immediately to the calculation of the value of lives, and only in an indirect manner to the question of the continuation or increase of the species. It may however be of use in enabling us to compare our conclusions respecting the population of Sweden, with such as may result from whatever we happen to know concerning the state of mankind in this respect in other countries. The difference in longevity and the value of lives, between Sweden, Germany, France, and England, and indeed every other country in which civilization has arrived at a certain point, and the climate is temperate, will not be found to be material, and therefore the same rules, so far as our enquiry is concerned, may be expected equally to apply to any of these countries.

A more essential observation, and which indeed applies to the foundation of our subject, will be suggested by a comparison of the number of women proper for child-bearing in each year, with the number of the born in that year. The births, for example, of 1757 were 81,878, and the number of women capable of child-bearing, of all ages, according to the returns for that year, were 436,542. Hence it appears that every five child-bearing women throughout the country in that year, gave a little more than one child to the state. In 1760 the births were 90,635, and the women capable of child-bearing 444,092; so that in that year every five child-bearing women gave somewhat less than one child. In 1763 the births were 90,152, and the women capable of child-bearing 458,236; so that in that year every five child-bearing women gave one child, with a fraction of excess considerably smaller than in 1757 [c].

[c] The proportion of one child born annually to five marriages, is recognized by Wargentin, Sussmilch, and Malthus. Sussmilch, vol. I. p. 231. Malthus, vol. I. p. 413.

This is a most material circumstance for enabling us to decide upon the propagation and increase of the human species. Taking this for the foundation of our speculations, our inference will be that every child-bearing woman, taking one with another, may be expected to bring four children, if the period of fruitfulness is of twenty, and five if it is of twenty-five years' duration. But the truth lies between the two. If we take the age of marriage at twenty, then the female does not become a mother till twenty-one: to which we may add, that a certain consideration is to be had of the diminishing fruitfulness of the human female during the concluding years of this period.

Let us try the argument afforded us by our information respecting Sweden in another point of view. Let us compare the number of the annual births in that country, with the number of females that annually arrive at twenty years of age.

From the Tables for 1757 it appears that the females then living, between the ages of twenty and twenty-five, were 104,872. I might here apply the rules furnished by Dr. Halley and Dr. Price for the calculation of lives, to enable me to determine how many of these might be supposed to be between twenty and twenty-one, and so forward. But the difference at this early period of life would be so small, that I prefer the simpler method of dividing the whole number by five, and concluding that 20,974 was the number of females who at the time of the enumeration in 1757 had completed the twentieth year of their 'age. The births for 1757 were 81,878, that is, not quite four to every female who in that year had completed her twentieth year. In 1760 the females completing their twentieth year were 20,723, and the births were 90,635, affording an average of 4⅜ to 1. In 1763 these females were 21,023, and the births 90,152, affording an average of 4²⁄₇ to 1.

Hence it follows, that in Sweden the females annually arriving at twenty years of age, may be considered as nearly equal to one fourth of the annual births; or, which is the same proposition in another form, that there are four births for every woman annually arriving at twenty. It is true, that the women who arrived at twenty in the year 1757 or any other year, were not the mothers of those births: other women between the ages of twenty and forty-five, if I may so express myself, bore these children for them: but it is a computation which will never be found belied in the annals of Swedish population, that the births of every year amounted to four times, or perhaps a small fraction above four times, the number of females who in that year arrived at twenty years of age. This has been the regular process: a certain number of females arrived every successive year, with a very small variation from year to year, at the age of twenty, and the births of that year have been found pretty exactly to quadruple the number of those females. Of consequence I may say, give me the number of females at twenty in any year in the community, and I will tell you the number of births. For ever, as far as we have yet had an opportunity of ascertaining, we shall have four births for every woman arriving at an age proper for child-bearing. What will be the effect of this, whether it will diminish, or keep up, or increase the population of a country, may be a subject of separate consideration.

A third reflection to the same purpose will be suggested to us, if we compare the amount of marriages and births according to Mr. Wargentin's Tables. He has given us[d] a statement of numbers under each of these heads for fifteen years, from 1749 to 1763 inclusive. The number of births added together amounts to 1,299,290 and the number of marriages to 315,482; that is, pretty exactly 4¼ births to a marriage.

And here, by way of confirming what we have seen of Sweden, I will introduce, though somewhat prematurely, what appears on the subject in the population-abstracts of England and Wales. The registered births for 1810 are stated as 298,852. Of these I will take for granted that half are females, or 149,426. According to Dr. Price's calculations founded on the Swedish Tables[e], of ten thousand females born, 5800 may be taken as living to complete the twentieth year of their age.   Let us then apply the rule of proportion, and say, If 10,000 female births yield 5,800 females living to the age of twenty, what number of such females may we expect from a stock of 149,426 births? the answer is 86,667. Now the registered marriages for 1810, as given from the same authority as the births, are 84,470. —From this specimen I should be apt to conclude that, if we knew as much of the population of England as of that of Sweden, we should find them to a great degree parallel to each other.

Hence it appears, that, whether we compare the births to the whole number of women capable of child-bearing, or to the females annually arriving at twenty, or to the registers of marriages, we are equally led to the same conclusion.

Another important observation is suggested to us by the view of Mr. Wargentin's Tables. The marriages for 1757, according to the Tables, were 18,799, and the number of females arriving in that year at twenty 20,974.   The marriages for 1760 are set down at 23,383, while the females arriving at twenty were only 20,723.   Finally, the marriages for 1763 appear to have been 20,927, and the females arriving at twenty 21,023. Thus in one instance we find the number of marriages exceeding the number of females who in that year arrived at the marriageable age.   But it must be obvious that that could not continue to be the case through any considerable series of years. The infallible inference then from this view of the subject is, that almost all the women in Sweden marry at some time of their lives. Or, to speak more precisely, there are nearly as many marriages annually, if we take for our foundation a series of fifteen or more years, as there are annually females arriving at twenty years of age.

And this position of the general prevalence of the marriage tie f, will, when we come to reflect upon the subject, appear in its own nature sufficiently probable. The tastes of men are so various, that nothing is more common to observe, than that the homeliest women, as they may appear in the eye of a connoisseur, get husbands. Those females, whose destination in life seems to

---

f When I say general, I mean so far as the female is concerned. The following extract from Graunt's Observations on the Bills of Mortality, p. 65, is not unworthy of attention, as it may be applied to this part of the subject.

Cum, quantis ovibus feminis sufficiat unus aries, experientia compertum sit, agnorum masculorum qualis proportio castranda sit, discimus: ex. grat. si viginti feminis illum sufficere concederemus, tum novemdecim castrandi forent. Nam si octodecim tantum castrarentur, duorum cum singulis feminis copulatio promiscua (in quantum duorum masculorum admissio id facere possit) incrementum impediret, sed si nulli castrarentur, verisimile est quod singulo viginti arietum cum singulâ feminarum copulante, minima, forsitan nulla, conceptio efficiretur.

I have thought the above passage worthy to be inserted in this place, because the subject of which I am treating cannot be thoroughly understood, without thus recurring to first principles. Be it observed however, that the theory of Graunt will only apply to man in a state of nature. The case is exceedingly different in societies constituted after the manner of European nations; as will more fully appear in the next chapter.

be to fill the situation of domestic servants, will perhaps be found very generally to marry, though a little later than they might otherwise have done. The females above the lower class, who, for want of the advantage of a portion, waste their years " in single blessedness," are enough in number to have the power of making their complaints heard, but are extremely few, when compared with the total amount of females in a state or nation.

CHAPTER VI.

BUT there is another view of the subject, equally worthy of notice, and well calculated to throw light upon the topic before us.

I have just stated that the annual number of marriages in any country, cannot, for any length of time, exceed the number of females annually arriving at a marriageable age.

Now let us take this question in another way. Though I have set out with considering the women capable of child-bearing as the soil or *nidus* in which the successive generations of mankind are reared, yet it is equally true, that husbands are necessary to the consummation of marriage, as that wives are so, and, at least in countries where polygamy is forbidden, that there can be no more marriages than husbands.

The same inference therefore should seem to follow as to males, which I have already drawn as to females, *viz.*, that the annual number of marriages in any country, cannot, for any length of time, exceed the number of males arriving at the age at which it is permitted, or rather at which it is usual for them to marry

But the number of males, though they are born in greater numbers, will be found at almost any age above childhood in all Tables of Population, and specially in those of Sweden, to fall short of the number of females.

In Sweden, the country we are here considering, there is a law, forbidding any individual of the male sex to marry, till he has completed the twenty-first year of his age [a].

To this consideration it may be added, that it will scarcely happen, that every male will be disposed to marry, as soon as he has completed the twenty-first year of his age. Perhaps, reasoning on this principle, the marriages which annually take place in Sweden cannot, for any length of time, be expected to exceed the number of males who annually arrive at twenty-five years of age. This will reduce the number of marriages, and consequently increase the number of females who spend their lives in the single state.

Such would appear at first sight to be the speculative principle of the subject, and would contradict what has been established respecting it in the former chapter. But let us see how it stands, as practically exhibited to us in the Swedish Tables. And here, as in the case of the fe-

---

[a] It is however allowed to a person of the male sex to marry at eighteen, provided he has any landed property, holds any office, or has in any other way the visible source of a regular income. *Handbok i Svenska Kyrkolagfaranheten,* or, Manual of the Swedish Ecclesiastical Law, Chap. 1. § 6.

N

males, I will take the fifth part of the males between
twenty and twenty-five in the year under consideration, as the number arriving in that year at
twenty or twenty-five years of age. The number
arriving at twenty-five will indeed be less than
the number arriving at twenty, in proportion
to the males who are found to die annually
between those periods of life. But this is not
the season of human existence most considerably
exposed to the accidents of mortality; and I will
wave for the present the taking that diminution
into the estimate.

The three years then, 1757, 1760, 1763, as
appears from the Tables, will stand as follows:

	Males arriving at the marriageable age.	Females becoming marriageable.	Marriages.
1757	18,292	20,974	18,799
1760	17,750	20,723	23,383
1763	18,460	21,023	20,927
Total	54,502	62,720	63,109

It has already been observed, that the females
becoming marriageable do in most years exceed,
as we should expect them to do, the annual
number of marriages. For, certainly, the marriages of any one year do not form a standard:
the marriages of any one year may exceed: my
proposition is, that the annual number of marriages cannot, for any length of time, exceed the
number of females annually arriving at the marriageable age.

Add to which, I have taken the marriageable age at twenty; but it is possible to marry before that age; and the Swedish law permits females to marry at fifteen [b]. Now the number of females annually arriving at fifteen is greater than the number of females annually arriving at twenty. If therefore the number of marriages exceeded the number of females annually arriving at twenty, the excess must necessarily be supplied from the females between fifteen and twenty.

But the case of the males is different; and they, as I have said, are forbidden to marry till they have completed the twenty-first year of their age. How then are we to account for the excess of marriages above the number of males annually arriving at twenty-one?

This difficulty will be found to be in a considerable degree removed by an inspection of the Upsal Table [c]. Few things are more striking in this Table than the excess of the number of widows above that of widowers. Adding together the whole series of nine years there exhibited, the number is

of widowers   20,567
of widows   108,537 :

the number of widows being more than five times the number of widowers. But married women, as may be judged from the Tables of Sweden in general, die with nearly as much ra-

---

[b] *Handbok, ubi supra.*
[c] Table VI, p. 159.

pidity as married men. The small number of widowers can therefore only be accounted for, by the infallible inference, that five times as great a number of widowers as of widows, are found to marry again. And from the same principle we are entitled to conclude, that they intermarry generally, not with widows, but with virgins, or what our law calls spinsters.

To apply this, let us observe that, if the diocese of Upsal in 1763 contained 11,874 widows, the whole of Sweden by the rule of proportion would appear to have contained 135,712. But, if we suppose as many men to have lost their wives as women to have lost their husbands, it would then follow that upwards of 108,000 men had married a second time, even without taking into account those who might a second time have become widowers. This affords an ample allowance for the deficiency there might otherwise appear in the number of marriageable males.

Having referred in this place to the Table of Population for the Diocese of Upsal, I will here comment upon one or two particulars in it, which seem to require explanation. This Table descends to a greater fulness of distinction and enumeration than any other that has fallen under my observation; and it is therefore particularly desirable that it should be well understood.

One circumstance which appeared to me at first view somewhat surprising, was the small number of Housholds in the last column, compared with that of the subsisting marriages in the fifth.   This indeed is in no way material to the question I am investigating; but it is right for the satisfaction of the reader that it should be cleared up.

I stated this difficulty to the intelligent Swede[d], who had the goodness to assist me in translating the heads of these Tables; and his explanation was as follows.   " By a houshold or establishment we understand, all those persons who eat at one table, or, more properly who are subsisted from one income or expenditure.   For example, at Sir Joseph Banks's there are various tables at which different persons are fed, but the whole expence is defrayed by one individual. This therefore is one houshold.   If, on the contrary, there are several families dwelling under one roof, but which are, so to express myself, not nourished from one common root, these would be counted in the Swedish enumerations as separate housholds.   Now in this country [Sweden], nothing is more common, particularly in the rural parts, than for the sons, after they are married, to live under the roof with their father, all together constituting one ample houshold.   This is the reason why, in the Table of Population for the Diocese of Upsal, there appears so much smaller a number of housholds than of subsisting marriages."

---

[d] Mr. Nairman, one of the librarians to Sir Joseph Banks.

Another circumstance which may need eluci-
dation is, that the number of unmarried males
and females above fifteen years of age, in the
eighth and ninth columns, may appear at first
sight greater, than from previous reasonings
might have been expected.

Upon this I would remark, first, that it is not
rational to suppose that there can be any substantial discordance between the Tables of Population for Sweden generally, and the Tables of
Population for one of its most considerable provinces.   The comparisons I have exhibited between the number of annual marriages and the
number of females annually arriving at twenty,
are expressly taken out of the Tables of Population for the kingdom of Sweden.

Secondly, every reader will perceive that there
is a vast difference between the setting down in
figures on the one hand, the number of females
arriving at twenty in any given year who shall
finally remain unmarried, and on the other the
setting down the number of females at all ages,
who at any given period shall be found unmarried, though they may happen to marry in the
next year or the next week.   The number in
the last case may be great, at the same time that
the number in the former may be exceedingly
small.

Thirdly, the unmarried in the Upsal Table include all who have passed their fifteenth birth-day,
at which age according to the Swedish law fe-

males are permitted to marry.   But in the extracts I have made from the Tables of Sweden
in general, I have taken the marriageable age at
twenty.   Therefore the Upsal Table swells the
number of the unmarried females by the whole
amount of those between fifteen and twenty, or
at least by the amount of such as shall not have
married between those periods. But the females
between fifteen and twenty will be found to
constitute nearly a twelfth part of the entire
female population.

The proposition which I have deduced from
the Tables of Sweden in general, is that the annual marriages nearly equal in number the females annually arriving at twenty ; or, in other
words, that there are nearly as many women
married every year, as there are women arriving
every year at that age. The only limit upon
that proposition would be in the number of women that shall end their lives in the unmarried
state.

But the column of unmarried females in the
Upsal Table, does not set before us the number
of females that shall live and die unmarried. In
the first place, it may well be supposed that the
greater part of the females between fifteen and
twenty, making a twelfth part of the entire
female population, will hereafter marry. In the
second place it is to be considered, that the total
amount of unmarried females in any kingdom
or province at a given period, will materially

depend upon the customary age of marriage. If every female throughout the state married the day she completed her fifteenth year, then it is self-evident that the column of unmarried females above fifteen would be left a complete blank. But, if on the other hand the marrying age were from fifteen to thirty-five, and no woman married till she was twenty-five, then all might marry, and yet half the females between fifteen and thirty-five would constantly appear in the column of the unmarried.

Another consideration is to be added, which I may thus illustrate. Let us suppose the females annually arriving at twenty to be 20,000, and that of these 19,000 marry, and 1000 continue in the single state. Let us suppose that there is some natural reason, of infirmity or otherwise, why this twentieth part of the female division of the community should not marry. There would thus be 1000 females to be placed in the column of the unmarried, for the year for which this account is taken. In the next year there would be one twentieth of the females arriving at twenty in that year, or 1000 more, to be added to the 1000 of the preceding year, except so far as this last number was diminished by death, and so on *ad infinitum*. Thus, as we said before, if every female throughout the state married the day she arrived at the marriageable age, the column of the unmarried would be blank; but, if one twentieth remained unmarried, and continued so, this in time would amount to one twentieth of all the females living in the state, who were beyond the marriageable age. It is unnecessary to say more on this point: every reader who is desirous of so doing, will be able to follow out the further particulars for himself.

There is another circumstance entitled to our consideration, before we finally determine what degree of authority is to be attributed to the Swedish Tables. In the reasonings I have exhibited, I have set down the women capable of child-bearing as one fifth of the whole community. At the same time it fully appears from the Tables, that the births are scarcely more than four to a marriage. Now, if of the number of the born only one in five is to be counted on to become a mother and give children to the next generation, it clearly follows that the number of women capable of child-bearing will in each successive generation perpetually diminish, and consequently that a population so circumstanced must be regularly advancing towards utter destruction. But the Swedish Tables, from which these two facts are taken, exhibit a progressive increase of the number of inhabitants. Either therefore this apparent contradiction must be reconciled; or the Swedish Tables must be admitted to be an imperfect authority on which to rest our conclusions.

In answer to this difficulty I would observe, in the first place, that one of the most irresistible

results of the Swedish Tables, is that there are
four births to a marriage.   But this proposition,
if true, must be equally true if taken in an inverse
form, and we state it—to every four births there
is a marriage, or, in other words, for every four
births there is a marriageable woman.   One of
these propositions cannot be true, and the other
false ; and the number of women of an age capable of child-bearing is hereby clearly established.

Secondly, it is proper to observe that, though
it was sufficiently reasonable to set down, as the
foundation of our inferences, the period in which
a woman is to be considered as capable of child-
bearing, as beginning when she is twenty years
of age, yet this proposition is by no means absolute and uncontrolable.   The Swedish law
admits of the female marrying at fifteen ; and as,
necessarily, more human creatures live to attain
the age of fifteen than of twenty, we have here
a considerable addition to the stock of possible
mothers.   The females between fifteen and
twenty form a sort of *corps de reserve,* from
from which the brigade of marriageable women
may be recruited in case of necessity.

Thirdly, it is to be remembered that we found
the number of births to a marriage exceeding the
amount of four by a small fraction [e].   Now this
fraction may at first sight appear scarcely worthy
of notice, yet, in its operation over a nation con-

---

[e] Page 172.

sisting of three millions of souls, and spread over a succession of years, it would doubtless have the effect of rendering that population progressive, which without this fraction would have been stationary. There is therefore nothing contradictory and irreconcileable between the different particulars exhibited in the Swedish Tables.

Here then we are presented, as far as it goes, with a solid basis of reasoning concerning the possible increase of the numbers of mankind. Of every other country in the world we may be said in this respect to know nothing. In Sweden great labour has been exerted on the subject; this labour has been continued through a series of years; and it has been prosecuted on the most enlightened principles. We learn therefore from this example, perhaps as nearly as possible, how fast the race of mankind, at least as society is at present constituted, can increase, and beyond what limits the pace and speed of multiplication cannot be carried.

Sweden is a country in every respect as favourable to the experiment as we could desire. Almost all the women marry. "The continual cry of the government," as Mr. Malthus expresses it, "is for the increase of its subjects[f]." And the soil is so thinly peopled, that it would require many ages of the most favourable complexion,

---

[f] Vol. 1, p. 391.

for the inhabitants to become so multiplied by the mere power of procreation, as to enable them to rear and to consume all the means of subsistence which the land might easily be made to produce.

CHAPTER VII.

RECAPITULATION OF THE EVIDENCE OF THE SWEDISH TABLES.

IT is time that we should resume the propositions relative to the multiplication of mankind, which appear to result from all the information that has been collected respecting the population of Sweden.

This information is the fruit of experience.

We are not enquiring respecting gratuitous and arbitrary suppositions, asking with Euler, what would be the consequence if the deaths bore a certain proportion to the births, which proportion either never occurred, or, if occurring " for short periods," is substantially the same as not having occurred at all. We are not asking with Franklin, what would be the consequence, if in a certain country the marriages were twice as numerous as with us in Europe, and each marriage produced, taking one with another, eight children.

We are not enquiring how the earth was originally peopled, for which purpose, according to Derham, it was necessary that the duration of the life of man should be about one thousand years [a].

Our question lies in a narrow compass, and relates to "man as he is." Owing to the great care and perseverance with which the observations on this subject have been pursued in Sweden, we have a large and a strong body of facts on which to proceed: and I believe it will not be found that any other country can produce a body of facts, which shall be at variance with those that have been collected in Sweden.

We know then, first, that the marriageable women in any settled community, or over the whole globe, do not exceed one fifth of the population.

Secondly, that the number of marriageable women does not increase from generation to generation, or increases in a very inconsiderable degree.

Thirdly, that the number of children born is pretty accurately in the proportion of one child annually to five marriages.

Fourthly, that the number of children born annually is nearly in the same proportion to the number of child-bearing women in the state.

Fifthly, that the number of births to a marriage, taken upon an average, does not exceed the proportion of four to one.

Sixthly, that the women who live to reach

---

[a] See above, p. 127.

the child-bearing age are found pretty generally to marry; and that, if the bridegrooms are sometimes a little advanced in age, this rarely happens to the brides.

Seventhly, that early marriages do not greatly tend to increase population. In Persia, where a woman frequently marries at twelve, she is often found to be old and past child-bearing at thirty.

These are some of the principal laws relative to the propagation of the human species, so far as we are acquainted with them : and they appear to be confirmed to us by all that we know of authentic profane history.

They do not seem to convey to us with any strong evidence, that there is a power of increase in the numbers of the human species.

But they do tend very strongly to assure us, that such power of increase is at least subject to very strict limitations, and that we have nothing to fear for the well-being of any particular nation, or of the human species in general, from the operation of that power.

APPENDIX TO CHAPTERS IV, V, & VI.

Upon looking back to the preceding Chapters on the subject of the population of Sweden, I am apprehensive I have granted too much on the point of the increase of the number of inhabitants in that country. Dr. Price, in his enquiry respecting the value of lives, was necessarily compelled to a very close study of the Tables of the Population of Sweden, these Tables being so greatly superior, in the judgment with which they were originally planned, the care and fidelity with which they have been executed, and the constancy with which they have been kept up and pursued, to any thing that is to be found of the same nature in any other part of the world.

The following is in part the result of Dr. Price's observations on the subject.

" The enumerations and deaths for the first nine years, from 1755 to 1763, included the whole kingdom of Sweden, consisting of twenty-six principalities or provinces. In 1764 there was a suspension of all the observations. In 1765 they were taken up again; but in this and the following years the enumeration of one of the provinces was omitted, together with the registration of the deaths in that province. In the three years from 1767 to 1770 three provinces were omitted in the enumerations and registers. In the three years from 1770 to 1773 there was also an omission of three provinces, together with the city of Stockholm. And in the remaining three years to 1776, four out of the fifteen dioceses in Sweden were omitted [a]."

---

[a] Price's Observations, Vol. II, p. 405.

" The whole number of males living in the three years from 1765 to 1767 [I apprehend the doctor should have said, " living, according to the enumeration for 1766"] was 1,182,848, and of females, 1,290,068.   I have said that one of the twenty-six provinces of Sweden was omitted in the observations for these three years.   The addition of this province will make the inhabitants of Sweden in 1776 above two millions and a half.   In 1757 they were 2,323,195.   They increased therefore at the rate of near 200,000 in nine years.   But it appears that this increase had not been of long continuance ; for, had it been so, a table formed from the decrements as given by the registers, and by taking the medium of annual deaths from 1755 to 1763 for the *radix*, would have given the probabilities of living much too small through the whole duration of life ; whereas it does so only in the first stages of life.   From 45 to 60 it gives them nearly equal ; and after 60 it gives them greater, which is a plain proof that about the beginning of this century [the eighteenth] Sweden was decreasing.   To the same purpose it appears from the enumerations, that, while the numbers living in the first stages of life were increasing fast, the numbers in the last stages were decreasing [b]."

In the preceding remarks Dr. Price had an

---

[b] *Ibid*, p. 407, note.

O

advantage in some respects, which I cannot pretend to. He was engaged in a regular corres-
pondence with Mr. Wargentin, to whom we
appear to have been in the first instance so much
indebted for the judicious conduct visible in the
collections of the registers and enumerations of
Sweden. That meritorious compiler transmitted to the doctor regularly the Tables of the
Swedish population for a series of years, which
are only given at irregular intervals in the Memoirs of the Royal Academy at Stockholm,
from which I have transcribed them : and he
appears further to have answered several queries
which Dr. Price proposed to him, as to particular points not to be found in the registers and
enumerations [c].

On this account I will not quit the subject
without inserting here a Table from Dr. Price's
book, similar to those I have already inserted,
but founded on an average of twenty-one years,
from 1755 to 1776 [d]. And it is sufficiently remarkable that the numbers in this Table fall
short, both in the amount of the child-bearing
women, and of the inhabitants generally, of
each of the enumerations exhibited by Mr.
Wargentin in the Memoirs of the Academy for
the early part of this period [e].

---

[c] Ibid, p. 251, 431.   [d] Ibid, p. 404, 405.
[e] See above, p. 154, 155, 156.

Annual Deaths on an average of 21 years, from 1755 to 1776.

	Males	Females
Under one year -	9664	8355
Between 1 and 3 -	3592	3531
3 — 5 -	1816	1774
5 — 10 -	1789	1672
10 — 15 -	898	802
15 — 20 -	741	714
20 — 25 -	874	776
25 — 30 -	879	872
30 — 35 -	955	1058
35 — 40 -	907	901
40 — 45 -	1119	1129
45 — 50 -	1077	958
50 — 55 -	1233	1127
55 — 60 -	1180	1163
60 — 65 -	1383	1597
65 — 70 -	1328	1510
70 — 75 -	1360	1935
75 — 80 -	1023	1527
80 — 85 -	784	1230
85 — 90 -	383	609
Upwards of 90 -	195	339
	33,180	33,579

Living on an average of seven enumerations, in 1757, 1760, 1763, 1766, 1769, 1772, and 1775.

	Males	Females
Under one year -	33882	33640
Between 1 and 3 -	62155	63005
3 — 5 -	62696	63551
5 — 10 -	121871	122460
10 — 15 -	117879	118419
15 — 20 -	103093	105845
20 — 25 -	91907	102306
25 — 30 -	82919	93315
30 — 35 -	78615	87129
35 — 40 -	70390	77077
40 — 45 -	63961	70405
45 — 50 -	52083	59580
50 — 55 -	44908	52689
55 — 60 -	36253	44211
60 — 65 -	30772	39416
65 — 70 -	21170	29610
70 — 75 -	14610	21776
75 — 80 -	8224	12515
80 — 85 -	4036	6418
85 — 90 -	1522	2492
Upwards of 90 -	486	869
Males -	1,103,432	1,206,728
Females -	1,206,728	
Total -	2,310,160	

The result of the whole then is, that there is some probability, but by no means a certainty, that the population of Sweden has experienced an increase in most periods of time, from the commencement of the enumerations in the middle of the last century, to the present hour. But it is impossible to ascertain the rate of that increase, since its very existence is by no means beyond the reach of doubt. And yet this is all we have, by way of evidence, from the source of enumerations, of the inherent power in man of augmenting the number of his species. Respecting Sweden we have something approaching to authentic information : we may safely pronounce, that if there has been any actual increase, it at least amounts to comparatively very little. Of the rest of the world, so far as relates to a comparison of the number of native inhabitants from parent to child in successive periods, we know nothing.

CHAPTER VIII.

POPULATION OF OTHER COUNTRIES IN EUROPE CONSIDERED.

THE reader however would have some reason to be dissatisfied with what has hitherto been delivered on the subject of European population, if I confined my observations to Sweden only.

I will here therefore subjoin a few remarks tending to shew that there is nothing which has been collected concerning the other countries of Europe, that in any respect weakens, but is rather calculated to confirm, the conclusions I have formed.

These remarks shall be particularly directed to two points: first, the proportion which the women capable of child-bearing exhibit to the gross population; and secondly, the proportion between marriages and births, as it is found in the different countries of Europe.

The best information that can be had on the first of these points, *viz.*; the proportionate number of the females capable of child-bearing to the whole of any mass of population, exclusively of the Swedish accounts, is to be found in the collections that have been inserted by Dr.

Price, in his Observations on Reversionary Payments. These I will take in the order in which they occur. At the same time it is proper to observe, that his conclusions are of little avail, in balance with those I have already exhibited; first, because they are in all cases built upon a very small number of persons compared with the enumerations of Sweden; and, secondly, inasmuch as those numbers are arbitrarily and artificially taken, and rest upon no better evidence than that of the bills of mortality for the respective districts and countries.

Dr. Price's object having been very different from that which we are here considering, I find myself under the necessity of subjecting his statements to a certain process, before they can be applied to the purpose of this investigation. The enquiry of that writer was respecting the value of lives, and the different probabilities that exist as to the age at which human creatures shall die. He therefore supposed a thousand, or ten thousand, or a hundred thousand persons to be born at the same time, and then calculated, according to certain observations, by what degrees the ranks of this brigade or legion of human creatures would become thinned. My business is not with an imaginary number of persons, all born on the same day, but with real human societies, as we find, or may conceive, them constituted. Real human societies, particularly in old established countries, are made up of persons of all ages, from the cradle to the extremity of decrepitude.   To find out therefore from Dr. Price's Tables how many women, between the ages of twenty and forty-five years, would be living in any community at any assigned period, 1 was reduced to the necessity of striking an average between the number of females that, according to Dr. Price, would reach the age of twenty, and the number that would reach the age of forty-five, and of thus settling the proportion that would be living in any community at a given time.   For example:

In Table the Eighth, shewing the Probabilities of Life at Norwich, in Dr. Price's work [a], it is calculated that out of 1185 births, there were 467 living at the age of twenty, and 311 at the age of forty-five, which gives an average of 389. Of these if half were females, we shall have females proper for child-bearing 195, about one sixth part of the whole.

Table the Ninth is Mr. Simpson's Calculation of the Probability of the Duration of Life in London, founded on the London Bills of Mortality for ten years, from 1728 to 1737 inclusive [b]. In this Table it appears that of one thousand births, 360 were living at twenty years of age, and 192 at forty-five, giving an average of 276. Of these, one half, or 138, may be taken to be

[a] Observations on Reversionary Payments, vol. II. p. 296.
[b] P. 297.

females proper for child-bearing, being one seventh of the whole.

It is easy in the same manner to ascertain the number of females proper for child-bearing in every Table of Population, in which the ages are specified. I shall therefore content myself with exhibiting the general results, which, being thus brought together, may readily be compared one with another.

——————

TABLE,

Shewing the Proportion of Females proper for Child-bearing to be found in Different Masses of Population.

Place.	Population.	Females between 20 & 45.	Proportion nearly	Reference to Price's Observations, vol. II.
Norwich	1185	195	1 to 6	Table VIII, p. 296.
London 1728 to 1737	1000	138	1 to 7$\frac{1}{4}$	Table IX, p. 297.
Ditto 1759 to 1768	1518	192	1 to 8	Table XV, p. 304.
Ditto 1771 to 1780	28,452	4005	1 to 7$\frac{1}{10}$	Table XVI, p. 305.
Northampton	11,650	2095	1 to 5$\frac{1}{2}$	Table XVII, p. 311.
Warrington	2700	459	1 to 5$\frac{9}{10}$	Table XLI, p. 384.
Chester	4066	1000	1 to 4	Table XLII, p. 392.
Holy Cross	966	230	1 to 4$\frac{1}{5}$	Table XLIII, p. 401.
Electoral Mark of Brandenburg	1000	215	1 to 4$\frac{2}{3}$	Table LI, p. 446.
Holland	1400	344	1 to 4	Table LIII, p. 456.
France	10,000	2449	1 to 4	*Ibid.*

Every one will perceive that there is nothing in these Tables in the slightest degree calculated to impeach the Swedish authorities. In France and Holland, where we have least reason to depend on the accuracy of the accounts, the women proper for child-bearing are stated as one fourth of the community. In London, on the contrary, they are only as one to seven, and one to eight. The average of the whole however is something under one to five.

The next question is as to the number of births to a marriage, whether any accounts that have been collected in other parts of Europe might lead to a suspicion that the Swedish Tables have put them down at too low an amount.

One of the most considerable authorities on this subject is John Peter Sussmilch, a German author, who is copiously quoted by Dr. Price in his Observations on Reversionary Payments, and by Mr. Malthus in the Essay on Population. The title of his work, first published in 1765 in two volumes octavo, and since enlarged into three, is *Die Gottliche Ordnung, &c.*; or, The Order of Divine Providence, as Displayed in the Births, Deaths, and Increase of the Human Race.—I may observe by the way, that the object of Sussmilch in writing was precisely the reverse of that of Mr. Malthus; his view being, first to shew the possibility of an increase in the population of the earth, and then to recommend the adoption of such means as he could suggest for realizing that increase.

This author appears to have exerted great in

dustry in collecting all the documents he was able to procure respecting the population of Europe in general, and particularly of the German dominions of the king of Prussia, whose subject he was.

The following is a part of his collections under the last of these heads. They begin with the year 1694, and end with 1759, comprising a period of sixty-six years.

In the electoral mark of Brandenburgh, the proportions of births to marriages were tolerably uniform, the extremes being only 38 to 10, and 35 to 10, and the mean about 37 to 10 [c].

In the dukedom of Pomerania the extremes of the proportions of births to marriages, in different periods of five or six years, were 36 to 10, and 43 to 10, and the mean about 38 to 10 [d].

In the new mark of Brandenburgh, the extremes of the proportions of births to marriages were 34 to 10, and 42 to 10, and the mean about 38 to 10 [e].

In the dukedom of Magdeburgh the extremes of the proportions of births to marriages were 42 to 10, and 34 to 10, and the mean 39 to 10 [f].

In the principality of Halberstadt the extremes of the proportions of births to marriages were 42 to 10, and 34 to 10, and the mean 38 to 10 [g].

---

[c] Essay on Population, vol. II. p. 180.   [d] P. 181.
[e] P. 182.   [f] P. 183.   [g] P. 185.

I have thought proper to give these extracts in the very words of Mr. Malthus.

From the *Tableau Statistique des Etats Danois* it appears, that the whole number of marriages for the five years subsequent to 1794 in the Danish dominions, was 34,313, and of births 138,799 [h]. This is a little more than four for one, or $4\frac{45}{1000}$ to one nearly.

In a paper, presented in 1768 by B. T. Hermann, to the Academy of Petersburgh, and published in their Transactions, Volume IV, a statement is given under fifteen heads, *viz.* Petersburgh, the government of Moscow, Twer, Novogorod, &c., of the number of children that a marriage yields in each of these provinces [i], which numbers, being added together, and then divided by 15, give a quotient of $3\frac{7}{15}$ children to a marriage.

The following Table of Proportions between Baptisms and Marriages in England and Wales, is exhibited by Mr. Rickman, in his Observations prefixed to the Abstract of the Answers and Returns made pursuant to the Population Act of 1811, and ordered by the House of Commons to be printed 2 July, 1812.

	BAPTISMS.		MARRIAGES.
1760	366	to	100
1770	361	to	100

---

[h] Malthus, vol. I. p. 385.   [i] P. 416.

	BAPTISMS.		MARRIAGES.
1780	356	to	100
1785	366	to	100
1790	359	to	100
1795	353	to	100
1800	340	to	100
1805	350	to	100
1810	360	to	100

From whence it appears that the average proportion of births to marriages in England and Wales during this period has been about 35 to 10.

It is a matter of some surprise, that, in all the accounts I have seen, the human species is more prolific in France than in almost any other country. Buffon says, that in Paris each marriage produced in his time four children upon an average, but that in the rural parts five at least, and often six, was a very common proportion[k]. The *Statistique Générale et Particuliere de la France*, published in six volumes, in the year 1803, gives the marriages for the year 1800 at 202,177, and the births at 955,430, affording a quotient of 4$\frac{7}{10}$ births to a marriage. The compiler however recommends, that we should make a deduction of the eleventh part of the number of births for illegitimate children[l], which if we do, we shall reduce the proportion to

---

[k] *Histoire Naturelle, Tome* XL. *p.* 47.
[l] *Tome* I. p. 130.

4$\frac{7}{10}$ to one nearly. Now I should lay it down as a
general maxim, that where chastity and an habi-
tual practice of the domestic duties most prevail,
there we should expect to see the most numerous families and the largest crop of children in
general : and I am yet to learn that France possesses the superiority in this respect over Russia,
Denmark, Germany, and Great Britain. I
therefore look with a particular degree of distrust
upon the French registers.

Meanwhile, be this as it will, the result of all
these statements appears clearly to be, that
throughout Europe, taking one country with
another, the average falls short of four children
to a marriage.

From the particulars stated in this chapter I
am entitled to conclude, that the accounts collected in all other European countries do not
contradict, but on the contrary strongly tend to
confirm, the conclusions suggested by the Swedish Tables.   On them therefore we have every
reason, which the nature of the case admits, to
rely.

CHAPTER IX.

PRINCIPLES RESPECTING THE INCREASE OR DECREASE OF THE NUMBERS OF MANKIND RESUMED.

THERE is a further point highly worthy of attention in the subject now under consideration, and our investigation will be incomplete if that is not distinctly adverted to.

We have found that, according to all Tables which have yet been formed upon the registers of births and marriages, the union of two persons of opposite sexes does not produce upon an average, in Europe at least, more than four births.

But it may be objected, that this rule applies to Europe only, and may have relation to some accidents or customs which belong peculiarly to this division of the globe. In other countries the proportion of the number of births to the number of marriageable women may be greater. In America Dr. Franklin proposes that we should set it down as eight to one.

It may be further objected, that this rule may at last prove fallacious, as being founded on nothing but the actual registers of births and marriages, which after all nobody will affirm to be perfect and infallible. [The question of the number of marriageable women stands on higher grounds.] To this we have hitherto given but one answer, resting on the surprising coincidence in this respect of all the registers which have hitherto been produced from different countries, governed by laws and modes of record extremely unlike to each other.

But, wherever any phenomenon universally prevails, there may be found a principle, built upon the whole mass of the observations that have been made, shewing why it ought to be expected universally to prevail. It is the glory and the privilege of the human mind to investigate such principles. This is the concluding step by which observation is reduced into science: and, if it can be effectually accomplished, then, and then only, the enquirer after truth arrives at a suitable state of repose. He knows what has been, not merely by a record of apparent facts, but by the more satisfactory method of analysis, and he is able with some degree of confidence to predict what shall be.

The first consideration that occurs, which is calculated to qualify our ideas on the subject, is what I would call the value of a marriage, or the number of years which a married life, taking married lives on an average, may be computed to endure. If the human species were immortal, or, more exactly speaking, if men and women in their greatest vigour and the most procreative period of their existence, were not exposed to the accident of death, then the value of a marriage, or the number of years that it might be computed to endure, would be twenty-five years.

But this is not the case. No period of human life is exempted from the great law of mortality; and this consideration plainly limits the number of children that a marriage, when we are engaged in the survey of a community or political society, may be expected to produce.

Some women die in the first year of their marriage. These may for the most part be regarded as leaving no offspring. Others die in the second, third, or fourth year of their marriage, and so on through the whole period of twenty-five years.

To the mortality of the women, we must add that of their husbands. It has appeared that a very small proportion of widows marry again, consequently the death of the husband may be considered as operating no less effectually to put a stop to the fruitfulness of a child-bearing woman, than the death of the woman herself.

All that relates to this part of the subject is susceptible of an exact calculation; and Dr. Halley and Dr. Price have furnished us with Tables of the probabilities of human life, from which may be easily extracted whatever may conduce to throw light on this question.

I have myself entered into some computations

founded on the *data* furnished by these authors, and one or two of my friends, more devoted than myself to matters of calculation, have furnished me with others, which I had intended to insert in this place.   But I am unwilling to give to a book, the express object of which is to correct a pernicious, and unhappily a widely diffused error, any portion of a dry and repulsive air, that can without injury be avoided.   Whoever is disposed fully to investigate the subject for himself, may easily form such computations as I have done.   The general result of my investigation has been, that marriages, taken one with another, are worth about sixteen years.

To assist any one who should be inclined to go over the same ground, it is proper however that I should mention the *data* upon which I have proceeded.   I have supposed one hundred thousand marriages to be solemnized.   I have taken for granted, that the females of these marriages were every one of them precisely twenty years of age.   As men are found to marry somewhat later in life than women, I have taken the bridegrooms as all of them of the age of twenty-five. This in reality produces a very slight difference in the result, from what it would have been if I had taken them also at twenty.   But in matters of computation one must fix one's foot somewhere.

With these premises I have proceeded upon the foundations afforded by Dr. Halley and Dr

P

Price, to calculate, among one hundred thousand men and one hundred thousand women of the ages above specified, how many would die annually through the whole period of twenty-five years. The result of my computation has been to fix the value of a marriage at about sixteen years.

Let us next consider the various circumstances in human society, which limit this absolute measure, and consequently bring the average amount of children that a marriage shall produce, or, more accurately speaking, the proportion to be borne by the number of births to the number of women capable of bearing children in any community, greatly within that which the period of sixteen years for the duration of a marriage might lead us to expect.

We have hitherto, in our community of one hundred thousand men and one hundred thousand women, taken for granted that all marry, and that the women all marry at twenty, and the men at twenty-five. But that is not really the case with any community that ever existed on the face of the earth.

First, all women do not marry. We have seen reason to believe, that the number of women who spend their lives in the single state is by no means so large, as our first reflections might have led us to suppose. They are however a considerable number, and constitute a real proportion of the number of females of an age adapted for child-bearing in every community.

Secondly, it is by no means true, that every woman marries at twenty, and every man at twenty-five years.   To marry earlier than twenty will not, I believe, tend to increase the chance of augmenting the population in any country. But many marry later from motives of prudence.   And, wherever a great proportion of females are employed in the capacity of domestic servants, this of course opposes a sensible obstacle to early marriage on the part of the female. But, in case the husband or the wife at the period of marriage is older than is above set down, the chance of the number of years that their union shall last is diminished; and in the case of the woman, the abstract period of twenty-five years in which we have supposed her capable of child-bearing, is reduced also.

Thirdly, we have reckoned death only, as a period putting a termination on the value of a marriage.   But there is a sickness not unto death. And, in a numerous community, the amount of the females who, under the influence of temporary disease, may for a longer or shorter time be prevented from bearing children will not be inconsiderable.

I may add here, that, in calculating the number of births to a marriage, we may reasonably take into our consideration the duty which nature imposes upon the human female of suckling her offspring. This is scarcely omitted in the lower and more numerous walks of life: and where it is, perhaps it always happens that some female is occupied in the care of the infant, who might otherwise by child-bearing have been engaged in increasing the numbers of the community.

Fourthly, a further deduction from the number of children born into the world, or from the average amount that we should otherwise find of births to a marriage, is produced by the number of women who in the experiment are found barren, and of marriages which afford no children: for debility in the man may equally be attended with that effect, as barrenness in the woman.

Fifthly, we must subtract from the number of women who might otherwise be expected to prove mothers a certain proportion of women, who by some defect of constitution have a fatal indisposition to produce any but abortive births, and who, though often with child, are never found to continue pregnant long enough to produce a living offspring.

Sixthly, there is a considerable number of married women, who may be placed in a class next above those last named, that, though not absolutely incapable of bringing a living child into the world, are yet found during the whole period of their marriage, though it should last from the age of twenty to the age of forty-five years, some never to produce more than one, and others not more than two children.

Lastly. When we take the term of twenty-five years, from twenty to forty-five years of age, as the period in which a woman is capable of child-bearing, we must not suppose that capacity to subsist in equal strength during the whole period. A woman, endowed with all the fruitfulness of the most fruitful of her sex, may for a time bear a child regularly within a certain interval. From twenty to thirty, we will say, she may do so. But this is less likely to happen after thirty; it is still more improbable after thirty-five; and the improbability is further increased after forty. It is not the march of nature immediately to step out of one state into another state essentially different. The colours of Nature are insensibly blended, and change by very gentle gradations, from one tint, to another of contrasted or opposite hue. Of consequence, forty-five may be the age at which a woman may be calculated on as ceasing to be capable of bearing children; but for a number of years before that, she is no longer the teeming mother, the prolific female, she was. This has happened repeatedly within my own knowledge, and similar cases will occur to every one, that the woman who in the flower of her age bore a child every second year, or perhaps, if she did not suckle her children, still oftener, comes afterwards to the condition of bringing a child after an interval of three, four, or even five years.

To illustrate this let us consider, that when we have taken sixteen years as the value of a marriage, this is an average duration, and implies that half of them last less, and half more than sixteen years. Of consequence the whole period of a marriage is by no means to be taken as belonging to a vigorous and prolific period of life, but as indifferently spread over the entire period from twenty to forty-five years of age. That we may understand the value of this consideration I would once more have recourse to the Swedish Tables, deducing from them a view of the number of women to be found in Sweden in 1763, of all the different ages that fall within the child-bearing period. To render this more intelligible to every reader, I will divide them into twenty-five classes, one for every year. I might have calculated the chances of survivorship from year to year according to the Tables of Halley and Price; but this would have made so little difference, that I have preferred the simple method of dividing the number of females between twenty and twenty-five, and so on, by five, and setting them down accordingly, as follows:

In their 21st year 21,023	In their 29th year 20,200
22nd. —— 21,023	30th. —— 20,200
23rd. —— 21,023	31st. —— 19,162
24th. —— 21,023	32nd. —— 19,162
25th. —— 21,023	33rd. —— 19,162
26th. —— 20,200	34th. —— 19,162
27th. —— 20,200	35th. —— 19,162
28th. —— 20,200	36th. —— 16,290

In their 37th year 16,290	In their 41st year 14,971
38th. —— 16,290	42nd. 14,971
39th. —— 16,290	43rd. 14,971
40th. —— 16,290	44th. 14,971
	45th. 14,971

Amount of fractions rejected   6

Total   458,236

Hence it appears that, out of **458,236** women, living in Sweden in **1763** within the child-bearing age, **74,855** had passed their fortieth year, **81,450** were between thirty-five and forty, and only **21,023** of the whole number were in the twenty-first year of their age. It is from these only that we can expect, if married, all the fruitfulness of which the human female, upon an average, shall be found capable. It is easy to see therefore what proportion of the whole were in the highest state of vigour and fecundity, and what deduction as to the chance of frequent child-bearing we are entitled to make, for the number of those with whom that state was entirely past. This of course forms a very considerable deduction from the average number we might otherwise expect of births to a marriage.

Let us put together the different considerations, which are calculated to persuade us that, from the number of women living at a given time in any country between the ages of twenty and forty-five years, a smaller number of children will be born, than from the mere calcula-

tion of the probability of the lives of the parties
we might at first have been led to expect.
1. All will not marry.   2. A great number of
brides are above twenty, and bridegrooms above
twenty-five years of age; and this reduces the
number of years that their union might otherwise have lasted, and the period in which the
woman might have been counted on as capable
of child-bearing.   3. A deduction will arise upon
the average of births, not only from the mortality of the child-bearing women, but from the
consideration of a certain number in every year,
that by ill health will be cut off from the chance
of becoming mothers.   4. There will be a cer
tain number of barren wives and imbecile husbands.   5. Some women have a predisposition
to produce only abortions.   6. Many women are
found never to bear more than one, or more
than two children.   7. Though the actual period
of the capacity of child-bearing may be stated
as from the age of twenty to the age of forty-
five years, yet the activeness of that capacity
will be found to be greatly diminished, for a
considerable time before it totally ceases.

The whole of these considerations, if accurately weighed, will perhaps lead to a conclusion,
similar to that which will be found suggested by
all the reports which have yet been collected of
all the marriages and births that take place in
European society, *viz.*, that four births to a
marriage are an ample average allowance.

Let us turn from these, which may be considered as constituting a sort of *à priori* reasonings
on the subject, to a summary of what may be
regarded as the result of every man's observation
and experience with relation to the question in
hand.

At first sight it is probable, that most men's
superficial impression on the subject will be at
variance with the conclusion above laid down,
and they will start with incredulity from the
average of four children to a marriage, as being
greatly under the truth. Every man has seen
within the circle of his acquaintance families of
eight, or perhaps ten children. It is not unex-
ampled that the same woman may have brought
sixteen living human beings into the world.

But then it is to be considered, that these
are remarkable cases, which every body notices,
and every body talks of. They are not one in
twenty, and add little to the average; not half
a child.

Though a marriage have only one, two, three,
or even no children, this may not be from barrenness in the ordinary sense, or from any of the
causes I have recently enumerated. The marriage may be unprolific from the removal of
either of the parties by death. But in the one
case as in the other it counts equally in the average against large families.

Large families, as I have said, always attract
a certain degree of observation. The marriages

which produce few, are extremely common, and therefore pass without remark. The woman who dies, is soon forgotten.

These remarks are susceptible of easy illustration. Let us take five marriages: one produces twelve children, one five, two four, and one none: the sum is twenty-one children; scarcely more than four to a marriage.

Again, let us take five other marriages: one produces seventeen children, two two children each, and two none: the sum is as before twenty-one; scarcely more than four to a marriage.

Here then, if any where, we are presented with the real checks upon population, as they may be supposed to operate under the most favourable circumstances. No one of the seven checks above enumerated, even if we add to them the limitation of the value of a marriage arising from the precariousness of life either in the wife or the husband, comes within the meaning of the terms, as used by Mr. Malthus, "vice and misery." They are indeed the Law of Nature, benevolently providing that we should not "live like Nature's bastards, but her sons," and not be cut off from our natural inheritance, from that food which is necessary to and the right of all that are born, through the crowding and elbowing and violence of the multitude of claimants. This is a Law of Nature, the reverse of that impiously set up in the Essay on Population. It is not a Law, "forbidding to marry," telling the new-born infant to " be gone" from the face of the earth, and pronouncing sentence that " there is no vacant room for him."   It is a Law, that is every where executed, in all places and at all times, constantly and in silence, no man's attention being called to its operation, no man's aid being required to its administration, and accompanied with no calamity, unless we should chuse to call our common frailty by that name, and reproach the God who made us, that he did not ordain us another species of beings than that which we are.

From the evidence then collected in this and the six preceding chapters it appears, that Nature takes more care of her works, than such irreverent authors as Mr. Malthus are apt to suppose,—indeed exactly that care, which elder and more sober writers were accustomed to give her credit for.   She has not left it to the caprice of the human will, whether the noblest species of beings that she has planted on this earth, shall be continued or not.   She does not ask our aid to keep down the excess of human population. And, however an ascetic and barbarous superstition has endeavoured in different countries and ages to counteract her genial laws, the propensity remains entire; and nothing but a despotism, founded at once upon the menaces of a dismal hereafter as the retribution of a breach of the vows of celibacy, joined with the utmost severity of temporal punishments, can suspend its operation.

Naturam expelles furca, tamen usque recurret.

And this happens, not as Mr. Malthus supposes, by an impulse, similar to that of hunger, and equally wild for its gratification. It answers better to the apostolical description of charity, or love. "It suffereth long, and is kind. It beareth all things, believeth all things, hopeth all things, endureth all things." It tranquilly postpones its purposes from month to month, and from year to year: but they are not the less firmly fixed: and both man and woman are intimately convinced, that they have not fulfilled the ends of their being, nor had a real experience of the privileges of human existence, without having entered into the ties, and participated in the delights of domestic life.

CHAPTER X.

OF THE POPULATION OF ENGLAND AND WALES.

BUT, in opposition to the conclusions and computations of the preceding chapters, the adherents of Mr. Malthus may allege the accounts which have been delivered by various writers, and lately published under the sanction of high authority, respecting the growing population of England and Wales.

There is no actual enumeration of the inhabitants of this country, except the two which were made by the direction of two acts of parliament in 1801 and 1811. These stand as follows.

Enumeration for 1801 —— 9,168,000
Enumeration for 1811 —— 10,488,000

For the amount of the population at other periods, different modes of computation have been resorted to.

First, the writer of the Observations prefixed to the Abstract of Population for 1811, as published by authority, has proceeded upon the amount of the registered baptisms for different periods, and calculated by the rule of proportion, thus: " If 263,409 baptisms, the average

medium of the baptisms for the five years preceding the enumeration of 1801, were produced
from a population of 9,168,000, from what population were 157,307, the baptisms of 1700,
produced?" And upon this basis he has constructed the following

TABLE OF POPULATION THROUGHOUT THE LAST
CENTURY.

ENGLAND AND WALES.	
In the year	POPULATION.
1700	5,475,000
1710	5,240,000
1720	5,565,000
1730	5,796,000
1740	6,064,000
1750	6,467,000
1760	6,736,000
1770	7,428,000
1780	7,953,000
1785	8,016,000
1790	8,675,000
1795	9,055,000
1801	9,168,000
1805-6	9,828,000
1811	10,488,000

A mode frequently resorted to by writers on
political economy, in estimating the population
of a country, has been by a calculation built on
the number of houses. The following is a Table
collecting the different accounts on this subject
under one point of view.

HOUSES IN ENGLAND AND WALES.

In 1660 ——————— 1,230,000 a

1685 ——————— 1,300,000 a

1690 ——————— 1,319,215 b

1759 ——————— 986,482 b

1761, or 1765 c,— 980,692 b

1777 ——————— 952,734 b

1801 ——————— 1,633,399 d

1811 ——————— 1,848,524 d

A third method, perhaps as satisfactory as either of the preceding, would be, to proceed upon the amount of the registered burials for different periods, and to calculate by the rule of proportion, thus, If 192,000 burials, the average amount for five years, from 1795 to 1800, were produced from a population of 9,168,000, from what population were so many burials, the registered amount of a remoter year, produced?

I am afraid however that the conclusion from all these computations will be, that no certainty, no consistent and plausible result, can be deduced by any of the modes hitherto devised.

We have the inference drawn from the registered amount of baptisms, as calculated by the editor of the Reports.

The calculation from the number of houses in England and Wales ought in all reason to confirm the Table founded upon the baptisms; or it

---

a Price, Vol. II. p. 140.   b *Ibid*, p. 163.
c *Ibid*, p. 141.   d Population Abstract.

must be allowed in a certain degree to weaken the evidence which that Table affords.

The amount of houses, as exhibited in the preceding page, is obtained as follows. The first three items are taken from the hearth-books, there being at that time a tax of two shillings for every hearth [e]. The next three are in like manner extracted from the returns to the tax-office, given by the surveyors of the house and window duties for the different departments [e]. And the last two are taken from the returns to the two population-acts for those years respectively.

Now, if I calculate the question of inhabitants to a house by the rule of proportion, and suppose as many persons to a house in 1690 as in 1811, to which I see no reasonable objection, the population of England and Wales at the former of these periods will appear to be upwards of seven millions. But Mr. Rickman, by his computation upon the register of baptisms, makes the population of England and Wales for 1700 and 1710 (for he has not extended his calculation beyond the commencement of the eighteenth century) to be only 5,475,000 and 5,240,000 respectively.

Another conclusion that would follow from our calculating on the number of houses, would be that the country was rapidly depopulating

---

[e] Price *ubi supra.*

from the Revolution at least up to the year 1777, a conclusion, which no reasoning founded upon any other consideration will incline us to believe.   It is obvious indeed, that, where there is a tax to be collected, a variety of circumstances will vitiate the returns, so as to make them very far from being entitled to implicit credit.   I should refer myself therefore only to the actual enumerations.   There the enquiry was directed to the clergyman or overseer in each parish, who could hardly be conceived to have any temptation to conceal the number of houses in his district : to which I may add that a house is a sort of commodity not easily hid.

Let us next look to the number of burials, a species of register, I should think, as little liable to error as that of baptisms.   Every human creature that is born is not carried to the priest of the parish to be baptised; but every human creature that dies, unless at sea, is consigned to the earth, and his obsequies are rarely unaccompanied with the ceremonies of religion.

The question abovestated was, If 192,000 burials, the average amount for five years, from 1795 to 1800, were produced from a population of 9,168,000, from what population were so many burials, the registered amount of a remoter year, produced?

But here we are stopped on the threshold by the information of the editor of the Reports,

Q

who assures us [f], that " the average number of
registered burials (though considerably fluctuating from year to year) has remained stationary
during twenty-one years, from 1780 to 1800;
the first five years of which period, as well as
the last five years, and all the twenty-one years
together, equally averaging at about 192,000
burials *per annum*."

Here then we have an evidence, perhaps as
strong as any ground of computation can afford
us, of a population that does not increase.

This however does not shake the faith of the
editor of the Reports, who steadily adheres to
his computation from the baptisms, and affirms
an increase of population within that period to
the amount of 1,215,000 persons.   For the five
years from 1805 to 1810, he states " the average
of burials to be 196,000 [g]," that is, to exhibit the
comparatively slender increase of 4000 *per annum*; and yet, according to him, the population of
the country, between the years 1780 and 1810,
has experienced an increase to the amount of no
less than 2,535,000 souls.

This circumstance would certainly have startled the faith of a more diffident speculator ; but
it has no such effect upon him. He indeed
brings forward an extraordinary solution for the
difficulty.   " The average number of burials,"
he says, " having remained stationary, or nearly

---

[f] P. xxii.   [g] *Ibid.*

so, while the population has been increasing by more than two millions and a half, authorises a satisfactory inference of diminishing mortality in England [h]."   Satisfactory indeed, but no less astounding than satisfactory, if no more persons are found to die now, when the population is 10,488,000, than died before in the year 1780, when the population is stated to have amounted to no more than 7,953,000.   Can any thing be more extraordinary than this ?   I had heard before of the improving salubrity of London, in consequence of its widened streets and the better arrangement of its buildings.   But that the whole climate of the country from the Land's End in Cornwal to Berwick upon Tweed should thus have improved, I confess is new to me.

But let us try the accuracy of these registers in another way.   Dr. Price in his Observations on Reversionary Payments has fixed the average medium of the probability of human life at thirty-three years [i].   Consequently, the number of those who are born, or those who die, annually in any country, multiplied by thirty-three, ought to yield us the amount of its inhabitants.

Now by Mr. Rickman's statement, the average amount of baptisms for the five years preceding the enumeration of 1801 is 263,409 [k].   This number, multiplied by 33, gives 8,692,497, a

---

[h] *Ibid.*   [i] Vol. II, p. 403.   [k] P. xx.

number, short by 475,500 of the enumeration for that period. This however would be a most unfair mode of calculation, since, I suppose, a great majority of the people of England in 1801 were more than five years of age, and those who were older, being born, according to Mr. Rickman, from a much thinner population, must have been born in years that yielded a much smaller number of baptisms.

From the same authority we learn, that the average of burials is 192,000, and this for twenty-one years, from 1780 to 1800. Now this number, multiplied by 33, gives no more than 6,336,000, a number short by almost three millions of the actual enumeration.

It is further worthy of remark, that, in the page of the Observations prefixed to the Returns of 1811, immediately preceding that from which the Table of Population throughout the Last Century is taken, the editor has presented us with a Table of the Proportions of Baptisms to Marriages [1], during the very period when, according to him, the greatest increase was taking place in our population. The highest of these proportions is 366 to 100, very considerably less than four to one. Now it is surprising that it did not occur to the editor, that, while this proportion obtained, there could be no increase of population; a point which has already been

---

[1] For this Table see above, p. 203, 4.

abundantly established. The return of baptisms therefore supports two opposite conclusions; first, in page xxiv of the Preliminary Observations, that there can have been no increase of population; and, secondly in page xxv, that the increase has been so considerable, as for the number of people to have doubled itself in the course of a century. The just inference is, that these returns of baptisms can in no way be relied on as a safe ground of reasoning.

From what has been stated, it seems fair to set aside all the conjectural and computatory accounts of the population of England and Wales, previous to the passing the act for 1801. But it will still be asked, what shall we oppose to the comparison of the two actual enumerations of 1801 and 1811, from which it follows that we gained in population in those ten years an accession of 1,320,000 citizens?

It appears indeed that the marriages, compared with the births, did not average four children born during this very period to one marriage taking place in it, that the burials were increased by an amount of only 3,019 *per annum* for the whole country, and that the number of those who died, according to this statement, was only such as implied a population of 6,435,627 persons.

But I may be told that all this is computation merely, and will be wholly vitiated by the supposition of the gross imperfection of the regis-

ters.   The population on the contrary is the sum
of the returns made from every parish or district by the resident clergyman or overseer, who
by the exertion of a certain diligence could not
fail to know the number of the actual inhabitants.   It was his business to go from house to
house, and learn from the head of each family
the precise number of his family or inmates.
At all events, though he should in some instances have reported too small an amount, it
can hardly be supposed that he counted a larger
number of heads than really existed.   The population of England and Wales therefore ought
to be taken at 10,488,000 for the year 1811.

I am myself more inclined to give credit in
this respect to the returns of 1811, than to those
of 1801.   There are very obvious reasons, that
might have made men cautious at first of giving
a true answer to an enquiry of this sort.   A
country like England, so deeply loaded with
taxes and exactions of all kinds, will naturally
have a people that regard with a certain degree
of jealousy the movement of their government
and their superiors.   We have heard of poll-
taxes, of pressing of seamen, of pressing of soldiers, and of the conscriptions of France, not
to mention the drawings for the militia at home.
The honest peasantry and manufacturers and
mechanics of this country, when first addressed
with questions as to the number of persons in
their family, of their inmates or lodgers, very

excusably looked shy upon the questioner, and recollected a maxim current in ordinary life, that truth is not always to be spoken. The second time, having experienced no ill consequences from the first experiment, they became more frank. It is therefore very conceivable, that there was not one human creature more in the country, when the population was returned as 10,488,000 in 1811, than when it was returned as 9,168,000 in 1801.

I have already said, that the enumerations of Great Britain in 1801 and 1811, were merely so much labour thrown away. Being taken with such inconceivable absurdity, all ages and sexes being confounded together, they can, in my conception, be made the basis of no reasoning. We are therefore reduced to conjecture merely, as to the cause of the inequality of amount in the two enumerations. If the population had been divided into classes according to every five or ten years' difference of ages, as in Sweden and in the United States, the truth would have flashed upon us at once. The added numbers by direct procreation in the enumeration of 1811 would have been all under ten years of age, and of consequence the number of such children in 1811 would have exceeded the number in 1801 by the precise amount of 1,320,000. This would have been an evidence that could hardly have been called in question.

Is England more or less populous now, than

it was a hundred years ago, or than it was forty years back ? Each man answers this question according to his preconceived opinions.

Man is a migrating animal. He removes from one place to another, from the town to the country, and from the country to the town, as he shall happen to be impressed with the notion that in this or in that he shall be most likely to find his well-being.

London I am persuaded is more populous now, than it was at any remote period : but is England more populous ?

The life of man is too short for any accurate ideas on such a question ; and in this respect it is not true, that " one generation telleth to another." Our fathers thought, it may be, that their country was well peopled and prosperous. But did these words convey the same image to their minds as to ours ? The observation of man is too narrow to scan a country, 580 miles in length, and 370 in breadth. We see that one spot becomes more crowded, and another thinner of people ; but we do not see how far the one does or does not balance the other.

The observation of the same individual varies from youth to age. Our ideas become modified from day to day, and we do not observe the variation ; and the notion that the same set of words excites in us at twenty, and at fifty, is essentially different. Things alter, and appear to us the same, and continue the same, and appear to us materially changed.   I remember a friend of mine[m], who after a lapse of ten years visited the house where he had resided when he was a boy : he was persuaded that the garden was inclosed with a wall that effectually cut off the view of the circumjacent country, and felt much surprised at his return to find this wall scarcely higher than his breast : if he had continued all the time on the spot, it is probable he never would have perceived the alteration.   Our minds change much as our bodies do, in which it has been computed that not a particle remains the same after a lapse of twenty years.

We are like children at a juggler's exhibition, who, while their attention is craftily called to a particular point, look only there, and see nothing of the general scene, and of what is passing elsewhere, that it was more material to observe. We see the high days, and the holiday-making, and how men crowd together to shows, and courts, and prosperous cities, but what passes in the obscure nooks and corners of the state we do not see.   If I travel from London to York, I can count up the cottages, and observe how many carts and carriages and foot-passengers go along the road within a given number of miles, and what appearance there is of populousness and activity, or the contrary ; but I do not

---

m The reverend Joseph Fawcet, the friend of my youth, my first companion of imaginative soul and luxuriant ideas, whose name it is gratifying to me to record, though on so trivial an occasion.

know what Addison, and Swift, and Congreve, and the most competent observers saw, when according to the Table of Houses there was an appearance of the greatest numbers of mankind, though their local arrangement was different from that of the present day. Nay, if I had myself performed the journey twenty years ago, the memory of man is of so irretentive a texture, and his judgment so easily seduced, that I shall not now distinctly call to mind what I saw then, and shall be bribed insensibly to accommodate the comparison to that system of political economy, whatever it is, that I have happened to embrace. The collation we attempt, is either at too near intervals, when it is not reasonable to expect any considerable alteration, or at too remote ones, when the image which was once distinct in the mind, has become so obscure and faded, and has suffered so much from the injury of the seasons, and the variety of scenes and impressions which have intervened, that a wise man would hardly have the courage to rely upon it.

It is difficult to conceive how the notion of the increasing population of our country has become so generally prevalent. Is the population of the world increased? Have the numbers of the human species been increasing from the earliest accounts of time? There is nothing, to speak moderately, in the history of the earth, to authorise this opinion.

Is England then an exception to the general succession of ages and nations ? If so, the reasons should be assigned that authorise us to regard it as an exception.

Much confusion of ideas exists on this subject.

First, we read in holy writ that all mankind sprung from a single pair, and this unavoidably inclines us to believe in a progressive increase.

To this I have answered, first, from Derham and other theological writers who affirm the population of the earth to be now at a stand, that we are informed from the same divine authority, that in the early ages the life of man was nearly of one thousand years' duration, which, says Derham, was absolutely necessary for the first peopling of the world. Secondly, Mr. Malthus confines his enquiries to human authorities and statistical documents, and I cannot reasonably be blamed for following his example in my refutation of his Essay. Thirdly, this would have implied an invariable increase, or nearly so, an assumption as much in opposition to all the evidence of history as can well be imagined.

A second consideration which has impressed a majority of those to whom I address myself with the idea of the growing population of this country, is to be found in the progress of refinement. We compare our accommodations with what appear to us the aukward shifts to which the generations that preceded us were reduced,

and we persuade ourselves that our advantages
in this respect necessarily imply a greater number of human beings to partake of them. We
pass in imagination at one leap, from the refinements introduced or existing in the early
part of the nineteenth century, to a period of
absolute barbarism, like that of the naked Afri-
cans and North American Indians, and picture
to ourselves men wasting a disconsolate life in
immeasurable solitudes, where the presenting
one human being to the eyes of another might
be supposed to constitute an epocha.

But this is all a delusion. Civilisation as surely destroys its myriads, as the rudest and most
unpolished state of existence. Immense wealth
has a natural tendency to spread a comparative
desert around it. A simple and tranquil form
of social existence is not hostile to population.
Of this we might be sufficiently convinced from
the accounts given us by the first discoverers of
the West India islands, and of the empires of
Mexico and Peru. Of this we have still more
incontestible evidence in the statements of the
present population of Indostan.

But, though the notion of the increasing population of our country has been the current notion of our political writers, this increase was never viewed as an evil till the year 1798. It is the
geometrical ratio, that has produced all this confusion and uproar in the brains of politicians.
Till the present age, these men flattered them

selves with an increase; but it was an increase by moderate and slow degrees. They knew that the earth was capacious of inhabitants, immeasurably beyond the present numbers of mankind. They believed that, as nations advanced in numbers, they would also advance in ingenuity. They relied upon emigration as a resource, when any country or corner of a country should become inconveniently furnished with inhabitants. They regarded this, like the circles that the pebble makes in a lake; and they could contemplate no end to this vast, and perhaps frequently interrupted, expansion. They regarded the earth as an inexhaustible storehouse for the food of man, science and the practical application of science as indefatigable and endless, and the subsistence of human creatures and the progress of social improvement as a contemplation fraught with perpetual hope and exultation. But we have learned to fear that, which it is perhaps impossible should ever occur, and to give up all our present advantages, and those which a little before with confidence we anticipated, because the day will hereafter arrive, or not arrive, which will baffle and supersede all the calculations of human wisdom.

CHAPTER XI.

PROOFS OF THE GEOMETRICAL RATIO FROM THE PHENOMENON OF A PESTILENCE.

ONE frequent source of the mistakes that have been made on the subject of population, has been derived from the consideration of a pestilence. It has been said, that, when a nation has been laid waste by this great scourge of mankind, the loss is speedily made up, the lands are again cultivated, the cities repeopled, and the country grows as flourishing as ever. The received idea is, that, if you happened not to be a spectator of the distress while it lasted, and if you returned to the country that had been visited by such a calamity after an interval of ten years, you would know nothing of the matter. Influenced by these conceptions, it has been inferred by Hume, one of the most subtle of all reasoners, that, " if the restraints which the desire and power of propagation lie under were completely removed, the human species would more than double in every generation [a]." I have that deference for the great authority of

---

[a] Essays, Part II, Essay xi.

Hume, that for this reason principally I have determined to devote a chapter to the question.

Let it be remembered then, that, when London or any other considerable town became thinned by the plague, this was not entirely the consequence of the numbers that died. Every one that had the power, and almost that had not, fled from the dreadful scene; London was indeed a melancholy solitude. Her citizens migrated in multitudes to the country parts of England; but, when the infection was at an end, they migrated back again.

If, in consequence of a calamity of this sort, there appears, when it is over, eligible place for more inhabitants, this eligibleness will tempt population from the remoter parts of the empire, or from foreign countries. Wherever there is soil well prepared for cultivation, and a country, desirable to dwell in, but ill provided with inhabitants, thither human creatures will feel prompted to remove. Man is a being that wanders from Dan to Beersheba, from Copenhagen to Jerusalem, and from Europe to America, in pursuit of happiness. But of these migrations no European government takes an account; and the new comers speedily become consolidated with the old inhabitants. We must have regulations, such as are said to exist in some parts of Asia, forbidding every man to quit the district in which he was born, before we can easily obtain accurate notions of population.

And here it may be useful to recollect what was proved some time back, that there can be no real increase of population, but by an increase of the number of women capable of child-bearing. The rest of the society, the old and the young, except so far as they contribute to this, may come and go as they please. They are useless adjuncts, drones in the great hive of population, and in the point of view now under consideration not worthy to be counted. Mr. Malthus has taken infinite pains in comparing the number of births and deaths in given situations and periods, and is of opinion that, if in one year and another many more human beings are born than die, the population is substantially increased. But all this pains (so far as " short periods" are concerned) is thrown away. If indeed, as Mr. Malthus expresses it, " the population is continually pressing hard against the limits of subsistence," and we are in want of food sufficient to nourish us, it may then be desirable that the infirm and the useless should die off as soon as they could ; and we might be incited, except so far as we were restrained by religion or humanity, to imitate what is related of some savage nations, to bury our grandfathers and grandmothers alive, or tie them to a tree, and leave them to starve. But their protracted existence adds not an atom to the real power and source of population. In civilised society they may be useful, ornamental, admirable ;

but in the single question which Mr. Malthus has so successfully pressed upon general observation, they are mere weeds in the garden of society, a sort of annuals or biennials, that may drop off at pleasure, but add nothing to the substantial support of population, or to the chance that the nation or tribe to which they belong shall continue in their posterity.

" If you happened not to be a spectator of the pestilence while it lasted, and returned to the country after a lapse of ten years, you would not be aware of any alteration that had taken place." What would be the real state of the case? In ten years many of the men and women that existed in the beginning of the period would have deceased, according to the never sleeping, never to be suspended, course of nature. But in the mean time not one woman, not one man, would have been added to the population, by procreation only. Instead 'of this, we should see a fry of little children, the stay, and the single hope of the age to come. We must wait sixteen years at least, if not twenty, before we can look for a single mother from this quarter, to replace the race of mothers, who in the mean time have for the most part gone off the stage of efficient fecundity, since the pestilence ceased. A portentous gap, that might almost make us tremble for the continuance of the race. The only relief we have from this, is in contemplating the female children born before

R

the pestilence, some of whom, together with some of the married women, would have survived the general calamity. So clear it is, that we must rely upon the migrating principle in man, and not upon procreation, for any sudden restoration of numbers and prosperity, after a great scene of indiscriminate devastation.

DISSERTATION

ON THE

RATIOS OF INCREASE IN POPULATION,

AND IN

THE MEANS OF SUBSISTENCE.

BY MR. DAVID BOOTH.

———

SECTION I.

INTRODUCTORY OBSERVATIONS.

"IT has been said," says Mr. Malthus, " that I have written a quarto volume to prove, that population increases in a geometrical, and food in an arithmetical ratio; but this is not quite true. The first of these propositions I consi dered as proved the moment the American in-crease was related, and the second proposition as soon as it was enunciated. The chief object of my work was to enquire, what effects those laws, which I considered as established in the first six pages, had produced, and were likely to produce, on society; a subject not very rea-dily exhausted [a]." This, it must be acknow-

---

[a] Essay on Population, Vol. III, p. 343, 344, Note.

ledged, is meeting his adversary fairly in the open field. His means of defence are displayed before us; and we shall see if his " first six pages" form an impenetrable shield.

The argument of Mr. Malthus is founded on the comparison of numerical progressions; and, as mathematical science has always been held as the only one that is demonstrably true, this comparison of numerical progressions has been hastily allowed as infallibly certain, and has obtained for its author all that implicit faith, which has been granted by his disciples to the corollaries which he has drawn.

It may be premised however, that the science of mathematics is a science of certainty, only in as far as it is a science of abstraction;—that when it ceases to be abstract, and becomes what is termed " mixed mathematics," the numbers or quantities, assume definite designations; and the reasonings thence derived are true, or false, according to the accuracy, or inaccuracy, with which these numbers or quantities are designated.—Two times two, for instance, is four, because four is the term by which we have agreed to denominate the result of this multiplication; but when, in measuring surfaces, it is said that two feet multiplied by two feet will make four feet, there is an error in the syllogism; because the word " feet" in the product, has not the same meaning that it has in the factors:—in the latter it is lineal, and in the former superficial.

In application then, mathematical reasoning partakes of all the uncertainty of the branches of knowledge with which it is combined; and hence the numerous paradoxes which, even in this science of demonstration, have puzzled the pupils, and have scarcely been explained by their masters. These observations are not foreign to our purpose, when we have to speak of the ratio of increase in human population.

Mr. Malthus, if he himself understood; the subject, has taken it for granted that his comparison of ratios would escape the notice of mathematicians. He asserts that human population, if allowed to expand freely, would increase in a geometrical ratio, in the order of

1, 2, 4, 8, 16, 32, 64, 128, 256, &c.

Now it is obvious that this series can represent no connected chain of the expansion of human life. The quantity represented by 1 (the first term in the series) does not at any moment become 2 (the second term), but there are an indefinite number of terms of different magnitudes to be interjected between these terms (and so between every two other successive ones) to fill up the links of the chain. This then supposes time: time therefore, the most metaphysical of all metaphysical beings, is an ingredient mixed up with the consideration of the abstract numbers of the progression. This time Mr. Malthus has specified to be 25 years. The series then which denotes the increase of human beings in America, is thus represented.

First term, or original propagators,   1
2d,   in 25 years,   2
3d,   50 ——   4
4th,   75 ——   8
5th,   100 ——   16
6th,   125 ——   32
&c.   &c. ——   &c.

The philosophy of Mr. Malthus is not the method of induction. He perpetually appeals to principles which have never been brought into action, and which are opposed to all experience. He speaks of tendencies to human increase, and of powers of population, which " in no state that we have yet known have been left to exert themselves with perfect freedom [b]." This is exactly in the style of those dreamers, who predict of the future something unlike and opposite to what has ever appeared in the past. They too talk of secret springs, that have never yet displayed their elasticity,—of latent energies which have never been exerted.

Latent signifies concealed, and consequently the latent power of increase in the human species is what we shall never know; but, even granting for a moment that the 3 or 4 censuses which have been taken in America do exhibit something like a duplication in 25 years;—granting too that this increase

---

[b] Vol. I. p. 5, 6.

has arisen solely from propagation, independ
ent of emigration, there certainly exist no data
from which to infer the law of the series. We
have only 4, or at most 5 terms given us,—
some of them extracted at intervals of time by
no means regular,—from a series perpetually
flowing, and of the ebbs and floods of whose
motion we know nothing; and from these the
ordinary reader is presented with a picked set
of numbers, in geometrical progression, with
the ratio of two. From such an increasing series as the human race may be supposed to exhibit, any form of a progression may be taken :—
why not that of 1, 4, 9, 16, 25, &c. which increase as the squares of the terms 1, 2, 3, 4, 5,
&c. ? For aught that Mr. Malthus has discovered this may be the latent law of increase. All
that he has demonstrated, even granting his
American censuses, as we for the moment have
done, is that human beings are capable of increasing their numbers ; or, rather that they have
been found to do so for a specific time : but
the series which would mark the Law of that
Increase, he has either been unwilling or unable
to develop.

" The rate," says Mr. Malthus, " according to
which the productions of the earth may be supposed to increase, it will not be easy to determine. Of this however we may be perfectly
certain, that the ratio of their increase must be
totally of a different nature from the ratio of the

increase of population [c]." This passage is much more modest than that which we quoted at the beginning of this Dissertation, where he says, that food increases in an arithmetical ratio, and that he considered this proposition as proved the moment it was enunciated; but, as he proceeds, this modesty vanishes, and he comes to an undoubting conclusion that food can increase only in the series 1, 2, 3, 4, 5, 6, 7, 8, 9, &c. (an arithmetical progression whose ratio is one) and that the period between the terms, or time of increase, is also 25 years.

If the quantity of the food of man be increased, it is obvious that the increase will not be by starts every 25 years; but that it will be increased through many intervening times; and, consequently, even granting that such quantities as 1, 2, 3, 4, &c. were extracted from the flow of increase, at certain periods, the arithmetical progression thus exhibited would be a picked set of numbers, (as we stated respecting population) and might have been any other series rather than that which Mr. Malthus has chosen, for aught that experience has told him on the subject. The successive terms of all increasing series whatever present nothing but additions. The mathematician forms series at his own pleasure, where the additions are regulated by certain laws. It is not so with those of Nature.

---

[c] Vol. I. p. 9.

Whether her series alternately progress and re-
trograde;—whether they circulate, or decrease,
or flow in straight and eternal lines, is beyond
the ken of the philosopher. He snatches at intervals, a few links in the immeasurable and
ever moving chain of the universe; and dividing these links into such portions as are perceived by the glance of a moment, he cries out in
extacy, " I have found it !" This remark however is general. It refers to the boundaries of
human knowledge, and is applicable to a Newton as well as to a Malthus :—Our business is
with the latter.

Taking the series 1, 2, 3, 4, &c. as that of the
increase of human subsistence, or of any thing
else, we may, by picking the terms, extract from
it any progression we chuse : for instance, in —
1, 2, 3, 4, 5, 6, 7, 8, 9, 10, 11, 12, 13, 14, 15, 16, &c.
the 1st, 2d, 4th, 8th, and 16th terms, form the
precise geometrical progression, which Mr. Malthus has chosen to represent the increase of human beings. The progressions themselves then
would have signified nothing, had not Mr. Malthus assumed the principle, that an equal period
of time, 25 years, was to elapse between the
production of every subsequent term of either
progression. Thus arranged :

Population,   1, 2, 4, 8, 16, 32, 64, 128, 256
Food,   1, 2, 3, 4, 5, 6, 7,   8,   9
he believes that he has demonstrated that in 8
periods of time of 25 years each, the population

if unchecked, would increase to 256 times its present number, while the food would only be 9 times what it now is. Let us endeavour to view the grounds on which these different progressions have been raised.

SECTION II.

OF THE RATIO OF INCREASE IN THE MEANS OF SUBSISTENCE.

THE phrase, " means of subsistence," as applied to human beings is in the utmost degree loose and indefinite. In a general sense almost every thing that grows, walks, swims, or flies, is capable of being converted into the food of man, and hence every vegetable and every animal must cease to exist, before it can be said that his means of subsistence are exhausted; and, till then, the grown up man would always find sufficient to feed his young. In a particular view however, it may be, and often is otherwise. Man in society is a being of habits and prejudices He is moreover a slave. His food must be of a certain kind, dressed in a certain manner, and provided, not by the whole, but by a small portion of the species. In this situation a famine may occur while the world teems with animal and vegetable life [d].   He may starve in a work-shop, as well as within the walls of a dungeon; because, in neither case, has he any food except what is brought by his keepers.   It is food so prepared and so distributed, which constitutes the means of subsistence among the nations of Europe, where the labourer

> " Starves, in the midst of Nature's bounty curst,
> And in the loaden vineyard, dies for thirst."

As it is in America that Mr. Malthus has dis-covered his ratio of propagation, it is there also we should look for the ratio of increased subsistence; and in doing so we shall find reason to be asto-nished at his choice of an arithmetical one.   As far as animals constitute the food of man, its in-crease must be in the same sort of series as that of human beings : and, if a geometrical ratio ex-ist any where, it is surely in the vegetable pro-duce of the soil.   Animals and vegetables mul-tiply as rapidly at least as man, if submitted to his care and protection : and, as the love of his offspring is implanted in his nature, he would, if free, always exert himself to rear the food, which his children might require.   The limits of this production of food would not be discovered, as long as any land lay waste.   Until the whole were cultivated in the highest degree,—until the sea were drained of its inhabitants, and no wild beast or fowl were found upon the earth,

---

[d] Witness the horrible famine in India in 1771.

the food of man would always increase in an
equal ratio with the human race [e]. If America
have doubled its inhabitants every 25 years, the
prepared food must have increased in equal proportion : for all the inhabitants have plenty, and
are able to export grain to foreign countries.
In the only country then, where Mr. Malthus
has discovered any ratio of increase of human
population, the same, if not a greater ratio has
been observed in the increase of the means of
subsistence. As before observed, natural subsistence is indefinite, and prepared subsistence,
which is a manufacture from what nature has in
store, must always increase in quantity in proportion to the number of manufacturers employed, until the raw material can no longer be furnished ; and so long at least the ratios of human
increase and of the means of subsistence must
necessarily be the same. What will happen
when the prolific power of man shall enable him
to outstrip the fertility of the globe which he
inhabits : when the head of the serpent shall
bite off its tail, and no longer remain an emblem

---

[e] " If want alone, or the desire of the labouring classes to possess
the necessaries and conveniences of life, were a sufficient stimulus to
production, there is no state in Europe or in the world that would
have found any other practical limit to its wealth than its power to
produce ; and the earth would probably before this period have contained, at the very least, ten times as many inhabitants as are supported on its surface at present. But .... where the right of private
property is   tablished, &c. &c. &c.''

Vide Malthus on Political Economy, p. 348.

of the universe, we leave to the conjectures of those whose imaginations are able to people the universe with human beings [f]. Meantime, whether vice, misery, or (what Mr. Malthus never chooses to mention) the less extent of prolific power, and the shortness of time appointed for man upon the earth,—shall interfere with this peopling of the stars, we may rest assured that, until men can exist without food, the ratio of increase of population will never exceed that of the means of subsistence. Food may be reared beyond the wants of a people, and such a case has produced slavery and misery to the cultivators of Botany Bay [g]; but it is impossible that any term in the progression of subsistence can be less than its corresponding term in that of population, else that corresponding term would cease to be. Experience then never did nor ever can shew different progressions in population and in food, in favour of the former; and, as to the difference of inherent power (if a power which can never be exerted have a meaning), the power of increase in plants and animals is obviously equal to that of man.

---

[f] See Malthus on Political Economy, as quoted in page 484.
[g] See Wentworth's Account of that Colony.

SECTION III.

OF THE RATIO OF INCREASE IN HUMAN POPULATION.

WE have already observed that the progressions of nature are not formed like those of the mathematician. They do not start from one term to another, but proceed insensibly, so as to fill up all the interstices between the terms of the series; and it is only by catching at different points in the order of time, that progressions are extracted, to form (or oftener to suit) the theories of philosophers. It is known for instance that bodies fall to the earth with an accelerated motion. That acceleration has been assumed to be such, that the spaces described by the falling body shall always be in proportion to the squares of the times. Experiments were made on a petty scale to prove the truth of this theory, some of which appeared to coincide in a remarkable degree, while others presented very different results. It was then assumed that the ratio could exist only in a vacuum, on account of the resistance of the atmospherical air,—and as we have no means of making the experiment *in vacuo*, the principle still remains a mere *gratis dictum*. It is nevertheless considered as unquestionable; and is even made to guide the planets in their orbits.

In a similar manner, though with humbler claims to confidence, Mr. Malthus has adopted the principle, assumed by his predecessors, of a tendency to a continued geometrical ratio in the increase of human population; and has built upon this hypothesis, his theory of accounting for the vice and misery which exist among mankind. We have now to consider from what data this principle of increase has been inferred; but we may previously remark, that it is the tendency to this ratio of increase, and not the increase itself, which Mr. Malthus exhibits as the evil genius of the human race. This embryo of future famine—this being that is yet to be—is perpetually at war with the good genius of subsistence. The hand of industry is palsied, and the fruits of nature are shrivelled, by the touch of the demon. He hangs the ruin over our heads, and we are crushed by its weight before it falls.

Granting the power of increase to the human species, the methods of investigating the law of the series will vary according to our view of the origin of mankind. On this subject, however much men may differ in minute particulars, there are only two general and acknowledged systems of belief. The one is the peopling of the earth as recorded in the scriptures: the other is the aspect of human society as it appears to every succeeding generation, modified by the degree of confidence that such generation entertains in the traditions and uninspired written records of its ancestors. We will consider the case from each of these points of view.

On the first hypothesis the whole of the present race of men have descended from a single pair. In consequence, there is no question of the existence of a power of increase among the early inhabitants of the earth ; and the only point of controversy is, whether that power be not now diminished. But, however that may be, the investigator of ratios proceeds upon the same principle, and uniformly constructs his tables from a single pair. It is nevertheless evident that every table so constructed must proceed upon data furnished by the imagination. We have no complete genealogy of the first peopling of the globe ; and, as brothers do not marry their sisters in our times, the descendants of a single pair cannot now be kept separate from the population of a district. Such imaginary tables have notwithstanding been constructed ; and we give the following from Sussmilch, which was calculated by Euler. He takes a married pair of 20 years old, as the founders of his race. This pair have six children at three births (each birth producing twins—a male and a female) and these births are in the 22d, 24th, and 26th years of the age of the parents, who live till 40 years old, and then die. Every successive pair marry at 20, and have 6 children at 3 births, in their 22d, 24th, and 26th years, and live till the age of 40, as their parents did before them. The same succession of births, marriages, and deaths, continues from generation to generation, and the results are given for every 2d year, during a period of 3 centuries. These data are sufficiently extravagant. The Table presents, as might be expected, an abundant increase; and surely here, if any where, the geometrical ratio should be found.

In this Table the first column contains the years to which the numbers in the other columns respectively refer. The 2d column gives the number of the born in each particular year. The 3d column gives the number of the born altogether; which, if there were no deaths, would be the number of the living; but as all die in the 41st year of their age, the number of the dead is placed in the 4th column, which, subtracted from the whole number born as expressed in the 3d column, forms the 5th and last column, or the number of the living.

Year.	Number of the Born.	Number of the Whole.	Number of the Dead.	Number of the Living.
0	0	2	0	2
2	2	4	0	4
4	2	6	0	6
6	2	8	0	8
8	0	8	0	8
10	0	8	0	8
12	0	8	0	8
14	0	8	0	3
16	0	8	0	8

S

Year.	Number of the Born.	Number of the Whole.	Number of the Dead.	Number of the Living.
18	0	8	0	8
20	0	8	2	6
22	0	8	2	6
24	2	10	2	8
26	4	14	2	12
28	6	20	2	18
30	4	24	2	22
32	2	26	2	24
34	0	26	2	24
36	0	26	2	24
38	0	26	2	24
40	0	26	2	24
42	0	26	4	22
44	0	26	6	20
46	2	28	8	20
48	6	34	8	26
50	12	46	8	38
52	14	60	8	52
54	12	72	8	64
56	6	78	8	70
58	2	80	8	72
60	0	80	8	72
62	0	80	8	72
64	0	80	10	70
66	0	80	14	66
68	2	82	20	62
70	8	90	24	66
72	20	110	26	84
74	32	142	26	116
76	38	180	26	154
78	32	212	26	186
80	20	232	26	206
82	8	240	26	214
84	2	242	26	216
86	0	242	28	214
88	0	242	34	208
90	2	244	46	198
92	10	254	60	194
94	30	284	72	212
96	60	344	78	266
98	90	434	80	354
100	102	536	80	456
102	90	626	80	546

Year.	Number of the Born.	Number of the Whole.	Number of the Dead.	Number of the Living.
104	60	686	80	606
106	30	716	80	636
108	10	726	82	644
110	2	728	90	638
112	2	730	110	620
114	12	742	142	600
116	42	784	180	604
118	100	884	212	672
120	180	1064	232	832
122	252	1316	240	1076
124	282	1598	242	1356
126	252	1850	242	1608
128	180	2030	242	1788
130	100	2130	244	1886
132	42	2172	254	1918
134	14	2186	284	1902
136	16	2202	344	1858
138	56	2258	434	1824
140	154	2412	536	1876
142	322	2734	626	2108
144	532	3266	686	2580
146	714	3980	716	3264
148	786	4766	726	4040
150	714	5480	728	4752
152	532	6012	730	5282
154	322	6334	742	5592
156	156	6490	784	5706
158	72	6562	884	5678
160	86	6648	1064	5584
162	226	6874	1316	5558
164	532	7406	1598	5808
166	1008	8414	1850	6564
168	1568	9982	2030	7952
170	2032	12014	2130	9884
172	2214	14228	2172	12056
174	2032	16260	2186	14074
176	1568	17828	2202	15626
178	1010	18838	2258	16580
180	550	19388	2412	16976
182	314	19702	2734	16968
184	384	20086	3266	16820
186	844	20930	3980	16950
188	1766	22696	4766	17930

Year.	Number of the Born.	Number of the Whole.	Number of the Dead.	Number of the Living.
190	3108	25804	5480	20324
192	4608	30412	6012	24400
194	5814	36226	6334	29892
196	6278	42504	6490	36014
198	5814	48318	6562	41756
200	4610	52928	6648	46280
202	3128	56056	6874	49182
204	1874	57930	7406	50524
206	1248	59178	8414	50764
208	1542	60720	9982	50738
210	2994	63714	12014	51700
212	5718	69432	14228	55204
214	9482	78914	16260	62654
216	13530	92444	17828	74616
218	16690	109134	18838	90296
220	17906	127040	19388	107652
222	16702	143742	19702	124040
224	13552	157294	20086	137208
226	9612	166906	20930	145976
228	6250	173156	22696	150460
230	4664	177820	25804	152016
232	5784	183604	30412	153192
234	10254	193858	36226	157632
236	18194	212052	42504	169548
238	28730	240782	48318	192464
240	39702	280484	52928	227556
242	48126	328610	56056	272554
244	51298	379908	57930	321978
246	48160	428068	59178	368890
248	39866	467934	60720	407214
250	29414	497348	63714	433634
252	20526	517874	69432	448442
254	16698	534572	78914	455658
256	20702	555274	92444	462830
258	34232	589506	109134	480372
260	57178	646684	127040	519644
262	86626	733310	143742	589568
264	116558	849868	157294	692574
266	139126	988994	166906	822088
268	147584	1136578	173156	963422
270	139324	1275902	177820	1098082
272	117440	1393342	183604	1209738
274	89806	1483148	193858	1289290

Years	Number of the Born.	Number of the Whole.	Number of the Dead.	Number of the Living.
276	66638	1549786	212052	1337734
278	57926	1607712	240782	1366930
280	71632	1679344	280484	1398860
282	122112	1801456	328610	1472846
284	178036	1979429	379908	1599584
286	260362	2239854	428068	1811786
288	342310	2582164	467934	2114230
290	403268	2985432	497348	2488084
292	426034	3411466	517874	2893592
294	404348	3815814	534572	3281242
296	346570	4162384	555274	3607110
298	273884	4436268	589506	3846762
300	214370	4650638	646684	4003954

The mathematician, who is acquainted with
the data on which this Table is constructed,
knows that it presents a recurring series, the
law of which might be expressed by an algebraic
formula ; while the ordinary reader will be astonished at its ebbs and flows, and will labour in
vain, if he attempt to pick out an increasing
geometrical ratio from its numbers. There is
only one law in a geometrical progression, which
is, that every succeeding term shall have a certain fixed proportion to the preceding; and
hence, if, in a series of increasing numbers, every
set of equidistant terms (such as every 20th or
25th, &c.) presents a geometrical ratio, then all
the terms in the series are also in geometrical progression. Thus if in the numbers 1, 2, 4, 8, 16,
32, 64, 128, 256, 512, 1024, we take every third
term, beginning with 1, we shall have 1, 8, 64

512, a geometrical progression, where every succeeding term is 8 times that which went before
it.   If we chuse every second term we have, 1,
4, 16, 64, 256, 1024, a progression where the ratio is 4, and universally, pick as we will, if we
do so at equal distances, we shall always have a
geometrical progression : because the numbers
from which we have to chuse are all arranged in
that sort of series.   Before then a geometrical
progression can be picked, at regular intervals,
from any succession of numbers, every 3 or more
terms, that follow one another in that succession, must themselves be in geometrical proportion.   It is in vain therefore to look for a
doubling of mankind in certain periods, if there
be not an equable progression from year to year.
But, under any form of increase from a single
pair, this is impossible ; for the terms are only
numerically, not substantially the same.   The
number of the living in the Table before us
is doubled in the second year, tripled in the
4th, and quadrupled in the 6th year, but these
4, 6, and 8 persons, are not similar to the first
two.   The two are a man and a woman, while
the increase are children, who have to live a certain number of years before they can add to the
race.   The geometrical ratio therefore can never
exist under such circumstances.   In this Table,
though every contingency that could arise from
constitution, climate, or other causes, is studi-
ously rejected in the calculation, the " regular

confusion" is apparent, particularly in the 2d column, through a period of three hundred years; and though the numbers would not be so obviously irregular to common observers, they would never run into a geometrical ratio, though extended to as many centuries.

If the descendants of a single pair can never increase in a geometrical proportion, neither can those of a modern colony, for such a colony is only a certain number of grown up pairs; and besides, as they are real beings, they are liable to many accidents, defying all calculation, from which the preceding Table is by supposition free. A colony of grown up men and women insulated from the rest of the world, would resemble in a great degree the first parents of the human race. Society, as it exists in Europe, presents us with numbers of all ages from the cradle to the grave; and in gradations which could not exist in a colony, such as we have mentioned, for centuries. Mr. Malthus finds his geometrical ratio in America: but the least reflection might convince him that this ratio cannot possibly take place among the descendants of grown up propagators; and that, though it were supposed to exist, the continued influx of emigrants from Europe would so overwhelm it with stranger numbers, as to make it impossible to shew the progression. We are not, in this place, denying the assertion, that there has been an increase in America " from procreation only."

We only deny, and we do it peremptorily, that the increase is in any species of geometrical progression.

———————

We have hitherto considered the laws of the increase of human population, as originating from one or more pairs of grown up persons. We have now to contemplate mankind as they are found existing upon the earth;—as if they were beings but recently discovered by the philosopher. In this view, the origin of nations is lost in the mist of antiquity; and, we presume, it will be granted us, resting, as we must do, on the authority of profane history, that we have no conclusive evidence, whether the number of the inhabitants of the globe is greater or less now, than it was 2000 years ago. Of the whole population we observe only a small portion, and that for a very limited period of time.

Could we take an exact census of a populous nation, we should find it materially different in its construction from the enumeration of an infant colony, or the tabular genealogy from primitive progenitors. The multitude of human beings, whose origin is lost in history and who seem as it were indigenous to the soil, is composed of persons of every age from the moment of birth to the point of dissolution, including, in general, a period of about 100 years, that being the term which may ordinarily be considered as the extreme limit of human life. How many of these were born at every particular minute, hour, or day of the century immediately preceding the census, it is practically impossible to determine. The only Tables of any value on this subject are the population-lists of Sweden ; for there has never been a census in any other country on which there could be placed the least dependence, or from which any useful consequence could be drawn.

The population of Sweden, of which there have been frequent enumerations during the last 60 years, appears to be increasing, but certainly in no ratio approaching to geometrical. The irregularity of the increase is extreme, and occasionally we find a considerable diminution. How much of the increase may be attributed to a greater accuracy in taking the censuses, and how much of the irregularity may arise from the variations in its political boundaries, we must leave to the determination of the statesmen of that country. It is sufficient to say that they continually complain of the want of population. Our present business however is not with the increase itself, but with the law of that increase.

The following table is formed from the censuses for 9 years from 1755 to 1763 inclusive. Though it exhibits an increase, the population about that period may be considered as having

been nearly stationary [h] ; and certainly not increasing, if we keep in view the necessity of a
fund to supply the waste occasioned by those
unexpected convulsions of society, and calamities
of nature, which history records as having so
often retarded and diminished the population of
kingdoms.

---

[h] See the remarks of Dr. Price in Appendix to Chapters IV, V,
VI. p. 192, 193.

Population of Sweden in 1757, 1760, and 1763, the births being in each case the average of the 3 preceding years.

Age	Living in 1757			Living in 1760			Living in 1763		
	Males	Females	In all	Males	Females	In all	Males	Females	In all
Born	44,795	42,999	87,794	44,174	42,331	86,505	45,892	43,904	89,796
Under 1 yr.	33,731	33,459	67,190	37,323	37,272	74,595	36,094	35,453	71,547
1 to 3	63,954	64,883	128,837	66,034	66,860	132,894	66,059	67,234	133,293
3 — 5	64,380	65,045	129,425	65,828	66,923	132,751	66,464	67,701	134,165
5 — 10	123,984	125,175	249,159	128,627	129,332	257,959	130,019	130,758	260,777
10 — 15	114,605	114,203	228,808	119,514	121,525	241,039	126,696	128,021	254,717
15 — 20	95,254	100,087	195,341	97,621	101,633	199,254	108,312	109,985	218,297
20 — 25	91,460	104,873	196,333	88,752	103,613	192,365	92,299	105,115	197,414
25 — 30	86,947	99,780	186,727	85,001	100,614	185,615	88,056	101,003	189,059
30 — 35	82,716	90,880	173,596	81,432	92,153	173,585	85,936	95,811	181,747
35 — 40	68,516	75,563	144,079	70,773	79,066	149,839	74,826	81,453	156,279
40 — 45	58,990	65,443	124,433	61,158	68,645	129,803	67,448	74,854	142,302
45 — 50	50,658	58,162	108,820	59,339	51,407	110,746	52,398	59,551	111,949
50 — 55	43,500	51,973	95,473	43,807	51,872	95,769	47,298	56,646	103,944
55 — 60	39,091	48,599	87,690	37,224	46,402	83,626	37,086	45,537	82,623
60 — 65	29,557	39,580	69,137	32,329	42,647	74,976	34,892	44,925	79,817
65 — 70	22,293	33,559	55,852	21,438	30,169	51,607	20,649	28,964	49,613
70 — 75	16,390	24,913	41,303	15,102	25,299	40,401	15,454	23,159	38,613
75 — 80	9,236	14,679	23,915	9,096	14,265	23,361	8,858	13,556	22,414
80 — 85	4,060	6,786	10,846	4,418	7,337	11,755	4,620	7,487	12,107
85 — 90	1,690	2,932	4,622	1,513	2,571	4,084	1,508	2,694	4,202
above 90	583	1,026	1,609	555	1,019	1,574	527	988	1,515
	1,101,595	1,221,600	2,323,195	1,121,053	1,246,545	2,367,598	1,165,489	1,280,905	2,446,394

Table averaged from the preceding, together with the proportions calculated to a population of 10,000.

Ages of Living	Average of 9 years, from preceding Table	Proportioned to a population of 10,000
Births	88,032	370
Under 5 years.	334,899	1,408
5　to　10	255,965	1,076
10 — 15	241,521	1,015
15 — 20	204,297	859
20 — 25	195,371	821
25 — 30	187,134	785
30 — 35	176,309	741
35 — 40	150,066	631
40 — 45	132,180	556
45 — 50	110,505	464
50 — 55	98,395	414
55 — 60	84,646	356
60 — 65	74,643	314
65 — 70	52,357	220
70 — 75	40,106	169
75 — 80	23,230	98
80 — 85	11,569	49
85 — 90	4,303	18
above 90	1,566	6
Population	2,379,062	10,000

These Tables are formed from the comparison of 9 years; but, did they represent the average of centuries, they would then give us a fair view of the progress and waste of human life, in the state and climate of Sweden. We will suppose that they do so.

It appears then that 370 annual births are just sufficient to keep up a population of 10,000 persons. These 370 (or 1850 in 5 years) constitute a population of 1408, under 5 years of age, who are renewed by the births as they grow older or die. These 1408 are reduced by deaths to 1076 between the ages of 5 and 10, who are again reduced to 1015, being the number living between 10 and 15. In the same manner, from the continual supply by births and reductions by deaths, the different numbers of every age, making up the whole population, are regularly kept up throughout the century, which here appears to be the limit of the age of man. In actual existence these numbers will vary above or below the numbers of the Table, which are here given as an average proportion of a society of little or no increase.

The supply of this society is by children in nonage. The 370 annually born are expanded so as to keep up all the ranks of the different ages of which the 10,000 population consists; and for that purpose it matters not whether they be produced by the whole, or by a part of the tribe,—or whether they drop from the clouds.

In fact however these children are brought into the world by the child-bearing females. The period, during which women are capable of child-bearing is, in few cases, above 20 years,—rarely more than 25. Early marriages seem to produce no difference in this respect; because, the sooner they begin, the sooner they cease to be prolific. The whole range in Europe is between 15 and 45; and, in taking the numbers from the table, it matters little whether we count them between 15 and 40, or between 20 and 45: the amount is not materially different. Polygamy is not allowed in Sweden; and therefore these 370 children may be considered as produced by not more than the number of the population between 20 and 45; that is, by 3534 married persons. It will signify nothing that the husbands are occasionally of other ages, for the number (3534) would not thereby be increased: the females of these ages only being capable of child-bearing. Of these 3534, a proportion of women (diseased from birth or by after accidents) are never fitted for marriage; and it will therefore be no extravagant assertion to say that the married persons in this society will never exceed 3000, if ever they amount to that number. These 3000 persons then are the ever-during source from which this society flows. Their children fill up the vacancies of death, and recruit the ranks of propagators as they are invalided by age; but all the females, and a number equal to

all the males, above 45 years old, cease to be
useful in the continuation of the race. There
are 2108 persons above the age of 45 ; and if we
add to these the number who are too diseased
for marrying (of which we supposed 534 between
20 and 45) and the number of children, who,
though counted with the others, are doomed
never to swell the list of real propagators, we
speak within bounds when we assert, that of
these 10,000 persons, there are 3000 who are
useless in the work of procreation. These 3000
—more or less, according to healthy or unhealthy seasons,—form the fluctuating balance
of what would otherwise be a permanent population. The 370 children annually born, contain among their number the proportion neces
sary to keep up these 3000 useless adjuncts to
the hive : and, though all the 3000 were to
perish in a morning, so as to reduce the society
to 7000, the effective propagators would remain,
the births would continue the same, and the
3000 would gradually be renewed like the sever-
ed limbs of the polypus. As an example, we
will suppose that the 2108 persons above 45
years of age are all destroyed by accident or design. Their gradual renewal will be apparent
from the following Table :

Years.	Born.	Under 5.	5 to 10.	10 to 15.	15 to 20.	20 to 25.	25 to 30.	30 to 35.	35 to 40.	40 to 45.	45 to 50.	50 to 55.	55 to 60.	60 to 65.	65 to 70.	70 to 75.	75 to 80.	80 to 85.	85 to 90.	Above 90.	All the living.
0	1850	1408	1076	1015	859	821	785	741	631	556	—	—	—	—	—	—	—	—	—	—	7892
5	1850	1408	1076	1015	859	821	785	741	631	556	464	—	—	—	—	—	—	—	—	—	8856
10	1850	1408	1076	1015	859	821	785	741	631	556	464	414	—	—	—	—	—	—	—	—	8770
15	1850	1408	1076	1015	859	821	785	741	631	556	464	414	356	—	—	—	—	—	—	—	9126
20	1850	1408	1076	1015	859	821	785	741	631	556	464	414	356	314	—	—	—	—	—	—	9440
25	1850	1408	1076	1015	859	821	785	741	631	556	464	414	356	314	220	—	—	—	—	—	9660
30	1850	1408	1076	1015	859	821	785	741	631	556	464	414	356	314	220	169	—	—	—	—	9829
35	1850	1408	1076	1015	859	821	785	741	631	556	464	414	356	314	220	169	98	—	—	—	9927
40	1850	1408	1076	1015	859	821	785	741	631	556	464	414	356	314	220	169	98	49	—	—	9976
45	1850	1408	1076	1015	859	821	785	741	631	556	464	414	356	314	220	169	98	49	18	—	9994
50	1850	1408	1076	1015	859	821	785	741	631	556	464	414	356	314	220	169	98	49	18	6	10,000
55	1850	1408	1076	1015	859	821	785	741	631	556	464	414	356	314	220	169	98	49	18	6	10,000

From the foregoing table we find that, although we destroyed more than a fifth of the population, the whole are created anew in the course of 50 years. The 10,000 inhabitants are again brought forward, and the society ceases to have any further increase. If, in addition to the 2108 persons here cut off, all the diseased and inefficient had been likewise exterminated, the society would have been reduced to less than 7000. The apparent number of propagators would have thus been lessened, but the births would not therefore have been fewer; and in a certain number of years, as in the present case, every chasm would have been filled, and the original number of 10,000 human beings would have been brought again, and in the same order, to our view. There may therefore happen to be very extensive variations in the census of a society, in the germ of which there is no principle of permanent increase. They are precisely those adventitious beings who increase with favourable years, and who, when unfavourable seasons arrive, swell by clusters the bills of mortality. A series of seasons unfavourable to the vegetable productions of the earth, is also unfavourable to human life, particularly to that of the infirm and the aged. These die of disease, not of famine: for, except in the nauseous and hidden dens of a crowded and selfish metropolis, where man lies unseen and unpitied, there are comparatively few in Europe who perish of hunger. Of the

T

3000 who are old or diseased, two or three un-
genial seasons may sweep two thirds from the
earth. These two thirds are a fifth of the whole
population, and would leave a mighty blank in
the census of a nation. We see however that
this blank would be rapidly filled up, and a return of genial years might make them even
more numerous than they had previously been.

If, in the society which we have taken for our
example, we were to suppose that all those who
reached the age of 45 were to exist a thousand
years, while the law of population remained
otherwise the same, the elders of the society
would continue to increase during these ten centuries, when, after having risen to a number which
we will not now stay to calculate, the increase
would again come to a stand, and the census of
the nation would afterwards remain stationary.

Again : keeping in view our table of 10,000,
let us suppose a colony of 3837 persons, male
and female, between the ages of 15 and 40
(which we will take for the marriageable ages in
a new country), and in such proportions as they
are found in Europe. Let them be from Sweden, and be possessed of only the Swedish
powers of propagation. These persons then, being the exact numbers in our table of 10,000,
will form the nidus of a race, in the same manner as the persons at the outset of the immediately preceding Table; except that, until their
children arrive at the age of 15, the propagators

not being supplied by their growing successors, would diminish in numbers for a certain time. To remedy this, let there be an immigration, for the first 15 years, of 172 annually, or about a twenty-second part of the original colonists, which 172 will exactly keep up the number of our first column (those between 15 and 20) as they waste by age and death. The following table will shew the progress of the colony for the first 15 years :

Year of colony.	Born.	Under 5.	5 to 10.	10 to 15.	15 to 20.	20 to 25.	25 to 30.	30 to 35.	35 to 40.	40 to 45.	45 to 50.	50 to 55.	55 to 60.	60 to 65.	65 to 70.	70 to 75.	75 to 80.	80 to 85.	85 to 90.	Above 90.	Number of living.
0	1850				859	821	785	741	631												3837
5	1850	1408			859	821	785	741	631	556											5801
10	1850	1408	1076		859	821	785	741	631	556	464										7341
15	1850	1408	1076	1015	859	821	785	741	631	556	464	414									8770

At the end of these 15 years, the number of
the propagators will be continued the same, by
means of the grown up children, without further
importation. The society now exhibits an extraordinary increase. The original settlers were
3837, and the annual immigrants amount altogether to 2580. The latter however, as far as propagation is concerned, may be reckoned at only
half that number, because on an average they
have lived only $7\frac{1}{2}$ years in the colony. About
5000 propagators then have, in 15 years, increased their number by nearly 3000 additional
human beings, independent of those that have
been lost by death. It may be remarked too,
that we took our colonists from the general
mass between 15 and 40, which included the
blind and the maimed, the diseased and the dying. But such persons do not emigrate: and
this increased population might have sprung
from a colony much less numerous than what
we have here stated. In taking a census therefore of an infant colony, we need not wonder
that it should double its numbers in a very short
period. The emigrants, who arrive in small
numbers afterwards, are less observed than the
primitive founders; and it is extremely probable
that many such establishments may double their
numbers, apparently from propagation alone, in
less than 20 years. The principle however on
which this duplication rests, escapes the eye of
the common observer. The colony is not a society in the sense which we understand of a na-

tion. It is the first expansion of a set of picked propagators, without parents and without children, which two classes, together with the diseased and ineffective, constitute nearly three-fourths of the population of modern Europe. It is the body of the polypus without its limbs, which its inherent energies are able to renew. Till these are completed, the increase will continue. If our colony have no further accession of immigrants, it will increase until it muster its number of 10,000, after which it will continue permanent. Mr. Malthus catches the polypus in the middle of its growth;—he measures the length of limbs already attained, and, comparing these with time, he forms a ratio of increase, in which, he asserts, they will expand for ever !

A careful census of our 15 years' colony will give ample evidence that it increases solely because it is a society that is incomplete. In an indigenous society there are nearly a fourth of its numbers above 45 years of age. Here there are only 878 out of 8770, or about a tenth of the population. The higher ages,—the extremities of the polypus,—are not yet formed; neither, if immigration were continued, would they ever be. Of this the American censuses give sufficient proof. In none of the United States is the number of persons above 45 more than from 16 to 17 *per cent.* of the population, while in many of the newly settled districts they do not exceed 7 or 8, as will appear more particularly in the following table.

Proportion of white inhabitants, above and below the age of 45, (to a population of 10,000) in the different districts and territories of the United States of America in 1810, compared with the kingdom of Sweden from 1755 to 1763.

	Under 45.	Above 45.
Sweden	7892	2108
District of Maine	8867	1133
———— Massachussets	8391	1609
———— N. Hampshire	8610	1390
———— Vermont	8964	1036
———— Rhode Island	8387	1613
———— Connecticut	8308	1692
———— New York	8904	1096
———— New Jersey	8629	1371
———— Pennsylvania	8757	1243
———— Delaware	8961	1039
———— Maryland	8710	1290
———— Virginia	8771	1229
———— Ohio	9097	903
———— Kentucky	9044	956
———— N. Carolina	8895	1105
———— East Tennessee	9003	997
———— West Tennessee	9195	805
———— South Carolina	8963	1037
———— Georgia	9060	940
———— Columbia	8944	1056
Territory of Orleans	8833	1167
———— Mississippi	9210	790
———— Louisiana	9113	887
———— Indiana	9197	803
———— Illinois	9201	799
———— Michigan	8983	1017

Resting, as Mr. Malthus has done, the whole of the proof of his geometrical ratio on the censuses of the United States, it must be acknowledged that he has by no means stretched his evidence beyond what it would bear. The increase in the population of the new colonies between 1800 and 1810 is such as almost to stagger belief. The following Table is extracted from the censuses, but arranged so as best to elucidate our observations.

White inhabitants in Kentucky, Tennessee, Mississippi and Indiana in 1800 and in 1810.

	1800			1810			Ratio of increase in 10 yrs.
	Under 10 yrs.	Above 10 yrs.	In all	Under 10 yrs.	Above 10 yrs.	In all	
Kentucky	72,223	107,653	179,876	125,910	198,327	324,237	1.8
Tennessee	37,677	54,032	91,709	86,304	129,571	215,875	2.35
Mississippi	1,952	3,227	5,179	8,232	14,792	23,024	4.44
Indiana	1,645	2,932	4,577	9,478	14,412	23,890	5.21
Total	113,497	167,844	281,341	229,924	357,102	587,026	2.08

Here we have a population of 281,341 persons, which more than doubles its numbers in 10 years, while one division of this population is increased, within that period, to more than 5 times its original amount. These are ratios of which Mr. Malthus might boast, but of which he has not boasted.

When enumerations are taken every 10 years, it is obvious, exclusive of immigration, that in any particular census the persons living above 10 years of age must have all existed in the census immediately preceding. In that of 1810 for instance, all above 10 years formed part of the population of 1800 ; and are in reality the same, except inasmuch as they are diminished by death. Those under 10 have all been born in the interval between the censuses.

The whole population of 1800 in the preceding Table was 281,341. These in 10 years would be diminished to 200,000, under the most favourable laws that have hitherto been observed of human mortality :—but the number of persons above 10 years of age in 1810 were found to be 357,102; and therefore it is clear to a demonstration that this society must have been recruited by more than 160,000 immigrants: for, of these immigrants themselves many must have died, and besides, some of those under 10 years of age, may have been born in other countries

It may be said, and perhaps with truth, that many of these immigrants may have been from other parts of the United States, and not from Europe : but, comparing in the same manner the whole of the American census we shall find an astonishing extent of immigration : The white population of 1800 was 4,305,971. These in 10 years would be diminished by a fourth. It is very improbable that more than 3,200,000 would have been alive in 1810, for whatever proportion the births of that country may bear to the whole population, the proportion of deaths is certainly greater than in Europe.

These 3,200,000 then should have constituted the number of those above 10 years of age in the census of 1810, had there been no importation from other countries. But the actual census above 10 years of age was 3,845,389, giving a surplus of 645,389, which can be accounted for in no other way than by immigration The census of 1810 contains also 2,016,704 children under 10 years. Part of these too, as well as the deaths of immigrants since their arrival, should be added to the 645,389 above stated; and therefore of the 1,556,122 persons, which the census of 1810 exhibits beyond that of 1800, it is as clear as sunshine that nearly one half was added by direct immigration. Of the effects on the increase of population by the introduction of grown-up persons we have already spoken; and, adverting to these effects along with the statements now given, the additional population is completely accounted for, without supposing a power of procreation beyond what is found to prevail among European nations.

But it is needless to dwell longer on this part of the subject, for he, who will attentively examine the statistical tables of the United States, will discover in every line a marked distinction between them and those of Europe. At every step they announce a race, who, as has been supposed of their country, have but lately emerged from the waves. America has more resemblance to a camp than to a nation. Its in habitants are a band of adventurers, continually recruited by men like themselves, who seek for conquests in a new world, and have left their parents to perish on a distant shore. It is in vain therefore to look to that country for a geometrical or any other regulated increase of population. Immigration must cease for centuries, before such a law could be there developed, even allowing it to belong to human nature.

But it may be asked, if a colony were constituted of persons of all ages, such as they exist in Europe, and were the proportion of births raised in a great degree by the removal of the present checks to population, might not the inhabitants increase in a geometrical ratio, and double their numbers in 25 years? This is the only question that remains to be considered, and its discussion will close the present Dissertation.

In order to have a clear view of this proposition, we shall again refer to our Table of 10,000 which we proportioned from the Swedish population [a]. We must also remind our readers that this Table was formed from a society of little or no increase. We have already considered this society as stationary; but, whether so or not, it is equally effective for the sake of illustration.

We have before observed that the waste of these 10,000 is replaced by the 370 annual births; and that this perpetual flow of children

---

a Vide page 268.

successively fills up the ranks of the race, as
they are thinned by the hand of death. Where
man is indigenous, these are the gradations of
society; and, before it could be doubled, we
must have two for one of every age from the
cradle to the tomb. Now, by what means are
these additional human beings to be brought
upon the stage of life in 10, 15, or even in 25
years? Imagination may add birth to birth at
pleasure, but how shall our old men and old
women be so rapidly created, unless we can
close the gates of death, and hasten the flight
of time? Were we indeed to attend to numbers only, without regard to age, we might easily conceive an abundant increase; but it does
not therefore follow that this imaginary increase
must proceed in a geometrical progression.

Supposing that from some extraordinary for-
tuitous circumstances,—from an increase in the
genial powers of nature, or from a particular in-
terposition of Providence,—the females of our
little society were all at once to become doubly
prolific; and that thereby the annual births were
to be double what they now are, or 740 in
place of 370. It is plain that these additional 370
annual children would, independent of their own
progeny, form a new race, the exact counterpart of the old; and that the whole of the society would be thereby doubled in about 100
years. Were the original stock alone to be propagators, we should thus have an addition of

10,000 every century, being an increase in the ratio of 1, 2, 3, 4, &c. But at the end of 20 years (taking an average period) as many as remain alive of the 370 additional children that were born in the first year, will arrive at the marriageable age. The next, and every succeeding year, a like number will be added to the list of propagators, and will become the parents of a new race. The children of these last will become parents in their turn, thus engrafting a succession of scions, one upon the other, and all originally springing from a parent tree. Instead then of a geometrical ratio the period of duplication would be continually lessening, as the several scions were added to the stock. Supposing the new propagators to have the same prolific power that we have given to their progenitors, it would require 40 years for the first doubling, and about 30 for each of the two succeeding ones; and this period would become less and less, through a series of a very complicated form, though it would never be under 25 years. Besides, these duplications would be numerical only; for the numbers of the early ages would go on in an increasing ratio, but there would not be the same proportion of increase among those of riper years. We have calculated the progress of that series, but the Tables are too extended to be conveniently inserted in this place.

It is in vain to look for a geometrical ratio in the increase of any society, unless the society were originally constituted in that progression.

Assuming the females between 20 and 45
years of age to be the only source from which
the continuance of the race can be derived,
the series which would denote the varying numbers of those females, in the order of time,
would also denote the law of increase in the
censuses of the tribe or nation. All the females
now existing between 20 and 45 will be gradually erased from the list, by superannuation or
by death, in the space of 25 years. Their place
will be filled by others; and if the number of
the new mothers be not then double what they
now are, we may rest assured that the society
does not exhibit a permanent principle of increase, in the ratio and in the time prescribed by
Mr. Malthus. Had it been the order of Nature
that the human race should have originally been
arranged in a geometrical progression; had the
law been such that every year the births should
have increased in a fixed proportion to the preceding;—had the number of the living at every
succeeding age been increased in the same manner and in the same proportion: and, had the
whole frame of society been so constituted that
the child-bearing females should, by this regular succession of the inferior ages, have doubled
their numbers at equal periods, such as every
25 years;—then, and then only, could a geometrical ratio of the increase of population have
existed. But mankind have never been found
so arranged, and the laws that regulate the succession of human beings do not seem to be of

that feeble texture, which would warrant us in predicting that what has never been will ever be.

On the whole it is obvious that the assertion, that human population has a tendency to increase in a geometrical ratio, is, in the utmost degree, arbitrary. It is the mere *dictum* of Mr. Malthus, and when he finds, as he always does, that this ratio of increase has not hitherto acted, instead of doubting, as he ought, the truth of his hypothesis, he looks around for concomitant circumstances which, he says, have retarded or destroyed its operation: that is, for circumstances which have retarded or destroyed the operation of a principle, of which he has brought no evidence that it ever existed. But he even gives these retarding circumstances themselves as evidence. He calls them checks upon population, before he has proved that population required such checks. " There exist vice and misery in the world ; therefore these prevent mankind from doubling their number every 25 years !" Such is the reasoning.—The point in dispute is always taken for granted.

Were we to draw our inferences from a survey of the world and its history, we should come to no such conclusion as the principle of an unlimited increase. Man is individually a transient visitor of the earth. A few revolutions of the sun, and this proud being is thrust from the scene. Is the race then permanent? Many species of animals have disappeared, and fill our cabinets with their fossil remains. The mammuth no longer ranges over the globe, though for a time he must have lived with extensive power. What vice, misery or moral restraint has prevented the unlimited increase of the eagles in the air, or of the sharks in the ocean, where they reign paramount lords and masters? May not the law of increase—may not the duration of life itself diminish as it radiates from the primeval stock? Something of this kind is observed in vegetables, whose qualities deteriorate, and whose seeds more and more degenerate as they are distant from the parent tree. So far from having to frighten ourselves with the idea of an overwhelming population, have we not rather to fear that we are sinking by degrees into a degenerate race, which in the lapse of time may be swept from the globe? The earth itself is probably not immortal, and why should its puny inhabitants? All these, to be sure, are questions of mere possibilities, but they are as probable and as demonstrable, as the possibilities of Mr. Malthus. If the terms of the proposition do not involve a contradiction, there is no assertion, with regard to future contingencies, that can be proved to be untrue. But possibilities are inhabitants of the land of dreams. They may amuse in the closet, but they are useless in the conduct of life; and ought to be far beneath the notice of the legislators of nations.

TABLES

OF THE

AMERICAN CENSUS.

——

THAT the reader may be fully possessed of all the documents which should enable him to form correct notions on the subject, I have thought proper to insert here the Three Tables of the American Census, as they appear in Pitkin's Statistical View of the United States. I should have been glad to have printed from the Tables published by the authority of the American government; but I have been able to procure only those for 1810.

W. G.

TABLE No. 1.

Census of the Inhabitants of the United States in August, 1790.

	Free white males of 16 years and upwards.	Free white males under 16 years.	Free white females.	All other free persons	Slaves.	Total.
Vermont	22,435	22,328	40,505	255	16	85,539
New-Hampshire	36,086	34,851	70,160	630	158	141,885
Maine	24,384	24,748	46,870	538	none	96,540
Massachusetts	95,453	87,289	190,582	5,463	none	378,787
Rhode-Island	16,019	15,799	32,652	3,407	948	68,825
Connecticut	60,523	54,403	117,448	2,808	2,764	237,946
New-York	83,700	78,122	152,320	4,654	21,324	340,120
New-Jersey	45,251	41,416	83,287	2,762	11,423	184,139
Pennsylvania	110,788	106,948	206,363	6,537	3,737	434,373
Delaware	11,783	12,143	22,384	3,899	8,887	59,094
Maryland	55,915	51,339	101,395	8,043	103,036	319,728
Virginia	110,936	116,135	215,046	12,866	292,627	747,610
North-Carolina	69,988	77,506	140,710	4,975	100,571	393,751
South-Carolina	35,576	37,722	66,880	1,801	107,094	249,073
Georgia	13,103	14,044	25,739	398	29,264	82,548
Kentucky	15,154	17,057	28,922	114	12,430	73,677
Territory of the United States N. W. of river Ohio	6,271	10,277	15,365	361	3,417	35,691
					697,696	3,929,326

TABLE II.

Enumeration of persons in the several Districts of the United States in August 1800.

Names of Districts.	FREE WHITE MALES.					FREE WHITE FEMALES.					All other free persons except Indians not taxed.	Slaves.	Total.
	Under ten years of age.	Of 10 and under 16.	Of 16 and under 26, including heads of families.	Of 26 and under 45, including heads of families.	Of 45 and upwards, including heads of families,	Under 10 years of age.	Of 10 and under 16.	Of 16 and under 26, including heads of families.	Of 26 and under 45, includins heads of families.	Of 45 and upwards, including heads of families.			
New-Hampshire -	30,694	14,881	16,379	17,589	11,715	29,871	14,193	17,163	18,381	12,142	852	8	183,858
Massachusetts -	63,646	32,507	37,905	39,729	31,348	60,920	30,674	40,491	43,833	35,340	6,462	—	422,845
Maine -	27,970	12,305	12,900	15,318	8,339	26,599	11,338	13,295	14,496	8,041	818	—	151,719
Connecticut -	37,946	19,408	21,683	23,180	18,976	35,736	18,218	23,561	25,186	20,827	5,330	951	251,002
Vermont -	29,420	12,046	13,242	16,544	8,076	28,272	11,366	12,606	15,287	7,049	557	—	154,465
Rhode-Island -	9,945	5,352	5,889	5,785	4,887	9,524	5,026	6,463	6,919	5,648	3,304	380	69,122
New-York -	33,161	36,953	40,045	52,454	25,497	79,154	32,822	39,086	47,710	23,161	8,573	15,602	484,065
Supplemental return for New-York state }	16,936	7,320	9,230	9,140	6,358	16,319	6,649	9,030	8,701	5,490	1,801	5,011	101,985
New-Jersey -	33,900	15,859	16,301	19,956	12,629	32,622	14,827	17,018	19,533	11,600	4,402	12,422	211,149
Eastern District of Pennsylvania }	52,767	24,438	29,393	33,864	20,824	51,176	23,427	29,879	30,892	19,329	12,253	557	327,979
Western district of Pennsylvania }	50,459	21,623	24,669	25,469	17,761	48,448	20,362	24,095	22,954	14,066	3,311	1,149	274,566
Delaware -	8,250	4,437	5,121	5,012	2,213	7,628	4,277	5,543	4,981	2,390	8,268	6,153	64,273

TABLE No. II.—CONTINUED.

Names of Districts.	FREE WHITE MALES.					FREE WHITE FEMALES.					All other free persons except Indians not taxed.	Slaves.	Total.
	Under 10 years of age.	Of 10 and under 16.	Of 16 and under 26, including heads of families.	Of 26 and under 45, including heads of families.	Of 45 and upwards, including heads of families.	Under 10 years of age.	Of 10 and under 16.	Of 16 and under 26, including heads of families.	Of 26 and under 45, including heads of families.	Of 45 and upwards, including heads of families.			
Maryland, inclusive of Washington county, in Columbia	36,751	17,743	21,929	23,553	13,712	34,703	16,787	22,915	21,725	12,180	19,987	107,707	349,692
Additional return for Baltimore county	567	226	318	343	249	571	222	375	318	199	41	847	4,276
Eastern district of Virginia	57,837	25,998	32,444	34,588	19,087	54,597	25,469	34,807	32,641	18,851	18,194	322,199	676,682
District of Columbia, in Virginia	889	320	483	557	221	670	313	479	473	189	383	1,172	5,949
Western district of Virginia	34,601	14,502	16,264	15,674	11,134	32,726	13,366	15,923	8,639	15,169	1,930	23,537	203,518
North-Carolina	63,118	27,073	31,560	31,209	18,688	59,074	25,874	32,999	30,665	17,514	7,043	133,296	478,103
South-Carolina	37,411	16,156	17,761	19,344	10,244	34,664	15,857	18,145	17,236	9,437	3,185	146,151	345,591
Georgia	19,841	8,469	9,787	10,914	4,937	18,407	7,914	9,243	8,835	3,894	1,919	59,699	162,686
Kentucky	37,274	14,045	15,705	17,699	9,238	34,949	13,433	15,624	14,934	7,075	741	40,343	220,956
Territory N. W. river Ohio	9,362	3,647	4,636	4,833	1,955	8,644	3,353	3,861	3,342	1,395	337	—	45,365
Indiana territory	651	347	466	645	262	791	280	424	393	115	163	135	5,641
Mississippi territory	999	356	482	780	290	963	376	352	426	165	182	3,489	8,850
Tennessee	19,227	7,194	8,282	8,352	4,125	18,450	7,042	8,554	6,992	3,491	309	13,584	105,602

Grand Total, 5,309,768

TABLE No. III.

Aggregate amount of each description of Persons within the United States of America, and the Territories thereof, agreeably to actual enumeration made according to law, in the year 1810.

Names of the Districts and Territories	FREE WHITE MALES					FREE WHITE FEMALES					All other free persons except Indians not taxed	Slaves	Totals in each district
	Under 10 years of age.	Of 10 and under 16.	Of 16 and under 26, including heads of families.	Of 26 and under 45, including heads of families.	Of 45 and upwards, including heads of families.	Under 10 years of age.	Of 10 and under 16.	Of 16 and under 26, including heads of families.	Of 26 and under 45, including heads of families.	Of 45 and upwards, including heads of families.			
Dist. of Maine	41,273	18,463	20,403	22,079	13,291	39,131	17,827	21,290	21,464	12,515	969	108	228,705
Massachusetts	68,930	34,964	45,018	45,854	34,976	66,881	33,091	46,366	49,229	39,894	6,737	—	472,040
N. Hampshire	34,284	17,840	18,865	20,531	14,462	32,313	17,259	20,792	21,940	15,204	970	—	214,460
Vermont	38,082	18,347	19,678	20,791	13,053	36,621	17,341	20,983	20,792	11,457	750	—	217,895
Rhode-Island	10,735	5,554	7,250	6,765	5,439	10,555	5,389	7,520	7,635	6,372	3,609	108	76,931
Connecticut	37,812	20,498	23,880	23,699	20,484	35,913	18,931	24,973	26,293	22,696	6,453	310	261,942
New-York	165,933	73,702	85,779	94,882	53,985	157,945	68,811	85,139	85,805	46,718	25,333	15,017	959,049
New-Jersey	37,814	18,914	21,231	21,394	16,004	36,062	17,787	21,194	21,359	16,109	7,843	10,851	245,562
Pennsylvania	138,464	62,606	74,203	74,193	52,100	131,769	60,943	75,960	70,826	45,740	22,492	795	810,091
Delaware	9,632	4,480	5,150	5,866	2,878	9,041	4,370	5,541	5,527	2,876	13,136	4,177	72,674
Maryland	38,613	18,489	22,688	25,255	15,165	36,137	17,833	23,875	22,908	14,154	33,927	111,502	380,546
Virginia	97,777	42,919	51,473	52,567	35,302	90,715	42,207	54,899	51,163	32,512	30,570	392,518	974,622
Ohio	46,623	18,119	20,189	22,761	11,965	44,192	16,869	19,990	19,436	8,717	1,899	—	230,760
Kentucky	65,134	26,804	29,772	29,553	17,542	60,776	25,743	29,511	25,920	13,482	1,713	80,561	406,511

} 700,745

TABLE No. III.—CONTINUED.

Names of the Districts and Territories.	FREE WHITE MALES.					FREE WHITE FEMALES.					All other free persons except Indians not taxed.	Slaves.	Totals in each district	Total in the territories.
	Under 10 years of age.	Of 10 and under 16.	Of 16 and under 26, including heads of families.	Of 26 and under 45, including heads of families.	Of 45 and upwards, including heads of families.	Under 10 years of age.	Of 10 and under 16.	Of 16 and under 26, including heads of families.	Of 26 and under 45, including heads of families.	Of 45 and upwards, including heads of families.				
Dist. of N. Carolina	68,036	30,321	34,630	34,456	21,189	65,421	30,063	37,933	33,944	20,427	10,266	168,824	555,500	
East Tennessee	18,392	7,618	8,266	7,539	4,998	17,416	7,216	8,559	7,348	4,129	510	9,376	101,367	
West Tennessee	26,102	9,552	11,220	12,418	5,658	24,394	9,113	11,305	10,276	4,356	807	35,159	160,360	
South-Carolina	39,669	17,193	20,933	20,488	11,304	37,497	16,629	20,583	18,974	10,926	4,554	196,365	415,115	
Georgia	28,002	11,951	14,085	14,372	7,435	26,283	11,237	13,461	12,350	6,238	1,801	105,218	252,433	261,721
Ter. of Orleans	5,848	2,491	2,963	5,130	2,508	5,384	2,588	2,874	3,026	1,499	7,585	34,660	76,556	
Mississippi	4,217	1,637	2,692	3,160	1,144	4,015	1,544	2,187	1,753	675	240	17,088	40,352	
Louisiana	3,438	1,345	1,568	2,069	967	3,213	1,265	1,431	1,369	562	607	3,011	20,845	
Indiana	4,923	1,922	2,564	2,316	1,125	4,555	1,863	2,228	1,880	794	393	237	24,520	
Illinois	2,356	945	1,274	1,339	556	2,019	791	1,053	894	364	613	168	12,282	
Michigan	800	351	583	763	340	640	332	368	311	130	120	24	4,762	
Dist. of Columbia	2,479	1,158	1,530	2,107	866	2,538	1,192	1,653	1,734	832	2,549	5,395	24,023	
	1,035,278	468,183	547,507	572,347	364,736	981,426	448,324	561,668	544,156	338,378	186,446	1,191,364	7,239,903	

Total in the U. States, 7,036,562

Total in the territories. 203,340

Grand Total, 7,239,903

ENQUIRY

CONCERNING

POPULATION.

BOOK III.

OF THE CAUSES BY WHICH THE AMOUNT OF THE NUM-BERS OF MANKIND IS REDUCED OR RESTRAINED.

CHAPTER I.

FUTILITY OF MR. MALTHUS'S DOCTRINE RE-SPECTING THE CHECKS ON POPULATION.

IN the preceding Book I have taken for the subject of my enquiry the possible progress of mankind under peculiarly favourable circumstances, as to the increase of their numbers. I have produced the example of Sweden, as the most advantageous specimen of the kind that is contained in the records of history. I have not contented myself with this, but have proceeded

in the endeavour to establish certain principles
on the subject.   From the example of Sweden,
corroborated by views drawn from all other
countries of Europe, in which any progress has
been made in collecting Tables that have reference to population, I have sought to fix certain
maxims which may be of use to guide us in our
speculations on the subject.   To this I have
added some general reasonings, built upon the
nature of marriage, and the numbers and fruitfulness of human females, calculated to confirm
these facts, and to shew from the nature of
things why they should be found such as they
are.

But there is another question behind, which
will be of scarcely less importance in enabling us
to settle our opinions on the subject of this
work.   This is (to borrow the language of Mr.
Malthus), " What is it that checks population ?"

Or, I should rather chuse to express the enquiry upon which I am about to enter thus :

Population has been found, under peculiarly
favourable circumstances, for example in Sweden, to have a tendency to double itself in a little more than one hundred years.   But the
history of the world is not in accord with the
example of Sweden.   We have no reason to
suppose that the globe of the earth, at least so
far as it was then known, was at all less populous three thousand years ago, than it is now.

The inference therefore, in the point of view

in which we are here considering the subject, is, first, from the example of Sweden, that population, or the numbers of mankind, has a natural tendency to increase under particularly favourable circumstances, at the rate of a doubling in a little more than one hundred years; and, secondly, from the history of the world, that this increase is perpetually counteracted, so that we have no reason to believe that the earth is now more populous than at any past period of authentic history, or, from any thing that is at present going on on the face of the globe, that it has any likelihood to become so.

Population is kept down. This truth we learn from the history of mankind: and in this proposition I agree with Mr. Malthus.

But, in announcing this proposition, two questions occur to me. First, how is it kept down? Secondly, is it necessary for the common good, that any special attention should be given by governments and national councils, in the way of taking care that it should be kept down, or that the increase of the numbers of mankind should not be encouraged?

On the first question, [How does it happen that the population of the earth does not go on in a course of perpetual increase?] Mr. Malthus advances two propositions interchangeably, substituting the one for the other at his pleasure, as if they were only two ways of expressing the same thing: first, that population is kept down

by the intervention of vice and misery : secondly, that it is kept down, because the numbers of
mankind are, every where and incessantly, tending to increase beyond the limits of the means of
subsistence.

Now these propositions are so far from being
synonimous, and if I may apply the word somewhat out of its usual meaning, tautological, that
one of them may be true, and the other totally
and entirely false.

That vice and misery have a share in keeping
down the numbers of mankind, I will not deny.
There may also be other causes, as yet little adverted to, which may be concerned in producing
the same effect.

The most obvious causes which all history
forces upon our attention, are war, pestilence
and famine.   And here I would distinguish between
tween the two agents which in Mr. Malthus's
book are perpetually coupled, vice, and misery ;
or, as I would rather denominate them, vice,
and the visitation of calamity. Pestilence is
not vice ; famine can scarcely deserve to be called
by that name. War therefore, of these three,
is the agent for thinning the ranks of mankind,
which is best entitled to be denominated vice.

But how far are any of these concerned with
a scarcity of the means of subsistence ? Famine
indeed is a sweeping name, which expresses that
scarcity in its most aggravated degree. But
pestilence—is that only a lack of the means of

subsistence under another form?   Is the plague produced by hunger?   Is the yellow fever produced by hunger?   When our devoted country in former centuries was so often visited with the plague, were Englishmen in greater comparative want of the means of subsistence than at present?

War is, of almost any example that could be devised, well adapted to shew that Mr. Malthus's two propositions are of very different import. Do men go to war because they want the means of subsistence?   Far otherwise.   War in civilized countries is the offspring of pride, of wantonness, and an artificial method of thinking and living.   War cannot be carried on in such countries without a previous accumulation of the means of subsistence.   Money, it has often been said, is the sinew of war.   It would be more accurate to say, that provisions [*munition de bouche*] are the sinews of war.   The first care of a power going to war is to establish magazines.   I may add, that money itself is nothing, except so far as it can purchase the conveniences, and, *a fortiori*, the necessaries of life.

So far therefore as war is concerned, I allow that the numbers of mankind are thinned by vice: So far as famine and pestilence enter into the question, I admit that the same effect may be attributed to calamity.

But I totally reject Mr. Malthus's vice and misery in their obscure details.   I affirm, that we in the favoured countries of Europe have no more of them, than have occurred in the annals of the United States of America a. This will be sufficiently evinced in the subsequent divisions of this volume. The proper and ultimate appeal on this question is to the Bills of Mortality; and it must for ever redound to the disgrace of the followers of Mr. Malthus, that they have blindly adopted his propositions, without once having had recourse to so obvious a means of ascertaining the fact.

But the grand question, which embraces at once all the lucubrations of Mr. Malthus, is this, Does population require to be kept down?

All the legislators of antiquity, with one voice, and in the most authentic way, by their uniform practice, affirm the contrary.

To which I may add, first, that the proposition is absurd on the face of it; since the first element of civilization lies in this truth, that every human creature (except in cases of extraordinary corporeal imbecility) is endowed by nature with the power of producing a much greater quantity of that which nourishes human life, than is necessary for his individual subsistence.

After the experience, and the recorded history of several thousand years, we know that the

---

a Is it necessary to observe, that I would apply this to Great Britain as it was previous to the last peace, and not to the years of extraordinary calamity that have followed?

population of countries is for the most part in a state of flux and reflux.   As to the increase, in nations where it cannot be ascribed to the junction and mingling of the people of one country with the people of another, I will grant with Mr. Malthus that it is to be imputed to the power of procreation.   But what is the cause of the decrease?   Of this we know little; and Mr. Malthus has taught us nothing.   War, famine, and pestilence are real causes.   It is natural enough to think, that the race of mankind will have a tendency in some measure to increase where they are happy, and to decrease where they are unhappy.   But, as to Mr. Malthus's convenient and gratuitous causes, never to be defined, and never to be methodically traced by the lucubrations or the pen of the calculator or the political economist, but which he has always at hand to bring forward wherever he may happen to want them, these are wholly unworthy of a moment's serious consideration.   Why have so many nations and races of men wholly perished from the face of the earth?   Why have the natives of Mexico and Peru continually decreased, notwithstanding all the efforts and anxieties of government to keep up their numbers?   Why are the tribes of North American Indians to all appearance verging towards extinction?   These are questions which the Essay on Population affords us no assistance to answer.

What is the past history of mankind relatively

to the question of population? I grant, that those countries of antiquity where most attention was given by governments to encourage the increase of population, were from time to time exposed to the calamity (the vice, if Mr. Malthus pleases) of war. They were all very probably visited by pestilence and contagious diseases, carrying off their thousands and tens of thousands. If the author of the Essay on Population had confined his enquiry to the consideration of what would become of the numbers of mankind, when all vice and calamity shall have been abolished, and when every country of the earth shall be amply stocked with inhabitants, his argument would have taken a very different turn, and, if I had felt impelled to examine it, my reasonings would have been arranged in a different manner.

But Mr. Malthus knew, that if he had raised no other difficulty than this, his book would quietly have reposed on the shelves of the curious, and there would have been few, even of the most ardent speculators on the future improvement of mankind, who would not have contented themselves, as he expresses it, with leaving " an event at such a distance to the care of Providence b." It was therefore necessary for his purpose to affirm, that in old countries the population is every where and at all times

---

b Vol. II, p. 220.

pressing hard against the limits of the means of subsistence."

The fact however seems to be the reverse of this. All the legislators and governments of past ages, in proportion as they were supposed to be enlightened, and animated with a genuine zeal for the welfare of their subjects, were anxious to encourage population. Could they all be blind to the truth in this respect? Could they all be so obstinate and headstrong, that expe. rience itself could never enlighten them?

Let Mr. Malthus produce a single instance among these celebrated legislators, and in these famous countries, where that terrible reaction occurred which his hypothesis requires. According to him, the present administrators of Egypt and Syria ought to be considered as the genuine benefactors of mankind, while the efforts of those ardent patriots who directed their views to the increasing the numbers of their countrymen, would be seen to draw a long train of calamity and misery after them. I am unable to discern this. I cannot see the blessings and prosperity which attend upon and attest the wisdom of the existing governments of Egypt and Syria. And I must patiently wait for Mr. Malthus's information, as to whether the policy of Lycurgus, or Numa, or Zoroaster, or Confucius, affords the most apposite example of the misery that arises from encouraging population. In some instances he says " not thirty years would elapse [c]," before the most fatal and heart-sickening consequences would be produced. And the whole tendency of his book is to prove, that the expected disasters would be as rapid, as they were irresistible in their manifestation and their progress.

The inference certainly from all history is, that population does not challenge the vigilance of governments to keep it down. The inference from all history is, that those countries, other things equal, have been happiest, where the increase of mankind has been most encouraged, and those the most miserable, in which the power of depopulation has most fully displayed itself. If an author, in the beginning of the nineteenth century of the Christian era, comes forward, to teach us a new creed, and to persuade us to abandon that which the concurrent wisdom of ages had taught us, he should surely not attempt to do this by the sole aid of a few dogmatical maxims, but should have gone through the annals of antiquity, and have shewn us where in all famous nations and states the evil crept in. The fact is completely against him. The fact is, according to the evidence of all history, that population does not require the vigilance of governments to keep it down.

When once we have discarded this cardinal error, the rest of the subject becomes a topic of

---

[c] Vol. II. p. 269.

laudable speculation.   What tendency is there in the human species to increase their numbers? It cannot be disputed, that in some countries (Sweden for example) there appears to be a power in mankind to increase their numbers by procreation only.   Under what circumstances, and for how long a time, may this power be supposed to exert itself?   Under the most favourable circumstances, what would be the degree of the increase?   What are the causes that check the increase, and that produce a progress in the opposite direction? for the instances appear to be much more numerous and striking of a rapid depopulation.   At all events this is certain, that no governments, previously to the publication of Mr. Malthus's book, ever set themselves up for patrons of depopulation, and to "stop the propagation of mankind:" and it is scarcely less certain, that the population of the earth is not greater now than it was three thousand years ago.

If Mr. Malthus's doctrine were sound, and his novelties constituted a real discovery, the history of the population of the earth would be very different from the thing that it is.   But his theory sustains the common fate of every mere hypothesis ingeniously contrived to account for the phenomena around us.   It may look in some degree plausible in itself; but it will never truly tally with the facts it is brought to explain.   It

X

pays us with words; but it does not clear up a single difficulty.

The population of every old country, according to Mr. Malthus, is kept down by " pressing hard against the limits of the means of subsistence." If this were true, what would be the real state of the case in the history of all the nations of the earth? A periodical fluctuation.— That there is a change I admit, and that nations from time to time increase and decrease in the numbers of their people. But the cause of these changes has never yet been fully explained ; and least of all do they square with Mr. Malthus's hypothesis—To proceed in the statement and refutation of the views exhibited in the Essay on Population. Every country, as well as North America, in the proportion of its area and its soil is capable of subsisting a given number of inhabitants. When this capacity has been used, and the country has been replenished with men, that district or portion of the globe will refuse to receive a greater number. But it is perhaps the nature of every check or reaction, to operate somewhat beyond the extent of the impulse that gave it birth. Hence, we will say, comes the depopulation, which forms so memorable a portion of the records of universal history. That we may not fall into the error, so incident to the limited faculties of man, of confounding ourselves amidst the complication of very large numbers, let us take a district or an island fully competent to the subsistence of one thousand human inhabitants. The power of procreation, we will assume, continually tends to increase the numbers of mankind. The population of this district therefore, having arrived at one thousand, has an abstract tendency to extend itself further. But here it is stopped by the most powerful of all causes. Calamity invades this devoted race of men, poverty, examples of terrible distress, and the want of the means of subsistence. Hereupon follows, we will suppose, depopulation. No man need look far for the most impressive examples of depopulation. We will imagine the number of inhabitants reduced to five hundred. What will be the consequence of this? The area and the soil were fully competent to subsist twice that number. Strips and acres of land now seem to call loudly for the hand of the cultivator. The whole country pines and is sick for the ploughshare and the spade. Nothing therefore is more evident, upon Mr. Malthus's scheme, than that this region will speedily recover its lost population. Want of the means of subsistence put it down: that want being removed, the principle of increase inherent in the human species will raise it up again.

But is this really the case in the history of the earth? Let us look through all the depopulated countries enumerated by Montesquieu. They have been amply blessed in the remedy prescribed by Mr. Malthus, the reduction of the numbers of those who cried out for the means of subsistence. Why are they at present unconscious of their happiness, and why do they not diligently apply themselves to increase their numbers? I think I may venture to say that in no one instance has the thing happened as Mr. Malthus's theory requires. Wherever depopulation has once set up its standard, the evil goes on. In these countries we do not find, as according to the *dicta* of the Essay on Population we ought to find, a periodical flux and reflux of the number of their inhabitants [d], an elasticity by means of which, as soon as the pressure had operated to a certain point, the principle resumes its sway, and the energies mount again. On the contrary, wherever depopulation has operated to a great extent, and for a considerable length of time, I believe we shall never find that country resuming its preceding prosperity and populousness, unless by an actual planting and settling of a new race of inhabitants within its limits.

Hence it appears, that it is something else,

---

[d] This remark perhaps stands in need of explanation. I acknowledge a flux and reflux in the population of countries, as, for example, in Sweden. But I affirm that there is no instance of a country abundantly peopled, then reduced in its numbers through a scarcity of the means of subsistence, and afterwards from the depths of depopulation becoming populous again purely because the superabundance of its citizens was taken away.

and not merely or principally a rise and fall in the means that nature affords us for obtaining provisions and subsistence, that limits the population of a country, and causes that country in many instances to produce so much smaller a proportion of human beings, than it could boast in some preceding generation, or in some remote age of the world.

I would observe by the way, that a want of the means of subsistence, and a want of the means which nature affords to man for obtaining provisions and subsistence, are by no means synonimous. Much of Mr. Malthus's strength lies in his ambiguities. When the whole earth has been "cultivated like a garden [e]," we will suppose for a moment that this state of things puts a bar on the multiplication of mankind. But it is a very different question, and is well worthy of the enquiry of the political economist, Why Turkey in Europe, Turkey in Asia, Persia, Egypt, and a multitude of other countries, are so thinly inhabited now, to what they were in the renowned periods of their ancient history. Certainly it is not because their soil is exhausted. Certainly it is not because another blade of corn refuses to grow on their surface. We may venture, even in the infancy of the enquiry, to assert, that the cause is to be found in the government and political administration of these

[e] Essay on Population, Vol. II, p. 220.

countries. If a beneficent sovereign, the father of his people, were to arise among them, if a great genius, who loved his fellow-men, and in whom the ardour of his love generated enlightened attention, and fertilised the field of intellectual resources, were to mount the throne, if such a one were to apply all his energies to make his country what it formerly was, when it seemed to be the granary of the world, we may reasonably believe that his labours would not be in vain. The great mass of the people in that country would no longer be oppressed. Their sovereign, and inspired by him a long train of men in power inferior to the throne, would make it their ambition, that each father of a family who desired it, should have a portion of land subject to his own providence and discretion, and should possess the means of rendering the land he owned available to the purposes of human prosperity. The energies of the inhabitants of the country would be called forth, and men from other regions would be invited to settle on this advantageous soil. Hence it appears, that it is ill government, and not a want of the means of subsistence, that renders these countries a permanent scene of desolation.

But Mr. Malthus, that dark and terrible genius that is ever at hand to blast all the hopes of all mankind, will tell us, that Egypt, or whatever other territory we take for our example, will one day be " cultivated like a garden," and will refuse itself to any further increase of inhabitants.   Be it so: we will not dispute that for the present.   But is that any reason why, out of a generous care for a distant posterity, we should refuse the vast accession of happiness that shall be offered to us?   " Take the good the Gods provide thee."   I am disposed, like Mr. Malthus, to say, " An event at such a distance,"as that of a whole country, or the whole earth, having more inhabitants than its soil will maintain, " may fairly be left to Providence f." We have disarmed the Essay on Population of all its sting, when we have proved that, " at every period during the progress of cultivation, the distress for want of food will [not] be constantly pressing on all mankind," or, in other words, that the population of Europe, and the other parts of the Old World, is not necessarily " always pressing hard against the limits of the means of subsistence."

---

f Vol. II, p. 220.

CHAPTER II.

OF DEATHS AND THE RATE OF HUMAN MORTA-
LITY.

IT is the glory of modern philosophy to have
banished the doctrine of occult causes. Superstition and a blind deference to great names
taught men that there were questions upon
which we must not allow ourselves to enter with
a free spirit of research. In science, as well as
religion, we were told there was a sanctuary into
which it would be profaneness for ordinary and
unprivileged men to intrude. The αυτος εφη of the
master, was the authority upon which we were
directed to repose ourselves: and occult causes
were assigned, a sort of sacred names that could
not be defined, the operation of which was every
where to be recognised, and upon no occasion to
be subjected to investigation.

Lord Bacon was the mighty genius to whom
we are principally indebted for the destruction
of this fortress. He has taught us fearlessly to
bring all nature to the tribunal of science, and to
submit all her operations and phenomena to the
test of experiment. The path he pointed out
has since been indefatigably pursued by the in-

tellect of two successive centuries, and memorable is the progress that has been made.

The Essay on Population is an attempt to revive, in a particular case, that system of theorising which Lord Bacon had so successfully exploded. Vice and misery are Mr. Malthus's cabalistical terms; and he has treated us here, exactly as he has done in the question of the geometrical ratio. The whole of what he says on the matter is in reality comprehended in one dogmatical proposition, consisting of a subject, a predicate, and a copula—no more—which whoever will may believe, and whoever will may disbelieve; but which no man can reasonably either believe or disbelieve, without a body of evidence, such as Mr. Malthus has not attempted to produce.

If the population of the United States of North America has doubled itself every twenty-five years, and that by procreation only, Mr. Malthus should have shewn us how that procreation proceeded. He should have divided the number of children which his proposition required, to each wedded pair, their parents, should have first laid down how many children to a marriage were necessary to his hypothesis, and then have proved that that proportion of children was the actual produce of the United States. Mr. Malthus is said to be an expert mathematician: it would then have been an easy task for him, first, to have gone through, and next to have exhibited, this process.

In the same summary and oracular manner in which he delivers his doctrine of the geometrical ratio, he next introduces to our notice vice and misery, imaginary causes by which he wishes us to account for his imaginary effects. [I do not mean that vice and misery have no existence ; but I affirm that they are gratuitously assumed as causes of a given degree of energy, exactly commensurate to the producing a given effect, to wit, the suspension of the original law of the multiplication of mankind.] In other words, the human species, according to him, ought to double itself four times in a century : but, in Europe, Asia, Africa and South America, this is found not to be the case : therefore vice and misery must be the bars that are continually suppressing this progress. Vice and misery are good set terms : but one would think that a man must be desperately in love with them, who would give them credit for such stupendous effects, without allowing himself time for a little severe examination.

Here, as in the former case, the application of Mr. Malthus's attainments in mathematics is a main *desideratum.* He should have shewn us in what manner, and at what age, vice and misery destroyed the children that were born : for it must be as children that they are destroyed, since if they arrived at puberty, they might be the causes of an increased population in a following age, and if they continued to exist only ten or fifteen years, they would consume that quantity of food, which Mr. Malthus says is impossible to be supplied.   He should have chosen some country or some district of the earth for the subject of his experiment, and have brought forward in Arabic numerals the victims of vice and misery, as they fell in from year to year.

It happens however, most unfortunately for Mr. Malthus's hypothesis, that the subject of human mortality is not a new subject.   The avidity of mankind, the assiduous spirit of pecuniary calculation, and the desire inherent in the minds of the masters of families to make some provision for those who shall survive them, have gone a great way towards reducing this to a science, without the smallest idea on the part of those who cultivated it, that their proceeding was calculated to throw any light upon the moral government of the world.

Even before Dr. Price, and the other writers on annuities and reversionary payments, published their lucubrations, enough had been done to place in the clearest light that question, which Mr. Malthus has sought to involve in more than Egyptian darkness.   The author of the Essay on Population should have taken down Dr. Birch's Collection of the Yearly Bills of Mortality, and have extracted from thence a series of Tables of the victims of vice and misery.   If, in addition to this, he had procured and published Bills of Mortality for any of the most favoured

districts of the United States, we should have
seen with a glance of the eye to what extent
vice and misery prevail more in Europe than in
North America (for such is the whole question)
to destroy the infant offspring of the human
species.

This was a proper topic to be submitted to the
decision of figures. Here, as in the question of
the geometrical ratio, all should have been subordinate to the exhibition of actual facts. In
the enquiry respecting procreation, the author
should not have confined himself to bare enumerations, but should have shewn how his immense
augmentations of the species were procreated.
In like manner, in the destruction of the young
of mankind afterwards, it would by no means
have been attended with insuperable difficulty,
to have put down in columns the numbers destroyed from year to year; and I cannot understand how any man can reasonably acquiesce in
Mr Malthus's enormous and atrocious assertions,
without having first looked upon the subject
from this point of view. The author has chosen
for the field of his wild and disorderly *dicta* a
topic, which beyond almost any that can be
named is capable of mechanical exactness. The
whole question as to his vice and misery, their
terrible effects in old countries, and the suspension and neutralising of those effects in new, reduces itself to this, in what numbers do human
beings die, and when do they die?

Mr. Malthus says, " The proportion of births to marriages forms no criterion by which to judge of the increase of mankind[a]." But this is the grossest mistake that was ever made, by any person aspiring to proceed, as the author of the Essay on Population pretends to do, upon the principles of pure reason. There can assuredly be no other substantial and permanent increase of the human race, than the fruitfulness of marriages, or, to speak more accurately, of women capable of child-bearing.

In countries, where the forms of civilised life prevail, where men enjoy a moderate degree of security for person and property, and are unvisited by any overwhelming calamity, all the children or nearly all the children, are born, that the structure and frame of human nature can fairly lead us to expect:

In this we have Mr. Malthus completely with us. He says, " The passion between the sexes is necessary, and will always remain nearly in its present state[b]." He adds, " The principle of moral restraint has undoubtedly in past ages operated with very inconsiderable force, nor can we reasonably expect any future improvement, in which we are not borne out by the experience of the past[c]."

But we do not want the aid of Mr. Malthus, and his gross and degrading ideas of human na-

---

[a] Vol. II, p. 159.   [b] See above,   p. 31.   [c] P. 32.

ture, to establish our position. We have just seen that in many countries at least, Sweden and England for example, almost all the women marry, and that the marriages are sufficiently early to give us every reasonable chance of a numerous offspring.

When once therefore we have ascertained the fair proportion of births to marriages in any community, we have a just criterion by which to judge of the increase or otherwise of mankind in that community. Children in Europe are not smuggled out of the world, as Mr. Malthus's theory would require us to suppose. Give me the number of births annually or otherwise in any country; and I have the means of ascertaining, among civilised nations, how, in what proportions, and at what periods, they die. There is nothing mystical in this. It is in vain that the author of the Essay on Population offers me his vice and misery, killing their millions, of whom no account is taken, and who perish we know not how. I say, an account is taken of all. I say no more perish in Europe than in the United States; and that the value and probable duration of human lives, and the chances of surviving the mischiefs that beset us in infancy and youth, are no greater there than here.

Mr. Malthus indeed reduces himself to an express contradiction in terms, when he says on the one hand, that the increase of population in the United States is " by procreation only," and

on the other, that the number of births that a
marriage shall be found to produce, is " no criterion whatever of the rate·of increase." What
is procreation, but the production of a certain
number, increasing or otherwise, of births to a
marriage, or of births to the number of women
capable of child-bearing in any community ?

And, be it observed, all the calculations of
Dr. Price, and all other writers upon annuities,
proceed upon the negation *in limine* of the entire
system of Mr.·Malthus's book. These writers
have recourse to the bills of mortality, and the
reported numbers of those who die at every age,
and calculate from thence the value, or probable
duration of human life. If then in the United
States the population doubles itself every twenty-
five years by the natural force of the procreative
power, while in Europe it is at a stand, and if in
Europe all the children, or nearly all the children,
are born, that the structure and frame of human
nature can fairly lead us to expect, then it follows with the force of a demonstration, that human life is in the technical sense worth twice as
much in the United States as in Europe; and
that, if there are any societies for granting annuities in the United States, they must be
ruined in the shortest practicable period, if, upon
any given capital, they pay more than half the
amount *per annum*, that may safely and equitably be paid in this part of the world. I know
no way of evading this conclusion, but by sup-

posing that all this hideous excess of mortality, which distinguishes the Old World from the New, falls upon very young children, whose lives are seldom insured, and that, after having reached a certain age, human creatures die at much the same rate on one side of the globe as the other.

In the United States there must be, upon Mr. Malthus's hypothesis, only four deaths, for every eight that occur in a country in which the population is stationary [d]. This is as clear as any thing can be imagined to be. At what period of life do these deaths occur? To keep down the population effectually, it ought all to be of children. The death of a child, to speak in the spirit of Mr. Malthus's system, is worth five times, nay, I know not how many times, a death occurring at a later period. And indeed it is obvious all through, that Mr. Malthus trusts to the destruction of infants and young children, as the sheet-anchor of our hope to preserve the population of Europe from perishing with hunger. Surely, of all creeds that were ever greedily and unscrupulously received, this requires

---

d In the United States a given number of children die, and yet the population is doubled every generation. If as many children in proportion are born in China or any other country where the population is at a stand, as in the United States, it is clear that not only that number of children must die, but another number in addition, equal to the number of children that die in the United States, added to the number of mature persons that might be found necessary barely to keep up the race. See above, p. 50.

the greatest portion of faith, that twice as many, or, to speak more accurately, three or four times as many, young children perish through the direct operation of vice and misery in the most virtuous and happy countries of Europe, as perish through the operation of all causes taken together, in the United States of North America!

The theory of the Essay on Population poorly and precariously subsists upon two points, 1. That more human creatures are born from a given population in the United States than any where else. 2. That fewer human creatures die there, in a given population, or within a limited period. Mr. Malthus knows nothing of either. He has not dreamed of exerting any industry or enquiry about either. He has looked with a supercilious and hasty glance at the bare numbers placed on the territory of the United States, and has not thought of ruminating any further. He has talked about death, because death is the forked arrow with which vice and misery, according to him, consummate their purposes. And he talks about births, because the reading part of the public has not yet arrived at the perfection of believing in all cases, without requiring the exhibition of something that shall pass with them for a reason. But he has not even attempted to fix any thing specific, as to either the births or deaths of America. And with this unconcocted system, this abortive

Y

birth, this bear's whelp never licked into form, this hypothesis, which like the incomprehensible author of nature, dwells in clouds, and makes thick darkness its habitation, he has the modesty to require of us to reject every scheme that proposes to increase the sum of human happiness, to condemn all the wisest institutions that form the glory of the legislators of antiquity, and to send all philosophy to school again.

I am sensible that I leave the subject of this chapter unfinished. I am far indeed from placing an implicit reliance upon that species of records, known by the name of Registers [e]. I do not therefore think that much can be made of that species of argument, the favourite argument of Mr. Malthus, which consists in comparing the number of those that are stated to be born, with the number of those who appear from similar evidence to die, and thence inferring the increase or otherwise of mankind. We have seen the extraordinary conclusions that have been deduced by the editor of the Population Reports of England from the fact that no more are known to have died in 1800 than in 1780, in which period, according to him, the population had been increased by an addition of 1,215,000 [f].

---

[e] Perhaps we ought to except from this censure the Registers of Sweden, where so much enlightened attention seems to have been bestowed on all the questions connected with population.

[f] See above, p. 226.

Here, as in every question relating to the subject, where an accurate collection of facts is required, I know of no resource to which we have access, but the Tables of Population for Sweden. In these there is presented to us a digested abstract of the numbers that die, their periods of life, and the proportions of those who die at one age to those who die at another. To these we might add from the Bills of Mortality some hints respecting the diseases, by which human beings are cut off in the different stages of existence. I might therefore have constructed a Table founded on the Swedish reports, calculated to shew that there is no such mystery and inexplicableness in the affair as Mr. Malthus would have us suppose, but on the contrary that all goes on with a sort of regular march, in old countries, not labouring under the visitation of any singular calamity.

This Table I have not constructed. I wish to be considered as having merely sketched the subject, and left the outline to be filled up by those who come after me. All I have delivered on this head is new. No one has attempted before me by actual and patient investigation to ascertain any thing in the way of principle respecting the increase or decrease of the numbers of mankind. I claim nothing more than to have endeavoured to disenchant my fellow-men (I hope successfully endeavoured) from the unreal and fairy edifice in which Mr. Malthus had

sought to inclose them, and to have brought together some of the materials for erecting a fabric,
which hurricanes cannot demolish, nor floods
destroy.

CHAPTER III.

ATTEMPT TOWARDS A RATIONAL THEORY OF
THE CHECKS ON POPULATION.

SCARCELY any thing can be imagined more
likely to supply us with just views respecting
the past history of population, and of consequence to suggest to us sound anticipations as to
its future progress, than the comparing some
tract of country and period of time in which its
increase appears to have gone on with highest
vigour and health on the one hand, with all that
is known, as to its general aspect over the face
of the earth, on the other.

Mr Malthus has had recourse to certain wild
conjectures and gratuitous assertions respecting
the United States of North America, concerning whose population, and the effect of the
power of procreation among them, I may safely
affirm nothing is known, and has here taken his
stand, for the purpose of issuing his dogmatical
speculations. Upon this ground he erects his
monstrous proposition, that " the population of
the earth, wherever it is unchecked, will go on
doubling itself every twenty-five years, or will
increase in a geometrical ratio." Hence he sets

out on the hopeful task, the main business of all his pages, of shewing why this proposition of his has never been realised, or, I may rather say, why no approach has ever been made to it, in any settled country throughout the annals of the world.

I have chosen a different standard from that of Mr. Malthus. I have found that a very exemplary and elaborate account has been taken of the population of Sweden, in all those points most calculated to afford knowledge on the subject, for more than half a century. Here I grasp something real, and by which I can hardly fear to be misled. Here I find that the population of this division of Europe has gone on for fifty-four years, at a rate which, if in reality this subject would admit of any precise or mathematical measurement, would seem to promise a doubling in something more than one hundred years. The question therefore that is left me, is to consider why, in no country of the earth, the progress of population has advanced at this rate, perhaps for a single century; or, to take the question upon a larger scale, and where our evidence is more satisfactory, why the population of the earth, collectively taken, has experienced no increase, from the earliest records of authentic profane history to the present hour.

It is by looking at the subject in a comprehensive view, that I think we shall stand the best chance of attaining some sound principles concerning it.

For this purpose it may perhaps be worth while to direct our reflections to two points.

First, there are certain countries, which were once in an eminent degree populous and flourishing, that are now sunk into a state of comparative solitude and desolation. Such are Syria, Egypt, Greece, Italy, Sicily, that part of Asia which in ancient times was subject to the Great King, and the whole coast of Africa bordering on the Mediterranean. To these we may add the extensive empires of Mexico and Peru in the New World, together with the islands of the American Archipelago. What has reduced them to their present state of desolation?

Secondly, we may turn our attention to those countries, which for centuries past have not been subject to such violent convulsions, the countries which form what may be called the commonwealth of Europe, particularly England, Germany and France. Our thoughts will not then be of desolation, of vast and fruitful provinces rendered naked of inhabitants, but they will be turned to an enquiry not less interesting and useful, why, in none of these countries, population has advanced with that steady and uniform progress, of which, when regarded in the abstract, it seems to be capable?

Population, if we consider it historically, appears to be a fitful principle, operating intermittedly and by starts. This is the great mystery of the subject; and patiently to investigate the causes of its irregular progress seems to be a business highly worthy of the philosopher.

One of the first ideas that will occur to a reflecting mind is, that the cause of these irregularities cannot be itself of regular and uniform operation. It cannot be " the numbers of mankind at all times pressing hard against the limits of the means of subsistence."

Let us first look at those causes which may obviously account for a great and sudden diminution of the numbers of mankind. Those which are in every one's recollection, " familiar in our mouths as houshold words," are war, pestilence and famine. But there are other causes, more powerful and tremendous in their operation than war, pestilence and famine, at least than those calamities in their more ordinary and softened visitations. These are conquest, such as we find it recorded in certain periods of the history of mankind, and bad government, when carried to a certain degree of corruption and oppression. I say bad government, in the teeth of one of Mr. Malthus's most extravagant paradoxes, where he lays it down that " Human institutions, however they may appear to be the causes of much mischief to society, are in reality light and superficial, mere feathers that float on the surface, in comparison with those deeper-seated causes of evil, which result from the laws of nature and the passions of man a."

The truths I have here delivered, have in reality no novelty in them, but have been dwelt upon by every former political writer who has had much at heart the welfare and happiness of mankind. But there are truths, however obvious, that need to be from time to time revived in the minds of men. Human memory is a repository of so uncertain a tenacity, that the most important principles, the great land-marks of political and moral science, if not occasionally brought to our recollection, are in danger of being let go and forgotten.

I will produce therefore one specimen of the nature of conquest from the writings of Mr. Burke. I might have found as striking examples in fifty other authors, ancient and modern; but there is something in his language that enshrines truth, and imparts to it the immortality of the genius by which it is recorded.

" He drew," says he, speaking of the invasion of Hyder Ali in the Carnatic, "from every quarter, whatever a savage ferocity could add to his new rudiments in the arts of destruction; and compounding all the materials of fury, havock and desolation, into one black cloud, he hung for a while on the declivities of the moun-

---

a Essay on Population, First Edition, p. 177. Fifth Edition, Vol. II, p. 246.

tains.   While the authors of all these evils were
idly and stupidly gazing on this menacing me-
teor which blackened all their horizon, it suddenly burst, and poured down the whole of its
contents upon the plains of the Carnatic.   Then
ensued a scene of woe, the like of which no eye
had seen, no heart conceived, and which no
tongue can adequately tell.   A storm of universal fire blasted every field, consumed every house,
destroyed every temple.   The miserable inhabitants flying from their flaming villages, in part
were slaughtered; others, without regard to
sex, to age, to the respect of rank, or sacredness
of function; fathers torn from children, husbands
from wives, enveloped in a whirlwind of cavalry,
and amidst the goading spears of drivers, and
the trampling of pursuing horses, were swept
into captivity in an unknown and hostile land.
Those who were able to evade this tempest, fled
to the walled cities.   But escaping from fire,
sword and exile, they fell into the jaws of
famine [b]."

But, lest the exaggeration of the orator in this
passage should be suspected, I will subjoin an
extract from the authentic pen of the phlegmatic
Gibbon.

" In all their invasions of the civilized empires
of the South, the Scythian shepherds have been
uniformly actuated by a savage and destructive

---

[b] Speech on the Debts of the Nabob of Arcot.

spirit.   The laws of war, that restrain the exercise of national rapine and murder, are founded on two principles of substantial interest; the knowledge of the permanent benefits which may be obtained by a moderate use of conquest; and a just apprehension, lest the desolation which we inflict on the enemy's country, may be retaliated on our own.   But these considerations of hope and fear are almost unknown in the pastoral state of nations.   After the Moguls had subdued the northern provinces of China, it was seriously proposed, not in the hour of victory and passion, but in calm and deliberate council, to exterminate all the inhabitants of that populous country, that the vacant land might be converted to the pasture of cattle.   The firmness of a Chinese mandarin, who insinuated some principles of rational policy into the mind of Zingis, diverted him from the execution of this horrid design. But in the cities of Asia, which yielded to the Moguls, the inhuman abuse of the rights of war was exercised with a regular form of discipline. Such was the behaviour of the conquerors, when they were not conscious of any extraordinary rigour.   But the most casual provocation, the slightest motive of caprice or convenience, often provoked them to involve a whole people in indiscriminate massacre: and the ruin of some flourishing cities was executed with such unrelenting perseverance, that, according to their own expression, horses might run, without stumbling, over the ground where they had once stood. The three great capitals of Khorasan, Maru, Nisabour and Herat, were destroyed by the armies of Zingis; and the exact account which was taken of the slain, amounted to four millions three hundred and forty-seven thousand persons. Timur, or Tamerlane, was educated in a less barbarous age, and in the profession of the Mahometan religion; yet, if Attila equalled the hostile ravages of Tamerlane, either the Hun or the Tartar might deserve the epithet of the Scourge of God. Cherefeddin Ali, the servile panegyrist of the latter, would afford us many horrid examples. In his camp before Delhi, Timur massacred 100,000 Indian prisoners, who had smiled when the army of their countrymen appeared in sight. The people of Ispahan supplied 70,000 human sculls for the structure of several lofty towers; and a similar tax was levied on the revolt of Bagdad [c]."

These are a few of the most memorable examples of the achievements of savage conquerors. But we must not suppose that the desolation produced by conquests was confined to such as these. Cæsar, the elegant and accomplished Cæsar, whose humanity has furnished a topic to so many panegyrists, is computed to have conquered three hundred nations, taken eight hundred cities, and to have defeated three millions

---

[c] Decline and Fall of the Roman Empire, Chap. XXXIV.

of men, one million of which was left dead on
the field of battle. " Observe," exclaims Gibbon d, " with how much indifference Cæsar relates in his Commentaries of the Gallic war, that
he put to death the senate of the Veneti who
had yielded to his mercy (iii, 16); that he laboured to extirpate the whole nation of the Ebu-
rones (vi, 31); and that forty thousand persons
were massacred at Bourges, by the just revenge
of his soldiers who spared neither age nor sex
(vii, 27)."

The expressive style of Tacitus sums up the
whole of this subject in a very few words.
" *Proximus dies faciem victoriæ latius aperuit.*
Vastum ubique silentium, secreti colles, fumantia
procul tecta, nemo exploratoribus obvius e."

How often has this scene been acted over on
the face of the earth?   It was thus that " Babylon, the glory of kingdoms, the beauty of the
Chaldees' excellency, became as when God
overthrew Sodom and Gomorrah. It shall never
be inhabited, neither shall it be dwelt in from
generation to generation : neither shall the Ara-
bian pitch his tent there, neither shall the shepherds make their fold there : but wild beasts of
the desert shall lie there; and their houses shall
be full of doleful creatures, and owls shall dwell
there, and satyrs shall dance there : and the wild

---

d Ibid. Chap. XXVI, note 99.   e *Agricolæ Vita, cap.* 38.

beasts of the islands shall cry in their desolate houses, and dragons in their pleasant places f."

Surely all this is not "light and superficial, mere feathers that float on the surface of human affairs, in comparison with the evils which result from the laws of nature," and what Mr. Malthus deprecates by the name of " the passion between the sexes."

The next source of depopulation which I have mentioned is bad government.   It is not consistent with the object of this enquiry, to exhibit any of the subjects of which it treats, under false colours.   I have therefore said bad government; I have not said despotism.   Despotism is worthy of our fixed reprobation; but there have been despotisms so conducted, at least for a time, as not to produce the effects of depopulation.   On the contrary, the nations among which they prevailed, have appeared prosperous and flourishing.

I will confine myself under this head to a single example, which shall be taken from the work of Mr. Malthus.

" The fundamental cause of the low state of population in Turkey, compared with its extent of territory, is undoubtedly the nature of the government. Its tyranny, its feebleness, its bad laws and worse administration of them, together with the consequent insecurity of pro-

---

f Isaiah, Chap. XIII.

perty, throw such obstacles in the way of agriculture, that the means of subsistence are necessarily decreasing yearly, and with them, of course, the number of people. The miri, or general land-tax paid to the sultan, is in itself moderate; but by abuses inherent in the Turkish government, the pachas and their agents have found out the means of rendering it ruinous. Though they cannot absolutely alter the impost which has been established by the sultan, they have introduced a multitude of changes, which without the name produce all the effects of an augmentation. In Syria, according to Volney, having the greatest part of the land at their disposal, they clog their concessions [lettings, or admissions to tenantry] with burdensome conditions, and exact the half, and sometimes even two–thirds, of the crop. When the harvest is over, they cavil about losses, and as they have the power in their hands, they carry off what they think proper. If the season fail, they still exact the same sum, and expose every thing that the poor peasant possesses to sale. To these constant oppressions are added a thousand accidental extortions. Sometimes a whole village is laid under contribution for some real or imaginary offence. Arbitrary presents are exacted on the accession of each governor; grass, barley and straw are demanded for his horses; and commissions are multiplied, that the soldiers who carry the orders may live upon the starving peasants whom they treat with the most brutal insolence and injustice.

" The consequence of these depredations is that the poorer classes of inhabitants, ruined, and unable any longer to pay the miri, become a burden to the village, or fly into the cities; but the miri is unalterable, and the sum to be levied must be found somewhere. The portion of those who are thus driven from their homes falls on the remaining inhabitants, whose burden, though at first light, now becomes insupportable. If they should be visited by two years of drought and famine the whole village is ruined and abandoned; and the tax which it should have paid, is levied on the neighbouring lands.

" The same mode of proceeding takes place with regard to the tax on the Christians which has been raised by these means from three, five, and eleven piastres, at which it was first fixed, to thirty-five and forty, which absolutely impoverishes those on whom it is levied, and obliges them to leave the country. It has been remarked that these exactions have made a rapid progress during the last forty years; from which time are dated the decline of agriculture, the depopulation of the country and the diminution in the quantity of specie carried into Constantinople.

" The food of the peasants is almost every where reduced to a little flat cake of barley or doura, onions, lentils and water. Not to lose any part of their corn, they leave in it all sorts of wild grain, which often produce bad consequences. In the mountains of Lebanon and Nablous, in time of dearth, they gather the acorns from the oaks, which they eat after boiling or roasting them on the ashes.

" By a natural consequence of this misery, the art of cultivation is in the most deplorable state. The husbandman is almost without instruments, and those he has are very bad. His plough is frequently no more than the branch of a tree cut below a fork, and used without wheels. The ground is tilled by asses and cows, rarely by oxen, which would bespeak too much riches. In the districts exposed to the Arabs, as in Palestine, the countryman must sow with his musket in his hand; and scarcely does the corn turn yellow, before it is reaped, and concealed in subterraneous caverns. As little as possible is employed for seed-corn, because the peasants sow no more than is barely necessary for their subsistence. Their whole industry is limited to a supply of their immediate wants; and to procure a little bread, a few onions, a blue shirt, and a bit of woollen, much labour is not necessary. The peasant lives therefore in distress; but at least he does not enrich his tyrants, and the avarice of despotism is its own punishment.

" This picture, which is drawn by Volney, in describing the state of the peasants in Syria, seems to be confirmed by all other travellers in

Z

these countries; and, according to Eton, it represents very nearly the condition of the peasants in the greatest part of the Turkish dominions. Universally, the offices of every denomination are set up to public sale; and in the intrigues of the seraglio, by which the disposal of all places is regulated, every thing is done by means of bribes. The pachas, in consequence, who are sent into the provinces, exert to the utmost their power of extortion; but are always outdone by the officers immediately below them, who, in their turn, leave room for their subordinate agents.

" The pacha must raise money to pay the tribute, and also to indemnify himself for the purchase of his office, support his dignity, and make a provision in case of accidents; and as all power, both military and civil, centres in his person from his representing the sultan, the means are at his discretion, and the quickest are invariably considered as the best. Uncertain of to-morrow, he treats his province as a mere transient possession, and endeavours to reap, if possible, in one day the fruit of many years, without the smallest regard to his successor, or the injury that he may do to the permanent revenue.

" The cultivator is necessarily more exposed to these extortions than the inhabitant of the towns. From the nature of his employment, he is fixed to one spot, and the productions of agriculture do not admit of being easily concealed.

The tenure of the land and the rights of succession are besides uncertain.   When a father dies, the inheritance reverts to the sultan, and the children can only redeem the succession by a considerable sum of money.   These considerations naturally occasion an indifference to landed estates.   The country is deserted; and each person is desirous of flying to the towns, where he will not only in general meet with better treatment, but may hope to acquire a species of wealth which he can more easily conceal from the eyes of his rapacious masters.

" To complete the ruin of agriculture, a maximum is in many cases established, and the peasants are obliged to furnish the towns with corn at a fixed price.   It is a maxim of Turkish policy, originating in the feebleness of the government and the fear of popular tumults, to keep the price of corn low in all the considerable towns.   In the case of a failure in the harvest, every person who possesses any corn is obliged to sell it at the price fixed under pain of death; and if there be none in the neighbourhood, other districts are ransacked for it.   When Constantinople is in want of provisions, ten provinces are perhaps famished for a supply.   At Damascus, during the scarcity in 1784, the people paid only one penny farthing a pound for their bread, while the peasants in the villages were absolutely dying with hunger.

" The effect of such a system of government

on agriculture need not be insisted upon. The causes of the decreasing means of subsistence are but too obvious; and the checks, which keep the population down to the level of these decreasing resources, may be traced with nearly equal certainty, and will appear to include almost every species of vice and misery that is known g."

I shall wind up these extracts with repeating Mr. Malthus's remark, that "Human institutions, however they may appear to be the causes of much mischief to society, are in reality light and superficial, mere feathers that float the surface, in comparison with those deeper-seated causes of evil, which result from the laws of nature, and the passion between the sexes."

The theories of the Essay on Population have owed a very great portion of their success in the world, to the ambiguity of the terms employed in it. The multiplication of the human species has been checked and counteracted "by vice and misery." Who denies it? Yes, conquest is vice. Yes, bad government is vice. And, if these had been exiled from the face of the earth, we may reasonably believe that the human species and the globe on which we dwell would have worn a very different appearance from that which they actually present.

Having thus gained admission for his favourite

g Essay on Population, Vol. I, p. 255 to 263.

terms, the author of the Essay on Population immediately proceeds to put the change upon us.

First he affirms, that the increase of mankind, at least in old settled countries, is subject to an uniform and ever-active check. This we have no reason to believe; unless by a check we are to understand the uncertain tenure of human life, and the inevitable law under which we are placed, All men must die. In any other sense it is expressly contrary to the fact.

Secondly he finds, that, in the most memorable instances in which the multiplication of mankind is counteracted, there is generally great vice, and always much misery.

Having set up these two propositions, he bends them towards each other, that upon them he may repose a theory. The increase of mankind is subject to an uniform and ever active check [so says Mr. Malthus]: the known and most notorious checks upon population are vice and misery: therefore vice and misery are incessantly at work to prevent the multiplication of mankind: therefore vice and misery are indispensible ingredients in the permanent composition of the body politic. The ground of his theory is a gratuitous assumption; and, finding that there must be a check where there is none, he precariously compounds it of the best materials that offer themselves to his hand. He shews a very shadowy and inadequate founda-

tion for his first proposition, the geometrical
ratio.   He shews none at all for his second, by
which the stupendous multiplication of mankind
by a doubling every twenty-five years is reduced
at once, through the instrumentality of vice and
misery, to a stand ; but requires us to believe it,
simply because (as he says) it must be so.

CHAPTER IV.

ATTEMPT TOWARDS A RATIONAL THEORY OF
THE CHECKS ON POPULATION CONTINUED.

THUS far I have been considering those checks
on population, which operate with an out-
stretched power, and have in various instances
turned great cities and flourishing countries into
a desert. I proceed now to consider those regions, such as England, Germany and France,
which for centuries past have not been subject to
such violent convulsions.

What we appear to have most reason to believe under this latter head, is, that these countries, like Sweden, have from time to time gone
on for a certain period increasing their population
in a steady and moderate degree, and that then
certain events have occurred, which have arrested
this progress, and even reduced the population
considerably below the standard to which it had
lately attained. For instance, I will set it down,
that we have no very certain reason to believe
that England contains a greater number of inhabitants now, than it did in 1339, when Edward the Third commenced his expedition for
the conquest of France.

That the hypothesis just delivered, *viz.* that civilized countries, in possession of a reasonable degree of prosperity, have from time to time gone on for a certain period increasing their population in a steady and moderate degree, and that then certain events have occurred, which have arrested this progress, and even reduced the population considerably below the standard to which it had lately attained,—that this hypothesis, I say, is true, may be very strongly presumed from the example of Sweden.

To illustrate this, I will repeat here a Table which has already been laid before the reader in an earlier page of this volume.

The population of Sweden in 1805, as appears from the actual enumeration, amounted to 3,320,647.

Now let us suppose the population to have doubled in one hundred years, and let us take the half of this number as the sum of the Swedish people in 1705 ——— 1,660,323

By the same rule the population will be

in 1605 ———	830,162
in 1505 ———	415,081
in 1405 ———	207,540
in 1305 ———	103,770
in 1205 ———	51,885
in 1105 ———	25,942
in 1005 ———	12,971
in 905 ———	6,485
in 805 ———	3,242

in 705 ———— 1,621

in 605 ———— 810

in 505 ———— 405

So that by this way of calculation Sweden contained, at the time of the destruction of the Western Empire in 476, little more than three hundred souls, and, when this part of the globe began to send forth its hordes, which destroyed the power of the Romans, and changed the face of the world, it could scarcely boast a human inhabitant. There needs no argument, I presume, to prove that this is not the fact.

The progress of population indeed may be illustrated both ways, in its increase and in its decline, from the example of Sweden. In the year 1751, the precise period from which my accounts of the numbers of the Swedish nation commence, Adolphus Frederic of Holstein Gottorp, bishop of Lubeck, succeeded to the throne. He reigned during a period of twenty years, and was succeeded by his son, Gustavus III, who was assassinated by Ankarstroem in 1792. This event however occasioned little disturbance in the affairs of the nation: Gustavus III. was replaced in the government by his son, Gustavus IV, who reigned till 1809. Europe, during this period, was plagued with the war of 1756, the American war, and the wars which arose out of the French Revolution; but Sweden sustained less disturbance from these causes, than almost any other European state. The whole period was to her for the most part a period of tranquillity ; and accordingly we see a perpetual increase in the number of her inhabitants.

The close of the reign of Gustavus IV. was on the other hand eminently disastrous ; and we accordingly find it attended with corresponding effects. Not only Finland became lost to the Swedish crown, the population of which, by the returns of 1805, amounted to 895,773 souls · but, beside this reduction, the enumeration for the rest of the kingdom in 1810, instead of increasing, fell short by 47,000 and upwards, of the enumeration in 1805 [a]. From that period however the government was committed to the hands of Bernadotte, now Charles XIV, by whom the affairs of Sweden appear to have been conducted with some degree of prudence and moderation ; and accordingly we find, by the return for 1815, that the population is again upon the rise. Norway by a late treaty has been added to the Swedish dominions ; but the inhabitants of that country, amounting to about a million, are not included in the enumeration.

But I return to the question of population as it relates to my native country.

Now I say that the causes, which have kept down the population of the British Isles, and may, for aught we know, have prevent-

---

[a] I have been told by a Swede of good information that 90,000 persons perished in the disastrous campaign of 1809-10.

ed this country from arriving at a higher state of population at the present hour than it exhibited five centuries ago, may be principally reduced to these three, war, pestilence and famine, with the further addition of those calamities which bear a near affinity to them, *viz.* periods of general or local disturbance, contagious distempers of every description, unhealthy seasons, and occasions of eminent scarcity or public distress.

The question into which I am enquiring, is why England, having gone on for some time, at various periods, I shall suppose as Sweden has done, augmenting the number of its inhabitants, has also experienced such interruptions of this augmentation, as have very probably brought back the population to what it was before, thus presenting us with the image of a journey, such as often occurs in the incoherence of dreams, in which great advances have been made, but nothing has ultimately been gained. The ground on which we tread slides from under us, and at the end of the race we find ourselves precisely on the spot at which we set out.—As, by the hypothesis, the interruptions have been occasional, the causes of those interruptions must also have been of an intermittent, not a regular operation.

All this does certainly well accord with what we know of the system of the universe. If there were not a power of increase in the numbers of the human species, sometimes operating, and at other times existing as a power only without present agency, the human species in all probability must have been long since extinct. If, whenever famine, cruel war, or wide-wasting pestilence, had reduced the inhabitants of a country or a populous city to a mere remnant, as we frequently find to have been the case, of the population it boasted a few years or a few months before, there were no power in the constitution of man, of replacing by direct procreation with swifter or slower steps the numbers that had been swept away, it would be easy to see that every portion of the globe in its turn would have been changed into a desert.——To return.

In 1339 Edward the Third led forth an army for the conquest of France. He repeated the same proceeding in 1342, and again in 1346, while at the same time queen Philippa marched against the Scots, who were defeated in a great battle, in which twenty thousand North Britons were slain, and the Scottish king and many of his nobles were taken prisoners. The expulsion of the English from France in the latter end of the reign of Edward the Third, was probably more destructive than his conquests. To these events we must add the plague of 1348, of the victims of which fifty thousand are said to have been interred in one year, in a burial-ground now the site of the Charter House [b], beside

---

[b] Stow, *ad annum.*

those who died in other parts of London; this infection appears to have diffused itself impartially through every part of England.

The turbulent times of Richard the Second, the insurrection of the common people under Wat Tyler, and afterwards the contests between the king and his barons, could not have been favourable to population. The reign of Henry the Fourth was scarcely less disturbed than that of his predecessor.

Henry the Fifth acted over again the achievements of Edward the Third for the conquest of France; and these were followed by still more disastrous reverses in the reign of his son.

The series of events next brings us to the wars of York and Lancaster, upon which Hume observes[c]: "This fatal quarrel was not finished in less than a course of thirty years: it was signalised by twelve pitched battles: it opened a scene of extraordinary fierceness and cruelty, and is computed to have cost the lives of eighty princes of the blood, and to have almost annihilated the ancient nobility of England." What effect this had on the general population may easily be imagined. It is no less true of these wars, than of the war of Troy,

Quicquid delirant reges, plectuntur Achivi.

The reign of the Tudors may be conceived to have been on the whole favourable to population.

---

[c] A. D. 1455.

Not so the reign of the Stuarts. Charles the First never spared the blood of his people; and his conduct at length involved the nation in a civil war. The interregnum, with all its fluctuations and uncertainty of government, did not tend to increase the numbers of our countrymen; and the profligate and intolerant policy of Charles the Second could not have been beneficial to the nation.

At the Revolution commenced the system, of England making herself a principal in the wars of the continent. The long reign of George the Third has certainly had its full proportion of years of war.

Till the fire of London in 1666, Hume says [d], " The plague used to break out with great fury in this metropolis twice or thrice in every century."

From the reign of Elizabeth began the system of colonisation, the effects of which I shall have occasion more fully to unfold, when I come to treat expressly of the United States of North America. In the reign of George the Third we have not been contented to send out our planters to that side of the globe; we have settled an empire in the East Indies; and distributed our colonists profusely to other parts of the world.

Mr. Malthus may say what he pleases of the limited size of the earth, enabling it to subsist

---

[d] *Ad annum.*

only a limited number of inhabitants, and of its population " at all times pressing hard against the limits of the means of subsistence,"—nothing in the mean while can be more palpable than the inadequate population of this island, its imperfect agriculture, and the vast tracts of its soil, which have as yet been made to contribute scarcely any thing to the subsistence of man. In short it is universally admitted that the soil of this island would maintain its present population ten times told.

Meantime I have thought it proper to enter into this slight sketch of our history as connected with the numbers of our citizens, that it might serve in some degree as a corrective to the visions of Mr. Malthus. All this well accords with what we know of the history of population in Sweden. We know there, that it advances, and it retrogrades. It advances by slow and measured steps : and, in a country, not liable to the inroad of savage conquerors, nor to the perhaps still more destructive influences of a government framed for the misery of its subjects, absolute desolation is not to be expected. Here then we distinctly see the checks upon a growing population ; they are matters of record ; they form a distinct part of the great volume of our history. We are not left, in this (if in reality we knew nothing more of it than the Essay on Population supposes), misnamed science, to fill up its gaps with imaginary deaths, and still more imaginary births.

It will be seen that my question and Mr. Malthus's respecting the checks on population are altogether different. My question is, why the world, in its various climates, and its successive ages, does not produce human beings, at the rate Sweden is proved to have done for fifty-four years? His question, on the contrary, is why Sweden did not for those fifty-four years produce human beings, at the rate in which he exhibits them as produced, in his dream of the United States of North America?

The entire result of the arguments and facts collected in this and the preceding Chapter, is, that the causes that keep down the population of mankind, which otherwise might advance with a slow, but regular progress, are not silent, mysterious and concealed, but obvious and glaring, and that they operate by fits and at intervals. Though I am far from pretending in this place to have reduced the theory of the checks on population into a science, I have done something towards it. I have taken it out of the state in which Mr. Malthus left it, referring every thing, as he does, to occult causes, and holding the world in awe by the repetition, at due intervals, of two cabalistical terms, vice and misery, and have shewn that the real checks are palpable, recorded in the history of mankind,

and even capable of being reduced into somewhat of a tabulated form by the persons who
shall hereafter patiently study this important
branch of political economy.

A a

CHAPTER V.

MR. MALTHUS'S ELEVEN HEADS OF THE CAUSES
WHICH KEEP DOWN POPULATION CONSIDERED.

I HAVE complained, and with great reason, of
the vague and unsatisfactory style of generalisa-
tion in which Mr. Malthus treats his subject.
In one place however he makes an attempt at
being particular, and enumerates the checks to
population under eleven heads. I should therefore be doing injustice to his lucubrations, if I
did not bestow some attention on this passage.

The argument of the Essay on Population is
this. The population of some parts of the
United States doubles itself every twenty-five
years in regular series: the population of Europe
is at a stand, or nearly so: it is from the increase
in these parts of America, that we must infer
the inherent power and principle of population:
the different state of the numbers of mankind
in Europe must be owing to certain checks on
population, which operate here, and not in the
parts and countries alluded to. These checks
Mr. Malthus is for the most part contented to
speak of under the denominations of vice and
misery.

The passage which I am now going to offer to the attention of the reader is as follows. I transcribe it with no other variation, than the inserting in the proper places the Arabic numerals, for the sake of perspicuity.

" The positive checks to population are extremely various, and include every cause, whether arising from vice or misery, which in any degree contributes to shorten the natural duration of human life. Under this head therefore may be enumerated, 1. all unwholesome occupations, 2. severe labour, 3. exposure to the seasons, 4. extreme poverty, 5. bad nursing of children, 6. great towns, 7. excesses of all kinds, 8. the whole train of common diseases and epidemics, 9. wars, 10. plague, 11. famine [a]."

There is one thing that has been little, or not at all, adverted to by the disciples and favourers of Mr. Malthus. It is in no respect to the purpose, to produce a long catalogue of the vices that disfigure human society, or the miseries to which it is incident. This has nothing to do with our enquiry. Our only concern is with that vice and misery, or that degree of the one or the other, which exists here, and is not to be found in the northern parts of the United States of America.

I have already treated in a former chapter, of the three last of Mr. Malthus's checks, war, pes-

---

[a] Essay on Population, Vol. I, p. 21.

tilence and famine. They occur only incidentally in Europe or elsewhere. Their history fortunately may be traced. They are not in the
class of the obscure causes, among which Mr.
Malthus delights to dwell, and which, according
to him, are for ever active and awake to keep
down the population of mankind.

By this deduction then I reduce his eleven
causes to eight : and I appeal to every impartial
man to decide how pitiful a figure they make,
when assigned as the sources of such stupendous
effects as Mr. Malthus's theory requires from
them. But even here, just reasoning requires
that we should again subtract from this catalogue
all those causes, and all those modifications and
degrees of these causes, which are found to exist
in the United States.

There is still another and a portentous deduction which we are called on to make. It is but
too true, that extreme poverty has been found to
exist in some countries, and some periods in
certain countries of Europe. It is but too true
that England has exhibited a considerable portion of this evil for some years last past. Wherever extreme poverty lasts for any considerable
length of time, and spreads itself over a large
portion of mankind, it must be expected to
keep down population. But this is still nothing
to the purpose.

There are certain parts of Europe, where extreme poverty and beggary are scarcely known,

and in which there exists no such accumulation of wealth in the hands of a few individuals, as is to be found in more luxurious countries. Commerce has fortunately made little progress among them. Such a country is Switzerland; such a country is Sweden. Now what I require of Mr. Malthus is that he should shew such a difference in the operations of vice and misery, as should account for the republic of the United States doubling its population every twenty-five years in regular series by procreation only, while the population of Sweden perhaps exhibits no increase from century to century, and in its most favourable periods so small and drowsy an increase as that which is presented to us in the Swedish Tables.

This I say he has not done, and this I add neither he nor his followers will ever be able to do. We shall see in the next Book, how the case stands with the United States as to all those causes which are calculated to counteract the multiplication of mankind. Meanwhile, it will appear that I had great reason in the outset to call his theory a house of cards. Without any investigation into the subject he has affirmed that the population of a part of the United States increases successively in a geometrical ratio, and that by procreation only. This has never been proved, and shall be disproved. In the same manner he pretends to enumerate certain causes which keep down population to an

immense extent in Europe, and which have no
such operation (for here lies the pith of the question) in America. These causes, when narrowly
looked into, crumble into nothing. Mankind
do not increase, in the way in which he affirms,
and he never had any substantial reason for the
affirmation, in the New World. The increase
of the numbers of mankind is not counteracted,
in the way in which he affirms it is counteracted,
in the Old World. The two pillars of his system are wholly a delusion. And, this delusion
being blown away, we return to the same principles of good sense and philanthropy, by which
all the celebrated legislators of all antiquity
were guided as one man.

In addition to what is here alleged, be it further remembered that, as has already abundantly
appeared, it is the perishing of young children
only, that can answer the purpose of Mr. Malthus's theory for keeping down the population
of the Old World. This consideration entitles
us to strike out again from Mr. Malthus's Table
of checks, " severe labour," " exposure to the
seasons," and " excesses of all kinds," as having
little or nothing to do with the mortality of
young children.

CHAPTER VI.

OBSERVATIONS ON THE COUNTRIES IN THE
NEIGHBOURHOOD OF THE RIVER MISSOURI.

THERE are doubtless other causes, which
arrest, or which decrease population, more than
have yet been adverted to. In this question, in
the ark of which Mr. Malthus has set up an
image, that he requires all people, nations and
languages to bow down to and worship, but
which is in reality one of the newest and most
unconsidered in the whole circumnavigation of
human curiosity, it may be of some use to us
to look into unexplored paths, and to endeavour
to obtain instruction from quarters which have
hardly been resorted to.

A book has lately been published of the Travels of Captains Clarke and Lewis to the Source
of the River Missouri, and across the American
Continent to the Pacific Ocean. These men
wandered through countries, which had hardly
as yet been visited by any European. The citizens of the United States spreading themselves,
as they seem impelled to do, over every quarter
of the immense continent which has fallen to
them as by inheritance, it became interesting to

explore even this remote territory, and accordingly these officers were commissioned by the General Congress, to visit its tracts, and make report of what they saw. The book therefore which they have published, appears to be of singular authenticity.

These men, with their companions, wandered far and wide in the country they were appointed to survey. It appears to have exhibited a soil or extraordinary fertility, copiously and even magnificently watered by the hands of nature, but almost naked of inhabitants. Again and again captain Clarke, the survivor of the two appointed discoverers, by whom their observations have been published, speaks of various nations of the North American natives, the Ottoes, the Pawnees, and many more, who were once powerful races of men, but are now reduced to a feeble remnant of two or three hundred souls [a]. All these tribes, he observes, raise corn [a]. And, which may appear more extraordinary, he found among them in different places the ruins of fortifications, constructed with regularity and art, the plan of one of which he has inserted in his book.

The outline of this story is by no means extraordinary; but it comes before us in a new shape. The cities and empires which have successively disappeared from the face of the earth

---

[a] Vol. I, chap. ii, p. 44, 45.

form the counterpart of this. We visit the ruins of Balbec and Palmyra; we endeavour to trace the site of Babylon and Nineveh; and we do not feel that we are at a loss to account for the change that has taken place. We ascribe it to ruinous conquests, or to oppressive government. We may not always be right in this solution. We find marks of similar devastation on the banks of the Missouri; and we cannot impute it to desolating conquests, such as have frequently marked the history of Asia, or to bad government, of a nature like to that of which I have transcribed a specimen in the present state of Syria. It may be useful therefore to direct our attention specially to the banks of the Missouri.

It may tend somewhat to clear our ideas on the subject of population, if we divide the possible states of a country in this respect into three, increasing, decreasing, and stationary. There is every reason to believe that the aboriginal population of North America has long been decreasing, and is fast wearing out. It cannot have been always decreasing: that is an absurdity in terms. It once was stationary: before that, it is conformable to usual modes of reasoning on the subject, to suppose that it was on the increase.

Let us then assume a hypothetical period, when the numbers of the North American tribes began to diminish. This constitutes on many accounts a memorable era. Then first, according to Mr. Malthus, vice and misery may be conceived to appear among them. Who brought them? What caravan, crossing the vast deserts of snow which surround the North Pole, had the merit of importing the precious cargo? This idea of fixing a limit and a beginning to a thing, is of vast service to enable us to comprehend the probability or improbability of any hypothesis respecting it.

One of Mr. Malthus's theories respecting population (and he would fain have us believe that all his theories are in unison and harmony) is, that in old countries the numbers of mankind are kept down by a want of the means of subsistence. It is not so in new countries. This last is the reason, as he tells us, why the population of the northern part of the United States has gone on, " doubling itself every twenty-five years for a century and a half successively." The aboriginal inhabitants of the continent of North America were, I suppose, once a new people. They afterwards, it appears, changed their character, and became, according to Mr. Malthus's way of classing the inhabitants of the earth, an old people. When did this revolution take place?

The ideas we have usually been led to form of a race like the original tribes of North America, are that they are a wandering people, a nation of hunters. Hunting is certainly somewhat a precarious mode of providing the sustenance of human life; and we will suppose that, however plentiful the beasts used for food might be at first, a perseverance in the exercises of the chace may diminish their numbers. If this is the case, we might very naturally account for the decreasing population of a nation of hunters. But the nations on the banks of the Missouri all raise corn; their soil is peculiarly adapted for that purpose; and yet this tract of country is at this hour more thinly peopled than we almost any where read of.

But I shall perhaps be told by some, " War is the cause of this thinness of population; the nations in the vicinity of the Missouri are savages; and they occupy their time in cutting one another's throats." The speculators who are contented to assign this as the cause of the phenomenon, undoubtedly are persons who see a very little way. When did this spirit of warfare and murder begin? The inhabitants of this part of the world at one time probably went on increasing their numbers. At another time it may be they remained stationary in this respect. I suppose no one will be infatuated enough to believe, that from the very beginning of their existence they have gone on incessantly decreasing. We must therefore suppose that they were once a civilized and humane people, and then degenerated into cut-throats and cannibals.

This hypothesis therefore, that the thinness of

the population is to be accounted for by their wars, is entirely a gratuitous assumption. We have not the shadow of evidence of any change of character in the Aborigines of North America. We meet with a difficulty which we know not how to solve; and we invent this idea at random to account for it. Such a mode of proceeding bears no resemblance to reasoning, and is wholly unworthy of an answer.

It has already been observed, that, if a paucity of the means of subsistence is the cause that thins the ranks of mankind, it follows, as a corollary from this principle, that, when the agency of this cause has exerted itself to a given degree, the pressure should cease, and the former state of things return. It is somewhat of the same nature as the law of elasticity; want, severe necessity, according to Mr. Malthus, keeps down the propagation of mankind: but, when that want is removed, and every facility is afforded for procuring the means of subsistence, the principle of population ought to renew its strength like the eagle, and rejoice like a strong man to run his race. It is true, that in Europe every part and portion of the soil is allotted; the rich proprietor disposes of his land as he pleases. This is probably a reason why England and Europe have a very small number of inhabitants compared with that which the soil would maintain. But on the banks of the Missouri it is otherwise. There is no great landholder there, to say in every instance to his unfortunate neighbour, "This field is mine; and, whether I make an inadequate, or a perverse, or no use of it, you must not attempt to derive the smallest sustenance from it." The survey of the banks of the Missouri, is of itself a sufficient answer to this part of the Essay on Population.

Thus far I think I have proceeded with a reasonable degree of certainty. The facts observed by captains Clarke and Lewis on the banks of the Missouri will hardly be disputed. Their total discordance with the theories of Mr. Malthus is sufficiently evident. It happens in this, as in many other subjects, that while we confine ourselves to negatives, we tread on tolerably firm ground. When we endeavour positively to assign causes to account for the phenomena, we then begin to be bewildered. I will not therefore trifle far with my readers under this head. I will nakedly set down a cause which occurs to my mind.

May it not be, that races of men have a perpetual tendency to wear out? It is generally believed, both of men and animals, that a breed is materially improved by crossing, and by consequence that, where a breed is not crossed, it has a constant tendency to decline. May not the qualities of the present race of Europeans, such as we find them, be materially owing to the invasions of the Celts and the Cimbri, the Goths and Vandals, the Danes, the Saxons, and the Normans? Perhaps, when Daniel Defoe wrote his True-Born Englishman, and thought he was composing a satire, he was very unintentionally unfolding the causes which render the natives of this island in my opinion superior, in stamina of character, in constancy of action, in intellect, in humanity, and in morals, to the people of any other country now existing on earth.

If this be a true view of the case (and I state it only as a thing by no means impossible), it would be enough to lead a deep and searching mind, to consider the existence of the human species collectively, as in some degree precarious. If particular races of men wear out, why, in the vast revolution of ages, supposing the earth to last so long, may not the whole wear out? We have strong reason to believe that several kinds of animals, heretofore inhabitants of this globe, have become extinct. What is it that should for ever render man superior to the empire of mutability? Looking at the subject from this point of view, one might be almost tempted to say of the species, as of one individual, " Whatsoever thy hand findeth to do, do it with thy might; for there is no work, nor device, nor wisdom, nor knowledge, in the grave, whither thou goest."

But, whether the cause here mentioned for the disappearance of nations and races of men be a real cause or otherwise, I think I have a right to conclude from the contents of this Chapter, that is, from what is related respecting the Aborigines of North America, compared with a variety of similar facts recorded in the pages of ancient history, that there are other causes, which arrest, or which decrease from time to time the population of countries, more than have yet been adverted to.

ENQUIRY

CONCERNING

POPULATION.

BOOK IV.

*OF THE POPULATION OF THE UNITED STATES OF
NORTH AMERICA.*

CHAPTER I.

INTRODUCTION.

IN the Second Book of this work I have shewn
the absolute impossibility, so far as all the
Tables that have yet been formed respecting the
multiplication of mankind can be relied on, that
the increased population of the United States of
North America, " a doubling," according to Mr.
Malthus, " for above a century and a half successively, in less than twenty-five years," could
have been produced by the principle of " pro-

creation." We have seen that under the most favourable circumstances, and such as cannot be expected to continue in any country for any length of time, the increase is perfectly insignificant compared with the monstrous propositions of Mr. Malthus, and that from the constitution of human nature it must necessarily be so.

Here then I might have closed my argument respecting the principal topic of the present treatise. I might have rested my appeal with every strict and impartial reasoner, whether the phenomenon of the increased numbers of the people of the United States must not be accounted for in some other way, and not from procreation. But I know that many readers, and many persons calling themselves reasoners, are neither strict nor impartial. And I would willingly consent to depart a little from the rigid forms of logical deduction, if by so doing I can the more fully satisfy such as these.

There will doubtless be some who, struck with the preceding arguments, will feel as if they had before them two opposite demonstrations, that which results on the one hand from all that is known, or has been laid down by scientifical writers, respecting the multiplication of mankind, and that which results on the other from the actual enumerations and censuses of the inhabitants of the United States. That feeling will be erroneous. There cannot be opposite demonstrations: and, as has been already remarked,

B b

" A census or enumeration of human beings in any given country, or over the whole globe, can never constitute any term in the progression of the increase of mankind,"allowing for the moment that there is an increase[a].

The result is then, that I have sufficiently proved, so far as can be inferred from all the documents that have yet been collected respecting the supposed increase of mankind, that the augmentation of numbers in the United States of North America, to whatever it may amount, cannot have arisen from their own proper resources in the way of procreation. It will nevertheless, as I have said, be more satisfactory to many, that I should endeavour to shew affirmatively how it has arisen; and for the sake of such satisfaction the present Book shall be appropriated to the solution of that problem. The human mind in ordinary instances does not rest so well contented with a merely negative demonstration : it is the passion of the common run of enquirers into man or nature, to seek to account for every thing. I by no means promise that I shall in the present case do this completely; I am entering upon an altogether new topic; but I shall at least throw out some hints, which I have no doubt subsequent information will make out and confirm. And at all events I protest in the commencement, against any imper-

---

[a] See above, p. 147.

fectness in the present division of my treatise, as having the effect of vitiating the reasonings of the divisions immediately preceding.

I further trust that, if I shall not be able to make out to demonstration the precise sources of the increasing population of the United States, I shall at least shew in what follows, from a variety of considerations, exclusively of the thread of the argument of my Second and Third Books, that it is impossible that the source should be found in the principle of procreation.

CHAPTER II.

OF THE TOPOGRAPHY AND POLITICAL CONDITION OF THE UNITED STATES.

HAVING examined sufficiently the fundamental principle of our subject, and enquired into the facts which belong to it, as far as the other portions of the globe are concerned, it is time that we should proceed to the consideration of North America.

It is from this country that Mr. Malthus has drawn his portentous and calamitous doctrine of the geometrical ratio. He says, " In the northern states of America the population has been found to double itself, for above a century and a half successively, in less than twenty-five years ;" and he adds, This " has been repeatedly ascertained to be from procreation only."

Astonished at assertions so bold, for which I could perceive so very slender foundation, I wrote to Mr. Malthus, requesting him to state to me the precise authority on which his assertions were built. My Letter and his Answer are inserted in the First Chapter of the Second Book.

It will be obvious that the second assertion is the only one with which our question is con cerned. The first may perhaps demand some comment incidentally, but that only as it is connected with the second.

I knew however, when I wrote to Mr. Malthus, that it would be idle and almost ludicrous, to ask for his proofs for the second. I was in hopes they would in some measure be brought to light in our investigation of the proofs of the first.

The first observation then that forces itself upon our attention, is the impossibility of bringing any proof of the second assertion. And yet this, and this only, this little line, is all the ground that Mr. Malthus's system has to stand on. Every thing in the Essay on Population depends upon an original begging the question. Presumptions and probabilities, it might be supposed, would attend on the proposition: proofs there could be none.

To render Mr. Malthus's doctrine sound and complete, it would be necessary that the United States of America should be posited alone upon some island in the vast sea, and surrounded by inaccessible rocks, so that no vessel, not so much as a cock-boat, could make good a landing. How Mr. Malthus would have obtained his intelligence from this island, I would leave it to him to settle.

Next to such an island, the best country in which to try the experiment of the procreative power, would be such a country as China or

Japan, where it is understood to be death for any stranger to attempt a settlement. The United States is no such country. It is said, that they have not solemnly renounced all ideas of hospitality; and that a stranger may meditate a settlement there, without risking the loss of life or limb.

Well then : There can be no proof that the increasing numbers of the inhabitants of the United States came from procreation only.

If however we cannot have for the scene of our experiment such an island, or such a country, as I have described, it is to be hoped that at least the trial will be made upon a country seldom visited by voyagers, and almost never by any man with the intention of taking up his residence in it, a country that has an ill name over the rest of the globe, whose manners and superstitions are contemplated with horror, a country without activity or enterprise, where no man can hope to make his fortune, and the labourer must not expect by the sweat of his brow to earn the means of supplying the most indispensible wants of existence.

The United States of North America are the very reverse of all this. Let us take down the map, and look at the territory. It is one immense line of coast, presenting more multiplied commodiousnesses for taking land,—bays, harbours, navigable rivers, and creeks,—than any other country on the face of the earth. If the government of the United States, like those of China and Japan, had taken every precaution to prevent strangers from settling within their borders, it would have been in vain. The oldest inhabitants of the territory, a century or two back, were Europeans, speaking European languages. They have not yet acquired a physiognomy, a distinct character or set of manners, by which a native of North America can be distinguished from the emigrants settled in his vicinity.

But the government of the United States pursues no such train of policy. They know that they possess an immeasurable tract of country, and that that country, whatever we may talk of its population, is very poorly inhabited. They have very naturally the desire to become a mighty empire. Without imputing to them any vicious ambition, they might, from mere virtue, and benevolence of soul, wish to see the vast tracts, above, below, and around them on every side, adorned with a healthy, an industrious, a civilized, and a happy race of people. Their government is free; their institutions are liberal; and what they most obviously want is greater multitudes of men to partake these blessings. They are not converts to Mr. Malthus's philosophy; or at least not such converts, as to be disposed to make it their rule of action for the territory over which they preside. They are

not exactly prepared to trust for the future population of their domain, to " procreation only."

Long has the coast of North America been
looked to by the discontented, the unhappy, and
the destitute of every kingdom of Europe, as
the land of promise, the last retreat of independence, the happy soil, on which they might
dwell and be at peace. How could it be otherwise? Here every man, without let or moles-
tation, may worship God according to his
conscience. Here there are no legal infliction of
torture, no Bastilles and dungeons, no sanguinary laws. This is the sacred asylum of liberty.
Here land, by hundreds and thousands of acres,
may be had for almost nothing. Here the wages
of labour are high.

There are but two or three reasons, that prevent the whole lower and worst provided cast of
the inhabitants of Europe, from passing over to
the United States almost in a body.

First, the strange and nameless love which a
great majority of mankind feel for the spot of
earth on which they were born. To see it no
more, to meet no more the old familiar faces, never to behold again the trees and the hedge-rows,
the church, the hamlet, the chimney-corner and
the oaken-board, which have been our daily
acquaintance through life, is a divorce hardly
less severe than that of soul and body. In this
respect man is for the most part a vegetable,

with a slight shade of difference, and clings to his native soil with almost equal pertinacity.

A second reason why our poor do not generally remove to America, is that those to whom removal would be in a manner the necessary of existence, do not possess the means of accomplishing it. Without the possession of a little sum of money, they may look a thousand times with eager aspirations upon the waves of the Atlantic, but they can never ascend the bark that should waft them over.

CHAPTER III.

HISTORY OF EMIGRATION FROM EUROPE TO NORTH AMERICA IN THE SEVENTEENTH CENTURY.

THE discovery and the planting of North America form one of the most interesting epochs in the history of human nature. As long as there is tyranny and oppression among any of the governments of mankind, as long as it is possible for a human being to come under the burthen of unmerited disgrace, as long as there shall exist a pride in man that disdains servitude, and a spirit of industry anxious to free itself from vexation and constraint, so long will emigration form a feature in the history of our race. One of the blessings indispensible to the welfare of man in society, is the prerogative he shall possess of removing himself from the yoke of a government that, for whatever reason, has become intolerable to him. One of the great mischiefs of the Roman government under the emperors, was, that a man who had the misfortune to fall under the displeasure of the despot, or who could no longer brook the condition of the polity that ruled over him, had no refuge to which he could fly : the boundaries of the empire and of the known world were almost the same.   His situation was something like that spoken of in the Psalms of David : " If I take the wings of the morning, and dwell in the uttermost parts of the sea, even there thy right hand shall reach me."

The condition of the European world became greatly improved, in this respect, upon the dissolution of the Roman empire.   This favoured portion of the globe, by means of that event, was broken into several governments; and he who was dissatisfied with one, could remove himself into the sphere of another.   Yet the remedy was imperfect.   He who could not bear " the ills he had," might chance to " fly to others that he knew not of," and that might prove still more intolerable.   He removed himself, it may be, from the scene of his oppression, and he might come under a yet bitterer despotism and persecution.

The discovery of North America, and the manner in which it was planted, struck these objections to the root.   In proportion as the territory was cleared, and the savages retired back into the woods, here was a vast portion of the teeming earth, from Cape Breton north, to the boundaries of Florida, that opened wide her bosom, and tendered a hospitable welcome to every exile.   He whom the iron of oppression had pierced to the soul, and he whom visionary notions of civil or religious independence had driven from his native clime, equally found himself at home and at rest on the shores of North America. Here was no government to gall him. The refinements of oppression had not reached this happy soil: here was no scheme of civil policy, which, under the hollow pretence of a paternal care for its subjects, shackled the native freedom of enterprise, and sought to reduce the commerce of man with his God within the control of the " traditions of men."

The discovery of North America may almost be said to have added a new element to nature, and a new faculty to man.

One of the first considerable British settle·ments that was made in this part of the world, was effected in New England by the Brownists and Puritans, flying from the intolerance of king James the First, and still more of his son and successor, king Charles a. The foundations of Boston and some other considerable towns in that state, were laid in or about the year 1630 a. Charles dismissed his parliament early in 1629, with the declared intention of never calling another. Henceforth all that opposed his measures in church or state were laid at his mercy ; and it is well known that Laud and his colleagues dealt out nothing but tyranny to those whom they regarded as their enemies, in the shape of

---

a Robertson, History of America, Book X.

heavy fines, tedious imprisonment, and the pillory. It is computed that above fifteen hundred persons went into voluntary exile in New England in the year 1630, among whom were several of respectable, families, and in easy circumstances [b]. Shortly after, we read that the number of freemen greatly increased, so as to induce them, instead of attending the general courts in person, voluntarily to have recourse to the expedient of sending representatives who might transact business in their name [c]. In 1635, among crowds of new settlers, came Hugh Peters and sir Henry Vane [c]. In 1637 the government of Charles became so much alarmed on the subject, as to induce it to issue a proclamation, forbidding any one to emigrate to New England without leave from the court: and the first consequence of this proclamation was the stopping eight ships, in which were embarked sir William Constable, sir Arthur Hazelrig, Hampden, Pym, and Oliver Cromwel [d]. But, notwithstanding every precaution that could be used, the embarkations of the following year were more numerous than ever [e]: and it is computed that, from the first settlement of the Brownists to the year 1640, twenty-one thousand two hundred British subjects passed over to New

---

[b] *Ibid.*   [c] *Ibid.*

[d] Hume, Chap. LII. Chalmers, Annals of the United Colonies, p. 160.

[e] Robertson, *ubi supra.*

England, and two hundred thousand pounds, a vast sum for those days, were expended in fitting out ships, transporting settlers, and purchasing stock [f]. Thus did this colony not grow up by insensible degrees, but seemed to " rise like an exhalation."

Another colony which was planted about the same time was that of Maryland, by one of the most virtuous of mankind, Cecilius lord Baltimore. The colonists of Maryland were the Roman Catholics of the British dominions. This set of men, who faithfully adhered to the religion of their ancestors, were treated much more opprobriously, and experienced a bitterer persecution, than the Puritans ; while these last, themselves suffering from a similar cause, were the fiercest in calling for the execution of the sanguinary laws against men, who it was fashionable to say held principles incompatible with all civilisation and government. The first settlers in Maryland, who sailed from Great Britain in 1632, were two hundred Catholic gentlemen with their families and adherents [g]: but they were speedily followed by much greater numbers [g]; and during the first two years lord Baltimore himself spent the sum of forty thousand pounds upon his colony [i]. At the Restoration the inhabitants are said to have amounted to

---

f Robertson, *ubi supra.*   g Chalmers, p. 207.
i Chalmers, p. 208

twelve thousand persons [k], and in sixteen years afterwards to have increased to sixteen thousand [l].

Such was the recorded emigration to the coasts of North America from the island of Great Britain (stimulated by religious and political oppression), which was begun and nearly matured under the rule of Charles the First. It is exceedingly probable that the real number of emigrants from these considerations surpassed the number that is set down.

But it will perhaps be supposed, that when this cloud had passed over, the emigration ceased, and the colonies were left to what has been called their natural increase. Alas, where is the government, of which its subjects do not think they have reason to complain? Where is the history, every chapter of which does not abound with convulsions, intolerance, persecution, the calamitous defeat of one party, and the vindictive triumph of another? Where is the nation, multitudes of whose people do not suffer great adversity, and harbour in their minds grievous discontents?

While New England became thus considerable from the causes I have mentioned, another colony was established at the same time, or a little earlier, in Virginia. The first peopling of Virginia with British settlers appears to have

---

[k] Chalmers, p. 226.   [l] Chalmers, p. 363.

risen principally from the spirit of enterprise and
the general love of adventure.   But, when the
arms of king Charles sustained defeat in the
field, Virginia afforded as advantageous a retreat
for the cavaliers, as New England has before
done for the Puritans; and it prospered accordingly.

Meanwhile the victory of the republicans was
but temporary; the wheel turned round; and
Charles the Second was restored eleven years
after the death of his father.   Mr. Chalmers
says, this was " an age, when all men's minds
were inflamed either with the desire of emigration, because they were unhappy in England,
or with an anxiety to acquire distant territory,
because their sovereign was profuse of what cost
him nothing m."   And he adds elsewhere, " As
numbers during the reign of Charles II. suffered
more from what they dreaded than from what
they felt, they naturally deserted a land where
they were miserable, in order to enjoy that freedom and property which were now offered them
as the price of their change of habitation n."   I
have the misfortune to differ from Mr. Chalmers
in two of the sentiments conveyed in this last
sentence: first, I would say that where people
" are miserable," it cannot fairly be said that they
have nothing to complain of in point of "·feel-
ing ;" and secondly, I cannot admit, that under

m P. 635.   n P. 644.

the act of uniformity, the conventicle act, and the five-mile act, directed against a party, which had lately controled the state, and more recently had put the crown on the head of the sovereign, that party did not sustain grievances at least as substantial, as those experienced by the Puritans in the reign of the father. Be this however as it will, my subject is no otherwise concerned than with the fact, that " all men's minds were at this time inflamed with the desire of emigration."

Another memorable colony which gives lustre to the annals of Charles the Second, was led forth by William Penn, and founded the walls of the city of Philadelphia. This colony consisted almost entirely of Quakers, a sect, that in its origin was treated more contumeliously than almost any other upon record. Its founder was, " in prisons oft, in hunger and nakedness, whipped from tithing to tithing," and repeatedly drummed out of the cities and market-towns he thought proper to visit. At length a generous individual rose out of their own body, who found means to lead forth this despised people into the distant wilds of America, there to endow them with the rights of men, to enable them to worship God as seemed meet to their own consciences, to respect themselves and be respected, and so founded a tribe and an establishment of men, the simplicity of whose manners, and the sobriety of whose proceedings have

C c

been the wonder of the world. A certain number of these sectaries having sailed before, Penn himself embarked with two thousand adventurers in the year 1682. He immediately chose the site, and laid the foundation of his capital city ; and he " enjoyed the satisfaction of having completed the settlement of six-and-twenty sail of people to content, within the space of one year o." Speedily " it became a gainful branch of commerce from the West of England, to carry passengers to Pennsylvania, because the spirit of emigration pervaded a dissatisfied people p." Accordingly, the first assembly of the legislature of this colony, " consisting of seventy-two delegates from the six counties into which Penn had divided it," took place in the December of the very year, in which their great legislator first set his foot upon the Transatlantic shore q.

Such was the colonisation, from England only, in the course of the seventeenth century. I possess no such accounts of the emigration from Scotland and Ireland : but the much greater convulsions and calamities with which those parts of the British dominions were visited, leave me no room to doubt of its extent. The unhappy and beautiful country of Ireland has at all times been the victim of English ascendancy, and of the unsparing rigour of English des-

---

o Chalmers, p. 644.   p *Ibid.*   q Chalmers, p. 645.

potism. The barbarism and ignorance in which
we plunged our sister island, were the causes
why she did not keep pace with us in receiving
the light of the Reformation ; and the difference
of religious creed which sprung out of this,
afforded a new and abundant defence for all the
severities and all the tyranny which the govern-
ing country exercised towards contumacious
Papists. Whoever calls to mind the ferocious
manner in which the Irish rebellion, and as it
has sometimes been called the Irish massacre,
broke out in 1641, and the sanguinary proceedings employed by Cromwel and Ireton in suppressing it, will be at no loss for an idea of the
convulsions that shook that devoted country.
Again, in the close of that very century, Ireland
became the scene of new devastations. James
the Second made his last stand in the plains of
Ireland, and such was the system of the prince
who ravished from him his crown, that the Revolution under king William is remembered
with a horror and detestation by her natives,
equal to the love and veneration with which it
is contemplated by the friends of freedom in
England.

From Ireland let us turn to Scotland. Charles
the First found presbytery established as the national system of church-government there, and
he was persuaded by Laud and others, to set
out upon an adventure to establish episcopacy
and a liturgy in all their glory in his native

kingdom. The contention lasted for years, and
served as the first step in that memorable civil
war, which ended by depriving the king of his
head. After an interval came the Restoration
of Charles the Second : and this event served as
a signal, bringing on the Scots, who had been
foolish enough ten years before to fight for this
prince in the battle of Worcester, and so to lay
themselves bare to the vengeance of Cromwel,
one of the most atrocious specimens of mis-
government in the history of the world. The
act of uniformity, the conventicle act, and the
five-mile act, under which the presbyterians and
dissenters of England groaned, were but as the
little finger of tyranny, compared with what
was perpetrated beyond the Tweed. The names
of the duke of Lauderdale and others stand
upon record, as hardly to be matched but with
the Caligulas and Neros of Roman story.

The reign of king William, which was a
blessing to England, was scarcely less calamitous to some of the Scottish tribes, than it
proved to the Irish.

The year 1685 witnessed the revocation of
the edict of Nantes, under the auspices of which
the Protestants of France had possessed the
comforts of toleration for nearly a century. It
is well known to what a degree that measure
depopulated France of multitudes of her most
useful and industrious citizens, and not a few of
these went over and settled themselves in the

countries now bearing the name of the United States of North America.

The German settlements of persecuted Protestants, or otherwise, have been by no means inconsiderable.

I will conclude this chapter with extracting a short passage enumerating the various sets of adventurers, who originally constituted the population of this country.

" New England was settled altogether by Englishmen, except an Irish colony in the hilly part of one county of Massachusets, and a few Scottish and Irish settlements in New Hampshire. With these limitations, the New England population is at this hour entirely of English origin. The same source also supplies a great majority of the people in the middle, and a still larger portion in the southern states. The Germans make about a fourth of the population of Pennsylvania, and a part of the inhabitants of New York and New Jersey. They are however fast yielding their language, habits and customs to the predominance of the English. The same may be said of the Dutch, settled in New York, New Jersey, and Pennsylvania. A few French Protestants fixed themselves at New Rochelle and Staten Island in the state of New York, and at Charles Town in South Carolina. The Irish emigrants are found principally in Pennsylvania and Maryland ; and many are scattered over New York, New Jersey, Kentucky, and some other states. Those who are Catholics from the middle and south of Ireland, compose the bulk of the day-labourers in our large cities: the Protestants from the north of Ireland, generally become agriculturists in the interior of the country.

" The Scots, who are for the most part intelligent, industrious, good citizens, have settlements in New Hampshire, New York, New Jersey, Pennsylvania, and North Carolina. Some Swedes are found in New Jersey, Pennsylvania, and Maryland: and some Swiss have fixed their abode in the state of Indiana. Some small Welch settlements have been made in Pennsylvania and New York [r]."

---

[r] Bristed, America and her Resources, Chapter VII.

CHAPTER IV.

IT is not within the scope of the present treatise, to trace out all the different swarms and
hivings of emigration, by means of which the
United States have been raised to their present
populousness. I will therefore pass on without
further circumlocution, to what I find on the
subject in Dr. Johnson's Journey to the Western
Islands of Scotland. The Journey was performed in the year 1773.

This celebrated traveller appears to labour
under a want of words to express what he saw
and what he learned in this respect in his Scottish Tour. He talks of the " fever of emigration," the " epidemical fury of emigration." He
speaks of " the general dissatisfaction, which
was at that time driving the Highlanders into
the other hemisphere:" and mentions vessels,
which "lay waiting to dispeople some of the
Western Islands, by carrying the natives away
to America."

" Whether the mischiefs of emigration," says

he, " were immediately perceived, may be justly
questioned.   They who went first, were probably such as could best be spared ; but the accounts sent by the earliest adventurers, whether
true or false, inclined many to follow them ; and
whole neighbourhoods formed parties for removal; so that departure from their native country
is no longer exile.   He that goes thus accompanied, carries with him all that makes life pleasant.   He sits down in a better climate, surrounded by his kindred and his friends : they
carry with them their language, their opinions,
their popular songs, and hereditary merriment :
they change nothing but the place of their
abode ; and of that change they perceive the
benefit."

" The numbers which have already gone,
though like other numbers they may be magni-
fied, are very great, and such as if they had
gone together, and agreed upon any certain settlement, might have founded an independent
government in the depths of the western continent.   Nor are they only the lowest and most
indigent ; many men of considerable wealth
have taken with them their train of labourers
and dependents ; and if they continue the feudal
scheme of polity, may establish new clans in the
other hemisphere."

In former times " those who left the country
were for the most part the idle dependents on
overburthened families, or men who had no

property; and therefore they carried away only themselves. [The erroneousness of this idea has been seen in the preceding Chapter]. In the present eagerness of emigration, families, and almost communities, go away together. Those who were considered as prosperous and wealthy, sell their stock and carry away the money. Once none went away but the useless and the poor; in some parts there is now reason to fear, that none will stay but those who are too poor to remove themselves, and too useless to be removed at the cost of others."

The reader is aware that the scenes here described were the result of the great revolution in the Highlands and Islands of Scotland, which followed upon the defeat of the partisans of the House of Stuart in 1745.

I will add to the testimony of Dr. Johnson, a passage from a recent author, well known for his faithful and masterly delineations of the manners of Scotland, the author of the Tales of My Landlord.

"Serjeant Macalpin had seen hard service in various quarters of the world, and was reckoned one of the most tried and trusty men of the Scottish Train. Having lost his right arm in a peninsular campaign, he retired, with an allowance from Chelsea, and a small income, accruing from prize-money and savings, in the design to set himself down in the wild Highland glen, where, when a boy, he had been accustomed to herd black cattle and goats. To his recollection, this sequestered spot was unparalleled in beauty by the richest scenes he had visited in his wanderings. He came; he revisited the loved scene: it was but a sterile glen, surrounded with rude crags, and traversed by a northern torrent. This was not the worst. The fires had been quenched upon thirty hearths: of the cottage of his fathers he could· distinguish but a few rude stones: the language was almost extinguished: the ancient race from which he boasted his descent, had found a refuge beyond the Atlantic. One southland farmer, three grey, plaided shepherds, and six dogs, now tenanted the whole glen, which in his youth had maintained in content, if not in competence, upwards of two hundred inhabitants [a]."

Finally, the American war in 1775, and the Declaration of Independence, changed the scene in the Western World, and gave a new and powerful impulse to the tide of emigration. Hitherto it had been a fashion with many to regard the American colonies with a sort of scorn. Our courts of justice had been accustomed to sentence such as were found guilty of offences, in expiation of which it was not thought proper to inflict capital punishment, to be transported to the plantations. Forgetting therefore the way in which these colonies were first settled,

---

[a] Tales of my Landlord: First Series ; Old Mortality.

by men of generous enterprise, by conscientious men flying from religious persecution and political oppression, forgetting the virtues of lord Baltimore, Penn, and sir Henry Vane, and the meditated purposes of Hampden and his illustrious compeers, it was not uncommon to hear these settlements opprobriously called a land of convicts. This reproach was for ever obliterated by the Declaration of Independence, and the achievements by which thatDeclaration was rendered effectual. It was speedily seen that this quarter of the world was henceforth to be regarded as the asylum of freedom of thought and political liberty. Almost every human creature has as intuitive feeling of the connection between true manliness of sentiment and understanding, and republicanism. It was obvious that civilization in the European world was in its decay; and it was uncertain whether any happy convulsion would occur, by means of which we might hope to see it renovated. The United States of America looked, in the eye of the warm-hearted philanthropist, like a phoenix, in which we might hope to see revived all that was most valuable and lovely in ancient or modern history.

One of the most memorable results of the Independence of the United States of North America has been the practical extension of their territory. Before the commencement of the war between Great Britain and her colonies

in 1775, the territory actually settled was, with
a few exceptions, little more than a strip of land
extending along the shores of the Atlantic as
far as Florida south, of enormous length indeed,
but scarcely more than fifty or a hundred miles
in breadth. In consequence of this circumstance, one of the projects of the government
here was to burn and destroy all the towns along
the sea-coast, by means of which the colonies,
considered in their political and social existence,
would be in a manner annihilated, and the
wretched fugitives would certainly be reduced
to accept any terms which Great Britain in her
clemency might think proper to prescribe. Now
the territory of the United States is computed
to contain six hundred and forty millions of
acres[b]; and over the whole of this vast surface
the population is gradually spreading itself.
Formerly the planters cautiously dwelt near to
each other and to the succour of the governments, through fear of the inroads of the savage
Indians: now that mischief is at an end. At
the commencement of their Independence they
counted thirteen states: the tables of the last
census are distributed under twenty-six heads of
territory. The consequence of all this is, that
every emigrant, possessing a moderate sum of
money, is immediately allured by the acquisi-

---

[b] Morse, American Geography.

tion of hundreds and thousands of acres, to become a citizen.

Influenced by these considerations, multitudes no doubt from all parts of Europe shipped themselves for the territories of the United States, between the period of the Declaration of Independence in 1776, and the breaking out of the French Revolution in 1789. But this last was the event, that, if we trace its consequences through all their ramifications, may emphatically be said to have broken down the dykes which held in the population of Europe, and poured out the streams of its real or imaginary superfluity, to fructify the immeasurable plains of the Western World. All this I shall pass over in a summary manner. If I were to do otherwise, I must write the history of the convulsions of Europe for the last thirty years, and exhibit the essence of all the books of travels to North America which have been published within that period.

The commencement of the French Revolution was the commencement of a reign of terror. The whole nobility of the country, with a few exceptions, withdrew from their native soil: and the nobility of France was out of all proportion to ours, since every son of a noble father there became distinguished by a title. Many fled, from abhorrence of the intemperate spirit of innovation to which they saw all their ancient institutions a prey; and many more, because they could scarcely hope for safety in staying at home. All financiers and farmers-general, all administrators and collectors of the revenue, the whole numerous train that had been more or less connected with the court, found cause of reasonable alarm. Every one who had at that period arrived at years of discretion, can remember how the streets of London suddenly became crowded with French emigrants; and many of these emigrants found their way to North America.

There was enough of persecution and ill blood in France from the very commencement of the Revolution. But affairs changed inexpressibly for the worse, when the different sovereigns of Europe combined for the suppression of Gallic liberty, and the duke of Brunswick issued his proclamation, worthy to be remembered with eternal execration, in which he threatened, in the name of the allied sovereigns, to level Paris to the ground, and not to leave in her one stone resting upon another. This was the signal for the massacres of September 1792. This roused to desperation and frenzy every man in France (the partisans of despotism only excepted), who had any attachment to the independence of his natal soil.

One of the effects of the spirit thus roused was, that the duke of Brunswick was driven back with disgrace, that Flanders was con-

quered, and that in the following year the heads
of the king and queen fell upon the scaffold.

But there was no end to the convulsions of
that unhappy country. No sooner was the
cause of liberty triumphant, than her friends
burned with animosity against each other, and
republicans and monarchists indiscriminately
bowed their heads to the public executioner.

Nor were the disorders that rose out of this
memorable event confined to France. Every
kingdom in Europe, in any way neighbouring
to the scene, was convulsed by the spirit of general liberty, which every way propagated itself
from France as a centre; and, as has been already said, no country can suffer internal commo-
tions, without one of the most natural results
shewing itself in a spirit of emigration. To the
war of France for her independence, succeeded
the counteraction, in a series of expeditions on
the part of that power, for the subjugation of
Europe. The sequel brought forward the great
conqueror and spoiler of modern times, Napo-
leon Bonaparte. He conquered Italy; he conquered Germany ; he conquered Spain ; he conquered Poland; he proceeded far towards the
conquest of Russia. He menaced England.
The ancient republics of Europe, Holland, Switzerland, Venice, and Genoa, were prostrate at
his feet.

One of the results of the French Revolution
was the Irish Rebellion in 1798; and it is well

known how the soil of the United States has fattened on the miseries of Ireland.

Another of these results was the war of Great Britain against the United States in 1812. I understand that the soldiers we sent out in that war deserted in almost entire regiments, and became peaceable citizens of the republic.

CHAPTER V,

RETROSPECT OF THE HISTORY OF POPULATION IN THE UNITED STATES.

I PROCEED to the direct consideration of the present state of the population of the United States of North America. And that we may have the more accurate ideas on the subject, I will set it down in numbers, in two forms.

First, the different stages of the population, as given in Pitkin's Statistical View of the United States, and referred to by Mr. Malthus in his letter addressed to me, of the date of October 24, 1818. In this author there occurs:

1. An Estimate for 1749————1,046,000 [a].

---

[a] Page 12. I will indulge myself in only one remark in this place. Mr. Pitkin states the population in 1749 as 1,046,000 : Dr. Franklin, another of Mr. Malthus's authorities, in his celebrated paper to which I have so often had occasion to refer, says in 1731, " There are supposed to be now upwards of one million of English souls in North America." The difference between Dr. Franklin's statement and Mr. Pitkin s is nothing. What authority there is for either I know not. Mr. Pitkin gives a specious appearance of accuracy to his, by putting down a precise number for each of the twelve colonies, *seriatim*. But he does not tell us from whence he drew his information.

Now, comparing these two estimates, it would follow that, for sixteen years, the population of North America experienced no increase. Nay if we hold the two authors to the words of their respec-

D d

2. The Census of 1790————3,929,326 [b].

3. The Census of 1810 [omitting for the sake of perspicuity .that of 1800]————7,239,903 [c].

Secondly, Another view, materially connected with a just conception of the subject, will be suggested by a consideration of the annual increase, to be inferred from these *data*. I will take my stand therefore upon the period of lord Delawar's first expedition in 1610, and proceed on the principle that nothing worthy the name of a settlement, or that laid the just foundation of a European population of the North American continent, had occurred before that time.

The annual increase, upon that hypothesis,

from 1610 to 1749, will be ——   6973
from 1749 to 1790 ———— 70,325
from 1790 to 1810 ————165,527.

We should certainly proceed very idly in our examination of this question, if we did not admit that there is considerable difficulty. It was this difficulty that gave birth to the vain boasts of Dr. Franklin and Dr. Styles, and to the atrocious and heart-appalling theories of Mr. Malthus.

---

tive propositions, we might perhaps conjecture that the population had diminished. Dr. Franklin speaks of the number of " English souls ;" while Mr. Pitkin expressly takes in the " whole white population." What becomes then of Mr. Malthus's assertion, that " in the Northern States of America the population has been found to double itself, for above a century and a half successively, in less than twenty-five years ?"

  [b] See above, p. 290.   [c] P. 293, 4.

We have no choice in the solution of this question, but either to refer it to an inherent, rapid and incessant power in the human species to multiply its numbers, or to emigration. It has been the purpose of all that has gone before in this Treatise, and particularly of the Second and Third Books, to prove that the former of these is impossible.

The substantial part of the solution must therefore be from emigration. The present population of the North American continent, with one exception which will presently be mentioned, must have arisen from a direct transportation of the inhabitants of the Old World to the New.

In one point of view there is nothing wonderful in this. Let us take the present population of the United States at ten millions. What are ten millions of human creatures to the population of Europe? According to the latest geographers Europe is computed to contain 153,000,000 souls. Ten millions of these therefore, one would naturally say, might be taken away, and never be missed. But in some parts of Europe, at least, they are missed.

The difficulty therefore is not in supposing that ten millions of human beings, born in Europe, should have spent the middle or concluding part of their lives in the tract of country which now constitutes the territory of the United States. It lies merely in the astounding

conception of their passage over; and the wonderful in this is rather increased, than otherwise,
by the putting it in the form of an annual supply : such being the constitution of the human
mind, that we understand better, and reason
more clearly, upon any subject connected with
numbers, when those numbers have been so reduced that we can compass and wield them.   As
far as the population of the United States has
grown from emigration merely, it is necessary,
with one limitation which I shall presently mention, that 165,000 emigrants, upon an average,
should have passed over annually from Europe,
during the twenty years which elapsed between
1790 and 1810 [d].

The limitation I allude to lies in this.   The
majority of the emigrants that pass over from
Europe to North America may be supposed to
be in the flower of their life.   Now every such
emigrant is equal to two human beings, taken
indiscriminately among the population, or rather
among the rising generation, of an old established country.   For example, we have found that,
in four children born into the world, we have no
right to count upon more than one female who,
by child-bearing, can contribute to keep up or

---

[d] It is not unworthy of remark, that the first idea of a doubling
in perpetual series with short intervals, was started, when the number of new arrivals would have had nothing astounding in it.   It
was published by Dr. Franklin in 1731, and by Dr. Styles in 1761.
A considerable part of the interval between these two passed, according to Mr. Pitkin, without any increase.   See note a.

increase the numbers of mankind in the next generation.   But, of emigrants withdrawing themselves to America, as we have been informed
they usually withdraw themselves in families,
we have a right, if they go in the flower of
their lives, out of every four, to count upon
two females who, by child-bearing, may contribute to the future population of the country.
Those who pass over in the flower of their lives,
have already surmounted the dangers of childhood and early life, and the females among them
may immediately be counted in the roll of those
effective members of the community for the
purpose here treated of, who, and who alone,
(exclusively of such a number of males as may
be necessary to give effect to the procreative
principle in them) are of value in keeping up
the internal and proper population of a country.
Perhaps, in consideration of this exception, we
may reduce the number of emigrants necessary,
upon the principles of this treatise, to account
for the reported increase of population in the
United States for twenty years, from 1790 to
1810, from one hundred and sixty-five thousand
annually, to eighty or ninety thousand.

Emigrants for the most part pass away silent-
ly from their native shores, and make no noise,
except perhaps among their own immediate
neighbourhood.   Even so much as this does not
happen, in so far as they emigrate from among
the settled inhabitants of great towns and cities.

In this last case the process is something like
what Dr. Donne describes of the death of the
virtuous man,

> While some of his sad friends doe say,
> The breath goes now ; and some say, No.

It may be considered at this time as something
like an admitted principle, that the population
of great cities cannot be kept up without continual supplies from the rural parts of the state.
These again may be supposed to pass off by
emigration to foreign countries, and their places
a second and a third time to be filled by supplies from the rural inhabitants, while the whole
is no more adverted to, than the insensible tran-
spiration in the human body, by means of which
principally it has been supposed that perhaps
not a particle of the frame remains the same
after a lapse of twenty years.

One way of considering the subject, so far as
this island is concerned, is by comparing the
gross estimate of our merchant-ships at different
periods. We are told that, between the years
1630 and 1640, twenty-one thousand two hundred British subjects were computed to have
passed over to New England only. I have not
before me an account of the tonnage of the
merchant-ships of Great Britain at that period.
But the following is an extract from Anderson's
History of Commerce, as to the annual amount
of merchant-ships from the Restoration.

SHIPS CLEARED OUTWARDS.

Years.		Tons.
1663 }	———————	142,900
1669 }		
1774	———————	864,056
1780	———————	753,977.

Anderson's account ends with the year 1780. But, as our concern is particularly with the shipping of a later period, I have obtained a supplement in relation to more recent years, which I have no doubt may be relied on as correct [e].

SHIPS CLEARED OUTWARDS.

Years.		Tons.
1785	———————	1,182,479
1790	———————	1,573,831
1800	———————	2,130,322
1810	———————	2,762,801
1818	———————	3,072,409.

The simple deduction by the rule of three from the two extremes of this statement is, that if 142,900 tons yielded an emigration to America to the annual amount of 2000 persons, 3,072,409 tons in the year 1818, computing at the same rate, will yield an annual emigration, from Great Britain only, of 43,000 persons. It may be doubted however, whether the amount of shipping in the merchant service was so great between the years 1630 and 1640, as in the years 1663 and 1669, which Anderson has

---

[e] The following numbers are taken from the records at the Custom House, collated with the Returns annually laid on the Table of the House of Commons.

‚chosen. The victories of the Commonwealth of England over the Dutch, and the Act of Navigation, had occurred between. In that case, as 2000 settlers were conveyed to North America by a state whose annual shipping was much under 142,000 tons, a greater number of emigrants in proportion than 43,000 may be conceived to have been conveyed from a state whose annual shipping exceeded three millions of tons. I doubt also whether the impulse to emigrate, or, as Dr. Johnson calls it, " the fever of emigration," to the continent of North America, has not been twice as general in our days, as it was in the days of Charles the First. It must be remembered too that Ireland is wholly excluded from this statement. If then we allow only 43,000 annually for the emigration from Great Britain, that from Ireland, together with " the vast tide of emigration which is at present flowing from all parts of Europe to the United States of America," as I find it expressed by a late writer [f], will soon mount up the whole to as great a number, as any hypothesis on the subject can require.

In the investigation of this subject my attention was necessarily called to the encouragement held out by the government of Great Britain to induce the inhabitants of this island, or, what it has lately been fashionable to call, our " sur-

---

[f] Wentworth, New South Wales, Preface.

plus population," to transport themselves to North America. This has been one of the blessings immediately growing out of Mr. Malthus's theory, that, whereas the patriotic sovereigns and rulers of former times, sought to increase the number of their subjects, and deemed it their glory to preside over an industrious and numerous population, our governors have been taught that it is one of their first duties, to reduce the amount of their countrymen, and to render the thin population of this once happy island still thinner and more sparing than they found it.

The first circumstance of this kind that fixed my attention, was the publications of Mr. John Campbel, styling himself government-commissioner and general agent in Scotland for this business. His first manifesto or declaration on the subject is dated Edinburgh, 22 February 1815. I accordingly endeavoured to procure the most authentic information as to the plan and effects of his undertaking; and the account I have received is as follows.

The encouragements held out in the first year were, a grant of land to the settler, a free passage, implements of husbandry, and provisions for the first six months. These were afterwards discontinued, with the exception of the grant of land, on account of the great expence which was found to accrue.

A further inducement to such as might be

410 RETROSPECT OF POPULATION BOOK IV.

willing to transport themselves, is thus expressed : " Should any number of families, proceeding from the same part of the United
Kingdom, be desirous of settling in the same
neighbourhood in Canada, care will be taken to
allot them lands as nearly as possible contiguous
to each other; and a sufficient portion of land
will be appropriated, in the midst of such settlers, for a church, and for the maintenance of
a clergyman and a schoolmaster, and a salary of
one hundred pounds *per annum* will be provided
to the minister, and fifty pounds *per annum* to
the schoolmaster, for such period as shall afterwards be specified."

No accurate return could be furnished of the
number of settlers, who have availed themselves
of the encouragement thus held out to them;
but it is supposed, that about five thousand
persons went out as settlers to Canada upon this
plan in 1815, that an equal or greater number
emigrated in 1816, and that their numbers annually have not since diminished. Many also
have undoubtedly gone out, without being furnished with letters from the secretary of state,
the governors of the two provinces of Upper
and Lower Canada having a discretionary power
to make grants of land to persons applying for
them, not exceeding twelve thousand acres to
one person. It appears from a paper just put into
my hands, published by the Emigrant Society
of Quebec, and dated 11 October, 1819, that

" the number of emigrants arriving at that port, since the opening of the navigation for the present season, amounts to upwards of twelve thousand, which probably exceeds two-thirds of the population of the city itself," and that the consequence has been a great accumulation of distress.

I have received an official account from Ireland of the number of persons who emigrated from that country to North America in three years, ending 5 January, 1819. The total stands thus :

Number of persons emigrating from Dublin 6645
————————— from Ireland generally 35,633
Is there no chance that the persons actually emigrating, should even have exceeded the number officially reported under that head ?

The following is an extract of notices, appearing in Niles's Baltimore Weekly Register, a journal of the highest character for authenticity in the United States.

" August 16, 1817.

" Within the last two weeks, ending yesterday morning, we have received accounts of the arrival of twenty-six vessels, at the several ports of the United States, with two thousand five hundred and twelve passengers, viz.

From Amsterdam, Germans and Swiss — 1896
From England, Scotland and Ireland — 281
From the same, via Nova Scotia and
    Newfoundland ——————————— 238

From France ――――――――――――― 97

————

2512."

————

"**August 30, 1817.**

"EMIGRATION. The two weeks ending yesterday gave us accounts of the arrival of 21 vessels, with emigrants from Europe, *viz.*

From England, Ireland, and Scotland — 557
From Holland, Germans and Swiss —— 365
From France ――――――――――― 25

————

947.

————

"Of these "one hundred and seventy-one reached the United States *via* Halifax, though great inducements are held out to settlers there. As for instance, a Dutch ship which arrived at Philadelphia, put into that port for provisions, when the government offered to the passengers 10,000 acres of land, *gratis,* in fee simple, and farming utensils, if they would stay there; **but** they refused it. Many settlers, as they are called, arrive in Canada, from whence hundreds of them pass up the river, &c. and cross into New York and Ohio. It seems to be discovered, that it is more convenient to reach our country through the British colonies, than to come on direct. Facilities are afforded for the former, which are denied to the latter."

"October 25, 1817.

"EMIGRATION. The British ship, Mary Ann, has arrived at Boston in 50 days from London, with two hundred and four passengers. The Mary Ann was bound to St. John (N. B. e), but the passengers not wishing to go there rose upon the crew, and brought the vessel into Boston."

"September 12, 1818.

"The current of emigration from the British dominions to the territory of the United States, never was so strong as it is now. For the week ending 31 August, 2150 passengers, nearly the whole of whom were emigrants from Europe, arrived at the single port of New York; and for the subsequent week we kept an account of the passengers reported in the newspapers (which is far short of the number that arrived) and found them to amount to nearly 3000, for five or six principal ports,—and the aggregate may be fairly estimated at 6000 for the two weeks preceding the sixth of September. Of the six thousand, about 4000 were from England, 1000 from Ireland, and the rest from Scotland, Holland and France; about 100 only from the latter."

The Numbers of Niles's Register from which the above extracts are taken, are by no means a regular series; and for the use of these detached

e New Brunswick,

sheets I am indebted to the liberality of an American gentleman of high character in this country.

In Cobbet's Weekly Register for August 14, 1819, I find, in a letter by that gentleman, dated Long Island, in the state of New York, the following assertion: " Within the last twelve months upwards of a hundred and fifty thousand have landed from England to settle here." Now every one acquainted with Mr. Cobbet's writings must know, though he is an intemperate politician, and though his productions abound with the most violent and unqualified invectives, yet that he is a hard-headed man, entirely competent to observe bare facts and to report numbers, and that he has not perhaps been detected in misrepresentations of that sort.

I am aware that many of the statements I have last given belong to a period subsequent to the American Census of 1810 : but they will at least serve strikingly to illustrate the fact, of the vast number of emigrants from Europe that may be conveyed across the Atlantic, while at the same time a matter of such mighty importance, whether upon Mr. Malthus's hypothesis, or upon the ideas of national policy universally received till the year 1800, attracts a very inconsiderable share of public attention.

A circumstance worthy to be mentioned in this place is the great number of voluntary asso ciations, best known by the name of Emigrant Societies, which are found to exist in all the southern and middle states of the American Union. The object of these associations is two-fold, to assist the destitute emigrant when he arrives, and, by means of authorised agents, and certain fugitive publications of the most inticing and alluring contents, to induce him to leave his native home. In Philadelphia I find these associations under the following appellations; the Society for the Aid and Protection of Irish Emigrants, the St. Patrick's Society, the Hibernian Society, the St. Andrew's Society, the Scot's Thistle Society, the Welsh Society, the St. George's Society, the French Benevolent Society, and the German Society[f]. In New York there is an association of this sort, instituted by Thomas Addis Emmet, called the Shamrock. This society, about two years ago, presented a petition to Congress, praying that a right of preemption in a certain portion of the Illinois territory might be granted to emigrants of the Irish nation, which petition was rejected, on the ground that it was not the policy of the United States to separate their new citizens by districts and boundaries, but rather to blend them into one common mass. This association is accustomed, on two solemn days of the year, the day of their tutelary saint, and the anniver-

---

[f] Morse, Geography; Article, Pennsylvania; Section, Societies, Mellish, Travels, Chapter 24.

sary of the Declaration of American Independence, to parade the streets of New York, with colours flying, and to the sound of instrumental music, in commemoration of the happy period, when they left their native land, and resorted to the hospitable shores of the New World.

The American Congress, about the same time that they refused the prayer of the Shamrock Society, voted a special privilege to emigrants of the French nation, permitting them to obtain property in a certain district at a very low price, upon condition of their cultivating the vine and the olive.

There is an extreme fallacy in Mr. Malthus's language, when he talks, in his letter to me of October 1818, speaking of the population of the United States, of " foreign immigration." In the United States there is no idea, correspondent to the term, " a foreigner." This republic is properly *colluvies omnium gentium*. No native of any part of Europe will fail in one respect to find himself at home, the moment he has set his foot on the shores of North America; particularly the inhabitants of the British isles, who, according to Mr. Niles's collections, land there at the rate of two or three thousand *per* week. The term " foreign" in this case conveys to the mind a fallacious idea; since we are accustomed to see what Mr. Malthus calls " foreign immigrants" constituting a very trivial portion of the population of an old country. The American Congress in reality has done wisely in refusing to separate their new citizens by districts and boundaries, in cases where particular countries have sent out to them a great number of settlers, and chusing rather to blend them into one common mass; since, if they were allowed by such separation fully to keep alive their original prejudices, we might expect to see them one day overpowering the Creoles, or proper descendants of the old settlers, just as in some countries we read of slaves, that have become so numerous as to be able to put down and subjugate their masters.

The phrase, with which Mr. Malthus introduces his subject, and in the force of which lies the whole foundation of his theories, in the ninth page of his first volume, that " the increase of population in the United States of North America *has been repeatedly ascertained to be* from procreation only," is the most dark, cabalistical and unmeaning, that was ever inserted in any work pretending to reasoning. It may challenge any dogma in Jacob Behmen himself. Mr. Malthus tells us in one place that he expects his work to last many thousand years. [" As it is probable, if the world were to last for any number of thousand years, systems of equality would be among those errors, which will never cease to return at certain intervals, I really think there should be somewhere on record an

E e

answer to such systems founded on the Principle of Population ᵍ"]. But Mr. Malthus should
be told that his work is not constructed on the
plan of a Κτημα ις αιιι.

The inference from what is stated in this
chapter seems clearly to be, that the whole increase of the population of the United States
may be accounted for, without supposing with
Dr. Franklin, that, where there is one marriage
in Europe, in America there are two, or cre-
diting with him and Mr. Malthus, that, from
the superior fruitfulness of the marriage-bed in
the United States, the human species doubles its
numbers in twenty or five-and-twenty years,
while the population of Europe is at stand.

Was ever so stupendous and calamitous a
fabric erected upon so slender foundations ?

ᵍVol. II, p. 271, 3.

CHAPTER VI.

OF THE AMOUNT OF BIRTHS IN THE UNITED STATES.

IT has already appeared, I trust, to the satisfaction of every reader, that the only increase of the number of human beings in any community by procreation, must be by increasing the proportion of births to a marriage, or, more strictly speaking, to the amount of women capable of child-bearing in that community.

This is the essence of the question which the Essay on Population professes to treat. If Mr. Malthus, or any writer less presumptuous than Mr. Malthus, should hereafter undertake to deliver any thing sound and substantial on the subject, to this point it is necessary he should direct his investigation.

It should seem therefore as if the United States afforded us no ground to stand on: I have taken considerable pains to obtain information in this point, but have been unable to procure any thing satisfactory.

The only thing I have seen, that comes to the point in this essential question, is a paper in the third volume of the Transactions of the American Philosophical Society held at Philadelphia, entitled, Observations on the Probabilities of the Duration of Human Life, and the Progress of Population, in the United States of America, by William Barton, Esq, which paper was read in a meeting of the society, on the eighteenth of March, 1791.

These Observations are expressly written to support the principle first started by Dr. Franklin, Dr. Ezra Styles, and others, in laud and glory of the land of America.

The testimony of an adversary, if it should turn out to be in favour of the opinion I have delivered, is of double force; and on that account I value the testimony of Mr. Barton. In his paper he has the following remarkable passage.

Having asserted, that "the United States of America possess in a superior degree an inherent, radical and lasting source of national vigour and greatness; since it will be found that in no other part of the world (at least in none of those parts with which we are best acquainted) is the progress of population so rapid as in these States:" he enters into certain calculations; and then proceeds thus:

"From the foregoing statements it may be presumed, that four and a half persons to a house, and the same proportion of births to a marriage, are an allowance quite high enough for some of the healthiest parts of Europe. There is but one instance, in which I have been enabled to obtain the actual proportion of births to marriages in this country.   At the first parish in Hingham, in the State of Massachuset , during the course of fifty-four years, there were two thousand two hundred and forty-seven births, one thousand one hundred and thirteen deaths, and five hundred and twenty-one marriages; which gives the proportion of six and a quarter births to a marriage.   Therefore, the proportion of births to marriages in that parish having been taken out of so considerable a number of persons, and for so long a time, inclines me to think it may serve as a pretty just standard for the country-parts of the northern, and perhaps of the middle states."—It is to be observed that Mr. Barton comes down here from Dr. Franklin's vantage-ground of " eight being the average number of births to an American marriage."

Having Mr. Barton's numbers however before me, I thought it proper to try the justness of his conclusion by the Rule of Three. And, this being the very essence of the question, I shall here set down the steps of the process entire. Thus·

Divide 2247 births, by 521 marriages:

$$521)2247.\,000(4.312$$
$$2084$$

$$1630$$
$$1563$$

670

521

——

1490

1042

——

448

And the result will be **4.312** births to a marriage.—How Mr. Barton came to imagine that six and a quarter was the quotient, instead of four and a fraction somewhat above a quarter, it is impossible for me to divine.

It is particularly to be observed that Mr. Barton's numbers for births, marriages, and deaths, are printed in words at length; so that we may be tolerably certain that no error of the press lurks in the statement.

Now this brings us down at once to something like the European standard. And it is sufficiently remarkable that four and a half births to a marriage, a proportion somewhat greater than what is here brought out for " the first parish in Hingham in the State of Massachusets," is Mr. Barton's allowance for " the healthiest parts of Europe."

Mr. Malthus was the first to detect the error in Mr. Barton's statement, though he lets himself down as softly as he can, by calling the true quotient $4\frac{1}{2}$ [a].

————

a Vol. II, p. 151.

———

Since writing the above, I have had transmitted to me by my valued friend, Mr. Joseph Valence Bevan of Georgia, reports of the marriages and births in Portsmouth, the capital of New Hampshire, for six years, from 1804 to 1809, drawn up and published on the spot by Dr. Lyman Spalding. These are the more important, as they relate to those Northern States of America, upon the increase of population in which by procreation only, Mr. Malthus has thought proper to lay his principal stress. They are as follow.

Years.	Marriages.	Births.		Total.
		Males.	Females.	
1804	64	163	130	293
1805	67	138	157	295
1806	63	128	128	256
1807	62	151	133	284
1808	56	141	134	275
1809	69	146	153	289

Now in these reports, if I take the latest year, it will give me something less than $4\frac{1}{4}$ births to a marriage: and, if I add the whole six years together, the proportion will be found to be $4\frac{44}{100}$ to one.

My friend at the same time transmitted to me a paper of the Return under these heads for the city and suburbs of Philadelphia:

but this is only for the one year 1818, and
does not distinguish the sexes of the born:
the result is, "Marriages (as far as obtained)
792; Baptisms 2221:" yielding a quotient
of fewer than three births to a marriage. It
is somewhat remarkable that this Return concludes with a memorandum, that "the baptisms of this year were decreased by 282, and
the burials increased by 64."

Thus, the further we enquire into the subject, the more we find the progress of the numbers of mankind by procreation in the United
States, conforming itself to the model of Europe. In rural situations, such as Mr. Barton's
parish in Hingham, and Dr. Spalding's Portsmouth in New Hampshire, the fruitfulness of
marriages appears to be such as we might expect
in rural and healthful situations in the Old
World. But, when we come to large capitals,
such as Philadelphia, the progress of population
is reduced; and we are led to conclude of North
America, as of Europe, that the number of inhabitants in great towns would not be kept up,
without a perpetual influx of new citizens from
distant quarters.

If therefore it is true, that the increase of
population "by procreation only," can arise in
no other way than that of an increased number
of births, then it is as plain as the operations of
arithmetic can make it, that in every instance
where the evidence has come to our hands, the

fruitfulness of the human species in the United States does in no way materially differ, from what occurs on the subject in many countries of Europe.

CHAPTER VII.

OF THE PERIOD AT WHICH MARRIAGES ARE FORMED.

DR. FRANKLIN, in his Observations concerning the Increase of Mankind, Peopling of Countries, &c, where he says, " If in Europe they have but four births to a marriage, we in America may reckon eight," inserts a slight parenthesis, in which he assigns one solitary reason, to account for this amazing disparity, and to reconcile the mind of the reader to so extraordinary an hypothesis. This may be the case, says he, because " many of the European marriages are late."

Mr. Malthus in like manner lays great stress upon the question of early marriages, and seems to think that, if " moral restraint," of the efficacy of which he entertains " very inconsiderable hopes," could once be brought into action, so as to prevent this evil, the mischiefs to be apprehended from overpopulation might then be prevented, with very little, or perhaps no need of the aid of his established confederates, vice and misery.

It is therefore just that we should bestow

some consideration, on the difference that is likely to arise in the peopling of countries from early and from late marriages.

Marriage takes place, in some countries, when the parties are sixteen years of age, or even earlier: we may suppose the marriageable age to be twenty: or we may carry it on, with Mr. Malthus, to the age of twenty-seven or twenty-eight [a].

The opinion of Sussmilch on the subject is thus expressed [b].   "Too early and too late marriages are both of them injurious to population. Experience shews this in animals : as, for example, among great cattle, the cow which has a calf when too young, never comes to the size and strength which she otherwise would have done."

Tacitus speaks to the same purpose in his treatise *De Moribus Germanorum* [c].   "The young men marry late, by which means their virility is preserved ; nor is the female in greater haste to engage in the nuptial tie.   They come together with similar vigour, in complete stature, and with well matched force ; and thus it happens that the offspring fails not to inherit the robustness of its parents."

Cæsar, treating of the same Germans, delivers his sentiments in a similar manner [d].

---

[a] Vol. III, p. 92.   [b] Vol. I, p. 184.
[c] §. 20.   [d] *De Bello Gallico, Lib.* VI, *cap.* 19.

"Those who remain longest without the knowledge of the other sex, bear the greatest praise among them. They believe that this increases their stature, their force, and their muscular energy. To have intercourse with the female before the age of twenty, they regard as in the highest degree disgraceful."

It seems indeed sufficiently probable that the female of the human species is endued with a certain degree of fecundity : and I believe it will be found in a majority of instances, that the woman who is called upon early to afford that species of nutrition from her frame which the unborn infant requires, sooner grows old, and ceases sooner from the power of child-bearing, than the woman in whom this faculty is not called forth till a later period.

There is another consideration of material consequence, as connected with this question, whether early marriages contribute to forward, and late marriages to retard, the increase of mankind. Dr. Franklin talks of " the frequent lateness of marriages in Europe." I should be glad to have had the opportunity of asking him, what he meant by " a late marriage?" We should then have seen, whether the difference of the age at which marriage is contracted in Europe and in the United States, had almost any tendency to account for a superior fecundity on the other side of the Atlantic.

It is true that, where a country is in great

distress, and the means of subsistence are difficult to be procured, there marriage will often
not take place at so early a period, as it might
do in countries which are placed in more favourable circumstances.   But then there is another
point to be considered.   The period of marriage
usually depends on the male.   When a woman
is solicited in wedlock, it will 'very rarely happen that her parents, or the female for herself,
will decline the proposal, because she is not yet
twenty-eight or thirty years of age.   When we
talk of a late marriage, in nineteen instances out
of twenty we refer exclusively to the age of the
husband.   When an old man desires to marry,
how often does it occur that he insists upon a
wife as old as himself?   No : whatever be the
age of the bridegroom, he is almost sure to look
out for a young bride; and then, unless he be
indeed stricken in years, the chance of offspring
is nearly the same, as if he had been himself as
young as the woman he leads to the altar.

CHAPTER VIII.

THE two preceding Chapters are to be considered as an application of the principles of my
Second Book, respecting the power of increase
in the numbers of the human species, to the
particular case of the United States. I will
proceed in this Chapter to apply the principles
of my Third Book to the same subject, in the
form of a review of the causes by which the
amount of the numbers of the human species is
reduced or restrained. If it shall appear that
the United States possess scarcely any advantage in this respect over the established kingdoms of Europe, this will add great accession
to the force by which Mr. Malthus's theory is
to be taken away and destroyed.

There are only two ways in which the population of any country can be increased from procreation : first, by a greater number of births ;
or secondly, if of those who are born a smaller
number are prematurely cut off by disease or
otherwise. Now, I say, a greater number of
children are not born to a marriage in the Uni-

ted States than in Europe: this has been the topic of the two preceding Chapters. To which I here add, that a smaller number are not prematurely cut off, by disease or otherwise, in the United States than in Europe: this is the proposition I seek to establish in the present Chapter.

The first disease I will mention is Consumption. Mr. Warden, late consul for the United States at Paris, in his Statistical Account of that republic, published in 1819 [a], says, " At Portsmouth in New Hampshire, one fifth of the cases in the bill of mortality for 1801 is of this description [b]. In the city of New York the cases of consumption of the lungs occupy nearly one fourth of the tables of diseases for the year 1802; and nearly one fifth in the years 1803, 1804 and 1805. In the year 1816 the number of consumptive cases was 678, exceeding by 60 what took place in 1815."

The second disease I will mention is Dysentery, ordinarily known in the United States by the name of the Summer Complaint. This disease, according to Mr. Warden [c], " is seldom fatal." But, according to my information, it is much otherwise. A very respectable lady, who has returned to England after seventeen years'

---

[a] Part I, chap. vii.

[b] The proportion is exactly the same in the bill of mortality for the same place in 1809.

[c] Ibid.

residence in Pennsylvania, assures me, that a great proportion of the children in that state are carried off by it under three years of age, and that upon her return to Great Britain it was matter of surprise to her, to see, as no uncommon thing, families with seven or eight children. Another lady, a native of Boston, and wife of a gentleman filling an official situation, added to this, that it was not unfrequent in her part of the Union, for two or three children in a family to be taken off at once with this complaint.

A further evidence of the unhealthiness of the climate of the United States, of which much has been heard, is the Premature Decay of Teeth. Volney, in his View of the Climate and Soil of the United States [d], remarks, " Of a hundred persons under thirty, it may be affirmed you will scarcely find ten entirely unaffected in this respect. It is particularly lamentable to observe almost generally, that handsome young women, from the age of fifteen or twenty, have their teeth disfigured with black spots, and frequently great part of them gone." The lady from Pennsylvania whom I mentioned above, stated to me, that the citizens of that state, male and female, were generally found to decline from their youth and strength at twenty-five or thirty years of age. She further expressed herself as having no doubt that the con-

---

[d] Chap. XII,

tinuity of population from their own proper
sources was less full there than in England : for
which she assigned four reasons ; first, that the
mothers suckle their children longer ; secondly,
that in Pennsylvania there are few old people ;
thirdly, that more children die ; and lastly, as
above observed, that a large family of children
is a rare phenomenon there.   She added, that
the native Americans, both male and female,
are easily distinguished by the sallowness of
their complexions ; and she further mentioned
as a corroboration of her idea, that the quakers,
the original founders of Philadelphia, now constitute very considerably less than one fourth of
the population of that city, that there are no
new colonists of that sect, and that the obvious
consequence has followed, that notoriously the
number of quakers in that part of the United
States do not increase.

I will say little on the subject of the Yellow
Fever, which, according to Volney, " grows
more and more common in the United States,"
and which is known, in point of devastation,
and the rapidity of its progress, only to fall
short of the plague.

It is indeed notorious, that a new settled
country is always an unhealthy one.   North
America abounds with swamps.   Mr. Warden
undertakes to assign " reasons why the country
of the United States has been generally considered as unhealthy."   He remarks, that " in

F f

Carolina the country was found to be more sickly, in every situation where the surface was recently broken up for agricultural purposes." Volney observes, " Intermittent autumnal fevers and agues prevail in the United States to a degree of which it would be difficult to form a conception. They are particularly endemic in places recently cleared, in valleys, and on the borders of waters, either running or stagnant. In the autumn of 1796, in a journey of more than seven hundred miles, I will venture to say that I did not find twenty houses free from these diseases. In a journey of two hundred and fifty miles from Cincinnati to Fort Detroit, in a company of twenty-five persons, we did not encamp one night, without at least one of the party being seized with an intermittent fever. When we arrived at Detroit, there were only three of our company in health. At Grenville, the head-quarters of the army that had just conquered the country, of three hundred and seventy persons or thereabouts, three hundred had the fever. These attacks are not immediately fatal, but they undermine the constitution, and gradually shorten life. Other travellers have observed before me, that in South Carolina for instance, a person is as old at fifty, as in Europe at sixty-five or seventy; and I have heard all the Englishmen with whom I was acquainted in the United States, say that their friends, who had been settled a few years in the southern or even the central States, appeared to them to have grown as old again, as they would have done in England or Scotland."

I conclude this chapter with asking, What probability is there, that a people, circumstanced as has here been described, should have afforded a phenomenon, as to the rapid multiplication of the species from their own proper resources only, which never occurred in any other country or age of the world?   In reality it seems perfectly obvious that, at least in the middle and the southern States, the population could not have maintained its stand from one generation to another, without a perpetual succession of supplies from abroad.

Mr. Malthus indeed is willing to confine his imaginary doubling of the population by procreation only, to " the Northern States."   But this is another of the numerous fallacies that start upon us from every side in the examination of this subject.   The doubling, according to the Census, extends over the whole Union.   If the New England States of themselves furnish this universal doubling, and spread forth their colonies incessantly to the west and the south, while the southern and middle states remain in a neutrality in this respect, then Mr. Malthus has put down his increase of population there, and consequently the principle of increase inherent in human nature, vastly shortly of the truth : and I should think that he might with sufficient modesty have ventured, instead of a doubling, to have affirmed, that, " in the Northern States the population has been found to quadruple itself, and that from procreation only, every twenty-five years."

CHAPTER IX.

REPORTS OF THE POPULATION OF THE UNITED STATES ANALYSED AND EXAMINED.

I NOW come to the principal point in my whole subject. It was America, that by the inaccurate representations that were made of her population, gave occasion to Mr. Malthus's theory of the geometrical ratio. The United States of America have since exerted a laudable and enlightened diligence in collecting an accurate account of their population. Mr. Malthus indeed, in the letter with which he favoured me of the date of October 25, 1818, appeals to " the three regular censuses of 1790, 1800, and 1810," as " more than confirming" his statement respecting the manner in which the population of that country has increased. Upon that point I join issue with him. I am ready to refer the whole question to the figures that are given in the statements of the American Census.

In Mr. Booth's Dissertation on the Ratios of Increase in Population and in the Means of Subsistence, the reader will find many important remarks on the Tables of the Census, shewing, from the numbers of the po-

pulation of that country under the heads of the
different ages of human life, compared with the
population of Sweden, that the United States
cannot be a country increasing its inhabitants in
regular series through the power of procreation [a]. I shall confine myself in what I have
here to offer, to a single, but a very conclusive
particular in the case.

In this mutual appeal therefore we are of
course to take it for granted on both sides, that
the reports of the American Census are accurate.

Let us first then recollect what is the question we have to examine. If the publication
of the Census is accurate, we are inevitably
agreed that the population of the United States,
as it was found in the year 1810, amounted to
7,239,903 persons. That is not the question.

I will also admit, if Mr. Malthus pleases,
(though I look upon the Census of 1790, which
exhibits no distinction of ages or classes, with a
certain degree of suspicion) that the population
of the United States in that year amounted to
no more than 3,929,326, affording an increase
in twenty years of 3,310,577 persons. That is
not the question.

The number of the inhabitants of the United
States, whatever it amounts to, proves nothing.

The rapid increase of that number, whatever

---

[a] See above, p. 279, et seqq.

be the measure of that rapidity, proves nothing.

The question between us is the cause of that increase. Mr. Malthus says, that it " has repeatedly been ascertained to be from procreation only." I say, the cause is emigration.

Now fortunately the contents of the reports of the American Census seem to set that question for ever at rest. Certainly, if those reports may be depended on as accurate, I see no way of escaping from the conclusion I draw from them.

Wherever there is an increase of mankind from procreation, the number of the born must be proportional to that increase.

Wherever there is an increase of mankind " from procreation only," to such a degree as " to double the population in less than twenty-five years," the proportion of the number of the born must be correspondently great. The number of the born will always be a symbol denoting that increase: the two facts will necessarily harmonise with each other.

Dr. Franklin says, that, in order to effect a doubling of numbers by procreation every twenty years, it is necessary that we should " reckon eight births to a marriage :" and I believe he is right.

I have shewn, in the Sixth Chapter of the First Book, treating of China, that, wherever " marriage is greatly encouraged," there must

be as many children born, as in those countries
where the population is supposed " to double
itself, for one hundred and fifty years successively, every twenty or twenty-five years."   All
the difference is, that in countries, like China,
where the population is at stand, three-fourths of
the born must be murdered, destroyed by vice
and misery, or cut off by some of those " various causes, which, some sooner, and some
later, contribute to shorten the natural duration
of human life :" while, in the countries where
the geometrical ratio operates, with full effect,
the utmost care is taken of, and the utmost success attends upon, the rearing of children.   To
keep up the population of a country we must
reckon upon four births to a marriage ; to double
the population we must reckon upon eight.
Where there are four births to a marriage, the
number of births must double the number of
procreants : where there are eight, it must quadruple it.   Thus, as I illustrated in the case of
China, if a country has three hundred millions
of inhabitants, we may fairly reckon upon half
the population, or one hundred and fifty millions, as adults.   These adults must procreate the
double of their own number, or three hundred
millions of children : otherwise the population
would decline.   But, if they are capable of
doubling their number every twenty or twenty-
five years, they must then procreate six hundred
millions of children.

The authors of the American Census for 1800 and 1810 have fortunately classed the " free white inhabitants" according to their ages, and thus enabled us to ascertain the number of adults and the number of children. This is the most important piece of information relatively to our subject, that can be conceived. According to the Census of 1810, the " free white inhabitants under sixteen years of age" throughout the Union amount to 2,933,211, and the " free white inhabitants above sixteen years of age," to 2,928,882, placing those under and above sixteen years of age as nearly as possible on an equality. Hence it inevitably follows, that throughout the Union the population, so far as depends on procreation, is at a stand, and that there are not on an average more than four births to every female capable of child-bearing. This is altogether as satisfactory, as if we had a table of births and marriages for every State of the Union, as particular as Sussmilch's Tables for the German dominions of the king of Prussia. It may be considered as equivalent to a general reduction and summary that should be made of the results of such tables when they had once been constructed : and, as being made on a larger scale, it may seem to be less liable to error.

I have more than once complained of the pictureless generalities of Mr. Malthus's theories. If it were not for this quality, it is impossible that they should have obtained credence for a

moment. If it were true, that the population of
the United States had "been found to double itself, for above a century and a half successively,
in less than twenty-five years;" and that this had
been "repeatedly ascertained to be from procreation only;" it is absolutely certain that in that
country the children would outnumber the
grown persons two or three times over. It would
have been a spectacle to persons from other parts
of the world of the most impressive nature.
The roads and the streets would have seemed
covered with children. It would have appeared
a nation of children. I should have expected that,
as I have read respecting some schools where the
pupils have been extremely numerous, the children would have risen in rebellion, and over-
powered their elders, would have erected a parliament and legislature of their own.

There is nothing more deceitful than the eye
of man, when by its aid only we endeavour to
form an estimate of numbers. A traveller in
New England, or even a native, would go into
one family and another, and see six, eight, ten
or twelve children, all brothers and sisters, and,
especially if he had been previously initiated in
the mysteries of Mr. Malthus's book, would become perfectly satisfied of the actual operation
of the geometrical ratio. The Census sets all
this at rest for ever. It assures us from the
highest authority, that there are no more children
in the United States than there are grown per

sons. Of consequence, supposing all to marry agreeably to Dr. Franklin's hypothesis, the average number of births to a marriage is remarkably small: four must be an ample allowance. I own, for myself, I felt some scepticism as to the European account of four births to a marriage; I thought that still there might be some latent error: but, with respect to the United States, I do not see how we can resist the evidence before us;, four births to a marriage must be the utmost that occurs in that country.

ENQUIRY

CONCERNING

POPULATION.

BOOK V.

OF THE MEANS WHICH THE EARTH AFFORDS FOR THE SUBSISTENCE OF MAN.

CHAPTER I.

OF THE PRESENT STATE OF THE GLOBE AS IT RELATES TO HUMAN SUBSISTENCE.

THE pith of all Mr. Malthus's speculations lies in establishing a geometrical ratio for the power of increase in the human species, and an arithmetical ratio for the power of increase in the means of subsistence: and his capital inference is, that, at least in all old settled countries, or rather in all countries, except those where land is to be had freely, or at a very low rate, and agriculture is understood, the popula-

tion is continually limited and kept down by
the limits of the means of subsistence, and there
is always a somewhat greater number of inhabitants, than the food of the country will fully
and wholsomely nourish.

We have already enquired into the solidity of
the doctrine of the Essay on Population, respecting that excessive tendency of the human
species to increase, which it represents as " a
source of mischief to mankind, in comparison
with which all the evils entailed upon us by human institutions, however erroneous or oppressive, are in reality light and superficial," and
scarcely deserve the name of calamity. We
have seen, that it is at least problematical, whether there is a tendency in the human species to
increase, and that, for any thing that appears
from the enumerations and documents hitherto
collected, it may be one of the first duties incumbent on the true statesman and friend of
human kind, to prevent that diminution in the
numbers of his fellow-men, which has been
thought, by some of the profoundest enquirers,
ultimately to threaten the extinction of our species.

It is proper that we should now proceed to
examine the other branch of Mr. Malthus's doctrine, that which relates to the means of subsistence; concerning which he will be seen to
have fallen into errors not less ill-founded and

pernicious, than those which concern the possible
numbers of mankind.

I might indeed content myself to dismiss this
part of my subject with all possible brevity.
Having, I trust, for ever put to rest Mr. Malthus's geometrical ratio for the increase of
mankind, I might rest satisfied with his arithmetical ratio for the increase of the means of
subsistence, as abundantly sufficient to satisfy
all the demands which the human species are
ever likely to make upon it. But there are
many reasons why I do not think proper to stop
here.—To proceed then.

The first thing perhaps that would arrest the
observation of an enlightened enquirer, who
should set himself down to survey the globe we
inhabit according to the latest authorities, is the
scanty and sparing way in which man, of whose
nature we are, and in many respects with good
reason, so proud, is scattered over the face of
the earth. What immense deserts, what vast
tracts of yet unconquered forests, the asylum
only of wild beasts, or of the most pernicious
and contemptible animals, have we occasion to
observe! When I travel even through many
parts of England, it seems to me that I pass
through a country, which has but just begun
to be reclaimed from the tyranny of savage nature. I believe I may venture to affirm that there
is one third of the island which does not yet feel
the hands of the cultivator; not to mention the

very imperfect and inadequate manner in which the other two-thirds are turned to use. Man seems formed to subdue all these, to chase the wild beasts and either to tame or destroy their species, to fell the forests, and to render the most ungrateful soil productive. If indeed we are qualified to " increase, and multiply, and replenish the earth," it might be hoped that, at a period however distant, the whole surface of all lands might be " cultivated like a garden." But, for some reason or other, the very reverse of this is glaringly and deplorably the case.

And it is in a world, thus cheerless and melancholy in the point of view in which we are considering it, that Mr. Malthus has thought it opportune to blow the trumpet of desolation. He tells us, that the chief evil we have to fear is from the too great increase of population, and that this evil not only threatens to fall upon us, when the whole earth shall be subdued and turned to use, but that, " at every period during the progress of cultivation, from the present moment to the time when the whole shall become like a garden, the distress for the want of food will be, more or less, constantly pressing on mankind a."

---

a Vol. II, p. 220.

CHAPTER II.

OF THE NUMBER OF HUMAN BEINGS WHICH THE GLOBE IS CAPABLE OF MAINTAINING ON OUR PRESENT SYSTEMS OF HUSBANDRY AND CULTIVATION.

I AM desirous, on the present occasion, of shutting out every thing conjectural, and which therefore by a certain class of reasoners might be called visionary. One practical way of looking at the subject is this. The habitable parts of the globe are computed to occupy a space of thirty-nine millions of square miles, and its human inhabitants to amount to six hundred millions. Of this surface China is said to constitute 1,300,000 square miles. Now, let us admit the present population of China to stand at three hundred millions of souls. How fully China is cultivated I do not know; but I have as little doubt as Mr. Malthus appears to have, that the soil of that empire might be made greatly more effective for the purposes of human subsistence, than it is at present[a]. But let us assume, for the sake of argument, the

---

[a] It has already been mentioned that there are large forests within the boundaries of China. Book I, Chapter VI,

cultivation of China for the standard of possible cultivation, and consequently its population for the standard of possible population. The earth then, if all its habitable parts could be made as fertile as China, is equal to the sustaining a population of nine thousand millions of human beings. In other words, wherever one human being is now found in existence, the earth is capable, not in theory only, and according to conceived improvements no where yet realised, but judging from approved facts, instead of that one, of subsisting fifteen.

The majority of men seem to have laboured under some deception as to the population of China. It is principally in the vast extent of an empire said to be every where so flourishing, that China is worthy of admiration. Taking from Pinkerton the dimensions of China on the one hand, and of England and Wales on the other, I find that, if the latter were as well stocked with citizens as the former, it would contain 13,461,923 inhabitants, that is about three millions beyond the returns to the population-act of 1811. Now it has been admitted by the most phlegmatic enquirers, that England and Wales might easily be made to maintain double their present number of inhabitants. Of course such enquirers proceed on the assumption, that there are tracts incapable of being profitably applied to the purposes of human subsistence. By parity of reason therefore the soil of China

G g

itself is very far from being turned to all the profit of which it is susceptible, for the subsistence of the human species.

The latter end of Mr. Malthus's system is of a character extremely discordant with the beginning. The author of the Essay on Population has been understood as proceeding upon the impression, that the surface of the earth was limited, containing only so many square miles, but that the power of population, upon the assumption of his geometrical ratio, was unlimited, and that the greater was at any time the actual number of human beings, the greater would be the power of increase.

I cannot but think that the first contemplation that would have suggested itself to an enlightened philanthropist, proceeding on these premises, would have been something like the following.

Man is an admirable creature, the beauty of the world, which, if he did not exist in it, would be " a habitation of dragons, and a court for owls; the wild beast of the desert would cry to the wild beast of the islands; baboons would dance there; and its pleasant places be filled with all doleful creatures." How delightful a speculation then is it, that man is endowed by all-bountiful nature with an unlimited power of multiplying his species! I would look out upon the cheerless and melancholy world which has just been described, and imagine it all cultivated, all improved, all variegated with a multitude of human beings, in a state of illumination, of innocence, and of active benevolence, to which the progress of thought, and the enlargement of mind seem naturally to lead, beyond any thing that has yet any where been realised.   I would count up the acres and the square miles of the surface of the earth, and consider them all as the estate in fee simple of the human intellect.   I would extend my view from China and England, countries already moderately, and but moderately peopled, to the plains of North America, of South America, of Africa, of many tracts of Asia, of the north of Europe, of Spain, and various other divisions of the prolific world.   I should contemplate with delight the extensive emigrations that have taken place to North America [b], and plan and chalk out, as far as my capacity and endowments of study would permit me, similar emigrations to other parts of the world, that should finally make the whole earth at least as populous as China is at present.

Whatever may become of the great question

---

[b] Emigration becomes a less pleasing object, in proportion as we are induced to doubt of the increase of the numbers of mankind; and however agreeable it may prove to the country (North America for example) by which the emigrants are received, it would be sedulously counteracted by all means of benevolent and parental treatment in the enlightened statesmen of the country from which they proceeded.

of the increasing or diminishing numbers of mankind, I own that the temper of my mind still compels me to cling to the picture here delineated. Mr. Malthus has constrained me to examine with severity the evidences that hitherto exist on the subject: but, however the conclusion to which those evidences have led me, may serve as a seasonable antidote to the loathsome theories of the Essay on Population, it is, I confess, a conclusion painful and adverse to my feelings. If it be just, the friend of man must then be contented, to hope to see the comparatively small handful of mankind scattered on the face of the earth, ultimately become enlightened and benevolent and happy, instead of seeing those blessings participated by fifteen or thirty times (upon a moderate computation) the numbers of the present inhabitants of the earth, and must console himself by the purity of their enjoyments for the fewness of those who possess them.—To this it might be added, that, if war and the other atrocious follies of society were abolished, we should have reason to expect, that if the numbers of mankind were not enlarged, at least they would not then decrease.

But Mr. Malthus takes a very different view of the subject, and instead of considering the alleged power of multiplication in man, when combined with the imperfect and scanty population of the earth, as a subject of congratulation, he finds in it cause of " lamentation and

much weeping." Under a wise and honest administration of human affairs, I do not doubt that
the power of multiplication in man, however extensive, might for centuries to come be rendered
the source of an immeasurable increase of happiness on the face of the earth. Indeed, in
this point of view, I hold Mr. Malthus as having penned a satire upon the existing constitu-
tions and laws of society, infinitely bitterer than
any thing that has yet been produced, by all the
Utopianists and visionaries that ever existed.
Those who possess the direction of human affairs, might, if they pleased, by wise concert,
by persuasion, by developing grand views of
the true interests of civilised man, and by a
faithful discharge of the duties of their station,
diffuse populousness through every region of
the globe, and multiply thirty-fold the number
of beings susceptible of human contentment,
while by the same operation they would remove
our oppressions, and give to every man a degree of competence and independence hitherto
unknown. But the kings and the rulers of the
earth prefer gratifying their bad passions, their
ambition, their love of war, and their love of
ostentation, by reigning over a comparative desert.

But Mr. Malthus leaps this interval of long
happiness, which upon the principle of multiplication, and with a moderate degree of wise
management, seems altogether not to be avoid-

ed, and passes at once to the period when the earth shall be replenished in all its parts. He then supposes that society will be heedlessly and brutishly bent upon multiplying as rapidly as possible; and, having first drawn the fair picture of a community where reason presides, and benevolence is first minister to execute her decrees, proceeds to exclaim, " This beautiful fabric of the imagination vanishes at the severe touch of truth. The spirit of benevolence, cherished and invigorated by plenty, is repressed by the chilling breath of want. The hateful passions that had vanished reappear. Violence, oppression, falshood, misery, every hateful vice and every form of distress, which degrade and sadden the present state of society, seem to be here generated by the most imperious circumstances, by laws inherent in the nature of man, and absolutely independent of all human regulations [c]."

Elsewhere however Mr. Malthus seems to be aware, that by this kind of argument he would stand but a small chance of making converts, and that the number of persons would be inconsiderable, who would zealously enlist themselves in the cause of vice, misery, and whatever other checks upon population he has been able to discover in the successive editions of his Essay, from a contemplation of the calamities that

[c] Vol II, p. 255, 6.

might occur, when the globe was too full of inhabitants. "If," says he, "a beautiful system of equality were in other respects practicable, and if no difficulty would arise from the principle of population, till the whole earth had been cultivated like a garden, and was incapable of any further increase of produce, I cannot think that our ardour in the pursuit of such a scheme ought to be damped by the contemplation of so remote a difficulty. *An event at such a distance might fairly be left to Providence* d."

Mr. Malthus is certainly extremely skilful in what logicians call the *argumentum ad hominem*. When the business is to demolish a scheme of happiness founded upon a philosophical principle of equality, he conceives this sufficiently done by displaying the folly of the wise, and the selfishness of the benevolent. But turn back a few pages, and you find him candidly acknowledging, that he "cannot think that our ardour in the pursuit of such a scheme ought to be damped by the contemplation of so remote a difficulty, and that an event at such a distance might fairly be left to Providence."

This is very much of the same nature, as the justification which he elsewhere sets up of the goodness of God, in inflicting upon us all the miseries which he traces to the principle of population. He rests this justification upon the

---

a P. 220.

way in which excessive population might be kept down, without vice and misery, by the mere operation of human forbearance and discretion :—and then adds, " I believe few of my readers can be less sanguine in their expectations of any great change in the general conduct of men on this subject than I am; and the chief reason why *I allowed myself to suppose* the general prevalence of virtue, was, that I might endeavour to remove any imputation on the goodness of the Deity [e]," by shewing, that, if he had made man a creature such as Mr. Malthus thinks man never was or will be, many of the miseries of this sublunary scene would have been removed [f].

---

[e] Vol. III, p. 103.

[f] Great mistakes seem to have been made respecting the actual population of the earth, which it is perhaps worth while to mention. There is a spirit gone forth among mankind, whose favourite gratification it is to abolish the beautiful, and to paint all that is, or that has been, however in appearance prosperous or admirable, under humiliating colours. Pride has a gross and undistinguishing appetite, that feeds at one time upon honour, and at another upon disgrace. Impelled by this spirit, some writers have been disposed to set down the population of China at one hundred and fifty, instead of three hundred millions, as reported by Du Halde and Sir George Staunton. But they appear to have had little reason on their side. If the received account is accurate, the population of China amounts to 230 persons to a square mile. But the inhabitants of England rate at 200, the county of Lancaster at 476, and the district of Burdwan in Bengal at more than 600. [*See above* p. 54, 55.] A particular district however can never be taken for the standard of a country of large dimensions.

CHAPTER III.

CALCULATION OF THE PRODUCTIVE POWERS OF
THE SOIL OF ENGLAND AND WALES.

FINDING therefore that he has done little,
by his strange hypothesis of the misery to grow
out of universal happiness, and the irresistible
reign of self-love to occur as soon as " benevolence had established her reign in all hearts," or
within thirty years after [a], which hypothesis, in
the very next contiguous chapter to that in
which he sets it up, he ingenuously acknowledges to be a " difficulty, that ought not to
discourage us in our pursuit, and an event that
might fairly be left to Providence,"—Mr. Malthus changes his ground, and assures us, that,
" at every period during the progress of cultivation, from the present moment to the time when
the whole earth has become like a garden, the
distress for the want of food, will be, more or
less, constantly pressing on mankind." Indeed
this is the sole subject of one very large division
of his work, to shew that in all countries, America only excepted, population, as he phrases it,

---

[a] Vol. II, p. 269.

" continually presses hard against the limits of the means of subsistence."

In what is to come in this and the following chapters, I am obliged to proceed upon the assumption, that there is in the human species a tendency towards increasing population. Few persons would be inclined to dispute, that, supposing population at a stand, and setting aside this imputed tendency to increase, it would not be an unconquerable problem, to find, in this or any other known country, the means of raising the subsistence, so as fully to meet the wants of its present number of inhabitants.

A sober enquirer would be disposed to begin with the examination of the country in which he lives. To assist us in this, and enable the reader to compare the subsistence actually raised in England and Wales, with the present number of the inhabitants, I will subjoin a few extracts from Mr. Middleton's Survey of Middlesex, published by authority of the Board of Agriculture.

In the ninth section of his seventeenth chapter, entitled, " Supply and Consumption of South Britain," Mr. Middleton states the

	Acres.
Cultivated Land of England and Wales at	39,100,000
Commons and Waste Land at	7,816,000
Total	46,916,000

In the same page of his book (642) he rates the consumption of the inhabitants, men, women and children, upon an average, thus:

Food, per head annually:	Acres.
In bread, the produce of ————	$\frac{1}{2}$
In liquids ————————————	$\frac{1}{8}$
In animal food ————————	2
In roots, greens, and fruit ————	$\frac{1}{8}$
Total	$2\frac{3}{4}$

Proceeding on this calculation, and taking the population of England and Wales at ten millions of souls, their total consumption, *per annum*, would be

	Acres.
In bread, the produce of ——	5,000,000
In liquids ————————	1,250,000
In animal food —————	20,000,000
In roots, greens and fruit ——	1,250,000
Add to this, that Mr. Middleton computes that we employ 1,200,000 horses in agriculture, which devour the produce of four acres each, making —————	4,800,000
Miscellaneous, or unaccounted for ———————	6,800,000
Total	39,100,000

Now if we take this last item of 6,800,000 acres, and divide it by $2\frac{3}{4}$, we shall find that it affords food for 2,054,380 human beings, which added to the ten millions before named, gives a total of 12,054,380, that is, a number exceeding by nearly two millions the amount of the inhabitants of England and Wales, according to the returns to the population-act of 1810.—It is to be observed, that in this calculation I have wholly omitted all consideration of the 7,816,000 acres, which Mr. Middleton states as consisting at present in commons and waste lands, but which are certainly in part capable of being diverted to the sustenance of human life.

I have the rather chosen to present these extracts to the reader, as they naturally lead to several interesting reflections on the subject of human subsistence, independently of the question under present consideration.

I was however originally anxious to have given here, instead of the above, a Table of the actual produce of the country, under the heads of the different articles of human nutriment. But I did not find that I could obtain, with sufficient accuracy, the materials of such a Table. Mr. Middleton proceeds on a ground, peculiarly unfavourable to the result of which I was in search. He computes the quantity of land, appropriated to grazing and tillage, and from thence reasons downward to the food of a human being. I do not doubt, that if I could have procured an account of the actual produce, it would have shewn the wealth of the country, and the extent of its power in sustaining a number of human beings, in a much more striking light.

At present, for example, England produces annually a certain number of quarters of corn, and so on of the other means of human subsistence. If Mr. Malthus intends to say that this quantity of corn and this stock of provisions will subsist only a given number of human beings, and that, supposing all importation and exportation to be suspended for one year, the whole of this stock may be *bona fide* applied to the subsistence of the people of England, he is or may be delivering a truth; but he is merely delivering a truth of the most obvious and trivial nature, while he affects with much solemnity to be laying down a principle.

The proper question is, why, if this quantity of provisions is not sufficient for the subsistence of the people of England in the year under consideration, or as they might be found in the subsequent years, a greater quantity of provisions does not go on to be produced?

And here the first certain and incontrovertible answer, is the negative one, that it is not the limited dimensions of the globe, or of any of its considerable divisions, and that it is not that the earth refuses itself to the producing a more considerable quantity. The lands of England have never yet been tasked to produce all the means of human nourishment of which they are capable: the men of England have never yet been

called forth to exert all that agricultural industry, of which the number of hands existing in
the country are susceptible. It is neither the
want of soil, nor the want of hands to cultivate
it, that limits the quantity of provisions which
England annually produces. It must therefore
be something different from both of these.

CHAPTER IV.

CAUSES OF THE SCARCITY OF THE MEANS OF HUMAN SUBSISTENCE.

THERE lurks an ambiguity under the term " means of subsistence ;" and, but for that ambiguity, I conceive that Mr. Malthus's doctrine upon this head could never have been listened to for a moment.

The earth is, in a liberal point of view, the " means of subsistence" to man ; and, till her prolific bosom has been exhausted, and her soil has been so cultivated, that the store of provisions she is able to afford can be no further enlarged, there can be no danger to free and unshackled, and at the same time civilized man, on the score of the means of subsistence.

In another, and a very restrained sense, the provisions actually collected from the surface of the earth, may be called our " means of subsistence ;" and in this sense Mr. Malthus always chuses to understand the term.

If this ambiguity had been attended to, every one would have felt the absurdity of talking of " population pressing hard against the limits of the means of subsistence," in any intermediate

period, till the "whole earth had been cultiva-
ed like a garden."

To place this fact in a more striking point of
view, let us set apart from each other the two
great modes of the existence of man, the civilised, and the savage state.   For the present I
will confine myself to the former.

Civilised man, is man not living upon the
wild fruits of the earth, or the wild animals of
the field, but for the most part upon that which
is matured by human industry.   Here therefore
every man that is born into the world, is a new
instrument for producing the means of subsistence, in the sense of provisions ; and every member added to the numbers of the community, is
a new instrument for increasing those means.

The basis of civil society, at least as it exists
in those countries with which we are best acquainted, will be found in the truth of this proposition, that man in society is capable of rearing
a greater quantity of provisions than is necessary for his own subsistence.   Till this was the
case, all mankind were shepherds or husband-
men ; and if the case had not been altered, such
we must for ever have remained.

It is to this supererogatory power in man,
that we are indebted for all our improvements,
our refinements, and elevation.   The result has
been, the dividing the members of civil society
into two great classes, the one, who are employed in rearing the fruits of the earth, and the

other, who live in idleness, or who are employed in other kinds of industry, not immediately connected with the production of food.

How profound therefore the absurdity of talking of " population pressing hard against the limits of subsistence," till the earth, and the different parts of the earth, have been " cultivated like a garden !"

Let us look to the continent of North America, whose real or fabulous history has had the shame to give birth to Mr. Malthus's hypothesis. There, we are told, every man considers each additional child that is born to him, as so much added to his wealth, to his means of subsistence, or rather to his means of indulgence and of accumulating a moderate fortune. There, it has over and over again been pretended, the population doubles by procreation only, in fifteen, twenty, or five-and-twenty years. There, we are assured, the number of inhabitants in 1749 was one million, and at the present hour is ten millions. [I grant the increase; but I deny that there is such a progressive and permanent increase from procreation only.]

Why is all this? For one simple reason. Because on the continent of North America there is a vast quantity of productive land, yet uncultivated, which may be had *gratis*, or at a low price, so as to be, with a little patience and industry, within the reach of every man to obtain.

H h

It is clear therefore, that, so long as there is in any country cultivable land, yet unapplied to the purposes of human subsistence, or not yet improved to those purposes to such a degree as is easily within the reach of existing science and skill, population may be checked, but it is not checked by any thing that is connected with a paucity of the means of subsistence. In other words, till the whole earth has been cultivated like a garden (for the power of such cultivation is in proportion to the number of human beings naturally capable of agricultural labour), or till some one of its considerable portions has been so cultivated, and the inhabitants will not be persuaded to seek their fortune elsewhere, there can be no cause, inherent in the nature of things, why population should not go on to increase, to any extent to which it has the power of increasing.

Nothing therefore can be more insolent, or more groundless, than to talk to an unportioned man, who has come into the world in obedience to the great laws of nature, and without his own consent, of his having come into a " world, where every thing is appropriated." Appropriated indeed it is, but not to the wisest and most honest purposes, not to purposes most conducive to the diffusion of human happiness. He has only to lift up his eyes, and survey our heaths and our forests, our parks and our pleasure-grounds, and he must see that the world is not appropriated, as the simple, but never to be confuted, laws of nature direct us to appropriate it. I am not now enquiring whether the appropriation made by the institutions of society has or has not good reasons to defend it : but I say, that as long as that appropriation operates in its present form, population is not kept down by the want of the " means of subsistence."

We may indeed venture to affirm, without fear of reasonable contradiction, that there is no country, known at present to exist on the face of the earth, where population is imperiously checked, but by one of two causes, ignorance, or the positive institutious of society.

The savage tribes of mankind are thinly scattered over a vast extent of soil, of which they have never discovered the true and most beneficial use.. They subsist precariously upon the wild animals of the forest, or the fruits and roots which accident may offer to their acceptance. They make little provision against the time when these precarious means of subsistence may not be presented to them. A run of what is vulgarly called ill-luck, may starve whole families to death. Man is an animal that, whatever Mr. Malthus may say to the matter, requires to be tenderly treated. In the beginning of existence the infant can scarcely be reared without anxiety and care ; and in the decline of life we perish soon, unless we are supplied with accommodations and indulgencies. The latter of these

circumstances, as I have shewn, does not diminish the source of population; but the inadequate means which savages possess for rearing
their offspring, and the distress which must be
supposed to occur from their want of magazines,
do so diminish it.   Even in maturity the being
continually subjected to all the variations of the
elements must be materially injurious; and,
though uncivilised man does not feel these variations so sensibly as we do, they must, in a
vast multitude of instances, tend to cut short
the thread of human existence.   Undoubtedly
the life of a savage is, to my conception of the
thing, a miserable life.

The only other cause, beside ignorance, that
can tend imperiously to check the progress of
population, in a world so imperfectly peopled as
that we inhabit, arises from the positive institutions of society.   So long as there are vast portions of land, in this or any other country,
wholly uncultivated, or not so cultivated as to
supply to a considerable extent the food of man,
it is a solecism to say that population is kept
down for want of the means of subsistence.
Arguments may undoubtedly be offered why a
country should not be cultivated to its utmost
extent: it may be alleged in various ways to
conduce to the highest virtue and improvement
of man, that there should be differences in rank,
and inequalities of fortune: and it is perhaps
better that human creatures should exist in in-

ferior numbers, but in the noblest and most admirable state of which we are capable, than that the numbers of mankind should be carried to their utmost extent, while in intellect they should be brought down nearer to the brutes. I am not now disputing about the most eligible form of human society. But I claim, in the language of a homely proverb, but full of good sense, that the " saddle should be put on the right horse."

The chief object of this work is to restore the old principles of political science, to scatter the clouds, and set aside the paralogisms, with which Mr. Malthus has obscured them. I claim therefore peremptorily to infer from what has been said, that population is not kept down, in the different countries of Europe, provided it has a tendency to increase, by a want of the means of subsistence, but by the positive institutions of society. I claim to reverse the celebrated maxim of Mr. Malthus, and to say, that " human institutions, if erroneous and oppressive, are the mighty and tremendous sources of mischief to mankind, while the progress of population is, in the comparison, light and superficial, a mere feather that floats upon the surface" of the Essay on Population, and hardly worthy of serious consideration any where else.

What is the great difference between the continent of North America, and the principal divisions of the European quarter of the world ?

That in America I can say to a man, as God said to Abraham, " Go forth into the field, and look to the east, and the west, and the north, and the south," and chuse where thou wilt for the place of thy inheritance. In Europe, the destitute man, and the man that is inclined to draw forth the resources of his industry, may in like manner look to all the winds of heaven, and see many tracts uncultivated, or not rendered available to the subsistence of man ; but he sees this in vain. If he drives in a spade, or sets up a pale, another will presently come, and pointing to the soil, say, " This is mine," and will bring his writ of ejectment, or chase out the new-comer with the *posse* of his companions and dependents in a more summary way. He not only cannot obtain an inch of land *gratis,* but, if he wants a small portion, cannot obtain it, perhaps at any price, or at any price which, in his circumstances, would make it an available speculation. The land indeed, as Mr. Malthus says, is " wholly appropriated ;" but it is not appropriated to the genuine uses of natural man.

CHAPTER V.

CAUSES OF THE SCARCITY OF THE MEANS OF HUMAN SUBSISTENCE CONTINUED.

LET us resume for a moment, and endeavour to set in a still clearer light this proposition of Mr. Malthus, The population of the earth is continually kept down in all old countries by a want of the means of subsistence.

The weakness and folly of this idea seem to exceed every thing that could previously have been imagined of the extent of human credulity. A man must be lost beyond redemption in a labyrinth of sophistry, before he can become its victim.

The eunuch of the queen of Ethiopia said to the apostle, Lo, here is water; what hinders that I be baptised? In the same manner we may represent to ourselves an unsophisticated man of plain understanding saying, Lo, here is land; what hinders that I cultivate it? To make the case a fair one, the plot of earth concerning which his question is framed, shall be one of those many portions to be found in our native country, which have never felt the plough, and have scarcely in any degree worth mentioning, been applied to the purposes of human subsistence.

The merest driveller can answer this question, What hinders me, is civil institutions, and the law of the country.

What can be plainer? If I cultivate this land for my own use and the use of those most closely connected with me, I shall hardly rob any one of the means of subsistence, more than I should have done by cultivating a few acres in the wildest parts of North America. And this plot of land that I speak of, is a thousand times more easily to be improved by me, than a similar plot in the back-settlements of America. It will want a certain degree of preparation, before it can be rendered productive. But the correspondent plot in North America is first to be cleared of its native woods, the aborigines of the soil. The implements of husbandry in the one case are to be transported across the Atlantic; in the other they are to be procured at the same price, and without any expence of freight, at the adjacent market-town. The capital which is required for inclosing a farm and rendering the soil available in America, might equally suffice to the cultivator in his native country, but for the prohibition that hangs over him, and the impossibility under which he labours of buying or hiring the portion of land he wants at home.

Divers authors have reasoned learnedly respecting the origin of property. The explana-

tion given by Locke has been exceedingly
admired; and there is a very striking passage
of Rousseau in his Emilius on the same subject.

Mr. Malthus has set aside all the speculations
of his predecessors on this momentous topic.
He says, or rather his argument requires him
to say, The law of property originates in the
geometrical ratio.   The founders of nations had
an intuitive feeling of the unlimited and rapid
multiplication of mankind, and therefore set up
this fence in time, to keep down the population
of the earth.   It is true, that it must be civil
institutions after all, that cause the soil of this
island to be so inadequately cultivated, in a degree, according to Mr. Malthus, which is un-
equal to the wholesome and competent nourishment of all its inhabitants.   But then, if we
admit the theory of the Essay on Population,
civil institutions may justly stand discharged of
all blame on the subject, for this reason ; because
they are guilty of no caprice, they exercise no
discretion; they are the blind and necessary instruments of a higher power, of the great, inherent and indefeasible law of the multiplication
of mankind.   The great axiom of Mr. Malthus
will therefore still remain unimpeached: " Human institutions, however erroneous or oppressive, though they may appear to be the causes
of much mischief to society, are in reality light
and superficial, mere feathers that float on the
surface, in comparison with those deeper-seated

causes of evil, which result from the laws of nature and the passion between the sexes."

The more closely we look into the Essay on Population, the greater reason shall we find to be convinced, that it exhibits a theory of the most airy and unsubstantial nature that was ever obtruded on the public. It sets out in a grand style with the arithmetical and geometrical ratios, and undertakes to shew that, let the earth be cultivated and improved to however great a degree of perfection, the produce could never suffice to supply the wants of all the human beings that, by the principle of multiplication in man, would be engendered upon it.

This is the shewy and dazzling part of Mr. Malthus's theory, set forth to amaze his readers; and with this he has contrived to delude and mislead a countless multitude of followers. But this has nothing to do with the practical part of his doctrines, the essence of which lies simply in one proposition, *viz.* that "in all old countries, where the land is already appropriated, the population is at all times pressing hard against the limits of the means of subsistence."

Now, if in all old countries the population is at all times pressing hard against the limits of the means of subsistence, it must be so in countries where population is at a stand, for it is at a stand probably in most countries of Europe. Nay, which is more, and which Mr. Malthus has been at great pains to make out, it must be so in countries where population is actually on the decline.

The arithmetical and geometrical ratios therefore of the Essay on Population, are upon a par with the curls of the wig of Sterne's Parisian barber. " Immerge them in the ocean, exclaimed he, and they will stand."

" What a great scale," says Sterne, " is every thing upon in this city !   The utmost stretch of an English perriwig-maker's ideas could have gone no further than to have ' dipped it into a pail of water.' The pail of water standing beside the great deep, makes certainly a pitiful figure in speech : but, it will be said, it has one advantage ; it is in the next room, and the truth of the buckle may be tried in it without more ado in a single moment."

What Mr. Malthus advances on the subject of population in his Essay, is the exact counterpart of this.   " If a beautiful scheme of social happiness," says he, " were in other respects practicable, I cannot think that our ardour in the pursuit of such a scheme ought to be damped by the contemplation of so remote a difficulty, as might arise when the whole earth had been cultivated like a garden, and was incapable of any further increase of produce.   An event at such a distance might fairly be left to Providence.   But the truth is, that, at every period from the present moment, the distress for want of food will be constantly pressing on all mankind."

If then the truth is, that in all old countries, there is at all times, when the question is fairly weighed, a dearth of the means of subsistence, and at no time a sufficient supply for the full and wholesome nourishment of all, then the smallest assignable increase in the number of those who claim a share will be a serious calamity. Away then with the pompous procession of Mr. Malthus's ratios, which serve in this matter for parade only, and to perplex the minds of the readers! The true practical difficulty, the only question worthy the consideration of those whose concern is with the affairs of real life, is whether any remedy can be found for this disparity between the amount of the means of subsistence in all old countries, and the claims of those, who, being in existence, naturally desire to subsist. Mr. Malthus says, the remedy is in keeping down the population, the number of claimants. Another man may, with equal plausibility and appearance of right, say, that the remedy lies in increasing the amount of the means of subsistence, in a different administration of those capacities which the earth holds forth for the subsistence of man. It is between these two schemes of reasoning that we are called upon to decide.

The question does not, as Mr. Malthus unjustly endeavours to make us believe, depend in the smallest degree upon the extent to which the power of multiplication in man might possibly be carried. This has nothing to do with the matter. The geometrical ratio is a mere *ignis fatuus*, serving to no purpose but to lead us astray, through " fens, bogs, dens, and shades of death—a universe of death." Be the power of multiplication in man whatever it may, its actual operation is arrested, if arrested, by something else than the effects of its own excessive rapidity. The chariot of Nature has not yet been set on fire by the velocity of its motion. Let the principle of increase in man be the smallest that can be imagined, still, according to Mr. Malthus, that minute increase is for ever " pressing hard against the limits of the means of subsistence." Let us then, undazzled and undismayed by the prodigious prologue which the Essay on Population sets before this dry and simple proposition, enquire into the truth of the proposition itself.

Mr. Malthus's great practical proposition is, The population in all established states always presses hard against the limits of the means of subsistence ; or, in other words, the excessive tendency there is in human nature to increase in numbers, renders every attempt to increase the means of human subsistence, that is, provisions, abortive at least, if not rather pernicious.

Now there are three very simple reasons

which may be assigned to prove that this is not the case.

First, because, in many such states, there is no increase, but the population is at a stand : in some it actually decreases, without any public benefit arising from that circumstance.

Secondly, because, according to Mr. Malthus's famous doctrine of the parallel ratios, the two first terms in each coincide. The population, he informs us, has a tendency to double itself in twenty-five years; but then he grants that the means of subsistence may in the same time be increased by a quantity equal to itself. Thus far the arithmetical and geometrical ratios coincide. For the period of the first duplication of population in any country, all is safe. The fears of Mr. Malthus, and the fears which can reasonably be entertained by those who espouse his principles, are for the subsequent periods. Well then, let us grant the first period. Upon Mr. Malthus's own shewing, during all the time that we are advancing towards the first doubling things may go on tranquilly and prosperously. The population increases; but then the means of subsistence (unless Mr. Malthus's concessions are hollow and treacherous, promising us all good and desirable things, like the song of the Sirens, the better to destroy) may be expected equally to increase.

The express doctrine of the Essay on Population, when stripped of all false colours, and separated from the false prophecies, the accomplishment of which we have certainly no present reason to expect, is that the country of England, for example, where Mr. Malthus and I have written our treatises, may go on well, till the population it now contains, say, ten millions, becomes doubled, becomes twenty millions. Take the words of the Essay on Population " In the first twenty-five years the population would be twenty millions [he says, twenty-two millions], and the food being also doubled, the means of subsistence would be equal to this increase a." This is no trivial statement thrown out at random. This is the arithmetical and geometrical ratios themselves. This is the very basis of all Mr. Malthus's speculations, " which except every one do keep whole and undefiled, without doubt" he is a mere interloper and impostor in the school of the Essay on Population.

But let us suppose that the population of England does not become twenty millions in so short a period as twenty-five years. For every thing in Mr. Malthus's ratios, simple as they may appear to a cursory observer, depends upon time. If mankind do not double in every generation, the venom of the doctrine of the Essay on Population is extracted, the poison is neutralised. The improvements in the art of pro-

a Vol. I, p. 14.

ducing the means of subsistence, the very foundation of the arithmetical ratio, are intimately
bound up with the consideration of time. Mr.
Malthus's express doctrine is, " Be it allowed
that the subsistence for man which the earth affords might be increased every twenty-five years
by a quantity equal to what it at present produces b." It is so written down in the bond. If
then mankind do not double their numbers in
twenty-five years, if they only double in fifty,
or seventy-five, or a hundred years [or, if, as we
know from experience in the Old World, they
do not double at all; for it is with a real and not
a possible doubling that we are concerned; possible men do not eat, though real men do], the
increase in the means of subsistence by additions
of its own quantity every twenty-five years may
go on, and the geometrical ratio, advancing by
different periods of time, may be a long, an indefinite period, in overtaking the arithmetical.

Nothing therefore can be more clear than that
the doctrine of Mr. Malthus, as laid down in the
Essay on Population, is the farthest in the world
from being a practical doctrine. It is a theory
in the clouds, for the amusement of those who
delight to dwell in an element remote from the
affairs of men. It is on a par with Dr. Price's
illustration of the inherent power of the principle of Compound Interest. " One penny," says

---

b P. 13.

this author, " put out at our Saviour's birth to
five *per cent.* compound interest, would, in the
year 1791, have increased to a greater sum than
would be contained in three hundred millions of
earths, all solid gold [c]." Now it would be as reasonable for us to take the alarm at the despotic
and uncontrolable power over all mankind, that
might be supposed to fall to the rightful heir by
primogenitureship of the man who put out one
penny to compound interest at our Saviour's
birth, as that we should disquiet ourselves about
the issue of Mr. Malthus's ratios.   I should say
to him who felt terrified at the first, Wait, till
you have seen in sober earnest the penny become
one thousand or ten thousand pounds.   And I
should say to the man, the tranquillity of whose
repose was seriously disturbed by the dream of
the geometrical ratio, wait at least, till you
have seen the ten-million population of this island become twenty millions ; for up to that
period we have the authority of the Essay on
Population to say, " The food being also doubled, the means of subsistence would be equal
to this increase."   Till we see the first step of
the geometrical ratio in England realised, we
have no reason to be discomposed ; and Mr.
Malthus's statements have in the mean time as
much to do with the realities of life, as the old
adage which says, " When the sky falls, we
shall catch larks."

---

[c] Observations on Reversionary Payments, Vol. I, p. 314.

Thirdly, let us consider a little attentively how it is that the increase of population, by procreation only, is to produce the effect of making provisions too scanty. The first start of this increase must be by an addition to the number of infants. But infants do not in their first years consume any great quantity of animal or vegetable food. The increasing demand therefore for the means of subsistence can only come upon us gradually. And the means of subsistence, by the doctrines of the Essay on Population, are susceptible of an increase, regular, progressive and unlimited, though only in an arithmetical ratio. It is not therefore any actual increase in the number of candidates, that renders the means of subsistence in an old country too limited for the fair supply of its inhabitants. But, if it is not any thing actual, then it is something apprehended. To this conclusion we must come at last. If it is the tendency to increase in population beyond the practicable increase in the means of subsistence that keeps down the numbers of mankind, then it must be the apprehension of that increase. But how can that be, since Mr. Malthus in the year 1798 had the honour to discover the geometrical ratio, and since all the statesmen of ancient and modern times up to that memorable era, were persuaded, with Dr. Paley, that " the decay of population is the greatest evil that a state can suffer," and considered the main *desi-*

deratum in politics as being, to increase the number of their fellow-citizens? Thus it has been no reality, but the apprehension of what no man apprehended, that has carried on the most extensive system of infanticide, and strangled the progeny of the human race, to an amount which it is difficult to conceive, but which any man who will be at the trouble of applying the geometrical ratio from the first planting of this island, or peopling of the world, may easily put down, if he can procure a sheet of paper large enough to contain the figures that represent it.

To help the imagination of the reader in this point, I will present him with two authentic calculations on the subject.

The first is to be found in Morse's American Gazetteer. Under the article, " New York City," he has the following words: " Should the population of this city proceed in the same ratio through this century, as it has the last twenty years, the number of its inhabitants will be 5,257,493 :" thus raising by anticipation, in the course of less than a century, a comparatively humble town, with a population, at the moment of the author's writing his book, as it appears, of 83,500 persons, to somewhat towards the double of the computed population of Pekin.

My next example shall be taken from the pen of Mr. Malthus himself, who, in a book just published, entitled, Principles of Political Economy Considered, has the following passage.

" If any person will take the trouble to make the calculation, he will see that, if the necessaries of life could be obtained without limit, and the number of people could be doubled every twenty-five years, the population, which might have been produced from a single pair since the Christian era, would have been sufficient, not only to fill the earth quite full of people, so that four should stand upon every square yard, but to fill all the planets of our solar system in the same way, and not only them, but all the planets revolving round the stars which are visible to the naked eye, supposing each of them to be a sun, and to have as many planets belonging to it as our sun has [d]."

And this is the doctrine, which has seriously deluded the gravest statesmen of England and of Europe for the last twenty years, has reared its motley front in courts and parliaments, and been judged worthy to be made the foundation of legislative measures, and of codes of practical administration and jurisprudence to mankind!

The spirit of Mr. Malthus's theory bears a striking resemblance to the policy employed in training coach-horses, upon whose heads their manager is accustomed to fasten a pair of blinkers, that they may attend to nothing on either side, but see only straight before them. It is

[d] Principles of Political Economy, p. 227.

surely worth while that we should endeavour to
trace the effects of the geometrical ratio, as it
must have operated in ages past.   We live, as I
have often had occasion to repeat, in an unpeopled world.   How comes this, upon the principles of the Essay on Population ?   What was
it that stopped the increase of population in ancient times before the existence of records ?

I have abundantly shewn, if population is
kept down by the narrow limits within which
the means of subsistence are at present confined, that this restraint arises out of civil institutions, the inequality of mankind, and the accumulation of property, landed property especially,
in few hands.   But this system of policy had a
beginning.   It is the offspring of refinement.
The soil of the earth was once as free, once probably a great deal freer, than it is now in the
territory of the United States of North America.   Every man might have land at a very
cheap rate.   Every man might have land perhaps for nothing.   And then, by the principle
I have already explained, that each man in civilised society is born with the power of producing a much greater quantity of food than is
necessary for his own subsistence, I see nothing
that upon the principle of the Essay on Population should have arrested the progress of population, till the earth, the known world, was
" cultivated like a garden."   I call on Mr. Malthus to explain this phenomenon.   I call on Mr.

Malthus to account for what we see, an unpeopled world.

But perhaps the disciples of the geometrical ratio will say that, in this state of things, population was not arrested, as the fundamental principle of the Essay on Population affirms that the operation of this ratio is not stopped in North America. Perhaps the whole world once " swarmed with human beings," as the eye-witnesses of the first discovery of South America affirm of that quarter of the world, " as an ant-hill swarms with ants." If this is true, surely the thought of it is enough to make one serious. The earth might easily, upon our present systems of husbandry and cultivation, be made to subsist thirty times the number of human creatures that now inhabit it. Therefore it did contain thirty times the number of its present inhabitants. Therefore twenty-nine thirtieths of the human race have already been struck out of the catalogue of the living. And it is in this wreck of a world, almost as desolate as if a comet from the orbit of Saturn had come too near us, that Mr. Malthus issues his solemn denunciations, warning us on no consideration to increase the numbers of mankind.

The reader is aware that he is not to take the above statements as the enunciation of my own opinions. I give them only as the fair consequences of the theory of the Essay on Population. I give them only as results which Mr.

Malthus must either account for or elude.   And I therefore give them as considerations to which I might have trusted singly for the overthrow of Mr. Malthus's positions, if the world had not appeared so infatuated on the subject, as to impose on me the necessity of an elaborate re- futation of the most groundless paradoxes that ever were started.

CHAPTER VI.

OF THE IMPROVEMENTS OF WHICH THE PRO-
DUCTIVENESS OF THE GLOBE FOR THE PUR-
POSES OF HUMAN SUBSISTENCE IS CAPABLE

IT is with some diffidence that I would enter
upon the theoretical part of the question, and
enquire how far the earth may be rendered more
productive to the purposes of human subsistence
than it is at present. This branch of the subject however would be left imperfect, if that
consideration were wholly omitted.

To the improvements of man, more particularly in art, and the application of human industry, there is no end. No sooner therefore
shall we have got rid of the geometrical ratio,
and the still more absurd doctrine (if indeed
there be any degrees between these) of " population necessarily and constantly pressing hard
against the limits of subsistence, from the present moment to the time when the whole earth
shall be cultivated like a garden," than our
prospects will grow very cheering indeed.

Mr. Malthus, in the commencement of his
theory, is willing to grant, that in twenty-five
years the means of subsistence, i. e. the amount

CHAP.VI. SPECULATIONS ON THE MEANS, &c. 489

of provisions, through the whole earth, or in
any given country, might be doubled, in fifty
years tripled, in seventy-five years quadrupled,
in one hundred years quintupled, and so on in
an infinite series. Perhaps in some steps of this
series he supposes too much, and we can scarcely bring our minds to believe in an absolutely
infinite progression. It is this apparently candid spirit of concession, as much at least as any
other cause, or all other causes put together,
that has given to Mr. Malthus's theory so astonishing a success with his contemporaries. They
said, the writer must be very sure of his ground,
who grants to his antagonists more than any antagonist would venture to ask. But I do not
relish any of Mr. Malthus's ratios.

Timeo Danaos et dona ferentes.

Let us come down then to the regions of common sense. And, to attain a greater degree of
perspicuity in our views, let us take for the object of our consideration the countries of England and Wales.

In what is to come it must by no means be
forgotten, that, as far as the laws of nature are
concerned, there is no difficulty arising from the
increasing numbers of mankind, if there be any
increase, till a very remote period. The idea of
" pressing hard against the limits of subsistence," where the cultivation of the earth is understood, and as long as there shall be any

portions of a country cultivable, and not yet cultivated, is, I trust, banished for ever.

In the first place then I would observe, that, after what has been stated, it will hardly be denied, first, that the food produced in England and Wales, if equally distributed, is more than enough for the present number of the inhabitants; or, secondly, that many tracts of land in these countries might be rendered more efficient for the subsistence of man, than they actually are.

The problem now under consideration, is, how shall a given tract of country be made to subsist more men? The problem that seems for more than a century past in England practically to have occupied the attention of those in whose direction the affair was placed, has been, How shall a given tract of country be made effective only for the subsistence of a smaller number of men?

Dr. Price mentions two causes, operating in this country, which are eminently calculated to produce this effect; the engrossing of farms, and the progress of luxury.

" A large tract of land," he observes, " in the hands of one man, neither yields so great a return, nor does it employ so many people [as it would do if divided to a number of proprietors]ᵃ." And, in illustration of this, he mentions two parishes in the Pays de Vaud; one of

---

ᵈ Observations on Reversionary Payments, Vol. II, p. 139

which, once a little village, having been bought
by some rich men, was sunk into a single demesne; and the other, once a single demesne,
having fallen into the hands of some peasants,
was become a little village. " How many
facts," he adds, " of the former kind can Great
Britain now furnish a !"

With respect to the progress of luxury, he
produces the following striking particulars. " In
the year 1697 wheat was at three pounds *per*
quarter, and other grain proportionably dear.
But there was no clamour, and the exportation
went on. At present [1773], though the quantity of money, or what passes for money, is
doubled, yet when wheat is below this price,
there is an alarm, the poor are starving, and exportation is prohibited.

" The true reason of this seems to be, that
the high price of bread was not, at the time I
have mentioned, of essential consequence to the
lower people. They lived more upon other
food, which was then cheap; and, being more
generally occupiers of land, they were less under the necessity of purchasing bread. Whereas now, being forced, by greater difficulties, and
the high price of all other food, to live principally or solely upon bread, if that is not cheap,
they are rendered incapable of maintaining
themselves.

" In confirmation of this account I will men-

---

a *Ibid*

tion, that though, during the whole seventeenth century, corn was generally dearer than it has been at an average for the last forty years, yet flesh-meat was at about half its present price. In an act of parliament, 25 Henry VIII, beef, veal, pork, and mutton are named as the food of the poor, and their price is limited to about one halfpenny *per* pound. Beef and pork, in particular, were sold in London at two pounds and a half, and three pounds, for a penny; at the very time that wheat was seven and eight shillings *per* quarter, bearing the same proportion to the price of flesh, that it would bear now, if it were about four pounds *per* quarter [b].

"Upon the whole, the circumstances of the lower ranks, and of the day-labourer, are altered in almost every respect for the worse, while tea, fine wheaten bread, and other delicacies, are become necessaries, which were formerly unknown among them [c]."

To this it may be added, that the labours of agriculture were then generally performed by means of cows and oxen, which were afterwards used as food, whereas the almost universal employment of horses at present, which consume, according to Mr. Middleton, upon an average the produce of four acres of land each, must materially diminish the quantity of food which is left for the use of man.

---

[b] P. 148, 149.   [c] P. 159, 160.

Mr. Malthus repeatedly calls our attention, and with great propriety, to the period when the whole earth, or any considerable division of it, shall be "cultivated like a garden." Till that shall be the case, it is perfectly clear that there can be no permanent deficiency in the means of subsistence, except what is produced by the restrictions imposed on us by human institutions.

I feel inclined in this place shortly to mention the agricultural improvements of Mr. Coke of Norfolk. This gentleman may be considered as a sort of rural father of his country; and it is a pleasing task to any one who writes on the means of subsistence and •the welfare of mankind, to commemorate his merits.

Mr. Coke's Norfolk estate, when he came to the succession more than forty years ago, was regarded as some of the worst land in the country. A great part of it was leased out at three shillings an acre. The entire rental amounted to £2200 *per annum.* By his example and encouragement its produce is now so far raised, that it may serve as a sort of model to the whole island. The rental has increased ten-fold: the cultivators are happy: the population is tripled. They have no longer need for a poor-house, which has accordingly been pulled down. The very land, which was lately an object of so much contempt, now produces five or six quarters of wheat, and ten of barley, *per* acre d.

---

d Rigby, Holkham and its Agriculture.

Mr. Coke is however at this moment a sort of phenomenon in the island.   The majority of our cultivators, even in the naturally fertile counties of Shropshire and Cheshire, go on in the method of their fathers, without improvement; and, at the very time that Mr. Coke was gathering the crops abovementioned, the average produce of wheat among them was not more than two quarters *per* acre [e]   Thus we see that by a very simple process, the example of which we have under our eye, the produce of our island might be much more than doubled.   The consciousness of this, one would have thought, would have prevented any sober man, in this ill-omened hour for so unhallowed a purpose, from preaching up Mr. Malthus's doctrine of depopulation.

I mention this example for two reasons. First, because it is a pleasing task, to do justice to the merits of a public benefactor. Secondly, because there is a numerous class of persons, well disposed to do justice to an actual experiment, at the same time that they turn a deaf ear to what comes before them in the shape of speculation. For these reasons I have recorded the proceedings of Mr. Coke, though these are doubtless extremely trivial, compared with what I conceive, and with what Mr. Malthus assumes, of the capacity of the earth for affording subsistence to mankind.

---

e Rigby, Holkham and its Agriculture.

It is a sentiment commonly in the mouths of those who wish well to human prosperity, " Success to the plough." But, if I dared indulge in the hope of a rapid, but not (like Mr. Malthus's geometrical ratio) wholly impossible, multiplication of mankind, I should substitute for this sentiment, " Success to the spade." The productiveness of garden-cultivation over field-cultivation, for the purposes of human subsistence, is astonishingly great. Mr. Coke leases out his land at forty shillings an acre; but, judging from some examples within my own knowledge, I should conclude forty pounds an acre for some kinds of garden-ground, a very moderate estimate. Let us add to this the various expences of labour, manure, and several other sorts, necessary to render this acre of garden available, and we shall then form some conjecture, how many men's subsistence an acre of ground may represent.

I see only one objection to this cultivation of the spade : [that is, upon the supposition, hitherto wild and without rational support, that the earth, or any portion of it, shall become stocked with human beings, so as in that sense to realise what the benevolent mind is impelled to fancy of Utopia.]

The objection I allude to is built on the consideration that, in any very improved state of human society, I should desire to see the quantity of manual labour diminished, instead of increased. But I am afraid we must pass through a probation of extensive labour, before we can come at any thing better. The human species is not yet so far improved, as for the larger portion of mankind to know how to make an innocent and intelligent use of that which is, abstractedly considered, the most valuable of human treasures, leisure. When we are arrived at this improvement, there is no danger but that we shall be able to possess ourselves of the means by which to exercise it. It is one of the most certain features of human progress, the invention of machinery; and there is no reason to suppose that there is any species of industry, which may not ultimately be abridged by the application of this faculty.

To the speculations already mentioned upon the means of human subsistence, is to be added the sea. The sea occupies two-thirds of the surface of the globe: it is every where full of animal life, and nearly all that life may be rendered subservient to human subsistence. This is a species of crop that we are not called upon to sow; it needs no manure; and the farmer who takes care of it, will seldom have occasion to observe the face of the heavens, and send to the parish-minister to solicit a prayer for fine weather, or a prayer for rain. There is no long watching the progress of growth, but one fine day will be sufficient for him to bring in his stores. It has been ascertained, particularly as to the salmon-fishery, that no drafts upon this stock, however immense, occasions the smallest sensible diminution of the crop for the next season. It is upon the confidence of this fact, that some of the most serious transactions are founded, in the countries to which the question relates. Thus, in some parts of Scotland, where the drain has for years been the most considerable, the rents for a right of fishing for a certain distance, have lately been raised tenfold above what they had been. Add to which, that salmon and other fish, when cured, may be kept for almost any time, and be carried any distance up the country.

Before we quit this branch of the subject, it will be worth while to look back to Mr. Middleton's estimate of the present mode of human subsistence. He states each man to consume upon an average, *per annum*, "in bread the produce of half an acre, in roots, greens and fruit the produce of one eighth of an acre, in liquids one eighth of an acre, and in animal food two acres." Here we are presented in a striking view with the knowledge, of how much would be economised as to human subsistence, by the general substitution of the vegetable for the animal productions of the earth.

Thus we are led to observe two grand steps of practical improvement as to the subsistence of man ; the first, by substituting the plough in the room of pasture : the next, as we have

K k

said, by causing the spade to supersede the plough.

When it has been demonstrated, that there is an actual increase in the numbers of mankind, it will then perhaps be time enough to calculate what may be gained by these two improvements.

Meanwhile enough has been said, to deliver any rational followers of Mr. Malthus, from the fear of any speedy deficiency in the means of subsistence. Nature has presented to us the earth, the *alma magna parens*, whose bosom, to all but the wild and incongruous ratios of Mr. Malthus, may be said to be inexhaustible. Human science and ingenuity have presented to us the means of turning this resource to the utmost account. " Rest, rest, perturbed spirits !" Your anxieties are vain, and infinitely more senseless than those of the proprietor of a province, who should fear that, by some unexpected turn of fortune's wheel, he should be compelled to die in a workhouse.

A very natural objection to what has been stated in the few preceding pages, is that such a statement was wholly unnecessary, as Mr. Malthus grants an arithmetical ratio to the multiplication of the means of subsistence, which is as much as can be desired. He grants that the present produce of the earth may be doubled in twenty-five years, tripled in fifty, quadrupled in seventy-five, and quintupled in a century.

But these concessions are hollow and treacherous; and the author might have known them to be so.   He instantly buries his arithmetical, under the ponderous weight of his geometrical ratio.   He might safely make these concessions; for they have had no weight with any body. He merely gives us a " commodity of good words." The only effect they have had, is to gain him a specious character of candour, the better to destroy us.   The author is admired for his generosity; while his fortune exceeds that which our ancestors ascribed to charity ; for in fact the more he gives away, literally the more he gains.

Mr. Malthus's concessions are indeed valueless. They are composed of air, and can be blown away, whenever the author or his adherents find it convenient to get rid of them.   The great defect of every part of his system, is that, though it professes to be every where conversant with human affairs, it conveys no image to the mind.   1 have therefore found it necessary to go over the above particulars, that my readers may have something to think of, something to go back to whenever they have occasion, in a word, something that the author of the Essay on Population has not the power to give, nor the power to take away.

There is however one other circumstance that requires to be mentioned, before the subject can properly be considered as exhausted.   Of all the sciences, natural or mechanical, which within the last half century have proceeded with such gigantic strides, chemistry is that which has advanced the most rapidly. All the substances that nature presents, all that proceeds from earth or air, is analysed by us into its original elements. Thus we have discovered, or may discover, precisely what it is that nourishes the human body. And it is surely no great stretch of the faculty of anticipation, to say, that whatever man can decompose, man will be able to compound. The food that nourishes us, is composed of certain elements; and wherever these elements can be found, human art will hereafter discover the power of reducing them into a state capable of affording corporeal sustenance. No good reason can be assigned, why that which produces animal nourishment, must have previously passed through a process of animal or vegetable life. And, if a certain infusion of attractive exterior qualities is held necessary to allure us to our food, there is no reason to suppose that the most agreeable colours and scents and flavours may not be imparted to it, at a very small expence of vegetable substance. Thus it appears that, wherever earth, and water, and the other original chemical substances may be found, there human art may hereafter produce nourishment: and thus we are presented with a real infinite series of increase of the means of subsistence, to match Mr. Malthus's geometrical ratio for the multiplication of mankind.—This may be thought too speculative; but surely it is not more so, than Mr. Malthus's period, when the globe of earth, or, as he has since told us, the solar system, and all the "other planets circling other suns," shall be overcrowded with the multitude of their human inhabitants.

CHAPTER VII.

OF THE PRINCIPLES OF A SOUND POLICY ON
THE SUBJECT OF POPULATION.

BEFORE we dismiss the question of subsistence, it is however proper to consider it in another point of view, in a point of view, not originating in the visionary theories and wild chimeras of Mr. Malthus, but in facts.

The only substantial evidence which has thus far been collected on this branch of political economy, teaches us, that the numbers of mankind have no permanent tendency to increase [a]. The population of Europe, of Asia, of Africa, is at best at a stand. In some countries it is certainly diminished; and we have, I believe, no sound reason to think that in any it has increased. The solitary example of North America is produced against this mighty mass of

---

[a] When I say no permanent tendency to increase, I speak from experience the genuine guide on this subject. Population has perhaps increased for a time in Sweden; but it is not less probable, that Sweden is not more populous now, than it was five centuries, or ten centuries ago. Mr. Malthus may indulge in the dream of his ratios, and I in my hopes of gradual change and improvements in human society': but practical statesmen ought to be governed in the ordinary course of their measures, by what they find recorded in the pages of genuine history.

experience, North America, a country, which for a century past has been the receptacle of almost all the emigrations that have been made from all parts of the world. Even in North America the inhabitants of the British dominions have not increased; and the negroes have not increased. A man must be the free citizen of a republic, before he is entitled to the benefit—for benefit there it is considered to be—of the geometrical ratio.

But what is most material,—for enumerations, after all, are an obscure and uncertain kind of evidence,—is, that it is the result of all the collections that have yet been made in all the countries of the world, that the wedlock of two human beings does not produce upon an average more than four children. In America we have seen that the ratio in this respect is the same as in the old world. This indeed is the true kernel of the question : and, if there is any real increase in the numbers of mankind, it is thus only that we can be rationally convinced of it. This is the way in which alone, as Mr. Malthus phrases it, " it can be ascertained to be from procreation only." Wherever it shall be found that there are only four children to a marriage, it appears to be clearly demonstrated, there can be no actual increase, and we have more reason to fear a decrease, of the numbers of mankind ; least of all can there be an increase in the United States, where we are assured that half the population is under sixteen years of age.

I by no means undertake to assert, that there is absolutely no tendency in the human species to increase, though I certainly think, that the idea of guarding ourselves against the geometrical ratio, is just as sagacious and profound, as that of Don Quixote's fighting with the windmills. All I affirm is, that the evidence we yet possess is against the increase : and I think it is the business of the true statesman and practical philanthropist in the mean time to act on such evidence as we have. It will be time enough to hunt our species out of the world, and " stop the propagation of mankind," when we see such danger, as no man up to the present time can have any solid reason to apprehend.

The business therefore of the true statesman and practical philanthropist under this head is extremely simple. Let us take it for granted that England and Wales at this moment contain ten millions of inhabitants. Let us assume with Mr. Malthus, that there are not at present provisions within the country to subsist this number. Certain it is, that, practically speaking, and looking to the distribution only, all are not adequately subsisted. The proper enquiry is, how this is to be remedied : and scarcely any man, considering the state of our soil, its cultivated and uncultivated parts, will venture to deny that a remedy may be accomplished, whether it shall be by certain wise changes in the mechanism of society, or by breaking up more ground, and rendering that which is already inclosed more available to its genuine purposes.

This speculation brings us back to the feelings of unsophisticated humanity, which it is the clear tendency of Mr. Malthus's theory to expel out of the world. He says, No, we must not increase the happiness of our contemporaries, lest by so doing we should immeasurably increase the candidates for happiness and subsistence. He would starve the present generation, that he may kill the next.

In the mean while, the idle dream of his ratios being dispelled, human nature is itself again. We return to the morality of our ancestors. We return to the morality of the Christian religion, and of all the religious leaders and legislators from the beginning of the records of mankind. Wherever I meet a man, I meet a brother. I recognise in him the image of the all-perfect. I see a creature, "fearfully and wonderfully made," and admire the exquisiteness of the workmanship. I do not think of effacing God's image, or of neglecting and superciliously setting light by that on which he has affixed his seal. I do not seek to suppress the most natural impulses of a human being, and turn the world into a great monastery. No: if it is ever unwise for man to marry (and unfortunately this is too true in a variety of instances), it is not owing, as Mr. Malthus impiously would have us to believe, to any thing in the original and indestructible laws of nature, but to the partiality and oppressiveness of human institutions.

It is the duty of legislators, and was always so understood, till Mr. Malthus came with his wild theory, built upon the erroneous construction of what was seen in one corner of the earth, and in flagrant opposition to all other evidence, and upon his perversion of the idea of subsistence,—I say, it is the duty of legislators, to deal tenderly with the life of man, not brutally and rashly to extinguish that, which all their art can never revive again, to cherish it as the apple of the eye, to believe that when they cut off a man, they impair so far the nerves by which a nation is sustained, and to tremble and hesitate before they take on themselves so awful a responsibility. Mr. Malthus's theory on the contrary would persuade us to hail war, famine and pestilence, as the true friends of the general weal, to look with a certain complacent approbation upon the gallows and massacre, and almost to long for the decimation of our species, that the survivors might be more conveniently accommodated.

ENQUIRY

CONCERNING

POPULATION.

BOOK VI.

OF THE MORAL AND POLITICAL MAXIMS INCULCATED IN THE ESSAY ON POPULATION.

CHAPTER I.

CHARACTER AND SPIRIT OF THE ESSAY ON POPULATION DELINEATED.

I HAVE now entered somewhat copiously into the three grand topics of Mr. Malthus's work, the progressive increase of the numbers of mankind, the causes [checks, in the language of the Essay on Population] by which the amount of the numbers of the human species is reduced or restrained, and the means which the earth affords for the subsistence of man.

Under these several heads I have endeavoured
to shew, 1. that we have no authentic documents to prove any increase in the numbers of
mankind, and that, if there is any tendency to
increase, exclusively of the counteracting causes
that are to be traced in the annals of history,
which is by no means certain, that tendency is
of the most moderate description : 2. that the
counteracting causes are neither constant nor
regular in their operation, and have nothing in
them of an occult and mysterious nature : and,
3. that the means which the earth affords for the
subsistence of man, are subject to no assignable
limits, and that the nourishment of human
beings in civilised society, can never, unless in
the case of seasons peculiarly unfavourable, sustain any other difficulty, till the whole globe
has been raised to a very high degree of cultivation, except such as arises from political institutions.

Having done thus much, I might well close
my volume, and put an end to this, perhaps the
last labour of no idle and unstrenuous life.   But
Mr. Malthus's book forms an era in political
speculation.   I should not chuse, like its author,
to talk of placing certain principles " on record,"
with a provident care lest, " if the world were
to last for any number of thousand years [a]," they
might then be wanted.   But I do think, that

---

[a] Vol. II, p. 271, 3.

some monument should be erected, to shew, for as long a time as such monuments might be expected to last, what extravagant and monstrous propositions the human mind is capable to engender, when once men shall be prompted, upon a fable, a gratuitous and wholly unproved assumption, to build a system of legislation, and determine the destiny of all their fellow-creatures.

Mr. Malthus has delivered a political system. His work is placed on our shelves, by the side of those of Plato, and Aristotle, and Sidney, and Locke, and Montesquieu, and Adam Smith. It may not therefore be uninstructive, setting apart for a moment the question of the truth or falshood of its principles, to enquire into its merits and complexion as a theory merely.

One of the most natural divisions of any work which takes human affairs upon a general scale for the subject of its research, is, 1. to lay down certain evils and imperfections to which human society is liable, and, 2. to treat of the remedy for these evils. Let us see what the Essay on Population has done under each of these heads.

The evil which it was the professed business of Mr. Malthus's work to lay open to the world, was, the tendency of the principle of multiplication in mankind to produce an increase, beyond the possible increase of the means of human subsistence. "The first of the propositions,"

into which this view of the condition of man
on the globe may be divided, namely, the rapid
increase of which the human species, abstractedly taken, is susceptible, so as to enable it (as
appears from the author's latest statement), in
less than two thousand years, to people the
whole visible universe at the rate of four men
to every yard square, Mr. Malthus "considered
as proved the moment the American increase
was related b:" and " the second proposition,"
namely, the comparatively slow possible increase
of the means of subsistence, as proved, " as
soon as it was enunciated b."

Here then is a very plain statement of the evil
which hangs over human societies, and which, according to the Essay on Population, is every
moment producing the most important effects.
It has the advantage of being placed before us
in a small compass, and easily intelligible to the
meanest capacities.

Mr. Malthus therefore, as he informs us, has
not written a work of very ample dimensions,
to prove these points. They are dispatched in
" the first six pages c;" and " the chief object of
his work c" is to display the consequences of
these two propositions, to enquire into the duties of those to whose care the public welfare is
intrusted, and to shew how this immense disparity between the number of possible candi-

---

b Vol. III, p. 344, note.   c *Ibid.*

dates for food, and the possible means of subsistence, has been, and must be obviated.

Now the remedies, according to the Essay on Population, by which the disparity between the power of increase in man, and the power of increase in the means of human subsistence, is to be cured, are chiefly vice and misery.

I am persuaded, that Mr. Malthus wrote his first little octavo, which was published in 1798, merely as an exercise of wit, a piece of pleasantry which, whatever should be its fate in other respects, might deservedly obtain for its author the praise of ingenuity. To his great surprise the world received his communications as a very serious affair.

When his speculations were first published, the author was at no pains to disguise the odiousness of their features. In proportion however as he proceeded to consider them in a more serious way, and to imagine that he was laying down a code for the regulation of nations, and deciding upon the fate of a distant posterity, he " so far differed," as he tells us, in his enlarged work from the original sketch, " as to *suppose the action* of another check to population, which does not come under the head either of vice or misery, and to endeavour in other respects to *soften some of the harshest conclusions* of the first Essay d."

d Preface, p. ix.

Mr. Malthus's three checks upon increasing population by his latest statement, are therefore vice, misery, and moral restraint.

The original infirmity however of his first Essay adheres to all the subsequent editions. In making the alterations above described, Mr. Malthus expresses an anxious " hope, that he has not violated the principles of just reasoning, nor expressed any opinion respecting the probable improvement of society, in which he is not borne out by *the experience of the past* [e]." Indeed it plainly appears, that the variations introduced are mere sacrifices at the shrine of decorum, without any alteration of opinion on the part of the author. The whole work is built in that contempt for human nature, from which so many men, both through the press, and in private circles, have sought for the reputation of superior wisdom, an opinion that, however refined may be our reflections, we shall in practice always blindly obey our appetites, and that consequently, whatever improvements may be effected in matters purely of science, no future generation of men will ever conduct themselves with more virtue and discretion than the past.

What Mr. Malthus's real opinion is of the efficacy of moral restraint to prevent an excess of population, plainly appears from various pas-

---

[e] *Ibid.*

sages of his work.   Take the following examples.

" But Mr. Godwin says, that if he looks into the past history of the world, he does not see that increasing population has been controled and confined by vice and misery alone. *In this observation I cannot agree with him.* I will thank Mr. Godwin to name to me any check, which in past ages has contributed to keep down the population to the level of the means of subsistence, that does not fairly come under some form of vice or misery,——except indeed the check of moral restraint, which I have *mentioned* in the course of this work, and which, *to say the truth*, whatever hopes we may entertain of its prevalence in future, has undoubtedly *in past ages* operated with very inconsiderable force [f]."

This passage is omitted in the last edition of Mr. Malthus's work.   Not certainly from any alteration of opinion in the author : but " it was suggested to him some years since by persons for whose judgment he has a high respect, that it might be advisable, in a new edition, to throw out the matter relative to systems of equality, to Wallace, Condorcet and Godwin, as having to a considerable degree lost its interest [g]." He has accordingly met these advisers half-way, and omitted one of the chapters on this point, from

[f] Quarto Edition, 1803, p. 383.   [g] Vol. II, p. 271.

which chapter the above passage is taken. But he could not consent to relinquish his antagonists altogether, and " really thought that there should be somewhere on record an answer to systems of equality, founded on the *principle of population.* It cannot," he adds, " be matter of wonder, that proposals for systems of equality should be continually reviving. After periods when the subject has undergone a thorough discussion, or when some great experiment in improvement has failed, it is likely that the question should lie dormant for a time, and that the opinions of the advocates of equality should be ranked among those errors, which had passed away, to be heard of no more. But it is probable, that if the world were to last for *any number of thousand years,* systems of equality would be among those errors, which, like the tunes of a barrel-organ, will never cease to return at certain intervals ᵍ."

Again. " I do not see," says Mr. Malthus, " how it is possible to escape the conclusion, that moral restraint is the strict line of duty. At the same time I believe that few of my readers can be *less sanguine than I am,* in their expectations of any sudden and great change in the general conduct of men on this subject: and the chief reason why in the last chapter I *allowed myself to suppose* the universal preva-

---

ᵍ Vol. II, p. 271, 3.

lence of this virtue, was that I might endeavour
to remove any imputation on the goodness of
the Deity[h],"—by supposing something that
would never take place.

One more extract to the same purpose. " In
my review of the different stages of society, I
have been accused of not allowing sufficient
weight in the prevention of population to moral
restraint. But, when the sense of the term,
which I have here explained, is adverted to, I
am fearful that I shall not be found to have
erred much in this respect. I should be very
glad to believe myself mistaken [i]."

If any man says, that " increasing population
can be restrained by any thing but vice and
misery alone," Mr. Malthus " cannot agree with
him."   " Few of his readers," and among them
no doubt are the licentious and the profligate,
such men, as I have heard talk, and have heard
others applaud, and loudly too, who vehemently
affirm that there is no woman chaste,—" Few
of his readers," I say, " can be less sanguine
than he is, in their expectations of the efficacy
of moral restraint."   He finds that this principle " has in past ages operated with very inconsiderable force ;" and he is not visionary enough
to entertain " any opinion respecting the future
improvement of society, in which he is not
borne out by the experience of the past."

_____

h Vol. III, p. 103.   i Vol. I, p. 22, note.

This is then the precise outline of Mr. Malthus's system. The evils against which he would guard are hunger and famine; the remedies for these evils are vice and misery.

Now certainly, when the doctrine of the Essay on Population is thus stated in all its nakedness, I shall probably make no hazardous assertion when I say, that it is the most extraordinary work ever presented to the world. The author may without the smallest breach of modesty affirm, that Plato and Aristotle and Sidney and Locke have done nothing that can enter into comparison with his achievements, and that his view of human affairs differs fundamentally from the views of any philosopher that ever existed

The converts to Mr. Malthus's speculations, as far as I am acquainted with them, are of two sorts.

The first are those who admit the doctrines of the Essay on Population unwillingly. These men are in their hearts lovers of virtue, votaries of the dignity of man, persons who would anxiously desire to see great improvements introduced in society, and who were not previously disposed to set limits to the progress of human understanding, or to the melioration of human institutions. These men are convinced against their will. They look with a certain unconquerable aversion upon the doctrines of the Essay on Population; but they find themselves unable to resist the luminousness of its statements

The second class of the adherents of Mr. Malthus, and these are considerably numerous, consists of persons, who hail his discoveries as an invaluable and a grateful acquisition. They are ready to erect statues to him as a public benefactor. They conceive it of the highest importance to put down once and for ever all impracticable speculations for the improvement of the political condition of man, and are anxious, not only that no overt attempts should be made towards such improvement, but that we should be deprived, if possible, of the dangerous indulgence of dreaming of it in the privacy of meditation and solitude. They regard the author as having performed an inestimable service by putting an end at once to all hopes of mankind ever bettering themselves. He has taught us an admirable lesson, by inducing us to rest satisfied as we are, and not to spend our strength in efforts, at once fruitless in the purposes at which they aim, and mischievous in the result. He has shewn us the path of sobriety and reason. These persons even consider the Essay on Population as a vindication of the goodness of God, and a demonstration of the doctrine of a Divine Providence [k].

---

[k] " An original well-head of political truth." " The great merit and the everlasting value of his work." " The high moral and religious blessings which lie involved in this germ." " But I must

To return.   Hunger and famine are the evils :
vice and misery are the remedies.

It is a trite observation, that the remedies
which the members of the medical profession
administer to our bodies, are for the most part
nauseous and offensive to the human palate. In
this point then Mr. Malthus has sufficiently
vindicated his claim to the appellation of a phy-
sician.

Surely that system ought to be attended with
an irresistible and overpowering evidence, of
which the choicest gifts that are tendered to us
are vice and misery.

But why these gifts ?   And what is to induce
us to accept them ?   A remedy can have no
claim upon our reception, but inasmuch as it is
better than the disease.   Now vice and misery

---

beware how I yield to this captivating theme." " It was natural
indeed to think, that all truth would be harmonious and consistent,
and that the universe was not constructed on a plan altogether pre-
posterous. It is the high distinction of the Essay on Population to
have demonstrated this."

This author expresses his astonishment and horror, that in the
year 1797, only one year before the first appearance of the Essay
on Population, the immortal Pitt introduced a bill laid before parliament, with such words as, " that those who had enriched their
country with children, might feel that they had a claim on its support."

See A Second Letter to the Right Honourable Robert Peele, M. P.
    for the University of Oxford, said to be written by the Rev.
    E. Coppleston, D D, Provost of Oriel College in that Univer-
    sity.

are the names for all we fear, and all we hate. What is that worse thing, which by taking these to our bosom we shall be enabled to defend ourselves against?   Over-population itself why should we fear, but because it is said to bring vice and misery in its train?

But I am unwilling that the subject should thus rest in general terms.   The human mind is an essence of a peculiar sort; and the effect of whatever is presented to it depends very much on the principle of novelty.   The most powerful stimulus may be administered to it so often, as to lose its efficacy: the most appalling and terrific considerations may by this means be made to " pass by us, like the idle wind which we respect not."

I will take my illustrations of the true bearings and import of these portentous terms, vice and misery, from the Essay on Population itself.

" The positive checks to population are extremely various, and include every cause, whether arising from vice or misery, which in any degree contributes to shorten the natural duration of human life[1]."   I call upon every conscientious speculator upon the state of man on earth, seriously to pause on this enunciation.

Mr. Malthus truly observes, " Every loss of a child from the consequences of poverty, must

---

[1] Vol. I, p. 21.

evidently be preceded and accompanied by great misery to individuals [m]." Most surely it must. Independently of the child, who languishes, and at length perishes, for want of sufficient nourishment, what must be the sensations of the parents, who are compelled thus to be the murderers of their own offspring, who occasionally give it something from the food which is necessary for their own sustenance, who see it craving and pining for more, who witness its gradual and premature destruction, and who are speedily destined to follow, partly for the want of that, which unavailingly they bestowed on the infant victim, and which eventually served for nothing but to prolong its miseries!

Yet this destruction of children, and that to an immense extent, is necessary, according to the principles of the Essay on Population, for the preservation of the human species. Alas, why on these principles are we preserved at all!

The same observations with little variety will apply to the whole of Mr. Malthus's eleven heads [n], under which he distributes his positive checks. The author of the Essay on Population sits remote, like a malignant Providence [Providence it seems we are bound to call it], dispensing from his magazine, all those causes, often arising from vice, always inextricably bound up with acute and exquisite misery,

---

[m] Vol. III, p. 299.   [n] See above, Book III, Chapter V.

which, some a little sooner, and some a little
later, " in various degrees contribute to shorten
the natural duration of human life" [this is the
desideratum] : or rather, himself free from the
disturbance of our passions and frailties, he
points out to us the various particulars of our
lot, and closes the account with taking to himself this satisfaction, that he leaves us to perish
" by the hands of God, and not by the hands of
man."

Undoubtedly it would be better upon this
hypothesis, that we could cut off, in a summary
way, a proper number of children in the first
stage of their existence, as the cultivator of the
earth sets himself to hoe his turnips, clearing
the ground round each favoured plant, that it
may have room enough for growth and subsistence. But this is not consistent with Mr.
Malthus's ideas of Christian morality.

Vice and misery are necessary for the preservation of order, and the well being of the body
politic. Vice and misery are remedies sufficiently repulsive to the innocent and pure-
minded : surely Mr. Malthus ought not to have
been contented with a general recommendation ;
but like other physicians, who are obliged to
prescribe distasteful and dangerous ingredients,
he should have told us the precise quantity of
each that was necessary in the medicine. Perhaps we need not have recourse to the whole
eleven : perhaps, if we took rather a larger por-

tion of some of them, we might be altogether excused as to others.

Vice and misery are absolutely necessary for the well being of society : and Mr. Malthus has travelled into various regions of the globe, to shew us how they operate in different countries to keep down the excess of population. Surely, as from chapter to chapter he led us to observe the modes and institutions of different states, he had a most desirable opportunity to play the censor, and while he recommended to us the milder vices and oppressions, to enter his protest against the excessive. But no such thing. Provided only there is vice and misery, Mr. Malthus's purpose is sufficiently answered. Or does he mean, that, by the beneficent care of a superintending Providence, each country has exactly the sort and the quantity of vice and misery that are best suited to its wants?

If Mr. Malthus, instead of contenting himself with a vague and general recommendation, had entered into particulars, he might have supplied us with an instructive lesson. There would still have been room for great political improvements. Perhaps there is no state, at present existing on the face of the globe, England for example, that has not vice and misery enough to answer all wholesome purposes. If any one should be perverse enough to suppose that Greece and Rome, in the days of their greatest virtue and renown, were more happily circum-

stanced than England is at present, perhaps
even the people of Greece and Rome had vice
and misery enough, to serve them as a healthful
condiment, and save them from putrefaction.
Were it not that Mr. Malthus is a sworn enemy
to all cheerful and cheering prospects, here was
abundant matter to enable him to vary the
dreary and repulsive monotony of his volumes.
He might have gone over the different governments of the East, Turkey, Persia, and Egypt;
he might even have ventured upon some of those
of Europe; he might almost have made the circumnavigation of the globe; and, hailing, and
pouring his benediction upon every despotic
shore, he might have said, " All these countries
may be raised to the political level of England,
or even of ancient Greece or Rome, without
having too much to fear from the *principle of
population.*"   But, no: this does not accord
with his tone in writing.   It sounds more musical in his ears to pronounce, " Human institutions, however they may appear to be the causes
of much mischief to society, are in reality light
and superficial, mere feathers that float on the
surface, in comparison with those deeper-seated
causes of evil [*viz.* the propagation of mankind]
which result from the laws of nature and the
passions of man."

I own I am pleased with the condition in
which the author of the Essay on Population has
dismissed his subject.   He who has written three

volumes expressly to point out to us the advantage we obtain from the presence of vice and misery, would naturally leave the question in all the confusion in which Mr. Malthus has left it. This is as it should be.   It is scarcely conceivable that the man who recommends to us such bosomfriends and companions, should have much discrimination and choice as to the different species and degrees of each.

The subject which I quit in this place, will be further pursued in the Third Chapter of this Book.

CHAPTER II.

OF THE POSITIONS RESPECTING THE NATURE
OF MAN UPON WHICH THE ESSAY ON POPULA-
TION IS CONSTRUCTED.

THE theory of the Essay on Population may
be considered under two heads: first, as it respects human communities, such as we now find
them: secondly, as it relates to any improvement in society which may be supposed to be
effected hereafter.

I might omit the consideration of the latter
altogether; for the majority of Mr. Malthus's
readers, and all Mr. Malthus's disciples, never
think but of what they see, and of man as he
is.

But it is proper to take some notice of that
branch of the speculations of this work, which
relates to future and remote improvements in
human society: first, because all the reasonings
of the author began with this; his first thought
was to shew the impracticability of all cardinal
and substantive improvements: secondly, because the object of this last division of my
enquiry is to display the character and spirit of
the Essay on Population, and to shew to those

who have followed this leader so far, under what sort of banner they have marshalled themselves.

The fundamental error of Mr. Malthus's system, as far as the constitution and structure of man, independently of the geometrical ratio, is concerned, seems to me to lie in two propositions, which were explicitly stated in the first edition of his book [a], but which he has since withdrawn. These are, "First, that food is necessary to the existence of man; and, secondly, that the passion between the sexes is necessary, and will always remain nearly in its present state." Thus our author sets out with putting these two necessities, that of food, and of "the passion between sexes" upon a level with each other.

I would be the last man in the world to deny an author the benefit of his after-thoughts. If Mr. Malthus has since discovered, that food and the passion between the sexes are necessities not exactly alike and of equal force, that were well. But I cannot consent to his withdrawing his premises, while he maintains the conclusions built upon them. This seems to be one of the instances of "a passage expunged, that the author might not inflict an unnecessary violence on the feelings of his readers."

For instance: the Essay on Population retains its argument respecting the impracticability

---

[a] P. 11.

of a permanent state of equality among human beings, founded upon the parity of these two propositions, in its latest edition, *verbatim* as it stood in the first.

" Thus it appears that a society, constituted according to the most beautiful form that imagination can conceive, with benevolence for its moving principle instead of self-love, and with every evil disposition in all its members corrected by reason, not force, would from the inevitable laws of nature, and not from any fault in human institutions, degenerate, *in so short a period as fifty years*, into a society, where self-love would lord it triumphant, and every hateful vice and every form of distress, which degrade and sadden the present state of man, would reappear in their most malignant aspect b."

Again : " As we are supposing no anxiety about the future support of children to exist, the encouragements to have a family would be greater than even in America c."

In fine : Mr. Malthus repents of his concession in the preceding passage, and concludes, " If such a system of society were established in its utmost perfection, *not thirty years could elapse*, before its utter destruction from the simple *principle of population* d."

This is no other than saying, that man is un-

---

b Vol. II, p. 268, 256.   c P. 251, 252.   d P. 269.

alterably such a brute and insensible animal, that
no arguments addressed to his understanding,
no beauty and virtue existing in the forms of
society around him, no clear and incontestible
conviction of the pernicious consequences of indiscriminate indulgence, could prevent him from
sacrificing the happiest and most enlightened
condition of our being, to what the ancient
philosophers called the " gross impulses of the
lower part of our nature." Merely because the
care of his children did not fall exclusively upon
himself, he would feel the " encouragement to
have a family greater," than all the considerations
of interest and worldly advantage are supposed
to have produced in America.

It is likewise exactly the same sentiment, that
has led Mr. Malthus to affirm of moral restraint
generally, that it has " operated in past ages with
very inconsiderable force," and that we have no
right to entertain " any opinion respecting the
future improvement of society, in which we are
not borne out by the experience of the past."

But this sentiment is expressed in the highest
possible energy in the memorable maxim of the
Essay on Population : " Human institutions,
however they may appear to be the causes of
much mischief to society, are in reality, light
and superficial, mere feathers that float upon the
surface, in comparison with those deeper-seated
causes of evil, which result from the laws of
nature and the passion between the sexes."

It is necessary then that we should pause for a moment upon these two fundamental positions of Mr. Malthus, respecting " food," and " the passion between the sexes." They are like two counteracting weights in a machine : if they do not pull with equal force, and have not the same degree of activity, the whole scheme of Mr. Malthus's Essay, at least as it relates to a pure and equal form of society, and I believe in every other view, will be found to be rotten at the core.

Now, that " food is necessary to the existence of man," I feel no inducement to dispute. We know of no instance of a man living without food. The human frame is sustained by reple- tion and evacuation ; and we have no reason, so far as experience goes, to consider this as any thing else than an indefeasible law of nature. Man is like a clock, that must be wound up at stated periods ; otherwise all motion ceases, and the main spring becomes inert and ineffective.

But what parity is there between this neces- sity, and what Mr. Malthus calls " the passion between the sexes ?" As has been observed in the Enquiry concerning Political Justice, " No- thing is so easy as to extinguish this propensity, amidst the progressive voluptuousness of the most sensual scene. So conscious are we of the precariousness of the fascination of the senses, that upon such occasions we provide against the slightest interruption. If our little finger ached,

M m

we might probably immediately bid adieu to the empire of this supposed almighty power e."

Mr. Malthus says, " the passion between the sexes is necessary, and will always remain nearly in its present state."

In controverting the second member of this proposition, I would ask, What is its present state ?   The want of a precise explanation under this head, is a deficiency that goes to the heart of the system.   Mr. Malthus assumes something, that is perpetually shifting, that at no two periods, and in no two places, is alike, and treats it as if it were absolutely determinate, and that, the moment it is named, every one would have exactly the same idea of its strength and its weakness.

This member of Mr. Malthus's proposition, if explicitly unfolded, must mean, that " the passion between the sexes" always exists and acts, in all persons, in all countries, and in all ages of the world, under all institutions, prejudices, superstitions, and systems of thinking, in the same manner.

But, when the whole meaning that lies hid in this ambiguous proposition, has been thus unfolded, I suppose it will not find a single defender.

Will it be affirmed, that the most decent single women, in those countries of Europe, where

---

e Book I, chapter v, p. 73. Edition, 1797.

morality most steadily maintains its empire, are as prone to violations of chastity, as the most licentious men, or as the women of Cafraria or Otaheite? Are the Fakirs, who voluntarily exercise on their bodies the most tremendous severities, at the same time immersed in the most shameless voluptuousness? Have the most reverend bishops, in times when celibacy was ranked among the first of virtues and the most indispensible, led exactly the same lives, as a Mohammedan sultan in his seraglio, as Tiberius or Sardanapalus? Many satirical and cutting things have been invented against monks and nuns and hermits: but are we really to believe that all such societies, without exception, have been sinks of debauchery, and all such persons the most audacious and consummate hypocrites that ever existed?

Let us confine our attention for a moment, to the fair, and, as it has sometimes been denominated, the frailer sex. The female of the human species, it is admitted, arrives at maturity sooner than the male. Yet a considerable portion of the women of England do not enter into the marriage state, till two-and-twenty, perhaps till five-and-twenty years of age. Even when they do marry, I believe it will be found, that the majority of young women, at least of decent condition, and of a certain education, do not marry merely for the indulgence of their appetites. It is, I think, notorious, that the sober part of the sex, which may perhaps be found to constitute the majority, take it for the main subject of their meditations, how by marriage they may "better their condition?" This is the lesson that their mothers industriously teach them; and a great part of the daughters are not found untractable scholars in the question.

Does Mr. Malthus mean to say, that these prudent young ladies are accustomed to appease the "heyday of the blood," by indulging another set of lovers, not in the way of marriage? If this is his judgment, I shall leave him to settle that question with the numerous portion of the inhabitants of this island, who are believers in virtue, and in decency of heart, and who think with me, that "moral restraint has operated in past ages with considerable force, and that *for that reason* hopes may be entertained of its prevalence in future."

Such then, I believe, is clearly the state of the case as to the female sex. And yet, when we come to examine the constitutional character of the two divisions of our species, it will hardly be disputed, that woman is the weaker vessel, and more a slave to passion. "For well I understand," says Milton,

> in the prime end
> Of nature, her the inferior, in the mind
> And inward faculties, which most excel.

The weakness indeed of woman in this respect is in some points of view her fairest ornament.

She is the creature of impulse, and is for that reason the more bewitching; and, when her impulses are innocent and pure, it is not in the mind of man to imagine any thing more lovely. But resolution is " the pillar of true dignity in man :" he is " formed for contemplation ;" and

> His fair large front, and eye sublime, bespeak
> Firmness of soul.

It cannot therefore be supposed that there is any thing in woman, that should make her by nature more capable of abstinence and rigorous self-government than our own sex.

Nor on the other hand will any impartial enquirer affirm, that the passions of the male sex are stronger than those of the female, so as by that means, though we have more power to control our appetites, yet having a more forceful antagonist to contend with, we should for that reason be oftener subdued.

Let us grant then, that the laws of chastity in civilised countries are more rigidly observed by the women than the men : what is the reason of this? Not that they have more energy of understanding, or weaker passions, than ourselves : but simply on this account, because they are more under the influence of " moral restraint." In this affair of " the passion between the sexes," which Mr. Malthus puts on a level with the appetite of hunger, and seems to suppose that we have as little reason to believe, that any considerable variety can be produced in the

534 OF MR. MALTHUS'S POSITIONS BOOK VI.

operation of the one as of the other, the women have more cogent reasons of self-interest and self-preservation than we have, to submit to the regulations of a strict morality. Still it is reason, and reason only, that restrains them, that power of which Mr. Malthus speaks with so much contempt, and respecting which he says, that " the error which pervades Mr. Godwin's whole work [f]," is the considering man too much in the light of a being purely rational.

Nothing then, I think, can be more clear, than the immense power possessed by this principle of " moral restraint;" and nothing more irresistible, than the inference that, if as powerful motives to forbearance can be presented to the minds of the male sex as of the female, the operation of those motives will not be less conspicuous and certain.

Mr. Malthus may say, if he pleases, that man is a being exclusively selfish. He may say, as he has said, that no respects of " the fairest form of society that imagination can conceive," no certainty that this society will be ruined by the uncontrolableness of his indulgences, no foresight that the children he begets will perish for want of sufficient food in the midst of the common wreck, will prevent him from considering the " encouragements to have a family as greater," in such a society, than all the motives which

<hr />

[f] Vol. II, p. 245.

interest and worldly advantages are supposed to have generated in America. He may accuse, as he is never sparing to do, the governor of the world,—that, while he has furnished motives ample and all-powerful to the female sex to observe the laws of morality, he has left it impossible that such motives can ever be found and brought to bear on the mind of the male.

But neither Mr. Malthus nor his adherents can hereafter have a right to charge this defect, upon " the laws of nature [as they are usually understood], and the constitutional passions of mankind."

So much as to the female sex : but how is it in reality as to the male? Away with the licentious and unprincipled doctrines, that we are not in many cases as pure and beyond suspicion in these respects as the females! I visit the ruins of our ancient monasteries in a very different spirit, from that in which I can suppose Mr. Malthus to visit them. These were the great scenes of " moral restraint." However mistaken might be the principle of the virtue practised by their inhabitants, I have learned to love virtue under every form it can assume. When I consider these noble edifices as the great preservers of all that is admirable in the literature of ancient Greece and Rome, when I recollect that wonderful class of men, known by the name of the Schoolmen, their patient labours, their voluntary self-mortification, their generous

love of truth, and of a fame, pure, however
limited in its circumference among their contemporaries, their disdain of the inticements
and splendours of the world, their exquisite
subtlety of thought and accuracy of deduction
in questions almost beyond the bounds of human enquiry, I feel myself under no temptation to arraign the sincerity of their moral
professions, or to believe that, amidst their more
than human labours, they were victims to the
lowest sensuality and debauchery. I am thank-
ful indeed, that I am impelled to " consider man
too much in the light of a being purely rational,"
not to expose myself to Mr. Malthus's censure
and opprobrium. I know that these glorious
institutions fell into degeneracy. I know that
their professions of morality were too high, not
to make it impossible but that some individuals
should become faint in the way. I know that
these establishments have had their use and their
day ; and I am contented that they should be
abolished.

At the same time nothing, I believe, is more
certain, than that numerous professions, and
large bodies of man, have passed their lives in
as great chastity and reserve, as the most exemplary women. Women, Mr. Malthus would
say, are restrained by the fear of giving birth to
a bastard child. But the mind of our sex is capable of motives as cogent and effectual, as this
consideration may be supposed to prove to a fe-

male. The mind of man is a noble structure, and we are prone to love many other things, beside the gratification of our appetites. In fine, I never will believe that, if " a form of society the most beautiful that imagination can conceive" were brought into existence, it would degenerate into " violence, oppression, falshood, misery, every hateful vice and every form of distress, that have ever saddened the past," and be " destroyed in less than thirty years," from the uncontrolableness with which every man would hasten to gratify " the gross impulses of the lower part of our nature."

It is however no part of my present intention, to pursue this subject into its full development. I have merely introduced it here, because it is the object of this final division of my work, to present to my readers a complete survey of the character and spirit of the Essay on Population.

CHAPTER III.

OF THE DOCTRINES OF THE ESSAY ON POPULA-
TION AS THEY AFFECT THE PRINCIPLES OF
MORALITY.

THE proper tendency of Mr. Malthus's system, is to persuade us to sit still, or rather to
deliver ourselves bound hand and foot, into the
hands of the awful and mysterious power, that
presides over " those deeper-seated causes of
evil," in comparison with which human institutions are " mere feathers that float on the surface." For, as I have already observed, and
this I apprehend none of Mr. Malthus's disciples
will be disposed to contend with me, if human
institutions can do comparatively no harm, it
must, in fairness, and consistency of reasoning,
be admitted that they can do as little good.

To this doctrine of quietism there can properly, upon our author's principles, be but one
limitation ; and that is from the consideration of
the mischiefs to be apprehended from all attempts
at improvement. As the elder Cato concluded
all his speeches upon whatever subject in the
Roman senate, with, Remember Carthage ! so
Mr. Malthus is bound upon every occasion to

lift his warning voice, and exclaim, Remember Utopia! Reject every measure, however specious in its appearances, that looks that way! The proper question upon every new legislative proceeding that is suggested, is, Does it not interfere with " those causes, which contribute in whatever degree to shorten the natural duration of human life?"

When he had done all this however, and properly completed the mighty web of his theory, there was a latent sentiment remaining in the author's mind that all was not right. This doctrine of quietism, and of negatively presenting a front of resistance against all improvements, hardly amounted to his idea of a Treatise upon Political Economy. He was accordingly seized with the ordinary passion, that in ancient times modified the obsolete systems of Plato and Aristotle, and became desirous to be doing. Strangely therefore, and with an inconsistency hardly to be accounted for, but from the original infirmity of our nature,

> —— *veteres avias tibi de pulmone revello,*

towards the conclusion of his book he proposes to enquire respecting " our rational expectations with regard to the future improvement of society[a]." The checks for which he has pleaded through three ample volumes, strike him as somewhat too horrible, and he proposes certain restrictions to counteract these checks.

---

a Vol. III, p. 306.

The general head under which Mr. Malthus classes his restrictions, is not the least extraordinary part of his work. It stands thus : " In every point of view, a decrease of mortality at all ages is what we ought to aim at [b]." This, for an author who sets out with telling us that the human species, in all past ages, and in all ages to come, would have gone, and will go, on to double their numbers every twenty-five years, were it not for those checks, " whether arising from vice or misery, which in various degrees contribute to shorten the natural duration of human life," must be acknowledged to be pretty well. It is the increase of mortality, or of deaths, by which we are to be saved. It is the " decrease of mortality" that the Essay on Population now turns round to recommend. Mr. Malthus knows that moral restraint is a very feeble resource, that men will go on to marry and have children, notwithstanding all he can do to prevent them, and that death, the grand agent and first minister to the geometrical ratio, is all we have to rely on to keep down the numbers of mankind. On this occasion however he is desirous " to soften down some of the harsher conclusions of his first Essay."

Well then : in what manner is it that our author enters upon his new project of diminishing the mortality of mankind?

---

[b] P. 299:

He has several very different ways, which he proposes for this end. They may all however be reduced to two: 1, the securing that no child, and no human creature, in the lower walks of society, should be subsisted, but by his own labour, or that of his parents; and 2, the providing that the reward of labour, and consequently the power of every man to subsist either himself or his children, should to the operating hand be reduced within the narrowest bounds.

These are the restrictions that Mr. Malthus proposes, to check the excessive inroads of vice and misery upon mankind: and it may therefore reasonably be remarked, that the author of the Essay on Population has the talent, to render his benefits no less odious than his injuries.—Of each of these restrictions in its turn.

The first thing that Mr. Malthus attacks under this branch of his subject, is the poor-laws of England, upon which he pronounces the sweeping censure, that they are " an evil, in comparison of which the national debt, with all its magnitude of terror, is of little moment [c]." The national debt is in its capital amount eight hundred and fifty millions, and the interest forty-seven millions *per annum:* the poor-rates are put down by Mr. Malthus at three millions [d].

Since however this tremendous evil of a legal

---

[c] P. 175.   [d] Vol. II. p. 307.

provision for the necessitous poor of England is
in existence, Mr. Malthus is by all means for its
" very gradual abolition d."

" As a previous step to any considerable alteration in the present system," it appears to our
author, that " we are bound in justice and honour formally to disclaim the *right* of the poor
to support e."

And why have they no right?

There was an old maxim, the repetition of
which has been attended with some compunction
in the minds of the tender-hearted and humane,
" He that will not work, neither shall he eat." ·

But Mr. Malthus's proscription is of a very
different sort, and includes, 1. man in his infancy and childhood, whose little hands are yet
incapable of the labour that should procure him
the necessaries of life : 2. the aged, whom length
of years, and the hardships they have endured,
have finally rendered as feeble as helpless infancy : 3. the sick, the cripple, the maimed, and
those who labour under one or other of those
diseases, which make the most fearful part of
the picture of human life : 4. those who, being
both able and willing to work, are yet, by the
ill constitution of the society of which they are
members, or by some of those revolutions to
which perhaps all societies are liable, unable to
procure employment. These are the persons,

---

d Vol. III, p. 178.   e *Ibid.*

whom "in justice and honour" we are bound to inform, that they have no claim of right to the assistance of their prosperous neighbours.

There is no need of informing them, that they have no right, founded in political law, to assistance, except in those countries, and to that extent, where and to which a provision is made for that purpose, as by the poor-laws of England.

But Mr. Malthus's appeal is to a very different jurisdiction. He denies that they have any right in morality to the assistance of their neighbours.

There are two heads and springs of moral duty, as far as this country of England is concerned; the first of which is to be found in the records of the Christian religion, and the other in the instructions we derive from the light of nature. I should not think myself justifiable on the present occasion in over-looking the first.

The lessons of Christianity on this subject are plain and incontrovertible. We are there taught to " love our neighbours as ourselves," and to " do unto others as we would they should do unto us." When an ingenuous young man came to Jesus Christ, desirous to be instructed in his duties, he was referred to the commandments; and, having answered, " All these have I kept from my youth up; what lack I yet?" Christ bade him, " Go, sell all that he had, and give to the poor :" upon which " the young man went away sorrowful; for he had great possessions."

There is a kind of Oriental boldness in this, at least considered as a general exposition of the moral law : for it would be reasonable to answer, If it is my duty to render the greatest benefit to my fellow-creatures, and if my mind is well prepared to discharge this duty, it will probably be better done, by my devoting my income to this purpose, than by at once divesting myself of the principal.

But nothing can be more clear than the general tenour of revelation in this question. By it we are instructed that we are stewards, not proprietors, of the good things of this life, we are forbidden to pamper our appetites or our vanity, we are commanded to be fellow-workers with and impartial ministers of the bountiful principle of nature, and we are told that, when we have done all, we have done nothing of which we have any right to boast.

Such are the dictates of the Christian revelation in this particular : and in all this there is nothing new, nothing that the light of nature did not as clearly and imperiously prescribe, to every one who was willing conscientiously to enquire into the law of morality.

We are here then furnished with a complete answer to what Mr. Malthus says in another place, that " every man has a right to do what he will with his own f."

Indeed I was beyond measure astonished to find such a sentence as this, in a book professing itself to be a book of science, and in a part of that book treating of the rights of human creatures.

Mr. Malthus could scarcely intend by this any thing so futile, as to inform his readers, that the laws of all civilised countries protect a man, and justly, in the exercise of his own discretion as to the disposal of his property.

Did the author purpose then to be understood as speaking either as a moralist or a divine, when he said; "Every man has a right to do what he will with his own?"

The " right divine of doing wrong," was formerly confined to kings, the anointed representatives of the author of the universe : but Mr. Malthus extends it to every one who has the power.

In every moral question, or in other words, in every question where the pleasure or pain, the happiness or unhappiness of others is concerned, there is one thing that it is a man's duty to do, and he has no right to do otherwise.

The rich man therefore has no right to withhold his assistance from his brother-man in distress, except in the sense that he cannot reasonably be brought under the jurisdiction of a court of justice, for his breach of the moral law in this respect.

The rights of any man as to his treatment of his fellow-man, are rights of discretion merely: in other words, that no man must attempt to compel him to do, that which it is his duty to do. The appeal is exclusively to the judgment of him who is to act; but he is bound to inform his judgment to the utmost of his power, and rigorously to adhere to the unbiased decisions of that judgment. So far is it from being true, that " every man has a right to do what he will with his own."

These are the fundamental principles of moral law; and, though they are so plain, that the most uninstructed man may comprehend them as soon as they are announced, they cannot be repeated too often.

Thus stood the principles of morality, before Mr. Malthus wrote his Essay on Population.

The rich man believed in these principles; and, though he perpetually offended against them by the sums he wantonly expended upon his appetites and his vanity, his conscience always reproached him. This was still something.

The poor man believed in these principles; and, though he saw how little they prevailed in the world at large, yet he had the consolation to know what ought to be, and to compare it with what was. No man had yet approached him, perishing with cold and hunger under a shed, and taunted him with, This is exactly as it should be. The poor man is not a perfectly sound judge in his own case: he could not affirm, This is the very man, possessed of opulence, by whom I ought to be relieved; for he could not tell what claims that man had upon his power of affording assistance to others. But he could tell, when " lewdly-pampered luxury" consumed its heaps in " vast excess," that this was not well; and that " every man had not a right to do what he would with his own." He knew that he could not, in law or morality, compel the rich to part with their superfluity; but he did not less know that the poor, that is, the infant, the helpless old, the sick, and the man who cannot procure employment, has " a right to support."

In this belief he was borne out by the light of nature, and by the gospel. Neither the evangelists, nor apostles, nor the Holy Spirit that inspired them, were aware that all these maxims were subverted by the " principle of population."

Mr. Malthus indeed, as far as he has succeeded in his Essay, has changed the situation of the rich and the poor.

To the poor he has taught, that if they receive any relief, they owe it, not to any claim they had to relief, but to what he sometimes calls the spontaneous charity and pure benevolence of the rich; though, since, as he tells us, " private charity almost invariably leads to pernicious consequences [g]," he [should have said they owe it, to the want of fortitude and firmness in the rich, and to their vices.

To the rich also he has read an important lesson. A great portion of this class of society are sufficiently indisposed to acts of charity, and eminently prone to the indulgence of their appetites and their vanity. But hitherto they had secretly reproached themselves with this, as an offence against God and man. Mr. Malthus has been the first man to perform the grateful task of reconciling their conduct and their consciences, and to shew them that, when they thought they were allowing themselves in vice, they were in reality conferring a most eminent and praiseworthy benefit upon the community.

----

[g] P. 291.

CHAPTER IV.

OF THE DOCTRINES OF THE ESSAY ON POPULA-
TION AS THEY AFFECT THE CONDITION OF
THE POOR.

THUS far Mr. Malthus cannot justly be accused of having advanced any thing that should
tend to the "decrease of mortality," and that
by so doing should counteract the main purpose
and fundamental doctrine of the Essay on Population. When he has established the two memorable propositions which have been canvassed
in the preceding Chapter, that the poor "have
no right to support," and that the rich "have a
right to do what they will with their own," these
maxims will by no means in their practical application tend to the "decrease of mortality,"
except so far as famine and despair may arrest
the propagation of mankind. And it is an obvious and irresistible truth, that he who is not
born will never die.

Indeed it will be found all through, that when
our author speciously proposed a scheme for the
"decrease of mortality," he meant a scheme for
"thinning the ranks of mankind."

Mr. Malthus however has great hopes of ac-

complishing his point, so far as this country is
concerned by the abolition of the poor-laws.

Having therefore prepared the way, by " formally disclaiming," on the part of the community, " the right of the poor to support," he
is contented with what he calls a " very gradual
abolition" of the enactments by which that
right is recognised.

His plan is that of a law, " declaring, that no
child born from any marriage, taking place after
the expiration of a year from the date of the
law, and no illegitimate child born two years
from the same date, shall ever be entitled to
parish assistance [a]." " This," he says, " would
amount to a fair, distinct and precise notice,
which no man could well mistake [b]." " No individual would be either deceived or injured
and consequently no person could have a just
right to complain [c]."

For my own part, I profess myself at a loss
to conceive of what earth the man was made, by
whom this sentence was penned.

In the question of a child to be born into the
world, and of the fortune that shall attend it,
there are two parties concerned, the child and
its parents. I own I was ignorant enough to
imagine that the child was the most deeply
concerned of the two.

Tristram Shandy has trifled in a very whim-

---

a Vol. III, p. 179.   b P. 180.   c P. 190.

sical way with the idea of a scheme for baptising children before they are born. Mr. Malthus is the first man that has proposed the proclaiming children, and putting them out of the protection of the law, before they are born, for the purpose of preventing them from complaining afterwards. What has his " fair, distinct and precise notice" to do with them?

In the system of the globe we inhabit, and among the varieties of human fortune, it is an exclamation that has often been heard, and when urged in the depth of reflection, and amidst the agitations of agonised feelings, does not fail to be greatly pathetic: " Why am I thus? How have I deserved the series of misfortunes that incessantly pursue me? How came I into the world? I never desired it. My consent was never demanded. I was compelled to come; and perhaps have never enjoyed one day of real felicity. All to me has been darkness, pains of body, grief of mind, hunger, nakedness, depression and contempt."

I know that the order of the universe is too mighty for any human being to contend with: but I do not entertain exactly the same deference and awe for the systems of human law. Earthly legislatures may without sin be approached in the language of expostulation and remonstrance.

Here then is a child that perishes with want perhaps as soon as he is born. Or he may drag on the load of existence for a varied length of way, from one to fourscore years. However long he may exist, he shall bear about him for ever the miseries, which arise from his being half-famished in the first stage of existence. And Mr. Malthus comes and tells him he " has no right to complain," for a " fair, distinct and precise notice" was given two years before he was born.

If Mr. Malthus and his disciples were to tell him, that general considerations of human weal, and the " principle of population" required that he should be thus deserted, that would be somewhat different. But to say, that a " fair, distinct and precise notice" was given two years before he was born, and " *therefore* no person has a just right to complain," what a mockery is it !

The author of the Essay on Population goes on in a climax, in this instructive discourse on the *rights* of human creatures. He first " formally disclaims the *right* of the poor," the infant, the helpless old, the sick, and the man who cannot procure employment, " *to support*." He next assures us, that, a " fair, distinct and precise notice" having previously been given, " no person," and consequently not the child thereafter to be born, " can have a just *right to complain*" of any calamities that may afterwards overtake him.

Mr. Malthus however undertakes to reconcile the poor man to his lot by an allegory. "These are the unhappy persons, who in the great lottery of life have drawn a blank [d]." "A man who is born into a world already possessed, if he cannot get subsistence from his parents on whom he has a just demand, and if the society do not want his labour, has no claim of right to the smallest portion of food, and in fact has no business to be where he is. At nature's mighty feast there is no vacant cover for him. She tells him to be gone, and will quickly execute her own orders, if he do not work upon the compassion of some of the guests. If these guests get up and make room for him, other intruders immediately appear demanding the same favour. The report of a provision for all that come, fills the hall with numerous claimants. The order and harmony of the feast is disturbed; the plenty that before reigned is changed into scarcity; and the happiness of the guests is destroyed by the spectacle of misery and dependence in every part of the hall, and by the clamorous importunity of those, who are justly enraged at not finding the provision which they had been taught to expect. The guests learn too late their error, in counteracting those strict orders against all intruders issued by the great mistress of the feast, who, wishing that her

---

[d] Vol. II. p. 266.

guests should have plenty, and knowing that she could not provide for unlimited numbers, humanely refused to admit fresh comers when her table was already full ᵉ."

I pass over the humanity of the man who makes to himself an agreeable amusement, from the consideration of the unhappy wretches that are starving at his door. The best of it is, that it is totally false. Men are born into the world, in every country where the cultivation of the earth is practised, with the natural faculty in each man of producing more food than he can consume, a faculty which cannot be controled but by the injurious exclusions of human institution.

It is true that this passage is omitted by Mr. Malthus in his last edition; but it deserved to be preserved as a specimen of the strange extravagances to which the " principle of population" is liable to urge its disciples. It is indeed the most dreadful passage that ever poor printer for his sins was condemned to compose.

But let us follow a little more closely Mr. Malthus's scheme for the gradual abolition of the poor-laws.

" To give a more general knowledge of this law, and to inforce it more strongly on the minds of the lower classes of people, I should propose that the clergyman of each parish should,

---

ᵉ Quarto Edition, 1803, p. 531.

after the publication of the bans of marriage, read a short address, stating the strong obligation on every man to support his own children ; the impropriety, and even immorality, of marrying without a prospect of being able to do this ; the evils which had resulted to the poor themselves, from the attempt which had been made to assist by public institutions in a duty which ought to be exclusively appropriated to parents ; and the absolute necessity which had at length appeared of abandoning all such institutions, on account of their producing effects totally opposite to those which had been intended.

" This would operate as a fair, distinct and precise notice, which no man could well mistake f."

It must be admitted, that this is a strong measure. It strips human life of all those pleasing hues, and all that fascinating appearance, which, if not genuine, has at least served to reconcile thousands to their fate. Marriage is the grand holiday of our human nature ; and, if the rest of the path-way of life is too often involved in horrors or in shades, this is the white spot, the little gleam of pure sunshine, which compensates for a thousand other hardships and calamities. It is indeed a bitter homily to the poor man, that Mr. Malthus proposes. However fair may be his hopes, no one who lives by the sweat

_f_ Vol. III, p. 179.

of his brow, can be sure that he shall always be able, without assistance, to support a family. He has revolved, it may be, with considerable anxiety and deep meditation, before he took this decisive step; and he does not love to be reminded of it, thus publicly, in the face of the church, at a time when the good customs of our forefathers taught him to look out for congratulations. Even if, when I propose to be married, my circumstances are moderately easy, I do not like to be thus lectured, and put into uncomfortable speculations on the occasion; and I will take care, after the passing Mr. Malthus's law, always to be married with a licence, that I may not individually be the occasion for my fellow-parishioners to hear, three times repeated, this displeasing warning. I cannot forgive the author of the law, for thus reminding me, whenever I am disposed to enter into wedlock, that marriage in the abstract is *crimen læsi boni communis*, and that in certain cases of exception only it becomes innocent.

It is further right to remark in this place, that Mr. Malthus's plan for the frequent recital of his homily against marriage, is for ostentation only. He expressly says, that the principle of moral restraint " has undoubtedly *in past ages* operated with very inconsiderable force ;" and he protests against " any opinion respecting the probable improvement of society, in which we are not borne out by *the experience of the past*." If

the making a picture of this kind would answer
.he purpose, and prevent our being visited with
the reality, then (upon Mr. Malthus's principle
of the necessity for perpetual and powerful
checks against increasing population) it were
well.　But our author well knows,

> It is the eye of childhood only,
> That fears a painted devil.

The writer of the Essay on Population, in his
commonwealth, can by no means dispense with
the actual presence of misery.　It is on this
ground that he pleads against " a society, constituted according to the most beautiful form that
imagination can conceive."　He is like some of
our old divines, who are of opinion that the
happiness of heaven would be incomplete, unless its inhabitants had a far-off prospect of
the gulph of hell, and heard its tenants from
their place of torment exclaim, that so they
might be fully sensible of the fate from which
they had escaped.

The author of the work I am examining
plainly shuts himself up in the little circle of
what is passing in the world around him, without ever having recourse to the evidence of
past ages.　Had he opened the volume of history, he would there have learned many instructive lessons.

In the first place, he would have learned the
origin of our poor-laws.　They grew out of the
Reformation.　They were no new concession

made to the lower order of the people of England, but a substitute for something that the Reformation had taken away. We have been taught by our ancestors, the authors of that great revolution in human affairs, to look only on the dark side of all that preceded, as if it had been all pure and unmingled evil. But it was not so: nor is such the character of the ancient institutions of any civilised country.

Christianity, as it was understood for centuries before the Reformation, was a religion of charity and beneficence. The prelates of those times had large revenues; but it was universally conceived that they held these revenues, not to be expended in personal luxuries, but merely as stewards for the flock of Christ. It was expected of them by the faithful, that they should themselves live in primitive simplicity, and even voluntarily subject themselves to many privations and hardships. The use they were to make of a considerable part of their revenues, was to relieve the sick, to clothe the naked, and to feed the hungry. The monasteries of those times had large revenues; but their inhabitants were held by the charter of their institutions, to rise to midnight prayers, to feed sparingly, and to live upon the earth as strangers, whose only home was beyond the grave. The aid therefore derived by the distressed and unfortunate from the revenues of the monasteries, was of the greatest importance. Even the nobility and gentry of those times, won over by such examples, employed a considerable part of their incomes in acts of charity.

All this was reversed by the Reformation. The great multitude of monasteries and religious houses was swept away at once; and the maxims of that age, when this high stimulus and example was removed, were speedily changed. The consequence was the establishment of a great number of hospitals and public institutions, and the enacting of our poor-laws. These did not originate in the prodigal beneficence of the men of those days; but were a penurious and scanty substitute for the vast sources of relief that were taken away, and they were absolutely required by the nature and state of society.

How comes it then that England was not greatly overpeopled in the ages that preceded the Reformation, as it certainly would have been, if the human species were altogether so like rabbits, as Mr. Malthus represents them? The scheme for starving us out for our good, is altogether new; and I am apprehensive that mankind did quite as well in times that are past, as they are ever likely to do under the parental care of the author of the Essay on Population.

If Mr. Malthus had looked into the page of history, he might have derived instruction not only from the early history of England, but from the records of Ancient Greece. Her two most flourishing states were Sparta and Athens.

These were the countries in which to have tried
the geometrical ratio; and it was tried ᵉ. The
constitution of Sparta endured five hundred
years; that of Athens not so long. But, in defiance of the calculations of Mr. Malthus, " this
fair form of society" was not destroyed, and all
its institutions turned into " every hateful vice,
and every form of distress, that can degrade
and sadden" the worst pages of the history of
mankind, by the "mere effect of the principle
of population."

To conclude. The reader will do me the justice to observe, that the above pages do not
constitute a criticism upon, or a defence of, the
poor-laws of England. Mr. Malthus has brought
these laws into discussion, while illustrating his
principle, that " the poor man has no right to
support." This principle I deny; but upon the
poor-laws I have no design of pronouncing
judgment. In England, those who are supposed unable to maintain themselves are aided
from a general assessment: in France and some
other countries, they are provided for in a different way. In both however they are under
the protection of the law: I should prefer being
the citizen of a country, where the deserted and
the helpless should be *sufficiently taken care of*
without the intervention of the state. But in
England at least we are not yet ripe for this.

ᵉ See above, Book I, Chap. X, and again, p. 101, 102, 103.

CHAPTER V.

OF THE DOCTRINES OF THE ESSAY ON POPULA-
TION AS THEY AFFECT THE CONDITION OF
THE RICH.

THE principle of population is no less pregnant with conclusions in favour of the riot and
wastefulness of the rich, than for the oppression
of the poor. Mr. Malthus is no mean follower
of the celebrated precept of Horace,

Omne tulit punctum, qui miscuit utile dulci :

which, being translated into the language of
the Essay on Population, is, He may claim to
have produced a perfect system, who judiciously
blends the squandering of the rich with the
starving of the poor.——But let us take the idea
in Mr. Malthus's own words.

The first point then to be noticed under this
head is our author's denunciations against private charity, or the pecuniary donations of the
rich in aid of the poor.

" A man who is born into a world already
possessed, if he cannot get subsistence from his
parents on whom he has a just demand, and if
the society do not want his labour, has no claim
of right to the smallest portion of food, and in

O o

fact has no business to be where he is. At nature's mighty feast there is no vacant cover for him. She tells him to be gone, and will quickly execute her own orders, if he do not work on the compassion of some of the guests. If these guests get up, and make room for him, the order and harmony of the feast is disturbed[a]," and the worst consequences will follow.

"When Nature will govern and punish for us, it is a very miserable ambition to wish to snatch the rod from her hands. To the punishment of Nature therefore *he should be left*, the punishment of want. He should be taught to know, that the laws of Nature, which are the laws of God, have doomed him and his family to suffer, that he has no claim of right to the smallest portion of food, and that, if he and his family are saved from starving, he will owe it solely to the pity of some kind benefactor[b]," acting in disobedience to the laws of Nature.

In reality, when Mr. Malthus said, "The poor have no right to support," his design was to deliver a moral principle[c], however much it may be in opposition to the principles of those systems, which heretofore have gained the most gracious acceptance in the world. He bottomed himself upon the great law of utility. That

---

[a] See above, p. 553. [b] Vol. III, p. 181.

[c] To what department of didactic science his second law belongs, that the rich man " has a right to do what he will with his own," is another question.

the poor should be supported otherwise than by the labour of themselves or their near kindred, was, in his view of the case, a great evil, inasmuch as it tended to encourage population. The poor-laws of England were therefore " an evil, in comparison of which the national debt, with all its magnitude of terror, is of little moment." And, by parity of reason, the kind-hearted individual, who is prompted by the softness of his disposition to give to the starving and the distressed, is an offender. To support the poor generally, is the highest enormity Mr. Malthus is able to conceive : if we support them a little, we shall do a little evil. It is all a part of the same great law of the Essay on Population ; and each member and shred of its violation partakes of the attributes of the whole.

Mr. Malthus however informs us, that the impulse of benevolence is not to be classed in mischievous effects with the passion between the sexes : that is, it is not that " deep-seated evil, in comparison with which human institutions, however they may appear to be the causes of much mischief "to society, are "light and superficial, mere feathers that float on the surface."

" The passion between the sexes and the impulse of benevolence are both," according to the Essay on Population, " natural passions, excited by their appropriate objects, and to the gratification of which we are prompted by the pleasurable sensations which accompany them [d]." But "*there is less danger to be apprehended* from the indulgence of the latter than of the former [e]," of benevolence than of the sexual appetite, because the one is comparatively strong, and the other weak. And yet there is this other difference between them : that I believe Mr. Malthus would not in all cases disapprove the indulgence of the appetite of procreation ; whereas, "*if we act at all*," in the affairs of relieving the poor, " we must *necessarily* encourage marriage and population [f]," and by that means be the authors of mischief to mankind.

Well then, since the rich, *if they act at all* in the relief of the poor, must *necessarily* produce a certain degree of mischief, the question obviously occurs, What shall they do with the remainder of their income, when their own simpler wants as partakers of an animal nature, and their more refined wants as partakers of the higher endowments of intellect, have been fully supplied ? And upon this point Mr. Malthus does not leave them without instruction.

" Among other prejudices," says he, " that have prevailed on the subject of population, there have existed some against the *waste among the rich*, and the horses kept by them merely for their pleasure. But these things have in reality a little of the same effect as the

---

consumption of grain in distilleries, which was noticed before. On the supposition that the food consumed in this manner, may be withdrawn on the occasion of a scarcity, and be applied to the relief of the poor, they operate certainly, as far as they go, like granaries, which are only opened at the time that they are most wanted, and must therefore tend rather to benefit than to injure the lower classes of society [g]."

Again. " If the diffusion of luxury, by producing the check sooner, tends to diminish the distress, it is surely desirable [h]."

Never certainly was there so comfortable a preacher as Mr. Malthus. No wonder that his book is always to be found in the country-seats of the court of aldermen, and in the palaces of the great. Very appropriately has a retreat been provided for him by the commercial sovereigns of the regions of the East. What a revolution does his theory produce in the interior sentiments of the human breast! There were vices on the earth before Malthus. Men abounding in the good things of this world, indulged themselves unsparingly in all those caprices, which they well knew the mass of their species condemned, and which they more than suspected were worthy of condemnation. But they had a monitor, not only on their shelves, but in their bosoms, which said: " Rejoice, O thou

_____

[g] Vol. III, p. 50, 51.   [h] P. 301, note.

rich man, in thy wealth ; and let thy heart cheer
thee in the multitude of thy possessions ; walk
thou in the ways of thy heart, and in the sight
of thy eyes : but know, that for all these things
God will bring thee into judgment."

Mr. Malthus has reversed all this. He has
undertaken to shew, that while they thought
they were giving way to their vices, and were
drawing down the " curses, not loud, but deep,"
of the bystanders, they were in reality public
benefactors, and that the more they wasted, the
more they saved. He has encouraged them to
persist in their generous plan of conduct, undismayed by the lamentable misconstructions of
their starving fellow-creatures. Nature [not
Mr. Malthus's Nature] had planted within us a
secret monitor, which, when we wandered from
the path of decency and duty, admonished us
with a soft and gentle, but articulate voice, and
bade us recollect ourselves. But Mr. Malthus
stimulates us to drive away this better genius.
He reconciles us to the worst and most prodigal
appetites of our sensual faculty, and bids us call
them by the names of patriotism and philanthropy. It is sufficiently remarkable that, when
he enumerates the eleven ways in which vice
and misery act to keep down the excess of population [i], he does not betray his cause, or put the
extravagance of the rich and great into his catalogue. It is true, for this it seems is not vice.

---

i See above, Book III, Chapter V.

Yes: there were vices before Malthus. But woe to the age and the country, " that shall call evil good, and good evil, that shall put darkness for light, and light for darkness." As long as the sentiments of our moral nature are uncorrupted, there is hope even in our vices. We are not entirely turned, by the enchantments. of pleasure, into beasts. There is still a corner in our souls reserved for better thoughts. There are times when the whirl of temptations hurries us into guilt; but there are also times when recollection resumes her seat. Our actions, it may be, are wrong; but our written monitors, our books, the great fathers of intellect, tell us truth. But, when we shall once be persuaded that all we waste is only "like a granary, and tends rather to benefit than to injure our inferiors," our hearts will become seared indeed.

Mr. Malthus however is unwilling altogether to proscribe private charity, though the principles of the Essay on Population are clearly hostile to it in every form it can assume. As a clergyman of the established church, this might have seemed not altogether consistent with decorum : and, as a friend to the present constitution of things, he would have been thus cutting off the higher orders of the community from one of those modes of action, by which they can best secure their ascendancy over their inferiors. After therefore having solemnly pronounced of the poor man, " To the punishment of Nature *he should be left,* the punishment of want," he adds a feeble and irresolute postscript, " If however he and his family are saved from perishing, he must owe it solely to the pity of some kind benefactor, to whom therefore he ought to be bound by the strongest ties of gratitude."

What ignorant babble is this ! When this " kind benefactor" saved this man and his family from absolute want and the actually perishing with hunger, he either did a right or a wrong, he did his duty or the contrary : for every thing, in our treatment of our fellow-creatures, that is not duty, is of the nature of evil. If what he did was wrong, what sort of gratitude do I owe him, for this splendid wrong to the general interests of society, by which indeed I was the gainer ? This is a gratitude which tramples upon all moral distinctions. This gratitude, with its " strongest ties," while the poor famished wretch is stammering out his thanks, teaches him a memorable lesson indeed ! It teaches him the entire futility of all questions of right and wrong : it teaches him to admire an action, not because it is useful or just, not because it accords with the uncorrupted sentiments of the human heart, but because, whatever are its intrinsic merits or demerits, he at least has got something by it.

Mr. Malthus has here made a great stride, as I suppose many of them would be apt to think, in behalf of the more favoured part of the community. A certain bishop, standing in his place in the Upper House of the English Legislature [k], delivered the extraordinary aphorism, that "the people of this country have nothing to do with the laws, but to obey them." But Mr. Malthus, if he could carry the point now in hand, would gain a still more considerable step, and one that has long been anxiously desired. His doctrine is, that [the people of this country, or at least that portion of its inhabitants who have any chance of ever standing in need of the assistance of others, are to think only of their own duties, and never pry into those of their betters.] These would be happy times indeed ! They would be halcyon days, in which our inferiors, whatever were the decisions of the rich, should submit without repining if they were unfavourable, and be conscious to those peculiar emotions of gratitude, which might arise when they got something upon which they had not the smallest right in law, morality or religion, if they gained. The opinion of the world is one of the greatest sanctions of the moral law, and it is to be feared, as society is at present constituted, that affairs would go but ill, were it not for its mighty control. But why should not the rich, like our members of the house of lords, be judged only

---

[k] Samuel Horsley, Bishop of St. Asaph.

by their peers, without being subject to the censure of a vulgar jury? Let the common people of England learn, that they " have no eyes to see, nor tongue to speak," but as their superiors command them!

No just exception can be taken to this construction of Mr. Malthus's doctrine, unless it shall be answered that, when he said, the rich " have a right to do what they will with their own," he virtually denied that they had any duties whatever.

Fortunately however for all that is most valuable in human society, Mr. Malthus will never be able to carry this point. It is true, as has already been stated, that the rich man cannot be brought under the jurisdiction of a court of justice, for any breach of the moral law he may commit in the disposal of his property. But there is another court, the authority of which no man is stout enough to contemn, and whose decisions are regarded with more deference and awe by the honourable and well-disposed mind, than the technical decisions of a court of justice. The presiding authority in this court, is placed in the sober judgment of his neighbours. When a country-gentleman with an estate of a few thousands a year, dwells in the midst of a neighbourhood of an inferior class, it is of no small importance to him, that he should be popular among them, and that his conduct should meet their approbation. To encounter their view in that case is a delight to him ; while, if in their honest judgments they condemn him, he would travel by a thousand circuitous routes rather than meet the expression of their hatred. There is no man that cannot read the smiles of his fellow-creatures; and there is a tongue in their silent aversion, that speaks with a voice louder than that of a trumpet. He must be a man of no common fortitude, who can anticipate with indifference, that the hearse which conveys him to the grave will be covered with mud, and the mourners pelted with stones, by the sincere indignation of the vicinity. I know that the judgment of the lower orders of the community is often exercised in too indiscriminate and peremptory a style, that it is frequently not well informed, and that it is apt to be under the empire of caprice. I know too that it is liable to be corrupted, and that a few shewy actions will often in this court buy out the censure that is due to a series of misdemeanours. But, with all these imperfections, the empire of opinion is still of high value. The truly virtuous man stands in no need of this check. But there are thousands, who, in the intoxication of their unearned and unmerited elevation over the heads of their fellow-creatures, would be guilty of atrocities now unheard of, were it not for this salutary restraint which feelingly convinces them, that the rich man has no " right to do what he will with his own."

CHAPTER VI.

OF MARRIAGE, AND THE PERSONS WHO MAY JUSTIFIABLY ENTER INTO THAT STATE.

The world must be peopled.
SHAKESPEAR.

OUR examination of the practical doctrines of Mr. Malthus's work will be by no means complete, if we do not stop a little, seriously to examine, what it is that constitutes a fair " prospect of being able to support a family [a];" for the misery of all our author's reasonings upon human affairs is, that they are pictureless, and dwell entirely in abstractions and generalities. Yet this is a question of vital importance; for to the crime of marrying without this prospect, the author of the Essay on Population unpityingly awards a punishment, at the very description of which the heart of humanity sinks within our breast.

" Though to marry in this case," says Mr. Malthus, " is in my opinion clearly an immoral act, yet it is not one which society can justly take upon itself to prevent or punish [how merciful!]; because the punishment provided for it by the laws of nature [no; by the laws of mo-

---

[a] Essay on Population, Vol. III, p. 180.

nopoly] falls directly and most severely upon the individual who commits the act. When Nature will govern and punish for us, it is a very miserable ambition to wish to snatch the rod from her hands, and draw upon ourselves the odium of executioner. To the punishment of Nature therefore he should be left, the punishment of want. He has erred in the face of a most clear and precise warning [here society kindly came in to the aid of Nature], and can have no just reason to complain of any person but himself, when he feels the consequences of his error. All parish assistance should be denied him. He should be taught to know, that the laws of Nature, which are the laws of God, have doomed him and his family to suffer for disobeying their repeated admonitions; that he has no claim of right on society for the smallest portion of food, beyond that which his labour will fairly purchase [and employment for that purpose is often denied him]; and that, if he and his family are saved from feeling the natural consequences of his imprudence, he will owe it solely to the pity of some kind benefactor, to whom therefore he ought to be bound by the strongest ties of gratitude b."

To return to the question then,—What it is which gives a man a fair " prospect of being able to support a family," and may so render his

---

b Vol. III, p. 180.

contracting marriage not wnat Mr. Malthus calls
" an immoral act :" for be it observed it is as easy,
upon the principles of the Essay on Population,
for a poor man to do an immoral act, as it is
difficult, not to say impossible, for a rich one.
Indeed I believe, according to this doctrine,
there can be no immoral act on the part of a
rich man, except such against which he shall
find a prohibition in Blackstone's Commentaries
of the Laws of England c.

A fair "prospect of being able to support a
family," are words that run glibly off the tongue,
and will pass without hesitation with many a
rich man, when he comes to pronounce judgment on a poor one. But it is my cue to put in
a plea for the poor, and " him that hath none
to help him."

For this purpose I have enquired respecting
the wages given to the labouring hand in this
country ; and I am informed that the usual pay
to a man employed in tillage is eighteen pence
per day, and that the ordinary salary of an arti-
san is about twice as much.

Now, to begin with the peasant. Shall this
man marry, or shall he not? I will suppose,
that he is in perfect health, with a robust constitution ; and that, as agriculture is not likely
soon to go out of fashion, he may hope for tole-

---

c This is a mistake : I ought also to have excepted, " an act of
private charity."

rably regular employment. To give every advantage to my case, we will take for granted that the female on whom he has fixed his choice is as healthy as he, is sober, and shall be able, from her needle, or otherwise, to bring in something to increase the common stock. Yet nine shillings *per* week, with whatever addition may thus accrue, is but a scanty income, upon which to build a fair " prospect of being able to support a family."

Mr. Malthus, if I understand him, would advise this man to wait, and save up something from his earnings, before he enters into the solemn engagement of matrimony. His yearly income is twenty-three pounds eight shillings. How much he can save out of this I do not exactly know. But I will suppose that, by patience and perseverance, he has saved a whole year's income, twenty-three pounds eight shillings: what is this in aid of a fair " prospect of being able to support a family ?"

Perhaps Mr. Malthus means, that no peasant can marry without being guilty of " an immoral act," unless his father can give him an hundred or two hundred pounds to begin the world with. If this was his intention, I wish he had said so; as then we could have made some calculation of the number of persons who, upon the " principle of population," are permitted to marry, as well of those who are condemned to lead a life of constrained celibacy, upon pain of being guilty of a heinous breach of the laws of morality.

To understand this question more perfectly, let us consider a little what marriage is, according to the most exact deductions that have yet been made of the laws of political economy Every marriage, I will say, upon an average produces four children, some fewer, some none, some a much more considerable number. Shall he then be considered as having a fair " prospect of being able to support a family," who takes for the basis of his calculation, himself, a wife, and four children? Oh, no : for in this lottery no fortune-teller has yet been found, who could infallibly foretel to each man his lot : it may be this man's lot to have twelve children or more. —Add to this uncertainty, the chances of sickness, and the thousand other casualties that await us in the darkness of the future.

Well: this man has drawn an unfortunate and overwhelming ticket; and I bring him to Mr. Malthus's tribunal for remedy. There he shall learn a most instructive lesson. He is told, " To the punishment of Nature we leave you, the punishment of want. You have erred in the face of a most clear and precise warning, and can have no just reason to complain of any person but yourself, now that you feel the consequences of your error. All parish assistance is to be denied you. You must be taught to know, that the laws of Nature, which are the laws of God, have doomed you and your family to suffer for disobeying their repeated admonitions."

Perhaps the hand of private charity may afford some scanty aid to this unfortunate man and his family. If it does, all I can say is, that Mr. Malthus is no wise accountable for this heinous offence against the " principle of population d." His system, as I have fully shewn, teaches us, that private charity *necessarily* leads to the most pernicious consequences. Here then we have a man, who, because he did not listen to the warning three times repeated, is left, and " should be left," with his family to the punishment of want. Why indeed should he listen? The words he hears have no meaning, and fall a *brutum fulmen* on his ear. No labouring peasant has a fair " prospect of being able to support a family." Nay, I would add that, in Mr. Malthus's sense, no rich man, no nobleman, and no king has.

For, be it observed, the question is not here of a calculation of probabilities, or the doctrine of chances. The law of the Essay on Population is peremptory and absolute. It is like the laws of Draco, which were written in blood, and allowed of no mitigation. " All

---

d I am thoroughly aware that Mr. Malthus has several neat and well turned periods in favour of charity, under certain strict limitations. All I mean to say is, that they are diametrically in opposition to the cardinal principles of his work.

P p

parish assistance is to be denied him. He has no claim of right on society for the smallest portion of food. To the punishment of Nature *he should be left*." " They should not have families, without being able to support them [e]." If he takes a ticket in a lottery in which there are nine hundred and ninety-nine prizes, and but one blank, yet his ticket may be that blank. And the law has no ears: he is to be left to his own resources; and Mr. Malthus calls out to every one to stand aloof, and see what God will do unto him.

But, without taking this extreme case, the poor man may presume that he shall be able to support four persons in a family, and he may have six, or twice six. He may presume that he shall have health, and sickness may be his lot. He may presume that he shall not break a leg or an arm. He may presume that he shall have constant employment. He may presume that he shall not be the father of a cripple or an idiot. What poor man does not know that marriage is preeminently and in every sense a lottery? It is all one. " All parish assistance is to be denied him. He has no claim of right on society for the smallest portion of food. To the punishment of Nature he and his family *should* be left. When Nature will govern and punish for us, it is a very mise-

---

[e] Vol. III, p. 199.

rable ambition to wish to snatch the rod from her hands. The laws of Nature, which are the laws of God, have doomed him and his family to suffer."

Did he not hear the warning voice three times repeated? Has he not sinned against a " fair, distinct and precise notice?" Will then he or his children pretend after this, that, whatever happens, they have " a right to complain?" Mr. Malthus peremptorily denies it. Still further. He may presume that he shall live, and by his exertions form the principal support of his family. But he may die. The Essay on Population makes no provision for this. " They should not have families, without being able to support them." And, as to his children, " a fair, distinct and precise notice" was given, two years or upwards before they were born, and therefore, though perishing with hunger, they " have no right to complain." Suppose him a drunkard or a profligate, spending on his own vices that which should support his family. Society has nothing to do with that. His wife may consider it as the proper return for her mistake in accepting his·addresses; and his children for the crime of being born. It is " the punishment of Nature, " and they " have no right to complain."

Certainly never was a theory given to the world, that breathed so total a disdain of the condition of man upon the face of the earth.

We will suppose however that a poor peasant marries. We will allow nine shillings a week for the produce of his labour, with some addition from the industry of his wife. That we may go as far as we can in vindication of his prudence, we will suppose that, out of his savings, he is enabled to commence house-keeping with a fortune of twenty-three pounds eight shillings in bank. This might have served him to buy a couple of cows; but he may not happen to live near a common, upon which he might feed them. That however will presently appear to be out of the question. Twenty-three pounds eight shillings is little enough in all conscience to furnish the inside of his habitation, and to supply a few of the plainest necessaries, without allowing him the hope of adding a peculium *sub Jove pluvio*.

Our old-fashioned ancestors were accustomed to admire the light heart of this man, who, trusting in the Providence of God, and the benevolence, if need were, of his richer neighbours, embarked himself cheerfully in the stormy sea of the world. Youth and a good constitution made the future appear gay and sunshiny before him. He knew that he lived in a country, which, though not so bountiful as Athens [f], had yet taken care to make a legal provision for such of her sons as were overtaken by unfore-

---

[f] See above p. 101.

seen distress. Twenty-three pounds eight shillings, under these circumstances, appeared a mine of wealth in the eyes of his good-natured patrons and friends.

Alas! our old-fashioned ancestors knew nothing of Mr. Malthus's doctrines, and had not dreamed of the Essay on Population. Lulled in the kindly sleep of a benevolent heart, they did not anticipate the twenty-third homily, to be read hereafter as the constant accompaniment of the bans of marriage.

Human life is an awful thing; and wisely did Solon pronounce, that we must never declare any man happy, till he is dead. They that have learned to sympathise in the vicissitudes of this sublunary scene, will know well how to compassionate a fellow-creature in distress. The great earl Mansfield is said to have had a constant foreboding in his mind, that he should die in a workhouse; and, if he had gone no farther than to believe this possible, no sober man would have blamed it as a weakness. In the chequered scene of our frail existence, " no man knoweth" what calamities await him. " The race is not to the swift, nor the battle to the strong; but time and chance happeneth to them all."

Mr. Malthus's homily therefore is not framed to the state of man on earth. It is too much to say to the poor man, with his family starving about him : " To the punishment of Nature we leave you, the punishment of want. You must be taught to know [*taught!* how appropriate a word to the wretch, whose eyes are glazed with famine, and his lips parched with lack of moisture] that her laws, which are the laws of God, have doomed you and your family to suffer for the immorality of your disobedience." Indeed Mr. Malthus, whatever you may allege, I can never be brought to think, that it is a just admonition to this man to say : " You have no claim of right upon society for the smallest portion of food ; and, if you and your family are saved from perishing, you will owe it solely to the pity of some kind benefactor," which pity is a weakness, and, as the Essay on Population asserts, " almost invariably leads" to pernicious consequences.

In reality, if Mr. Malthus had fully considered the effect of his principles, and had then thought proper to speak out plainly, he would have told us in so many words, that no man had a right to marry, without being first in possession of a moderate independence. Two or three hundred pounds *per annum* legally secured to the parties and their heirs for ever, I should think might do. The adherents of the " principle of population" would not require that every married man in the community with his family should live entirely at his ease. I know that two or three hundreds *per annum*, nor indeed as many thousands, in the ups and downs of Euro-

pean life, would not fully secure their possessor
against the chances of standing in need of the
benevolence of his neighbours, nor even from
coming with his family to the parish, but that
that word is blotted out of the vocabulary of
the disciples of the Essay on Population. But
then, even at the worst, he has an advantage.
I have often observed, in the advertisements
addressed " to the charitable and humane," what
a nameless charm there is, if the petitioner has
seen better days, has fallen from a state that had
been attended with every comfort, or is distantly
allied to some sprig of nobility. In addition to
this, the number of such petitioners are comparatively few, while the starving and inglorious
peasants are so numerous, that the hand of " private benevolence" is tired out in the attempt to
relieve them. Mr. Malthus himself too would,
I conceive, pronounce this sort of liberality
exempt from the least shadow of blame, as it
would not " tend to the indiscriminate encouragement of marriage."

It also deserves to be remarked, that if marriage were considered as a privilege reserved for
the higher orders of the community, we should
still upon the " principle of population" have
enough of it. In following the speculations of
Mr. Malthus, we should never lose sight of the
geometrical ratio. If the present peasantry and
labourers of England were wholly rooted out,
we could on that basis easily calculate how soon

the country at large would become fully as populous as at present.   This would be a mode of
thinning the numbers of mankind, very analo-
gous to what was before mentioned of hoeing
turnips, without the disadvantage of our having
been obliged to have recourse to " every cause,
which might in any degree contribute to shorten
the natural duration of human life."   We should
stop the rising generation, which was crowding
into the " hall of existence" at so alarming a
rate, before they reached the threshold.   And
then the new population, not to mention the
genteel blood which would universally flow in
their veins, would have read so instructive a
lesson in the perishing of the old, that we
might hope they would get on, not indeed with
out vice and misery, but with somewhat a
smaller portion of each than was required for
their rude predecessors.

There is one view of the subject of this chapter too interesting to be entirely overlooked.   If
the ideas of Major Graunt, quoted in page 174,
are true, nineteen in twenty of the males of
mankind, if such had been the pleasure of the
author of the universe, might have been deprived of the power of procreation, and even
of the sexual appetite, without injury to the
source of human population.   Something like
this is said to be the condition of the bee.—*Sed
Dis aliter visum.*   We live in a system, if not
more favourable to the multiplication of man-

kind, at least more propitious to the cultivation of the affections of human nature. Upon the opposite system, the male would have been deprived of the larger portion of the pleasures of society, and the female would have been subjected to the degrading effects of polygamy.   It plainly appears therefore that the order of the world tends, not barely to the natural effect that the human species should exist in certain numbers on the face of the earth, but to the moral end that, by the union of one man with one woman, the happiness of our race should be increased, and the moral character refined and exalted.   This agrees with the doctrine of Christ and his apostles, that " Marriage is honourable *in all.*"   Hence it is that are derived to us " the charities of father, son, and brother:" and hence it appears, as was said in another place [a], that neither man nor woman has fulfilled the ends of their being, nor had a real experience of the privileges of human existence, without having entered into the ties, and participated in the delights of domestic life.

Let us then return at once, and return in earnest, to the long established and wholsome principles of policy and society on this subject, that it is one of the clearest duties of a citizen, to give birth to his like, and bring offspring to the state.   Without this he is hardly a citizen :

---

[a] P. 220.

his children and his wife are pledges he gives to
the public for his good behaviour; they are his
securities, that he will truly enter into the feeling of a common interest, and be desirous of
perpetuating and increasing the immunities and
prosperity of his country from generation to generation. *Sanguinis autem conjunctio et bene-
volentia devincit homines caritate : sed omnes
omnium caritates patria una complexa est.*

But if this duty is more peculiarly incumbent
upon one order of society than upon another, it
undoubtedly falls with greatest force upon that
order which is most numerous, and which constitutes the basis of the community, upon that
order which is necessary, while the others are
merely ornamental, upon that body of men,
who put their hands to the plough, or in other
ways participate in the aggregate of labour and
sweat by which the whole is sustained. Woe
to the country, in which a man of this class
cannot marry, without the prospect of forfeiting
his erect and independent condition! Woe to
the country, in which, when unforeseen adversity falls upon this man, he shall be told he has
no claim of right to be supported and led in
safety through his difficulties! We may be
sure there is something diseased and perilous in
the state of that community, where such a man
shall not have a reasonable and just prospect of
supporting a family, by the labour of his hands,
and the exertion of his industry, though he

begins the world with nothing. If he is disappointed in this, who is more worthy of the assistance of the friend of man ?

I know but of two principal exceptions to the law which affirms generally that it is the duty of a citizen to seek to become a husband and a father.

First, the profligate should not marry. It is true, he should cease to be profligate. I would encourage him to all possible good purposes, and exhort him to enter steadily into the limits of sobriety and virtue. But I cannot think that he should make a wife and a family the subject for the trial of his crude resolutions. This is indeed the only *pater familias* in a well constituted and well organised society, not in the convulsion of 'any extraordinary change, who can have reason (exclusive of the case of a bad wife or evil-disposed children) to repent that he has chosen this honourable condition. Profligacy, particularly in the lower walks of life, is the great bane of the married state. When the husband or the wife forget the duties which they have vowed to discharge, or spend in drunkenness and dissipation the means that are required for the weal of the establishment, theirs is indeed an unhappy and ill-fated family.

The second sort of persons upon whom it may not be incumbent to marry, are those who by high qualities and endowments seem destined to be distinguished benefactors to their country or their species. No man can be completely a judge of his own talents previously to the experiment: but every man can tell whether he feels within him an impulse to devote himself to public exertions. If he does, he is justly entitled to attend to that impulse. A superior duty controls that which is common. He who has an arduous career to run, should come unincumbered into the field. How many instances may be found of such as would have achieved great things, and have resigned themselves to obscure and unremunerated pursuit, if they had had only themselves to provide for, and had not been burthened with the cares of a family! This remark applies particularly to the earlier division of human life. I do not blame the man vehemently, who breaks through this rule; he only does that to which, in the abstract, man is destined. But I cordially applaud him, who having received a higher destination, cheerfully abjures every indulgence that would obstruct his progress.

There are other exceptions, beside these two, of men to whom it ceases to be a duty to seek to become a husband and a father. But let this suffice. I am not writing a *Ductor Dubitantium*, or seeking to compile a body of Cases of Conscience.

CHAPTER VII.

A FEW CONTRADICTIONS IN THE ESSAY ON POPULATION STATED.

It has not been the purpose of this work, to expose Mr. Malthus's contradictions. Never book afforded greater advantage in this way to an adversary, than the Essay on Population. Almost every page would be found upon a strict analysis to contain an answer to the page that went before. But I have had higher objects in view. It has been my purpose to assail his theory at the foundation. I have taken the main propositions of his volumes; and, without troubling myself with the question how often he has betrayed his cause, and thrown down the fabric he has raised, I have gone straight to the consideration of the truth or error of his principles.

There are however one or two points, immediately connected with the question now under consideration, where this spirit of contradiction is so glaring, that I am tempted by them to deviate for a moment from my general rule.

In vol. II, p. 309, Mr. Malthus expressly remarks, " No possible sacrifices of the rich could

for any time prevent the recurrence of distress
among the lower members of society." What
becomes then of the patriotism and philanthropy, to be displayed in living sumptuously and
keeping horses for pleasure, which we have just
been considering? Indeed it is observable, that
when he was expressly contending for this point,
his voice somewhat faltered. The words in
which he announces his position are, " The
waste among the rich, and the horses kept for
pleasure, have *a little* the effect of the consumption of grain in distilleries."

Mr. Malthus is an experienced pleader. He
knows how to sustain his temporary character
to a proper extent, and when it is becoming to
lay it aside. Just now he appeared before us as
an advocate for the poor. His theme was to
shew how much they were [ultimately gainers
by the luxuries of the rich. But, having made
a specious appearance with that argument, he
presently shews us what was his real object.
The business was to establish an apology for
luxury, and to furnish another corollary to his
memorable theorem, that " Every man," by
which he plainly means, every man that has
something that is worth calling his own, " has
a right to do what he will with it."—His plea
for the poor in this case, is exactly of the same
complexion, as the plea he elsewhere sets up for
God Almighty, of which he says, " The chief
reason why *I allowed myself to suppose* the

universal prevalence of this virtue, was that I might *endeavour* to remove any imputation on the goodness of the Deity," by supposing something, respecting which " no man could be less sanguine than he is," that it would ever take place.

The same contradiction that I have just shewn in what Mr. Malthus says respecting the luxuries of the rich, occurs in a still more striking manner in his observations respecting the poor-laws.

He sets out with the thundering position, that the poor-laws are " an evil, in comparison of which the national debt, with all its magnitude of terror, is of little moment [a]." If I at all understand the Essay on Population, the reason they are concluded to be such an evil, is because of their tendency to encourage marriage, and thus introducing some approximation towards the tremendous geometrical ratio.

Elsewhere however Mr. Malthus takes a very different view of the subject. " There are many ways," he says, " in which our poor-laws operate in counteracting their first obvious tendency to increase population [b]." Again : " The obvious tendency of the poor-laws is certainly to encourage marriage ; but a closer attention to all their indirect as well as direct effects, may make it a matter of doubt to what extent they

---

[a] Vol. III, p. 175.   [b] P. 294, note.

really do this [c]." And further on: " It will readily occur to the reader, that owing to these causes, it must be extremely difficult to ascertain, with any degree of precision, what has been their effect on population [d]."

The author at length winds up what he has to say on the subject with a most extraordinary note.

" The most favourable light, in which the poor-laws can possibly be placed, is to say that under all the circumstances with which they have been accompanied, they do not much encourage marriage ; and undoubtedly the returns of the Population Act seem to warrant the assertion. Should this be true, *many of the objections which have been urged in the Essay against the poor-laws will be removed;* but I wish to press on the attention of the reader, that they will in that case be removed, *in strict conformity to the general principles of the work, and in a manner to confirm, not to invalidate, the main positions which it has attempted to establish* [e]."

If this were told, would it be believed ? If Mr. Malthus had delivered the substance of what he has said on the poor-laws at a countymeeting, and I had thus attempted to arrest and record his " winged words," it cannot be but I should have been universally set down

---

c P. 373.   d P. 374.   e *Ibid.*

for a calumniator. Well and wisely did the patriarch Job conceive that memorable wish of his, "Oh, that mine enemy had written a book!"

Mr. Malthus sets out with pronouncing the poor-laws "an evil, incomparably greater than that of the national debt." He then proceeds with perfect consistency, in the strongest manner to urge their abolition. The subject however, he says, must be tenderly handled: the abolition must be "a very gradual abolition." We must begin with proclaiming that we are "bound in justice and honour formally to disclaim the right of the poor to support." And that for this reason, because, if they conceived they had any such right as is expressly recognised by our poor-laws, it would shortly become physically impossible, from the rapid multiplication of the species, to make this right the rule of our practice. The proposition, we are informed, is not less absurd, than if we were to say, "Every man has a right to live a hundred years f."

Having thus given to the poor "a fair, distinct and precise notice" of what they are to expect, we are next to proceed to put our gradual abolition into execution. "Every child that is born from any marriage, taking place after the expiration of a year from the date of this no-

---

f P. 154.

Q q

tice, and every illegitimate child born two years from the same date, " is to be for ever and in all cases cut off from the right to support." Mr. Malthus has discovered, that "no person could have a just right to complain" of this. " In the great lottery of life this child has drawn a blank." " The laws of Nature, which are the laws of God, have doomed him to suffer." " At Nature's mighty feast there is no vacant cover for him. She tells him to be gone; and if he does not make haste, she will quickly execute her own orders."

These are strong measures; but who can help it? The poor-laws, which are " an evil incomparably greater than that of the national debt," require to be abolished; and Mr. Malthus is persuaded that, " the principle, if not the plan," of the scheme he has delineated, is what we shall be " compelled by a sense of justice to adopt ᵍ."

This plan must necessarily make a great ravage of our species. The revolution is so considerable, that Mr. Malthus, " albeit unused to the melting mood," recommends that it be " very gradually" made. The sorrows, the agonies, the nakedness, the famine, that must come upon " the shorn lamb" of human society, before he has learned to bear the nipping blasts that shall blow upon him, are such, as I should not like to trust my pen to describe.

At length Mr. Malthus turns round to con-

ᵍ P. 178.

template the devastation he has made ; and he
ultimately comes to more than suspect there
was no need of this. All the passages I have
here quoted lie in the small compass of two
hundred pages : and the whole of this *pro* and
con on the poor-laws was published to the world
on the same day. When, though late, the author had discovered that, upon a supposition,
which he is inclined to believe to be " true,
many of the objections he had urged against the
poor-laws would be removed," and none of the
sad consequences he had predicted would follow, this does not induce him to cancel or re-
vise his preceding sheets: and he consoles
himself for all the inflictions he had recommended in his chapter of " gradual abolition"
by the curious remark, that if the poor-laws do
little or no harm, and if these inflictions were
unnecessary, still this happens " in strict conformity to the general principles of his work,
and in a manner to confirm, not to invalidate,
the main positions which he has attempted to
establish." There was a maxim imputed to the
celebrated and excellent Mr. Windham, " Perish commerce ! Live the constitution !" and I
confess I do not much differ from him in pre-
ferring the liberties of mankind to the wealth
of nations. In the same grand and magnificent style, but with some difference of impulse and character, I hear Mr. Malthus ex-
claiming, " Perish the human species ! Live the
Essay on Population !"

CHAPTER VIII.

OF WAGES.

IT remains to correct the errors of Mr. Malthus on the subject of wages.

All Mr. Malthus's errors are of the same complexion. He begins with considering man as a noxious species of vermin, whose race is to be kept down ; since, if it were not kept down, it would overrun the earth, to the destruction not only of other kinds of animals, but finally to its own destruction also. This is a new light that has broken in upon the world. It was not thus that moralists and divines were accustomed to consider the human species, " the paragon of creation." This view of our kind and its worth had scarcely been heard of, till the appearance of the first edition of the Essay on Population in 1798.

The rest follows of course. Man has an appetite never to be controled, so says Mr. Malthus, for the multiplication of his species. All the preachers of humility and self-abasement, previously to the Essay on Population, must " hide their diminished heads." We vainly dreamed that ours was an intellectual nature.

Even the great Pagan historian [a] began his immortal work with telling us, that it was the proper business of man, " to take care that he did pass through life in inglorious obscurity like the beasts, whom nature had formed with their faces towards the earth, and in subjection to their appetites; that our composition was twofold, consisting of mind and body, the office of the one being to rule, and of the other to serve." But the Christian divine who wrote the Essay on Population, teaches a different doctrine. He talks much at the rate of Shakespear's mad king **Lear**:

> To it, luxury, pell mell!
> The wren goes to it, and the small gilded fly
> Does lecher in my presence.
> Let copulation thrive!

Mr. Malthus indeed says, that these things ought not to be. But he is aware that " moral restraint has in past ages operated with very inconsiderable force;" and no one can be less " sanguine than he, in the expectation that future times will contradict the experience of the past."

In strict conformity therefore to these views of human nature, Mr. Malthus can find out no better remedy for the imaginary tendency to excess in population, than substantial vice and misery. All motives that address the higher part of our nature, act " with very inconsiderable force." All appeals to the human understanding are nu-

---

[a] Sallust, *In Bello Catilinario.*

gatory. However clearly and forcibly we have set before us what is virtuous, what is honourable, good for others, and good for ourselves, we shall live in the midst of these inducements, as if they had no existence. Brutes we are, and brutes for ever we shall remain.

Upon the principles here explained, and with the most perfect consistency, Mr. Malthus is upon all occasions an advocate for low wages. He says indeed, " There is no one that more ardently desires to see a real advance in the price of labour than himself [b]." Just so a minister of state, when he comes forward with a measure peculiarly oppressive and tyrannical, is sure to boast of the sincerity of his attachment to public freedom. And so Swift in his own poignant style observes, that, " when the court of Lilliput had decreed any cruel execution, the emperor always made a speech to his whole council, expressing his great lenity and tenderness, as qualities known and confessed by all the world : nor did any thing terrify the people so much, as these encomiums on his majesty's mercy."

The first passage I will select as a proper subject for a few observations, is as follows.

" Suppose that, by a subscription of the rich, the eighteen pence or two shillings a day which men earn now, were made up five shillings ; it might be imagined perhaps, that they would

[b] Vol. II. p. 324.

then be able to live comfortably, and have a piece of meat every day for their dinner. But this would be a very false conclusion. The transfer of three additional shillings a day to each labourer, could not increase the quantity of meat in the country. There is not at present enough for all to have a moderate share. What would then be the consequence? The competition among the buyers in the market of meat, would rapidly raise the price from eightpence or ninepence to two or three shillings *per* pound, and the commodity would not be divided among many more persons, than it is at present.[c]"

This is certainly the most extraordinary passage in the whole English library of books upon political economy; and Mr. Malthus must have felt himself very sure in his hold upon the disciples of the Essay on Population, before he could have ventured upon such a statement.

If this were true, then the equalization of property, of which poets have dreamed, and which many of the sanguine votaries of human improvement have imagined might one day be realized on earth, would be of no advantage to any one creature that should exist. The golden age would be an age of iron. The hopes of the human race would indeed be reduced to nothing.

But, without grasping at so mighty an object

---

[c] Vol. II, p. 307.

as the equalization of all property, it has been the universal cue of moral writers and divines, ancient and modern, to wish that property was not heaped with such vast monopoly in the hands of a few, and that the undowered labourer, perhaps with a large family, was not reduced to so scanty a pittance. Mr. Malthus comes to tell us, that this is but a pious delusion, of the sort to which all enthusiasts are exposed.

But this is not so. The author of the Essay on Population has here undertaken no less a task, than to argue us out of our senses, or rather out of that common sense, which, Pope says, " is, though no science, fairly worth the seven."

Observe : if five shillings a day would not give the labourer more than he has now, then neither would ten shillings, or twenty shillings. By parity of reason we may also argue downwards, and say that the labourer would do as well with a shilling or sixpence, as he does now with eighteen pence. It is all fairy-money, and serves to amuse us ; but when we come to apply it to use, we find, that when we thought we had it, we were not well awake. " Are we not in precious fooling ?"

The quantity of money, and of commodities that money will purchase, in any country at a given time, is a given quantity. The more money any one has, the better chance he has of obtaining the commodity he desires. Does Mr. Malthus mean to say, that if all the commodities in England were divided, to each inhabitant an equal share, the poorest man in the community would not have more than he has now?

It is undoubtedly true, that if every common labourer in England had five shillings a day, the price of commodities would rise. But he would go into the market, which contains a given quantity of beef and mutton, with two advantages: not only that he would possess more of that by which these commodities are commanded than he has now, but that the overgrown neighbour by whom he was elbowed almost into the desert, would have less. The rich man would be pampered with fewer luxuries; and the labourer, to express myself moderately, would approach nearer to competence.

But there is another radical mistake that Mr. Malthus makes in this argument, the same that lies at the foundation of his whole theory, viz. the seeing nothing in man but the two grossest accidents of his nature, hunger, and the sexual appetite. If every poor labourer at present in the kingdom had five shillings a day, which is more than three times his present income, he would not immediately go with it to the market, with a determination to carry home as much beef as it would purchase. The poor labourer is by nature as fond as his betters of the accommodations of life; and, if at present he confines his view to bare necessaries, it is the rigour of his condition that compels him to do so. Triple

his income, and he would immediately think how
he himself with his wife and children might be
better clad, with more comfort, with more neat-
ness, perhaps with a little ornament and show.
He would think how he should give his children
a better education.   He would think, that with
five shillings in his hand he might go to market
more economically, and not experience the truth
of that bold orientalism of holy writ, " From
him that hath not, shall be taken away, even that
which he hath."   He would think perhaps, for
the poor man is not necessarily without the
charitable affections of the human heart, however
he may now be forbidden from calling them into act, how he might help the widow and the
fatherless in their distress.   The price of meat
would certainly rise, upon this revolution in the
circumstances of the labouring hand; but it
would not, as Mr. Malthus has stated, " rapidly
rise to two or three shillings *per* pound."

There is another particular, which Mr. Malthus entirely overlooks in his view of the subject.   When a sudden, and we will suppose, a
beneficial change takes place in the circumstances
of a country, it does not immediately produce
all the good that may be expected from it.   It
takes some time for things to find their level in
this new position, and for matters to adjust
themselves to this altered state of affairs.   Mr.
Malthus says, " The transfer of three additional
shillings a day to each labourer, would not in

crease the quantity of meat in the country." Be it so.   There would be no immediate increase. But there is no more accurate feeling, than that which exists in persons bringing commodities to the market, as to the nature and extent of the demand.   More meat, as well as more of every thing else which the fortunate labourer would feel inclined to purchase, would speedily be produced.   Nothing could disturb this happy progress, but the geometrical ratio, an evil strong enough to disturb every thing, but which is nowhere to be found, and which exists only in the imagination of the libellers of the human species.

I am apprehensive that many of my readers will blame me for having laboured so plain a matter, and will be out of patience that I should have spent three sentences to refute so absurd a position, as that money is money only in the pockets of the rich, and that, the moment it is " transferred into that of the labourer," it turns out to be nothing.

I proceed to another passage of Mr. Malthus: a passage which is immediately preceded by his declaration, that " There is no one that more ardently desires to see a real advance in the price of labour than himself."   The sentiment I refer to, is thus expressed : " The price of labour, when left to find its natural level, is a most important political barometer, expressing the relation between the supply of *provisions*, and the demand for them [d]."

Here we are again presented with the same error, that man has no business in the world, but to eat, and to beget children. If the income of the labourer is spent upon any thing else but provisions, it cannot of itself constitute a measure of the price of provisions.

Mr. Malthus says, that, " if the income of the labourer were made five shillings a day, the price of meat would be rapidly raised to two or three shillings *per* pound." The price of labour in the United States is very nearly that which Mr. Malthus has here stated. The question therefore is reduced to a question of fact. Does butcher's meat in the American markets fetch two or three shillings *per* pound ?

The wages of the labourer depend on two things ; the demand for labour, and the price of the necessaries and conveniences of life [e]. The wages of the labourer must be sufficient to enable him to maintain himself and two children, or in other words, to attempt to rear four children ; otherwise the race of such labourers could not last beyond the first generation. They must therefore, at the lowest computation, be doubly what is sufficient to maintain himself [e]. This is the *minimum* of any settled or natural price of

---

[d] P. 325.   [e] Smith, Wealth of Nations, Book I, Chap. VIII.

labour; and if it goes below this, and is continued, the community in which this lower price is given, must verge rapidly to destruction.

It thus distinctly appears how low the price of labour can go; but there are many ages and countries in which this lowest price is not the price given. The fluctuations therefore above this lowest (wholesome, and permanently practicable) price, will depend upon another circumstance. That circumstance is the contract which can be effected between him by whom the labour is to be performed and his employer; and happy, in this particular at least, is the country, where the labourer is enabled to raise the price of his industry above this *minimum*, and to include in it a certain portion of those accommodations, which give comfort and complacence to the receiver, and raise him to a certain respectability in his own eyes and the eyes of others.

There are three parties to be paid out of all the labour that is performed in any civilized country, the landlord, in the form of rent, the capitalist, who possesses money enough to set the lower orders of the community to work and to supply them with materials, and the labourer ᵍ. The two former possess a great practical advantage over the latter; they can subsist for a given time without his aid. But the labourer in general has nothing in reserve; and

---

ᵍ *Ibid,* Chap. VII.

without employment he must perish. The actual price of labour will therefore be regulated by the question, at how cheap a rate the capitalist can get his work done ; this rate being checked, as was said before, by the price of the necessaries and conveniences of life. The landlord, and still more the capitalist, according to the present modes of thinking in human society, are disposed to make the most they can of what they possess. The price of labour in that case will depend upon the plenty or scarcity of hands in the market and the employer will give no more than he cannot help giving.

But, if Mr. Malthus, and a few other persons of his liberal way of thinking, could persuade masters to be less griping, and more generous in their contracts with those they employ, it is certain that nothing but what was beneficial would result from it. The number of mouths in the community, and of consumers in all kinds, would remain the same. The only alteration therefore would be, that the labourer would have more of those things which form the consolation of life, while the rich man would have fewer superfluities.

It ought not to pass without remark, that, while Mr. Malthus compares the price of labour to the mercury in a barometer, his single anxiety is lest, " when the common weather-glass stood at *stormy,* we should by some mechanical pressure raise it to *settled fair* [h]." He ought to have known, that the mercury was as liable by some irregularity to be depressed below, as to be raised above, the sound and proper point. But this is no part of the concern of the author of the Essay on Population. It is the depression of the mercury in the barometer of political economy, that leads in its most obvious concomitants to vice, or, what is still more effectual, to misery.

Mr. Malthus observes: " After the publication and general circulation of such a work as Adam Smith's, it seems strange, that men, who would yet aspire to be thought political economists [i]," should fall into such gross errors. This remark, in my opinion, well deserves to be retorted upon the author of the Essay on Population: and that this may be evident to every reader, I will subjoin a few passages from the Enquiry into the Wealth of Nations [k].

" In Great Britain the wages of labour seem to be evidently more than what is precisely necessary to enable the labourer to bring up a family. There are many plain symptoms that the wages of labour are no where in this country regulated by this lowest rate which is consistent with common humanity." The author then goes on to enumerate these symptoms, and subjoins, " The common complaint, that luxury

---

[h] P. 326.   [i] P 327.   [k] Book I, Chapter VIII.

extends itself even to the lowest ranks of the people, and that the labouring poor will not now be contented with the same food, clothing and lodging which satisfied them in former times, may convince us that it is not the money-price of labour only, but its real recompence, which has augmented.

" Is this improvement in the circumstances of the lower ranks of the people, to be regarded as an advantage or as an inconveniency to the society? The answer seems abundantly plain. Servants, labourers, and workmen of different kinds, make up the far greater part of every great political society. But what improves the circumstances of the greater part, can never be regarded as an inconveniency to the whole. No society can surely be flourishing and happy, of which the far greater part of the members are poor and miserable. It is but equity besides, that those who feed, clothe and lodge the whole body of the people, should have such a share of the produce of their own labour, as to be themselves tolerably well fed, clothed and lodged."

" The liberal reward of labour increases the industry of the common people. The wages of labour are the encouragement of industry, which, like every other human quality, improves in proportion to the encouragement it receives. A plentiful subsistence increases the bodily strength of the labourer; and the com-

fortable hope of bettering his condition, and of
ending his days perhaps in ease and plenty, ani-
mates him to exert that strength to the utmost.
Where wages are high, accordingly we shall
find the workmen more active, diligent and ex-
peditious, than where they are low; in England,
for example, than in Scotland; in the neighbourhood of great towns, than in remote coun-
try-places.   Some workmen indeed, when they
can earn in four days what will maintain them
through the week, will be idle the other three.
This however is by no means the case with the
greater part.   Workmen on the contrary, when
they are liberally paid by the piece, are very
apt to overwork themselves, and to ruin their
health and constitution in a few years.   A car-
penter, in London, and in some other places, is
not supposed to last in his utmost vigour above
eight years.   Something of the same kind happens in many other trades, in which the workmen are paid by the piece; as they generally
are in manufactures, and even in country-la-
bour, wherever wages are higher than ordinary.
We do not reckon our soldiers the most industrious set of people among us.   Yet when soldiers have been employed in some particular
sorts of work, and liberally paid by the piece,
their officers have frequently been obliged to
stipulate with the undertaker, that they should
not be allowed to earn above a certain sum
every day, according to the rate at which they

R r

were paid. Till this stipulation was made, mutual emulation, and the desire of greater gain,
frequently prompted them to overwork themselves, and to hurt their health by excessive labour. Excessive application during four days
of the week, is frequently the real cause of
the idleness of the other three, so much and
so loudly complained of. Great labour, either of
mind or body, continued for several days together, is in most men naturally followed by a
great desire of relaxation, which, if not restrained by force, or by some strong necessity,
is almost irresistible. It is the call of nature,
which requires to be relieved by some indulgence, sometimes of ease only, but sometimes
too of dissipation and diversion. If it is not
complied with, the consequences are often dangerous, and sometimes fatal. If masters would
always listen to the dictates of reason and humanity, they have frequently occasion, rather
to moderate, than to animate the application of
many of their workmen.

" In cheap years, it is pretended, workmen
are generally more idle, and in dear ones more
industrious, than ordinary. A plentiful subsistence therefore it has been concluded relaxes,
and a scanty one quickens their industry. That
a little more plenty than ordinary may render
some workmen idle, cannot well be doubted;
but that it should have this effect upon the
greater part, or that men in general should

work better, when they are ill fed, than when they are well fed, when they are disheartened, than when they are in good spirits, when they are frequently sick, than when they are generally in good health, seems not very probable. Masters of all sorts frequently make better bargains with their servants in dear than in cheap years ; and find them more humble and dependent in the former than in the latter.   They naturally therefore commend the former as more favourable to industry.   Landlords and farmers besides, two of the largest classes of masters, have another reason for being pleased with dear years.   The rents of the one, and the profits of the other, depend very much upon the price of provisions."   The inducement therefore, that leads them to this misapprehension and partial representation, is obvious.

The Enquiry into the Wealth of Nations is not a book much to my taste.   It is very proper that such subjects should be discussed ; but I own that there is something in the discussion that makes me feel, while engaged in it, a painful contraction of the heart. But it is refreshing to come to such sentiments as are here put down, after the perusal of such a book as that of Mr. Malthus.

CHAPTER IX.

CONCLUSION.

THERE can be no conclusion more natural or more profitable to such an enquiry as has formed the scope of the present volume, than an attempt to fix a just estimate of the state of man upon earth.

Man is perhaps the only animal in the world endowed with the faculty we call taste. Man is the only animal capable of persevering and premeditated industry, with the fruits of which the land and even the water of our globe are interspersed and adorned. Man is the only creature susceptible of science and invention, and possessing the power of handing down his thoughts in those permanent records, called books. Man has in him the seeds of sentiment and virtue, and the principle of comprehensive affections, patriotism and philanthropy. The human species is capable of improvement from age to age, by means of which capacity we have arrived at those refinements of mechanical production and science, which have been gradually called into existence; while all other animals remain what they were at first, and the young of no species becomes better or more powerful by the experience of those that went before him.

It cannot be but that a being so gloriously endowed should be capable of much enjoyment and happiness. Our tastes and our judgment are fitted to add indefinitely to our pleasures : we admire the works of God and the works of man. Our affections are to us a source of enjoyments, variegated and exquisite. Self-approbation and self-complacency are main pillars of human happiness. The consciousness of freedom and the pride of independence are inexhaustible sources of joy. There is a peculiar and an inexpressible delight which belongs to perseverance and a resolved constancy in the operations of science, in the cultivation of mind, and in a course of virtuous action. We are delighted with these things in solitude and intent application ; and society in such pursuits increases our delight. Indeed, when we do but name the word society, we touch a magical chord which introduces us at once to a whole volume of peculiar felicities.

Yet the state of man on earth is not a state of unmingled happiness. We have many pains and infirmities. Every stage of our existence from the cradle to the grave, has its peculiar compartment in this magazine of ills. Our cares and anxieties are innumerable. All those things which, presented to us in one aspect, are sources

of pleasure, may, if reversed, become equally
sources of affliction. The generous ambition of
the human heart, if disappointed, preys upon
our vitals. Our affections, those conduits of exquisite enjoyment, are often turned into the
means of agony. Man is an erring creature, and
may become the victim of remorse; or, if his
heart is hardened in this respect, he may be
made the object of the resentment and vengeance
of his fellow-creatures.

Beside all this, it is now time to add, that
human institutions may be the source of much
mischief to those they were framed to control.
There have been such things as despotism and
as tyranny. Society is the source of innumerable pleasures; without society we can scarcely
be said to live; yet in how many ways does society infringe upon the independence and peace
of its members. Man delights to control and to
inforce submission upon his fellow-man; human
creatures desire to exercise lordship and to display authority. One class and division of the
community, is taught to think its interests adverse to the interests of another class and division of the community. The institution of property has been the source of much improvement
and much admirable activity to mankind; yet
how many evils to multitudes of our species have
sprung from the institution of property. The
same may be said of the inequality of conditions.

All that is here stated is very much of the

nature of common-place. Every man has heard it; and every man knows it. Yet it is sometimes of great use that common-places should be recollected; and the author would deserve the name of absurdly fastidious, who should resolve upon all occasions to avoid them. Those which have been here introduced are particularly proper on the present occasion.

Between the advantages and disadvantages attendant on the state of man on earth there is one thing that seems decisively to turn the balance in favour of the former. Man is to a considerable degree the artificer of his own fortune. We can apply our reflections and our ingenuity to the remedy of whatever we regret. Speaking in a general way, and within certain liberal and expansive limitations, it should appear that there is no evil under which the human species can labour, that man is not competent to cure. This is a source of unspeakable consolation to us in two ways: first, we can bear with some cheerfulness the ill which for ourselves or our posterity we have the power to remedy: and, secondly, this power inherent in our nature is the basis of that elasticity and exultation which are most congenial to the mind of man. " We are perplexed, but not in despair; we are persecuted, but not forsaken ; we are cast down, but not destroyed." Man, in the most dejected condition in which a human being can be placed,

has still something within him which whispers
him, "I belong to a world that is worth living in."

Such was, and was admitted to be the state of
the human species, previously to the appearance
of the Essay on Population. Now let us see
how, under the ascendancy of Mr. Malthus's
theory, all this is completely reversed.

The great error of those who sought to encourage and console their fellow-beings in this vale
of tears, was, we are told, in supposing that any
thing that we could do, could be of substantial benefit in remedying the defects of our social
existence. "Human institutions are light and
superficial, mere feathers that float upon the surface." The enemy that hems us in, and reduces
our condition to despair, is no other than "the
laws of Nature, which are the laws of God [a]."

Nor is this by any means the worst of the
case. The express object of Mr. Malthus's writing was to prove how pernicious was their error,
who aimed at any considerable and essential improvement in human society. The only effectual
checks upon that excess of population, which,
if unchecked, would be sufficient in no long
time to people all the stars, are vice and misery.
The main and direct moral and lesson of the
Essay on Population, is passiveness. Human
creatures may feel that they are unfortunate and
unhappy ; but it is their wisdom to lie still, and

---

[a] Vol. III. p. 181.

rather " bear the ills they have, than fly to others that they know not of."

The two main propositions that are revealed to us by the Essay on Population are, 1. the kind of mortality and massacre that is continually taking place in the midst of us, without our having been aware of it: and, 2. the conduct which it is our wisdom to adopt under the unhappy condition of man upon earth.

It has been already sufficiently proved in the proper place, that, according to Mr. Malthus's principles, all the children in each generation on this side of the globe are born, that can be born [b]. The difference between the population of Europe on the one hand, and of the United States on the other, is not that a smaller number of children are born in the former case, but that a greater number are cut off in their infancy. If the present population of England and Wales is ten millions, it would twenty-five years hence be twenty millions, and so on for ever, were it not for the hitherto unobserved destruction of the young of the human species on this side of the globe. That man is mortal we sufficiently knew; we had studied and rehearsed, time out of mind, the various accidents that waylay us in every stage of our existence; and the thought of this was sufficient to make us sober, if not to make us sad: but Mr. Malthus has discovered

[b] P. 30, 31, 32.

to us the hourly destruction of millions upon millions more, of which we had no previous knowledge.   And how are they destroyed? " By all those causes, whether arising from vice or misery, which in various degrees and diversified manners contribute to shorten the natural duration of human life."   " Every loss of a child from the consequences of poverty [and, were it not for these losses, the population of England and Wales would double every twenty-five years] must evidently be preceded and accompanied by great misery to various individuals."

The second of the two main propositions that are revealed to us by the Essay on Population, is the conduct which it is our wisdom to adopt under the unhappy condition of man upon earth. Vice and misery are the main securities upon which we are to depend : it is they that make the condition of man upon earth so tolerable as we find it.   The most pernicious error into which we can fall, and which is beyond all others to be deprecated, would be the inconsiderate attempt materially to improve the state of society, to relieve the hardships under which the greater part of our species at present labour, and to introduce equality, or any approach towards equality, in the conditions of men. Since vice and misery are discovered to be the *mala bene posita,* the indispensible evils, without which the pillars of creation would tumble into ruins, we must be careful to touch them with the utmost tenderness, or rather we must be careful not to touch them on any account. They are the mysterious treasures, laid up in the sanctuary of the covenant between God and his creatures.

Look now upon this picture and on this, the faithful representment of two worlds! One is the world I was born in, and in which I lived for forty years: the other is the world of Mr. Malthus.

In the Old World (if I may be allowed so to denominate it) there was something exhilarating and cheerful. We felt that there was room for a generous ambition to unfold itself. If we were under the cloud or the grief of calamity, we had still something to console us. We might animate our courage with reflections on the nature of man, and support our constancy by recollecting the unlimited power we possess to remedy our evils, and better our condition. We felt, as I said before, that we "belonged to a world worth living in."

Mr. Malthus blots out all this with one stroke of his pen. By a statement of six pages, or rather of six lines, he undertakes to shew us what a fool the man is who should be idle enough to rejoice in such a world as this. He tells us that our ills are remediless, and that human institutions, and the resources of human ingenuity, are feathers, capable of doing little harm, and no more competent to produce us benefit. We are fallen into the hands of a remorseless step-mother, Nature: it is in vain that we struggle against her laws; the murderous principle of multiplication will be for ever at work; the viper-brood of passion, the passion between the sexes, the fruitful source of eternal mischiefs, we may condemn, but must never hope to control. He forbids us to augur well of the general weal, for all is despair; he forbids us to attempt to raise or improve our condition, for every such attempt is destructive.

I can liken Mr. Malthus's world to nothing but a city under the severe visitation of a pestilence. All philanthropy and benevolence are at an end. To serve our fellow-citizens is a hopeless undertaking. With hope, the very wish to serve them expires. We no longer love, where to benefit is impossible. " It were all one," as Shakespear says, " that I should love a bright particular star, and think to wed it." Our only refuge then is in pure self-indulgence, and an entire contempt for, and oblivion of our fellow-creatures. Boccaccio's description of some of his contemporaries in the great plague of Florence is excellently to this purpose. " The reflections of these men," says he, " led them to a determination sufficiently cruel : and this was, to shun and fly from their unfortunate and suffering countrymen. They shut themselves up in houses free from the infection, and sought to forget the very existence of their fellow-citizens.

They nourished themselves with the most delicate meats and the finest wines they could procure. Nay, they sung, they danced, they laughed, they jested, and considered this, as far as they were concerned, to be a sovereign remedy for every evil." It is wonderful how exactly this coincides with what is recommended in the Essay on Population, concerning the neglect to be shewn to the poor, and the wastefulness of the rich.

Till Mr. Malthus wrote, political writers and sages had courage. They said, " The evils we suffer are from ourselves; let us apply ourselves with assiduity and fortitude to the cure of them." This courage was rapidly descending, by the progress of illumination and intellect, to a very numerous portion of mankind; and the sober and considerate began deliberately to say, " Let us endeavour to remedy the evils of political society, and mankind may then be free and contented and happy." Mr. Malthus has placed himself in the gap. He has proclaimed, with a voice that has carried astonishment and terror into the hearts of thousands, the accents of despair. He has said, The evils of which you complain, do not lie within your reach to remove : they come from the laws of nature, and the unalterable impulse of human kind.

But Mr. Malthus does not stop here. He presents us with a code of morality conformable to his creed.

This code consists principally of negatives.

We must not preach up private charity. For charity, "if exerted at all, will necessarily lead" to pernicious consequences.

We must not preach up frugality. For the "waste among the rich, and the horses kept by them merely for their pleasure, operate like granaries, and tend rather to benefit than to injure the lower classes of society."

We must deny that the poor, whatever may be the causes or degree of their distress, "have a right to support."

We must maintain that every man "has a right to do what he will with his own."

We must preach down marriage. We must affirm that no man has a right to marry, without a fair "prospect of being able to support a family." "They should not have families, if they cannot support them." And this rule is strictly to govern our treatment of the married man in distress. "To the punishment of Nature he should be left, the punishment of want. He should be taught to know that the laws of Nature, which are the laws of God, have doomed him and his family to suffer for disobeying their repeated admonitions."

What havock do these few maxims make with the old received notions of morality!

It has not been enough attended to, how complete a revolution the Essay on Population proposes to effect in human affairs. Mr. Malthus is the most daring and gigantic of all inno-vators.

To omit all other particulars, if we embrace his creed, we must have a new religion, and a new God.

Mr. Malthus's is not the religion of the Bible. On the contrary it is in diametrical opposition to it.

> Increase and multiply, is Heaven's command.
> Who bids abstain, but our destroyer, foe
> To God and man?

Christianity is, and has always been called, a religion of charity and love. It is rigorous in prescribing the duties of the rich, as well as of the poor. It does not admit that we "have a right to do what we will with our own." On the contrary, it teaches that we have nothing that we can strictly call our own, that the rich are but stewards and administrators of the be-nefits of Providence, and that we shall be austerely called to give an account of every talent that is intrusted to us. We are taught to consider our fellow-creatures in distress as our brothers, and to treat them accordingly. " In-asmuch as ye have done it to one of the least of these, ye have done it to me."

But, if we embrace the creed of Mr. Mal-thus, we must not only have a new religion, but a new God.

The God of the Essay on Population, the God, as we are there informed, of Nature, and the author of her laws, has given us laws, " the deep-seated causes of evil," in comparison with which all that human ingenuity can effect of harm or of good, is but as a feather. These deep-seated causes of evil we can never counteract, nor can any thing extract their venom, unless we were capable of that moral restraint, which Mr. Malthus has in one instance " allowed himself to suppose," but which he has no expectation or belief that man ever will or can reduce into practice. Such are the laws, according to him, in conformity to which God has built the world, and such is the imbecil and impotent creature which he has planted here to inhabit it. The irresistible strength of these laws, and the weakness of man, are equally his work. It is his breath that has pronounced the fiat, " Vice and misery shall be the concomitants of the human species as long as they exist; I have made for them a law of multiplication so enormous, that the action of these causes shall be regularly required to cut off the excessive increase as fast as it appears." Lo now, and see, whether this is the God, which any system of religion on earth has taught men to recognise. Lo now, and see, whether this is the God, which serious men in enlightened Europe are prepared to praise and adore.

It is but just that those who adopt the creed of Mr. Malthus, should understand it in all its bearings, and be made aware of the full extent of the conclusions into which it leads; while, on the other hand, those by whom these conclusions are regarded with aversion, will perhaps feel themselves indebted to a book, by which the premises on which they are built, are, I trust, fully refuted.

The general inferences from the statements and reasonings of the preceding sheets are plainly these.   There is in man, absolutely speaking, a power of increasing the number of his species. Yet the numbers of mankind appear not to have increased on the whole within the limits of authentic profane history.   To speak from the best authorities to which we have access, the increase has never amounted to the rate of a doubling in one hundred years, nor has ever proceeded at that rate for a hundred years together.   And, till human affairs shall be better and more auspiciously conducted than they have hitherto been under the best governments, there will be no absolute increase in the numbers of mankind.   This is enough for Mr. Malthus, and the other adversaries of the dignity and honour of human nature.   For myself and those who hope better things, a doubling of the numbers of mankind once in an hundred years, has nothing in it, which can afford rational ground of alarm.   We have but too cogent reasons to believe, that a regular and uninterrupted progress of increase is a thing that cannot for a long time be looked for.   And, at all events, we may be as well assured, as it is possible to be upon a subject of this sort, that the progressive power of increase in the numbers of mankind, will never outrun the progressive power of improvement which human intellect is enabled to develop in the means of subsistence.

I am sensible that what I have written may be regarded in some respects as a book about nothing. The proposition of which it treats appears to have been established by universal consent from the days of Homer. I may perhaps however be allowed the merit of having brought new arguments in aid of old truth. In these times of innovation (innovation, one of the noblest characteristics of man) a pernicious novelty has been started, and has obtained for the time a general success. It seemed necessary that some one should stoop to the task of refuting it. Too happy, if I may flatter myself with the fate hereafter that Swift predicates of Marvel, whose "Answer to Parker is still read with pleasure, though the positions it exposes have long ceased to have any supporters." I have accordingly endeavoured that my volume should contain some reflections and trains of thinking not unprofitable for other purposes than those for which they were originally produced. Add to which, if I have contributed to place a leading point of political economy on a permanent basis, my labour may not in that respect be found altogether fugitive and nugatory.

THE END.

J. M'Gowan, Printer,
Great Windmill Street.